concept

A Xerox Company

We keep your business ticking along.

We are problem solvers, who love a good challenge

Our committed team use their skills and expertise to help discover your business needs.

With a wide range of digital print and document technology. From mono and full colour printers, to copiers and the latest wide format equipment, we've got you covered.

- **Multifunctional Printers**
- **Wide Format**
- **Production**
- **3D Printers**
- **Printers**

- **Remanufactured**
- **Digital Solutions**
- **Print Analysis**
- **Print Media**

Our concept is simple.

concept-group.co.uk

0345 241 2268

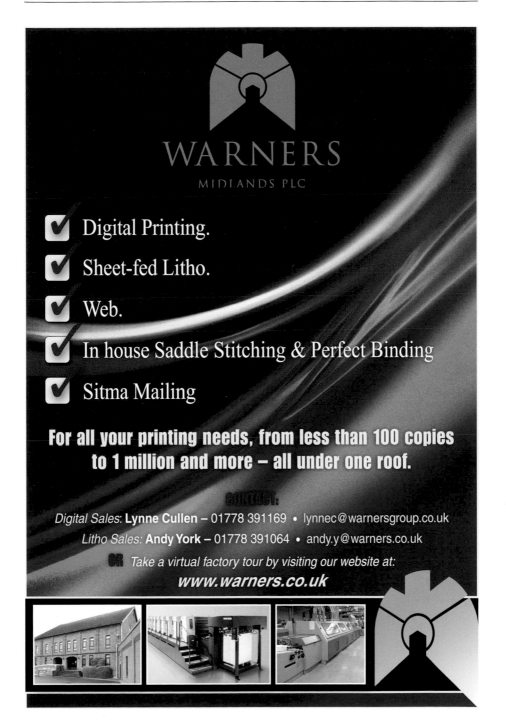

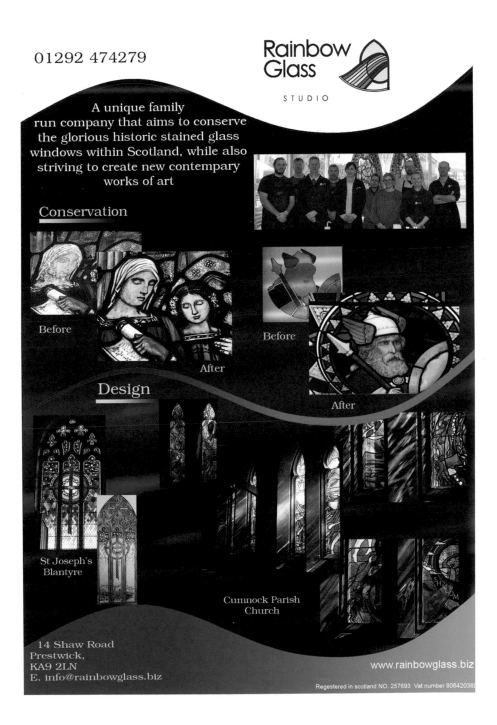

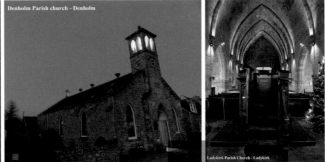

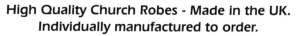

Rak Engineering
Sound Advice! - Sound People!

AV installation - induction loop - service & repair

phone: Tom Graham on **01698 283325**
or e-mail rakengine@blueyonder.co.uk

40 years experience installing systems in churches
"Preach the good word" but make sure it can be heard!

Check our website for more information: **www.rakengineering.com**
75 Cadzow St, Hamilton ML3 6DZ

REQUEST A SPEAKER

For over 70 years MAF has supplied a solution for the problem of poverty in isolation, delivering a lifeline for isolated communities in 27 countries across the developing world.

Arrange a speaker to your church, work or small group, and hear more about MAF's life-saving work. We cater for groups of all sizes across Scotland, completely free of charge.

Email scottishoffice@maf-uk.org or phone 0141 332 5222 to find out more.

Flying for Life

Registered charity in England and Wales (1064598)
and in Scotland (SC039107)
® Registered trademark 3026860, 3026908, 3026915

The Right Reverend Colin Sinclair
MODERATOR

The Church of Scotland
YEAR BOOK
2019–2020

134th year of issue

Editor
David A. Stewart

Published on behalf of
THE CHURCH OF SCOTLAND
by SAINT ANDREW PRESS
121 George Street, Edinburgh EH2 4YN

THE OFFICES OF THE CHURCH

121 George Street
Edinburgh EH2 4YN

0131 225 5722
Fax: 0131 220 3113
www.churchofscotland.org.uk

Office Hours:
Facilities Manager:

Monday–Friday 9:00am–5:00pm
Carole Tait 0131 240 2214

The following operate from the **Church Offices**, 121 George Street, Edinburgh EH2 4YN (0131 225 5722):

- Assembly Trustees
- The Church and Society Council   churchandsociety@churchofscotland.org.uk
- The Ministries Council   ministries@churchofscotland.org.uk
- The Mission and Discipleship Council   mandd@churchofscotland.org.uk
- The World Mission Council   world@churchofscotland.org.uk

The Social Care Council (CrossReach) operates from Charis House, 47 Milton Road East, Edinburgh EH15 2SR

0131 657 2000
Fax: 0131 657 5000
info@crossreach.org.uk
www.crossreach.org.uk

SCOTTISH CHARITY NUMBERS

The Church of Scotland: unincorporated Councils and Committees	SC011353
The Church of Scotland General Trustees	SC014574
The Church of Scotland Investors Trust	SC022884
The Church of Scotland Trust	SC020269

(For the Scottish Charity Numbers of congregations, see Section 7)

First published in 2019 by SAINT ANDREW PRESS, 121 George Street, Edinburgh EH2 4YN on behalf of THE CHURCH of SCOTLAND

Copyright © THE CHURCH of SCOTLAND, 2019

ISBN 978 0 7152 0980 6

British Library Cataloguing in Publication Data
A catalogue record for this book is available from the British Library.

Printed and bound by Bell and Bain Ltd, Glasgow

QUICK DIRECTORY

Action of Churches Together in Scotland (ACTS) 07527 433460
Assembly Trustees 0131 240 2229
Christian Aid Scotland 0141 221 7475
Church and Society Council.. 0131 240 2206
Church of Scotland Insurance Co. Ltd............................... 0131 220 4119
Conforti Institute... 01236 607120
CrossReach 0131 657 2000
Eco-Congregation Scotland 0131 240 2274
Ecumenical Officer.. 0131 240 2208
Gartmore House 01877 382991
Glasgow Lodging House Mission 0141 552 0285
Iona Community.. 0141 429 7281
IT Department Church of Scotland 0131 240 2245
Legal Questions Committee 0131 240 2240
Media Team (Press Office).. 0131 240 2268
Media Team (after hours)... 07854 783539
Old Churches House, Dunblane (formerly Scottish Churches House) 01786 823663
Pastoral Support Team (pastoralsupport@churchofscotland.org.uk).......... 0131 225 5722 ext 2419
Pension Trustees (pensions@churchofscotland.org.uk).................... 0131 240 2255
Place for Hope 07884 580359
Principal Clerk (pcoffice@churchofscotland.org.uk).................... 0131 240 2240
Priority Areas Office.. 0141 248 2905
Prison Chaplains... 0131 330 3575
Safeguarding Service 0131 240 2256
Scottish Churches Organist Training Scheme (SCOTS) 01592 752403
Scottish Churches Parliamentary Office.............................. 0131 240 2276
Scottish Storytelling Centre (The Netherbow)......................... 0131 556 9579
Work Place Chaplaincy Scotland................................... 0131 441 2271
Year Book Editor... 0131 441 3362

Pulpit Supply: Fee and Expenses
See www.churchofscotland.org.uk > Resources > Yearbook > Section 3F

Corrections and alterations to the Year Book
Contact the Editor:
yearbookeditor@churchofscotland.org.uk
0131 441 3362

GENERAL ASSEMBLY OF 2020
The General Assembly of 2020 will convene on
Saturday, 16 May 2020

CONTENTS

FROM THE MODERATOR

The Year Book, when it arrives each year, reminds me that I belong to a Presbyterian Church. Too easily, we simply think at a congregational level and impoverish both ourselves and our congregations. While our main focus is rightly at the local level, I have been immeasurably enriched by belonging to a Church which seeks to be faithful to Christ in a whole range of situations. In the bible we are called "to rejoice with those who rejoice and weep with those who weep". If we are going to stand with one another, pray for each other and engage with other places, we need information about them. The Year Book supplies that sort of detail, laying out the very diverse nature of parish life throughout Scotland and beyond.

For years it has been my "go-to point" for all kinds of useful contact details. I have always enjoyed lists since there was a craze for books such as "The Book of Lists" back in the 1970s. The Year Book has information on people and places, on the Councils and committees of the Church and on the most recent General Assembly. It also has all sorts of interesting articles about our church which can be found nowhere else. I am very grateful for the painstaking work that various Editors and their teams have put in to give us a snapshot of the Church at a particular moment in time.

I hope you find this volume useful in helping you to know more about our Church.

Colin A.M. Sinclair

BHON MHODERÀTOR

Bidh Leabhar na Bliadhna, nuair a ruigeas e gach bliadhna, a' cur nam chuimhne gum buin mi do dh'Eaglais Chlèireach.

Tha e ro fhurasta dhuinn a bhith a' smaoineachadh dìreach aig ìre coitheanail agus tha sin na chall dhuinn fhìn agus dhar coitheanalan. Ged a tha e ceart ar prìomh fòcas a bhith aig an ìre ionadail, tha mise air a bhith air mo bheairteachadh thar tomhais tro bhith nam bhall de dh'Eaglais a tha strì ri bhith dìleas do Chrìosd ann an caochladh mòr shuidheachaidhean. Anns a' Bhìoball tha sinn air ar gairm gu bhith "dèanaibh gàirdeachas leothasan a tha ri gàirdeachas agus caoidh leothasan a tha ri caoidh." Ma tha sinn dol a thoirt taic do chàch a-chèile, a dh'ùrnaigh dha chèile, agus a cheangal ri àiteachan eile, feumaidh fiosrachadh a bhith againn mun deidhinn. Tha Leabhar na Bliadhna a' lìbhrigeadh an leithid sin de dh'fhiosrachadh mionaideach, a' cur far comhair nàdar eadar-mheasgte beatha paraiste air feadh Alba agus thar a crìochan.

Fad bhliadhnaichean, 's ann thuige thionnndaidhinn airson gach seòrsa de cheanglaichean conaltraidh fheumail. Tha mi air a bhith dèidheil air liostaichean riamh on a bha fasan ann airson leabhraichean mar "The Book of Lists" air ais sna 1970an. Tha fiosrachadh ann an Leabhar na Bliadhna mu dhaoine is mu àiteachan, mu Chomhairlean agus mu chomataidhean na h-Eaglaise agus mun Àrd-Sheanadh mu dheireadh. Tha altan inntinneach de gach seòrsa ann cuideachd mu ar n-eaglais nach fhaighear ann an àite sam bith eile. Tha mi fada an comain an luchd-deasachaidh fa leth agus na sgiobaidhean aca airson an cuid saothrach eagnaidh ann a bhith toirt dhuinn mion-dhealbh dhen Eaglais aig àm sònraichte ann an tìm.

Tha mi an dòchas gum bi an leabhar seo feumail dhuibh ann a bhith gur cuideachadh barrachd eòlais a chur air ar n-Eaglais.

Cailean A. M. Mac na Ceardaich
Translation by Professor Boyd Robertson

EDITOR'S PREFACE

In the light of the decisions taken at the General Assembly of 2019, some changes have been made to Section 1 of this edition, and more will follow in subsequent editions.

I am grateful for the feedback from last year's edition, which helps the continued evolution of the 'Red Book', and to those who sent corrections and updates. Accordingly this year the following changes have been made:

- The lists of Prison Chaplains and University Chaplains have been restored to the printed book, and the names of full-time Church of Scotland health and work place chaplains added to the relevant chaplaincy lists. Chaplains to the Air Training Corps and Sea Cadets have also been listed.

- In the Presbytery Lists, the names of those ministerial and diaconal members not serving within a charge have been split into 2 groups: those 'In other appointments' and those 'Demitted', in order to allow readers to see at a glance those who are serving in (usually) full-time appointments. The 'Demitted' list of course encompasses many who continue to serve in active ministry in various capacities, including as locums.

- The annotations against the names of congregations in the Presbytery Lists have been expanded to indicate which congregations have Facebook pages (F), Twitter accounts (T) and websites (W). I have not included the full website addresses as these would clutter the layout and as people tend just to google the name of the congregation rather than rather type in a full www. address. As regards the annotations for hearing aid loops (H) and chair lifts/lifts (L) I rather suspect that more congregations now have these than listed – so I would welcome intimation of more.

- Last year contact details were listed (where permission was given under the General Data Protection Regulation) of Session Clerks for those congregations which were vacant or in guardianship where there was no other named person listed. That continues this year, save that in some cases Interim Moderators are listed instead. The aim remains that there should be a contact for every congregation.

One correspondent suggested that, as for ministers, the qualifications of Readers should be included in List 6-H (only some being included at present). I would be glad to include such if Readers would care to e-mail me accordingly.

As ever, around a hundred people contributed to the compilation, production and distribution of the Year Book. I again thank the Presbytery Clerks and their secretaries, the staff in the Church's offices (in particular my regular correspondents in the Ministries Council and the Communications Department), and those who compile some of the sections or subsections: Boyd Robertson (Gaelic), John Thomson (Forces Chaplains), Sheena Orr (Prison Chaplains), Roy Pinkerton (church grid references, parish and congregational changes, index of parishes and places, and editorial advice), Laurence Wareing (General Assembly report), Jennifer Hamilton (legal names and Scottish charity numbers) and Sandy Gemmill (statistics). Thanks also go to Claire Ruben of FairCopy (for assiduous copy editing) and to our contacts at Hymns Ancient and Modern who publish the book via the St Andrew Press.

Corrections, amendments and suggestions are always welcome.

David Stewart
yearbookeditor@churchofscotland.org.uk

SECTION 1

Assembly Trustees, Councils, Committees, Departments and Agencies

The symbol > used in website information indicates the headings to be selected as they appear

OFFICE OF THE PRINCIPAL CLERK

The Office of the Principal Clerk supports the General Assembly and the Moderator, and the Ecumenical Relations Committee. In addition, Departmental Staff service the following Committees (qv): Assembly Business, Legal Questions, the Committee to Nominate the Moderator, the Committee on Overtures and Cases, and the Committee on Classifying Returns to Overtures. The Clerks of Assembly are responsible for consultation on matters of Church Law, Practice and Procedure.

Principal Clerk:	Rev. Dr George J. Whyte
Depute Clerk of the General Assembly:	Ms Christine Paterson LLB DipLP
Executive Assistant to the Principal Clerk:	Ms Susan Taylor, 0131 240 2240
Senior Administration Officer (Assembly Arrangements and Moderatorial Support):	Miss Catherine McIntosh MA, 0131 225 5722 ext. 2250
Interfaith Programme Officer:	Ms Mirella Yandoli MDiv MSt
Ecumenical Officer:	Rev. Dr John L. McPake

Personnel in this department are also listed with the Councils and Committees that they serve. **Contact:** pcoffice@churchofscotland.org.uk   0131 240 2240   Fax: 0131 240 2239

OFFICE OF THE ASSEMBLY TRUSTEES

The Trustees have responsibility for governance, finance and stewardship, budgeting and general oversight of the agencies of the Church. They assist the General Assembly to determine the strategy and priorities of the Church, and seek to ensure the implementation of the policies, priorities and strategic objectives of the General Assembly through working with the agencies of the Church to achieve a collaborative approach to the nurturing of the people of the Church in their witness, worship and service. They are the Charity Trustees of the Church of Scotland (the Unincorporated Entities) Scottish Charity No. SC011353.

Assembly Trustees:

Convener:	Very Rev. Dr John P. Chalmers
Vice-Convener:	Norma Rolls
Administrative Trustee:	James McNeill
Other Trustees:	Brian Ashcroft
	Alan Campbell
	Sandra Carter
	Rev. George S. Cowie
	Jamie Lockhart
	Gary Macfarlane

Rev. Anikó Schütz Bradwell
Rev. Fiona E. Smith
Very Rev. Prof. Iain R. Torrance
David Watt
Raymond Young

Interim Head of Staff:	Rev. Dr H. Martin J. Johnstone
Head of Organisational Programmes:	Catherine Skinner
Executive Officer:	Catherine Forsyth
Audit and Compliance Officer:	Debra Livingstone
Worship Development and Mission Statistics Co-ordinator:	Rev. Dr Fiona J. Tweedie
Contact:	Carron Lunt, Senior Administration Officer clunt@churchofscotland.org.uk 0131 240 2229

Further information:
www.churchofscotland.org.uk > About us > Councils, committees and departments > Assembly Trustees

1.   COUNCILS

1.1   THE CHURCH AND SOCIETY COUNCIL

(As from 1 January 2020, a new body will be created, incorporating the work of the Church and Society Council and the World Mission Council.)

The Council seeks to engage on behalf of the Church in national, political and social issues through research, theological reflection, resourcing the local church, and by engaging with leaders in civic society, public bodies, professional associations and other networks. The Council seeks to put the wisdom of local congregations and those with lived experience of poverty and injustice at the heart of its work. Its focus for the next decade, after a consultation involving 10,000 respondents: investing in young people, local communities where people flourish, the health and wellbeing of all, caring for creation, global friendships, an economy driven by equality, doing politics differently.

Convener:	Rev. Dr Richard E. Frazer
Vice-Conveners:	Wendy Young BSc PGCE MLitt
	John Wilson BA DipHSM
Secretary:	Rev. Dr H. Martin J. Johnstone
	mjohnstone@churchofscotland.org.uk

Contact: churchandsociety@churchofscotland.org.uk   0131 240 2206
Further information:
www.churchofscotland.org.uk > About us > Councils, committees > Councils > Church and Society
www.churchofscotland.org.uk > speak out

1.2   THE MINISTRIES COUNCIL

(As from 1 January 2020, a new body will be created, incorporating the work of the Ministries Council and the Mission and Discipleship Council.)

The Council's remit is to recruit, train and support ministries in every part of Scotland, to monitor their deployment, working in partnership with ecumenical, inter-faith and statutory agencies, and giving priority to the poorest and most marginalised sections of the community.

Convener:	Rev. Rosemary Frew MA BD
Vice-Conveners:	Rev. Robert Mallinson BD
	Rev. Ruth D. Halley BEd BD PGCM
	Rev. Brian Porteous BSc DipCS
	Rev. Sarah L. Ross BD MTh PGDip

Council Secretary:	Vacant
Depute:	Mr Craig Renton
Education and Training:	Ms Kay Cathcart MA PGCE
Partnerships and Development:	Mr Daran Golby BA CIPD
Priority Areas:	Ms Shirley Grieve BA PGCE (0141 248 2905)
Recruitment and Support:	Rev. Dr Lezley J. Stewart

Contact: ministries@churchofscotland.org.uk 0131 225 5722

Further information:
www.churchofscotland.org.uk > About us > Councils, committees > Councils > Ministries Council
www.churchofscotland.org.uk > Serve > Ministries Council > Ministries in the Church
www.churchofscotland.org.uk/ascend
www.churchofscotland.org.uk > Serve > Go For It
Pulpit Supply Fees: www.churchofscotland.org.uk/yearbook > Section 3F

1.3   THE MISSION AND DISCIPLESHIP COUNCIL

(As from 1 January 2020, a new body will be created, incorporating the work of the Ministries Council and the Mission and Discipleship Council.)

The Council's remit is to stimulate and support the Church by the provision of resources nationally, regionally and locally in worship, witness, mission and discipleship. This includes the development of strategies and materials in the areas of adult education, resourcing elders, work with young adults, young people and children (including those with particular needs and disabilities), as well as in liturgy, and church art and architecture.

Convener:	Rev. Norman A. Smith MA BD
Vice-Conveners:	Rev. W. Martin Fair BA BD DMin
	Rev. Peter M. Gardner MA BD
	Lynne McEwen

Council Secretary:	Rev. Angus R. Mathieson MA BD

Church Without Walls:	Mrs Lesley Hamilton-Messer MA
Congregational Learning:	Mr Ronald H. Clarke BEng MSc PGCE
Resourcing Worship:	Mr Phill Mellstrom BA

Church Art and Architecture:	
Convener:	Rev. William T. Hogg MA BD
Contact:	gentrustees@churchofscotland.org.uk

Contact:	Lynn Hall
	mandd@churchofscotland.org.uk

Further information:
www.churchofscotland.org.uk > About us > Councils, committees > Mission and Discipleship
www.resourcingmission.org.uk

Church Art and Architecture www.churchofscotland.org.uk > Resources > Subjects > Art and Architecture resources

For Life and Work see below 2.15
For Saint Andrew Press see below 2.20
For Scottish Storytelling Centre (The Netherbow) see below 2.22

1.4   THE SOCIAL CARE COUNCIL
(CrossReach)
Charis House, 47 Milton Road East, Edinburgh EH15 2SR
0131 657 2000   Fax: 0131 657 5000
info@crossreach.org.uk   www.crossreach.org.uk

(In 2020 the Council is to become the Social Care Committee.)

The Social Care Council, known as CrossReach, provides social-care services as part of the Christian witness of the Church to the people of Scotland, and engages with other bodies in responding to emerging areas of need. CrossReach operates 72 services across the country.

Convener:	Mr Bill Steele
Vice-Conveners:	Ms Irene McGugan
	Rev. Thomas S. Riddell

Chief Executive Officer:	Viv Dickenson (viv.dickenson@crossreach.org.uk)

Director of Services to Older People:	Allan Logan (allan.logan@crossreach.org.uk)
Director of Adult Care Services:	Calum Murray (calum.murray@crossreach.org.uk)
Director of Children and Families:	Sheila Gordon (sheila.gordon@crossreach.org.uk)
Director of Finance and Resources:	Ian Wauchope (ian.wauchope@crossreach.org.uk)
Director of Human Resources and	
Organisational Development:	Mari Rennie (mari.rennie@crossreach.org.uk)

Further information: www.crossreach.org.uk

For sharing local experience and initiatives: www.socialcareforum.scot

1.5   THE WORLD MISSION COUNCIL

(As from 1 January 2020, a new body will be created, incorporating the work of the Church and Society Council and the World Mission Council.)

The aim of the Council is to enable the Church of Scotland – its members, adherents, congregations, and presbyteries - to participate effectively in the Mission of God in the world, following the example and priorities of Jesus Christ, and seeking the guidance of the Holy Spirit. The Gospel story of the walk to Emmaus (Luke 24) provides a paradigm for mission in the 21st Century as a shared journey; through listening to and walking with our partners on our shared journey of faith, the Council seeks to engage in a process of attentive accompaniment with the Church of Scotland's partners worldwide. This involves presence (an incarnational approach to mission in which relationships of mutual respect can be built); practical action (following Jesus' example in reaching out to the poor, the captive, the sick, and the oppressed); and proclamation (both the explicit proclamation of the Good News and being a prophetic voice for the voiceless and exercising advocacy on behalf of the powerless.) The Council is also the principal link with Christian Aid.

Acting Convener: Very Rev. Susan M. Brown BD DipMin DUniv
Vice-Conveners: Rev. Alan F. Miller BA MA BD
                   Mrs Maureen V. Jack MA MEd MSc

Council Secretary: Rev. Ian W. Alexander BA BD STM
Secretaries: Mrs Jennie Chinembiri (Africa and Caribbean)
                   Ms Carol Finlay (Twinning and Local Development)
                   Mr Kenny Roger (Middle East)
                   Mr Sandy Sneddon (Asia)

Contact: world@churchofscotland.org.uk   0131 225 5722
Further Information:
www.churchofscotland.org.uk > About us > Councils, committees > Councils > World Mission
www.churchofscotland.org.uk > Serve > World Mission

2.   DEPARTMENTS, COMMITTEES AND AGENCIES

2.1   ASSEMBLY BUSINESS COMMITTEE

Convener: Rev. Fiona E. Smith LLB BD
Vice-Convener: Rev. Donald G.B. McCorkindale BD DipMin

Secretary: Principal Clerk
                cmcintosh@churchofscotland.org.uk   0131 240 2240

Further information:
www.churchofscotland.org.uk > About us > General Assembly
www.churchofscotland.org.uk > About us > Councils, committees > Committees > Assembly
Business

2.2   CENTRAL PROPERTIES DEPARTMENT

Remit: to provide property, facilities and health and safety services to the Councils and
Departments of the central administration of the Church.

Property, Health and Safety Manager: Colin Wallace
Property, Health and Safety Officer: Jacqueline Collins
Property Officer: Eunice Hessell
Support Assistant: Joyce Anderson

Contact: cpd@churchofscotland.org.uk   0131 240 2254

2.3   CHURCH OF SCOTLAND TRUST

Chairman: Mr Thomas C. Watson
Vice-Chairman: Mr W.F. Stuart Lynch
Treasurer: Mrs Anne F. Macintosh BA CA
Secretary and Clerk: Mrs Jennifer M. Hamilton BA NP
                     jhamilton@churchofscotland.org.uk   0131 240 2222

Further information:
www.churchofscotland.org.uk > About us > Councils, committees > Departments > Church of
Scotland Trust

2.4   COMMUNICATIONS DEPARTMENT

Head of Communications: Ruth MacLeod 0131 240 2243
Communications Manager: Helen Silvis 0131 240 2268
Senior Communications Officer: Cameron Brooks 0131 240 2204
Communications Officer: Jane Bristow 0131 240 2204
Communications Officer: Laura Crawford 0131 240 2268

Web Editor: Jill Stevens
Web Developer: Alan Murray
Design Team Leader: Chris Flexen
Senior Designer: Steve Walker

Contact the Media Team after hours: 07854 783539
Contact department: 0131 240 2268
Further information:
www.churchofscotland.org.uk > About us > Councils, committees > Departments > Communications

2.5   ECUMENICAL RELATIONS COMMITTEE

The Committee includes six members appointed by the General Assembly, each attached to one of the five Councils of the Church and the Theological Forum, and two members with responsibility for the promotion of ecumenical work within the local Church, plus representatives of other denominations in Scotland and Church of Scotland members elected to British and international ecumenical bodies. The Church of Scotland trustee of ACTS and the co-chair of the Joint Commission on Doctrine attend as co-opted members. The General Secretary of ACTS attends as a corresponding member.

Convener: Rev. Alexander G. Horsburgh MA BD
Vice-Convener: Rev. Kevin Mackenzie BD DPS
Secretary and Ecumenical Officer: Rev. Dr John L. McPake
Senior Administrator: Vacant

Contact: ecumenical@churchofscotland.org.uk   0131 240 2208

Further information:
www.churchofscotland.org.uk > About us > Councils, committees > Committees > Ecumenical Relations Committee
www.churchofscotland.org.uk > Connect > Ecumenism
www.churchofscotland.org.uk > Resources > Subjects > Ecumenical Resources
World Council of Churches: www.oikumene.org
Churches Together in Britain and Ireland: www.ctbi.org.uk
Action of Churches Together in Scotland: www.acts-scotland.org
For other international ecumenical bodies see Committee's web pages as above
See also 'Other Churches in the United Kingdom' page 20

2.6   FACILITIES MANAGEMENT DEPARTMENT

Facilities Manager: Carole Tait
                       ctait@churchofscotland.org.uk   0131 240 2214

Further information:
www.churchofscotland.org.uk > About us > Councils, committees > Committees > Office
management

2.7   FORCES CHAPLAINS COMMITTEE

Convener: Rev. Dr Marjory A. MacLean
Vice-Convener: Carolyn Macleod MBE
Secretary: Vacant (Committee served by Ministries Council)
                   ministries@churchofscotland.org.uk   0131 225 5722

Further information:
www.churchofscotland.org.uk > About us > Councils, committees > Forces Chaplains
Committee
A list of Chaplains is found at Section 6 G

2.8   GENERAL TRUSTEES

Chairman: Mr Raymond K. Young CBE BArch FRIAS
Vice-Chairman: Mr Ian T. Townsend FRICS
Secretary and Clerk: Mr David D. Robertson LLB NP
Depute Secretary and Clerk: Mr Keith S. Mason LLB NP
Assistant Secretaries: Mr Brian Auld ChEHO MREHIS FRSPH GradIOSH
                           (Safe Buildings Consultant)
                           Ms Claire L. Cowell LLB (Glebes)
                           Mrs Morag J. Menneer BSc MRICS (Glebes)
                           Mr Brian D. Waller LLB (Ecclesiastical Buildings)
                           Mr. Neil Page BSc MCIOB
                           (Presbytery Strategy and Innovation)
Health and Safety Officer: Mr Andrew Barnet MA GradIOSH MIIRSM
Fire Safety Officer: Mr Robert Speedie GradIFE
Energy Conservation: Mr Robert Lindores FInstPa
Treasurer: Mrs Anne F. Macintosh BA CA
Finance Manager: Mr Alex Semple FCCA

Buildings insurance,   Church of Scotland Insurance Services Ltd.
all enquiries to   121 George Street, Edinburgh EH2 4YN
                           enquiries@cosic.co.uk   0131 220 4119

Contact: gentrustees@churchofscotland.org.uk   0131 225 5722 ext. 2261
Further information:
www.churchofscotland.org.uk > About us > Councils, committees > Departments > General
Trustees

2.9   THE GUILD

The Church of Scotland Guild is a movement within the Church of Scotland whose aim is 'to invite and encourage both women and men to commit their lives to Jesus Christ and to enable them to express their faith in worship, prayer and action'.

Convener: Marian Macintyre
Vice-Convener: Helen Banks
                     Andrea Houston
                     Margaret Muir
                     Mabel Wallace
General Secretary: Iain W. Whyte BA DCE DMS

Contact: guild@churchofscotland.org.uk   0131 240 2217

Further information:
www.cos-guild.org.uk
www.churchofscotland.org.uk > Serve > The Guild

2.10   HOUSING AND LOAN FUND

Chair: Rev. MaryAnn R. Rennie BD MTh
Deputy Chair: Rev. Dorothy U. Anderson LLB DipPl BD
Secretary: Hazel Bett LLB DipLP
                     Hbett@churchofscotland.org.uk   0131 225 5722 ext. 2310
Property Manager: Hilary J. Hardy
Property Assistant: John Lunn

Further information:
www.churchofscotland.org.uk > About us > Councils, committees > Departments > Housing and Loan Fund

---

2.11   HUMAN RESOURCES DEPARTMENT

Head of Human Resources: Elaine McCloghry
Human Resources Managers: Karen Smith
                              Angela Ocak
Human Resources Advisers: Sarah-Jayne McVeigh
                              Nicola Bird
                              Stephanie Thomson

Contact: hr@churchofscotland.org.uk   0131 240 2270

2.12 INFORMATION TECHNOLOGY DEPARTMENT

Information Technology Manager: David Malcolm
0131 240 2247

Contact: itdept@churchofscotland.org.uk 0131 240 2245

Further information:
www.churchofscotland.org.uk > About us > Councils, committees > Committees > IT

2.13 INVESTORS TRUST

Chairman: Mr Brian J. Duffin
Vice-Chairman: Mr Robert D. Burgon
Treasurer: Mrs Anne F. Macintosh BA CA
Secretary: Mrs Nicola Robertson
investorstrust@churchofscotland.org.uk

Further information:
www.churchofscotland.org.uk > About us > Councils, committees > Departments > Investors
Trust

2.14 LAW DEPARTMENT

Solicitor of the Church
and of the General Trustees: Miss Mary Macleod LLB NP
Depute Solicitor: Mrs Jennifer Hamilton BA NP
Senior Solicitor: Mrs Elspeth Annan LLB NP
Solicitors: Miss Susan Killean LLB NP
Mrs Anne Steele LLB NP
Mrs Jennifer Campbell LLB LLM NP
Gregor Buick LLB WS NP
Mrs Madelaine Sproule LLB NP
Gordon Barclay LLB BSc MSc MPhil PhD
David Stihler MA LLB DipLP NP

Contact: lawdept@churchofscotland.org.uk 0131 225 5722 ext. 2230; Fax: 0131 240 2246.

Further information:
www.churchofscotland.org.uk > About us > Councils, committees > Committees > Law

2.15 LEGAL QUESTIONS COMMITTEE

The Committee's remit is to advise the General Assembly on questions of Church and Constitutional Law, assist Agencies of the Assembly in preparing and interpreting legislation and arrange for the care of Church Records.

Convener: Rev. Dr S. Grant Barclay
Vice-Convener: Mrs Barbara Finlayson LLB WS
Secretary: Principal Clerk
Depute Clerk: Ms Christine Paterson LLB DipLP

Contact: staylor@churchofscotland.org.uk 0131 240 2240

Further information:
www.churchofscotland.org.uk > About us > Councils, committees > Committees > Legal Questions

---

2.16 LIFE AND WORK
the Church of Scotland's monthly magazine

The magazine's purpose is to keep the Church informed about events in church life at home and abroad and to provide a forum for Christian opinion and debate on a variety of topics. It has an independent editorial policy. Contributions which are relevant to any aspect of the Christian faith are welcome. The website, www.lifeandwork.org, includes up-to-date news, extracts from the magazine and additional features. To subscribe to the magazine through your church, speak to your Life and Work co-ordinator. To receive by post, call the number below or visit the website. A digital download, for reading on PC, tablet and smartphone, is also available.

Editor: Lynne McNeil   magazine@lifeandwork.org 0131 225 5722

Further information:
www.lifeandwork.org
www.churchofscotland.org.uk > News and Events > Life and Work

---

2.17 NOMINATION COMMITTEE

Convener: Ms Lynsey M. Kimmitt LLB DipLP NP
Vice-Convener: William M. Wishart BD
Secretary (Interim): Rev. Dr H. Martin J. Johnstone

Contact: Nominations@churchofscotland.org.uk 0131 240 2229

Further information:
www.churchofscotland.org.uk > About us > Councils, committees > Committees > Nomination Committee

2.18   PENSION TRUSTEES

Chairman:	Mr Graeme R. Caughey BSc FFIA
Vice-Chairman:	Mr Douglas Millar
Secretary and	
Pensions Manager:	Ms Jane McLeod BSc FPMI
Senior Pensions Administrator:	Mrs Fiona McCulloch-Stevenson
Pensions Administrators:	Mrs Marshall Rowan
	Ms Birgit Mosemann
	Mr Connor MacFadyen

Contact: pensions@churchofscotland.org.uk   0131 240 2255

Further information:
www.churchofscotland.org.uk > About us > Councils, committees > Departments > Pension Trustees

2.19   SAFEGUARDING SERVICE

The service ensures that the Church has robust structures and policies in place for the prevention of harm and abuse of children and adults at risk; and to ensure a timely and appropriate response when harm or abuse is witnessed, suspected or reported.

Convener:	Rev. Adam J. Dillon BD ThM
Vice-Convener:	Mrs Caroline Deerin
Service Manager:	Ms Julie Main BA DipSW

Contact: safeguarding@churchofscotland.org.uk   0131 240 2256

Further Information:
www.churchofscotland.org.uk > About us > Councils, committees > Departments > Safeguarding Service

2.20   SAINT ANDREW PRESS

Saint Andrew Press is managed on behalf of the Church of Scotland by Hymns Ancient and Modern Ltd and publishes a broad range of titles, ranging from the much-loved William Barclay series of New Testament *Daily Study Bible* commentaries to resources for the mission and ministry of the contemporary church. The full list of publications can be viewed on the Saint Andrew Press website (see below).

Contact: Christine Smith, Publishing Director christine@hymnsam.co.uk   0207 776 7546

Further information: www.standrewpress.com

2.21   SCOTTISH CHURCHES PARLIAMENTARY OFFICE
121 George Street, Edinburgh EH2 4YN

The Office exists to build meaningful relationships between churches and the Scottish and UK Parliaments and Governments, seeking to engage reflectively in the political process, translate their commitment to the welfare of Scotland into parliamentary debate, and contribute their experience and faith-based reflection on it to the decision-making process.

Scottish Churches Parliamentary Officer: Chloe Clemmons MA MA (Human Rights)
                                                chloe.clemmons@scpo.scot
Research and Resource Development Officer: Irene Mackinnon MA MLitt
                                                irene.mackinnon@scpo.scot

Contact: 0131 240 2276

Further information:
www.churchofscotland.org.uk > Speak out > Doing Politics Differently
www.scpo.scot

2.22   SCOTTISH STORYTELLING CENTRE (THE NETHERBOW)
43–45 High Street, Edinburgh EH1 1SR

The integrated facilities of the **Netherbow Theatre** and the **John Knox House**, together with the outstanding conference and reception areas, form an important cultural venue on the Royal Mile in Edinburgh. The Centre captures both the historical roots of storytelling and the forward-looking mission to preserve it: providing advice and assistance nationally in the use of traditional arts in a diversity of settings. Mission and Discipleship Council are pleased to host TRACS (Traditional Arts and Culture Scotland), a grant-funded body who provide an extensive year-round cultural and literary programme.

Contact: reception@scottishstorytellingcentre.com   0131 556 9579

Further information:
www.scottishstorytellingcentre.com

2.23   STEWARDSHIP AND FINANCE DEPARTMENT

General Treasurer:	Anne F. Macintosh BA CA
Deputy Treasurer (Congregational Finance):	Archie McDowall BA CA
Deputy Treasurer (Unincorporated Councils and Committees):	Bob Cowan BCom CA
National Stewardship Co-ordinator:	David J. Lynch BA
Finance Managers:	Lisa Erskine BA FCCA
	Elaine Macadie BA CA
	Alex Semple FCCA
	Leanne Thompson BSc CA

Contact: sfadmin@churchofscotland.org.uk
Further information and details of consultants:
www.churchofscotland.org.uk > About us > Councils, committees and departments > Stewardship and Finance
www.churchofscotland.org.uk > Resources > Stewardship > National Stewardship Programme
www.churchofscotland.org.uk > About us > Stewardship Finance and Trusts

2.24   THEOLOGICAL FORUM

The purpose of the Forum is to continue to develop and bring to expression doctrinal under-standing of the Church with reference to Scripture and to the confessional standards of the Church of Scotland, and the implications of this for worship and witness in and beyond contemporary Scotland. It responds to requests to undertake enquiries as they arise, draws the Church's attention to particular matters requiring theological work, and promotes theological reflection throughout the Church.

Convener:	Rev. Donald G. MacEwan MA BD PhD
Vice-Convener:	Sarah Lane Ritchie BA MDiv MSc PhD
Secretary:	Nathalie A. Mareš MA MTh

Contact: NMares@churchofscotland.org.uk
Further Information:
www.churchofscotland.org.uk > About us > Councils, committees > Committees > Theological Forum

SECTION 2

General Information

(1) GAELIC IN THE CHURCH
Professor Boyd Robertson

A' Ghàidhlig anns an Eaglais

Tha uallach air Comhairle an Àrd-Sheanaidh a bhith a' co-òrdanachadh na tha an Eaglais a' dèanamh airson leasachadh agus brosnachadh na Gàidhlig san Eaglais agus tha i a' faighinn taic san obair seo bhon Bhuidheann Ghàidhlig aig a bheil raon-dleastanais a chaidh aontachadh gu foirmeil aig Àrd- Sheanadh 2018. B' e aon de na chiad phrìomhachasan a chaidh a chomharrachadh leis a' Bhuidheann Plana Gàidhlig ullachadh. Tha am Plana a tha air nochdadh ag amas air dealas na h-Eaglaise gu fàs is leasachadh na Gàidhlig a shealltainn thar gach mìr dhe a raon-obrach. Ged is e misean na h-eaglaise is cur an cèill an Deagh Sgeul na prìomh chùisean, tha am Plana a' gabhail a-steach uile ghnìomhachdan làitheil na h-Eaglaise leithid conaltradh, sgiobachd is trèanadh. Tha farsainneachd is stoidhle a' Phlana Gàidhlig a' leantainn dreach phlanaichean co-ionann ris an deach gabhail le buidhnean eile ann an Alba.

Bha am Buidheann mothachail gum feumte maoineachadh gus am Plana a chur an gnìomh agus chaidh deagh adhartas a dhèanamh a thaobh seo le ionmhas air a sholar airson eileamaidean cudromach dhen obair a thoirt air adhart rè 2019-20. Chaidh tabhartas de £30k a thoirt seachad le Bòrd na Gàidhlig agus fhuaireas £15k bhon Eaglais fhèin bho mhaoin chuingealaichte. Cheadaich na tabhartasan sin le chèile Oifigear Gàidhlig fhastadh air bhonn co-chomhairleachaidh son bliadhna gus pìosan obrach sònraichte adhartachadh agus gus cosgais iomlan is priomhachas a chur air eileamaidean dhen Phlana mu choinneamh 2020-23. Bidh Donnchadh Sneddon, a tha na dheasaiche air Na Duilleagan Gàidhlig còmhla ri Liam Crouse, a' tòiseachadh mar Oifigear san Dàmhair 2019.

Tha Action of Churches Together in Scotland (ACTS) air tabhartas de £9k a bhuileachadh air dà phròiseact àraidh: solar riochd labhairteach Gàidhlig de na ceithir Soisgeulan agus stuthan Gàidhlig airson na h-iomairt ùrnaigh domhanta Thigeadh do Rìoghachd, nam measg eadar-theangachadh de leabhar-latha ùrnaigh agus craoladh pod goirid leis an Fhìor Urr Dr Aonghas Moireasdan a bha na Neach-Gairm air a' Bhuidheann chun na h-Ògmhìos 2018. Chaidh clàradh nan Soisgeulan a ghabhail os làimh le sgioba fo stiùir Nicola NicThòmais aig Sabhal Mòr Ostaig san Eilean Sgitheanach.

Tha am Buidheann Gàidhlig miannach a bhith ag obair le eaglaisean eile agus air buannachd fhaighinn bho cho-phàirteachadh is chomhairle an Oifigeir Uil-Eaglaiseil. Chunnacas eisimpleir ghasta de cho-obrachadh eadar-eaglaiseil leis an fhoillseachadh san Ògmhios 2019 de riochd Gàidhlig ùr dhen Tiomnadh Nuadh leis a' Chomann Bhìoball Albannach. Ghabh sgioba bho Eaglais na h-Alba, bhon Eaglais Shaor agus bhon Eaglais Chaitligich os làimh eadar-theangachadh bhon Ghreugais thùsail dìreach gu Gàidhlig an latha an-diugh thar deich bliadhna.

Tha am Plana Gàidhlig a' cruthachadh mòran chothroman airson cheanglaichean uil-eaglaiseil agus airson co-obrachadh. Bidh dùil gun obraich an t-Oifigear Gàidhlig an co-bhuinn ri eaglaisean eile far an urrainnear gus taic a thoirt dhan choimhearsnachd Ghàidhlig gu lèir is gus am bi goireasan is uidheamachadh nas fheàrr airson ministrealachd is misein aig luchd-labhairt na Gàidhlig anns gach eaglais. Ri linn seo, thèid prìomhachas a thoirt san ath sheisean do cho-labhairt nàiseanta, a' leantainn air an tachartas Ath Cheumannan 2015 a bheachdaich air àite na Gàidhlig ann an eaglaisean na h-Alba is mar a b' fheàrr a ghabhadh sin a neartachadh. Bheir tachartas 2020 sùil as ùr air dè tha dhìth agus dè na dòighean air ministrealachd is misean Gàidhlig adhartachadh agus bheir e taic is brosnachadh do mhinistearan Gàidhlig agus do neach sam bith a dh' iarradh an cuid Gàidhlig a leasachadh airson a chleachdadh taobh a-staigh na h-eaglaise. 'S e aon amas sònraichte gun tig fàs air an àireamh de sheirbheisean Gàidhlig a thathar a' cumail.

An t-Oll Boyd Robasdan
Neach Gairm Sealach, Am Buidheann Gàidhlig

GAELIC IN THE CHURCH

The Council of Assembly has responsibility for coordinating the Church's contribution to the development and promotion of Gaelic within the Church and is supported in this work by the Gaelic Group whose remit was formally approved by the General Assembly of 2018. One of the first priorities identified by the Group was the production of a Gaelic Language Plan. The Plan which has emerged is intended to reflect the Church's commitment to the growth and development of Gaelic across all of its work. Whilst the key areas of concern relate to the mission of the church and the proclamation of the Good News, the Plan encompasses the Church's day to day operations in areas such as communication, staffing and training. The breadth and style of the Gaelic Plan is in line with similar plans adopted by other organisations in Scotland.

The Group recognized that funding would be required to implement the Plan and significant progress has been made in this regard, with funding secured to enable key aspects of work to be progressed during 2019- 20. A grant of £30k has been awarded by the Gaelic development agency, Bòrd na Gàidhlig and, from within the Church, £15k has been provided from a restricted fund. These grants combined have allowed a Gaelic Officer to be appointed on a consultancy basis for one year to progress specific work and to fully cost and prioritise the elements contained within the Plan for the period 2020-2023. Duncan Sneddon, who edits the Gaelic pages of Life and Work with Liam Crouse, will take up the Officer's post in October 2019.

Action of Churches Together in Scotland (ACTS) has awarded a grant of £9k towards two specific projects: firstly, the production of a Gaelic audio version of the four Gospels and, secondly, for Gaelic resources for the Thy Kingdom Come global prayer initiative including a translation of a prayer journal and a short podcast by the Very Rev Dr Angus Morrison who convened the Group until June 2018. The recording of the Gospels has been undertaken by a team led by Nicola Thomson at Sabhal Mòr Ostaig, the National Centre for Gaelic Language and Culture, on the Isle of Skye.

The Gaelic Group is keen to work with other denominations and has benefited from the involvement and advice of the Ecumenical Officer. A splendid example of interdenominational collaboration led to the publication in June 2019 by the Scottish Bible Society of a modernised Gaelic version of the New Testament. A team drawn from the Church of Scotland, the Free Church of Scotland and the Roman Catholic Church undertook the translation from Greek into contemporary Gaelic over a 10 year period.

The Gaelic Plan provides many opportunities for ecumenical engagement and joint working. The Gaelic Officer will be required to work in collaboration with other churches wherever possible so that the Gaelic community as a whole is supported and that Gaelic speakers within all of the churches are better resourced and equipped for ministry and mission. In this regard, a priority for the next session will be a national conference, following on from the 2015 Next Steps event which looked at the place of Gaelic in Scotland's churches and how best to strengthen that. The 2020 event will further consider the needs and ways of promoting Gaelic ministry and mission and will offer support and encouragement to Gaelic speaking ministers and anyone who would like to improve their Gaelic for use within a church context. One specific aim is to see an increase in the number of Gaelic church services being held.

Professor Boyd Robertson
Acting Convener, Gaelic Group

(2) OTHER CHURCHES IN THE UNITED KINGDOM

THE UNITED FREE CHURCH OF SCOTLAND
Principal Clerks: Rev. Martin C. Keane and Rev. Colin C. Bown, United Free Church Offices, 11 Newton Place, Glasgow G3 7PR (0141 332 3435; office@ufcos.org.uk; www.ufcos. org.uk).

THE FREE CHURCH OF SCOTLAND
Principal Clerk: Rev. Callum Macleod, 15 North Bank Street, The Mound, Edinburgh EH1 2LS (0131 226 5286; offices@freechurch.org; www.freechurch.org).

FREE CHURCH OF SCOTLAND (CONTINUING)
Principal Clerk: Rev. John MacLeod, Free Church Manse, Portmahomack, Tain IV20 1YL (01862 871467; principalclerk@fccontinuing.org; www.freechurchcontinuing.org).

THE FREE PRESBYTERIAN CHURCH OF SCOTLAND
Clerk of Synod: Rev. Keith M. Watkins, Free Presbyterian Manse, Ferry Road, Leverburgh, Isle of Harris HS5 3UA (kmwatkins@fpchurch.org.uk; www.fpchurch.org.uk).

ASSOCIATED PRESBYTERIAN CHURCHES
Clerk of Presbytery: Rev. J.R. Ross Macaskill, Bruach Taibh, 2 Borve, Arnisort, Isle of Skye IV51 9PS (01470 582264; emailjrrm@gmail.com; www.apchurches.org).

THE REFORMED PRESBYTERIAN CHURCH OF SCOTLAND
Clerk of Presbytery: Rev. Peter Loughridge, 3b West Pilton Terrace, Edinburgh EH4 4GY (07791 369626; peterloughridge@hotmail.com; www.rpcscotland.org).

THE PRESBYTERIAN CHURCH IN IRELAND
Clerk of the General Assembly and General Secretary: Rev. Trevor D. Gribben, Assembly Buildings, 2–10 Fisherwick Place, Belfast BT1 6DW (028 9041 7208; clerk@ presbyterianireland.org; www.presbyterianireland.org).

THE PRESBYTERIAN CHURCH OF WALES
General Secretary: Rev. Meiron Morris, Tabernacle Chapel, 81 Merthyr Road, Whitchurch, Cardiff CF14 1DD (02920 627465; swyddfa.office@ebcpcw.org.uk; www.ebcpcw.cymru).

THE UNITED REFORMED CHURCH
General Secretary: Rev. John Proctor, Church House, 86 Tavistock Place, London WC1H 9RT (020 7916 2020; Fax: 020 7916 2021; john.proctor@urc.org.uk; www.urc.org.uk).

UNITED REFORMED CHURCH SYNOD OF SCOTLAND
Synod Clerk: Mr Bill Robson, United Reformed Church, 113 West Regent Street, Glasgow G1 2RU (0141 248 5382; brobson@urcscotland.org.uk; www.urcscotland.org.uk).

BAPTIST UNION OF SCOTLAND
General Director: Rev. Alan Donaldson, 48 Speirs Wharf, Glasgow G4 9TH (0141 423 6169; admin@scottishbaptist.org.uk; www.scottishbaptist.com).

CONGREGATIONAL FEDERATION IN SCOTLAND
Chair: Rev. May-Kane Logan, 93 Cartside Road, Busby, Glasgow G76 8QD (0141 237 1349; maycita1@virginmedia.com; www.congregational.org.uk).

RELIGIOUS SOCIETY OF FRIENDS (QUAKERS)
Clerk to the General Meeting for Scotland: Adwoa Bittle (Ms), 4 Burnside Park, Pitcairngreen, Perth PH1 3BF (01738 583108; adwoabittle@hotmail.co.uk; www.quakerscotland.org).

ROMAN CATHOLIC CHURCH
Fr. James A. Grant, General Secretary, Bishops' Conference of Scotland, 64 Aitken Street, Airdrie ML6 6LT (01236 764061; gensec@bcos.org.uk; www.bcos.org.uk).

THE SALVATION ARMY
Lt-Col. Carol Bailey, Secretary for Scotland and Divisional Commander East Scotland Division, Scotland Office, 12A Dryden Road, Loanhead EH20 9LZ (0131 440 9101; carol.bailey@salvationarmy.org.uk; www.salvationarmy.org.uk).

SCOTTISH EPISCOPAL CHURCH
Secretary General: Mr John F. Stuart, 21 Grosvenor Crescent, Edinburgh EH12 5EE (0131 225 6357; secgen@scotland.anglican.org; www.scotland.anglican.org).

THE SYNOD OF THE METHODIST CHURCH IN SCOTLAND
District Administrator: Mrs Fiona Inglis, Methodist Church Office, Old Churches House, Kirk Street, Dunblane FK15 0AJ (Tel/Fax: 01786 820295; DistrictAdmin@methodistchurchinscotland.net; methodistchurchinscotland.net).

GENERAL SYNOD OF THE CHURCH OF ENGLAND
Secretary General: Mr William Nye, Church House, Great Smith Street, London SW1P 3NZ (020 7898 1000; enquiry@churchofengland.org).

---

(3) OVERSEAS CHURCHES

See www.churchofscotland.org.uk > Serve > World Mission > Our partner churches

---

(4) HER MAJESTY'S HOUSEHOLD IN SCOTLAND
ECCLESIASTICAL

Dean of the Order of the Thistle and Dean of the Chapel Royal:	Very Rev. Prof. David A.S. Fergusson OBE MA BD DPhil DD FBA FRSE
Domestic Chaplains:	Rev. Kenneth I. Mackenzie DL BD CPS Rev. Neil N. Gardner MA BD RNR
Chaplains in Ordinary:	Rev. Norman W. Drummond CBE MA BD DUniv FRSE Very Rev. Angus Morrison MA BD PhD DD

Very Rev. E. Lorna Hood OBE MA BD DD
Rev. Alistair G. Bennett BSc BD
Very Rev. Susan M. Brown BD DipMin DUniv
Very Rev. John P. Chalmers BD CPS DD
Rev. George S. Cowie BSc BD
Rev. Elizabeth M. Henderson MA BD MTh
Rev. George J. Whyte BSc BD DMin

Extra Chaplains:

Rev. John MacLeod MA
Very Rev. James A. Simpson BSc BD STM DD
Very Rev. James Harkness KCVO CB OBE MA DD
Rev. John L. Paterson MA BD STM
Rev. Charles Robertson LVO MA
Very Rev. John B. Cairns KCVO LTh LLB LLD DD
Very Rev. Gilleasbuig I. Macmillan
      KCVO MA BD Drhc DD FRSE HRSA FRCSEd
Very Rev. Finlay A.J. Macdonald MA BD PhD DD
Rev. Alastair H. Symington MA BD
Rev. James M. Gibson TD LTh LRAM
Very Rev. Prof. Iain R. Torrance KCVO Kt DD FRSE

---

(5) RECENT LORD HIGH COMMISSIONERS
TO THE GENERAL ASSEMBLY

* deceased

1969	Her Majesty the Queen attended in person
1980/81	The Earl of Elgin and Kincardine KT DL JP
1982/83	*Colonel Sir John Edward Gilmour Bt DSO TD
1984/85	*Charles Hector Fitzroy Maclean, Baron Maclean of Duart and Morvern KT GCVO KBE
1986/87	*John Campbell Arbuthnott, Viscount of Arbuthnott KT CBE DSC FRSE FRSA
1988/89	*Sir Iain Mark Tennant KT FRSA
1990/91	The Rt Hon. Donald MacArthur Ross FRSE
1992/93	The Rt Hon. Lord Macfarlane of Bearsden KT FRSE
1994/95	*Lady Marion Fraser KT
1996	Her Royal Highness the Princess Royal LT LG GCVO
1997	The Rt Hon. Lord Macfarlane of Bearsden KT FRSE
1998/99	*The Rt Hon. Lord Hogg of Cumbernauld CBE DL JP
2000	His Royal Highness the Prince Charles, Duke of Rothesay KG KT GCB OM
2001/02	*The Rt Hon. Viscount Younger of Leckie KT KCVO TD PC
	Her Majesty the Queen attended the opening of the General Assembly of 2002
2003/04	The Rt Hon. Lord Steel of Aikwood KT KBE
2005/06	The Rt Hon. Lord Mackay of Clashfern KT

2007	His Royal Highness the Prince Andrew, Duke of York KG KCVO
2008/09	The Rt Hon. George Reid PC MA
2010/11	Lord Wilson of Tillyorn KT GCMG PRSE
2012/13	The Rt Hon. Lord Selkirk of Douglas QC MA LLB
2014	His Royal Highness the Prince Edward, Earl of Wessex KG GCVO
2015/16	The Rt Hon. Lord Hope of Craighead KT PC FRSE
2017	Her Royal Highness the Princess Royal KG KT GCVO QSO
2018/19	The Duke of Buccleuch and Queensberry KT KBE DL FSA FRSE

(6) RECENT MODERATORS
OF THE GENERAL ASSEMBLY

deceased

1992	Hugh R. Wyllie MA DD FCIBS, Hamilton: Old
1993	*James L. Weatherhead CBE MA LLB DD, Principal Clerk of Assembly
1994	James A. Simpson BSc BD STM DD, Dornoch Cathedral
1995	James Harkness KCVO CB OBE MA DD, Chaplain General (Emeritus)
1996	John H. McIndoe MA BD STM DD, London: St Columba's linked with Newcastle: St Andrew's
1997	*Alexander McDonald BA DUniv CMIWSc, General Secretary, Department of Ministry
1998	Alan Main TD MA BD STM PhD DD, University of Aberdeen
1999	John B. Cairns KCVO LTh LLB LLD DD, Dumbarton: Riverside
2000	Andrew R.C. McLellan CBE MA BD STM DD, Edinburgh: St Andrew's and St George's
2001	John D. Miller BA BD DD, Glasgow: Castlemilk East
2002	Finlay A.J. Macdonald MA BD PhD DD, Principal Clerk of Assembly
2003	Iain R. Torrance KCVO Kt DD FRSE, University of Aberdeen
2004	Alison Elliot CBE MA MSc PhD LLD DD FRSE, Associate Director, Centre for Theology and Public Issues, University of Edinburgh
2005	David W. Lacy BA BD DLitt DL, Kilmarnock: Henderson
2006	Alan D. McDonald LLB BD MTh DLitt DD, Cameron linked with St Andrews: St Leonard's
2007	Sheilagh M. Kesting BA BD DD DSG, Secretary of Ecumenical Relations Committee
2008	David W. Lunan MA BD DUniv DLitt DD, Clerk to the Presbytery of Glasgow
2009	William C. Hewitt BD DipPS, Greenock: Westburn
2010	John C. Christie BSc BD CBiol MRSB, Interim Minister
2011	A. David K. Arnott MA BD, St Andrews: Hope Park linked with Strathkinness
2012	Albert O. Bogle BD MTh, Bo'ness: St Andrew's
2013	E. Lorna Hood OBE MA BD DD, Renfrew: North
2014	John P. Chalmers BD CPS DD, Principal Clerk of Assembly
2015	Angus Morrison MA BD PhD DD, Orwell and Portmoak
2016	G. Russell Barr BA BD MTh DMin, Edinburgh: Cramond

2017	Derek Browning MA BD DMin, Edinburgh: Morningside
2018	Susan M. Brown BD DipMin DUniv, Dornoch Cathedral
2019	Colin A.M. Sinclair BA BD, Edinburgh: Palmerston Place

MATTER OF PRECEDENCE

The Lord High Commissioner to the General Assembly of the Church of Scotland (while the Assembly is sitting) ranks next to the Sovereign and the Duke of Edinburgh and before the rest of the Royal Family.

The Moderator of the General Assembly of the Church of Scotland ranks next to the Lord Chancellor of Great Britain and before the Keeper of the Great Seal of Scotland (the First Minister) and the Dukes.

---

(7) SCOTTISH DIVINITY FACULTIES

* denotes a Minister of the Church of Scotland

ABERDEEN

School of Divinity, History and Philosophy
50–52 College Bounds, Old Aberdeen AB24 3DS
Tel 01224 272366; Fax 01224 273750; divinity@abdn.ac.uk

Master of Christ's College:	Rev. Professor John Swinton* BD PhD RNM RNMD
	christs-college@abdn.ac.uk
Head of School:	Paula Sweeney MA PhD
Head of Divinity:	Professor Tom Greggs MA PhD PGCE FRSE FHEA
Co-ordinator,	
Centre for Ministry Studies	Rev. Kenneth S. Jeffrey* BA BD PhD DMin
	ksjeffrey@abdn.ac.uk

For teaching staff and further information see www.abdn.ac.uk/sdhp/

ST ANDREWS

University College of St Mary
The School of Divinity, South Street, St Andrews, Fife KY16 9JU
Tel: 01334 462850; Fax: 01334 462852; divinity@st-andrews.ac.uk

Principal and Head of School:	Rev. Stephen Holmes BA MA MTh PhD
Professor of Systematic Theology:	Rev. Professor Alan J. Torrance* MA BD DrTheol ARCM

For other teaching staff and further information see www.st-andrews.ac.uk/divinity/rt/staff/

EDINBURGH
School of Divinity and New College
New College, Mound Place, Edinburgh EH1 2LX
0131 650 8959; divinity@ed.ac.uk

Head of School:	Professor Helen K. Bond MTheol PhD BD MSt PhD
Principal of New College:	Rev. Professor Susan Hardman Moore* MA MAR PhD
Assistant Principal of	
New College:	Rev. Alison M. Jack* MA BD PhD
Professor of Divinty:	Very Rev. Professor David A.S. Fergusson* OBE MA BD DPhil DD FRSE FBA
T.F. Torrance Lecturer	
in Theology and Mission:	Rev. Sandy C. Forsyth* LLB BD DipLP MTh PhD

For other teaching staff and further information see www.ed.ac.uk/schools-departments/divinity/

GLASGOW
School of Critical Studies
Theology and Religious Studies
4 The Square, University of Glasgow, Glasgow G12 8QQ
Tel: 0141 330 6526; Fax: 0141 330 4943

Head of Subject:	Dr. Scott Spurlock
Professor of Divinity:	Rev. Professor George Pattison
Principal of Trinity College:	Rev. Doug Gay* MA BD PhD

For teaching staff and further information see www.gla.ac.uk Subjects A-Z. Theology and Religious Studies

HIGHLAND THEOLOGICAL COLLEGE UHI
High Street, Dingwall IV15 9HA
Tel: 01349 780000; Fax: 01349 780001;
htc@uhi.ac.uk

Principal of HTC:	Rev. Hector Morrison* BSc BD MTh
Vice-Principal of HTC:	Jamie Grant PhD MA LLB

For teaching staff and further information see www.htc.uhi.ac.uk

(8) SOCIETIES AND ASSOCIATIONS

1. INTER-CHURCH ASSOCIATIONS

ACTION OF CHURCHES TOGETHER IN SCOTLAND (ACTS) – Eaglaisean Còmhla an Gnìomh an Alba – was formed in 1990 as Scotland's national ecumenical instrument. It brings together nine denominations in Scotland who share a desire for greater oneness between churches, a growth of understanding and common life between churches, and unified action in proclaiming and responding to the gospel in the whole of life. The Member Churches of ACTS are in the process of transitioning the organisation into the Scottish Christian Forum, which would take forward the charitable purposes of ACTS. Interim General Secretary: Rev Ian Boa, Jubilee House, Forthside Way, Stirling, FK8 1QZ (07527 433460; ianboa@acts-scotland.org; www.acts-scotland.org).

The FELLOWSHIP OF ST ANDREW: The fellowship promotes dialogue between Churches of the east and the west in Scotland. Further information available from the Secretary, Rev. John G. Pickles, 1 Annerley Road, Annan DG12 6HE (01461 202626; JPickles@ churchofscotland.org.uk).

The FELLOWSHIP OF ST THOMAS: An ecumenical association formed to promote informed interest in and to learn from the experience of Churches in South Asia (India, Pakistan, Bangladesh, Nepal, Sri Lanka and Burma (Myanmar)). Secretary: Frances Bicket, 9/2 Connaught Place, Edinburgh EH6 4RQ (0131 552 8781; frances.bicket@gmail.com; www.fost.org.uk).

FRONTIER YOUTH TRUST: A movement of pioneering youth workers, committed to reaching young people on the margins. We host a mission community for youth workers. We are resourcing the church to take pioneering risks in their work with young people. And we are calling others to join the pioneer movement to reach young people on the margins. Contact us for training and coaching, or find practical resources on our website at www.fyt.org.uk. Contact us at info@fyt.org.uk, 0121 771 2328 or find us on social media.

INTERSERVE GREAT BRITIAN AND IRELAND: An international, evangelical and interdenominational organisation with 160 years of Christian service. The purpose of Interserve is 'to make Jesus Christ known through *wholistic* ministry in partnership with the global church, among the neediest peoples of Asia and the Arab world', and our vision is 'Lives and communities transformed through encounter with Jesus Christ'. Interserve supports over 800 people in cross-cultural ministry in a wide range of work including children and youth, the environment, evangelism, Bible training, engineering, agriculture, business development and health. We rely on supporters in Scotland for the work in Scotland and for sending mission partners from Scotland overseas. Scotland Ministry Facilitator: Grace Penney, 21 Park Avenue, Bishopbriggs, Glasgow G64 2SN (07971 858318; GraceP@isgbi.org; www.interserve.org.uk).

IONA COMMUNITY: We are an ecumenical Christian community with a dispersed worldwide membership of Full Members, Associate Members and Friends. Inspired by our faith and loving concern for the world and its people, we pursue justice and peace in and through community. Our new Glasgow centre hosts a growing programme of events, our work with young people, Wild Goose Publications and the Wild Goose Resource Group. The

Iona Community also welcomes guests to share in the common life in the Abbey and MacLeod Centre, Iona and Camas outdoor adventure centre, Mull. Joint Leaders: Ms Christian MacLean and Rev Kathy Galloway, 21 Carlton Court, Glasgow, G5 9JP (0141 429 7281, admin@iona.org.uk; www.iona.org.uk; Facebook: Iona Community; Twitter: @ ionacommunity). Iona Centres Manager: Rev Heinz Toller, Iona Abbey, Isle of Iona, Argyll, PA76 6SN (01681 700404; enquiries@iona.org.uk).

PLACE FOR HOPE: Our churches and faith communities face change, encounter difference and experience conflict at different stages and for a variety of reasons. In times of change or challenge, we know that practical support can help. Place for Hope, a body with its roots in the Church of Scotland and now an independent charity celebrating our 10-year anniversary, accompanies and equips people and faith communities where relationships have become strained and helps them move towards living well with difference. Through a skilled and highly trained team of Practitioners, we accompany groups navigating conflict and difficult conversations and resource the church and wider faith communities with peacemakers. Place for Hope can:
– support groups and individuals experiencing conflict
– facilitate sensitive or difficult group conversations, such as preparing for change or transition
– provide individual coaching
– host and enable community dialogues on difficult, potentially divisive issues
– offer training, workshops and resources for understanding and working with conflict and change.
Please get in touch for information, or a confidential conversation: 07884 580359; info@ placeforhope.org.uk; www.placeforhope.org.uk.

The ST COLM'S FELLOWSHIP: An association for all from any denomination who have trained, studied or been resident at St Colm's, either when it was a college or later as International House. There is an annual retreat and a meeting for Commemoration; and some local groups meet on a regular basis. Hon. Secretary: Rev. Margaret Nutter, 'Kilmorich', 14 Balloch Road, Balloch G83 8SR (01389 754505; maenutter@gmail.com).

SCOTTISH CHURCHES HOUSING ACTION: Speaks to churches and for churches on homelessness and its challenges; offers advice and support on establishing befriending services and other voluntary action; and provides consultancy advice on using redundant property for affordable housing. Chief Executive: Richard Howat, 44 Hanover Street, Edinburgh EH2 2DR (0131 477 4500; info@churches-housing.org; www.churches-housing.org).

SCOTTISH CHURCHES ORGANIST TRAINING SCHEME (SCOTS): Established in 1997 as an initiative of the then Panel on Worship, along with the Royal School of Church Music's Scottish Committee and the Scottish Federation of Organists, this is a self-propelled scheme by which a pianist who seeks competence on the organ – and organists who wish to develop their skills – can follow a three-stage syllabus, receiving a certificate at each stage. Participants each have an Adviser whom they meet occasionally for assessment, and also take part in one of the three or four Local Organ Workshops which are held in different parts of Scotland each year. There is a regular e-newsletter, *Scots Wha Play*. Costs are kept low. SCOTS is an ecumenical scheme. Information from Douglas Galbraith (01592 752403; dgalbraith@churchofscotland.org.uk; www.scotsorgan.org.uk > SCOTS).

SCOTTISH JOINT COMMITTEE ON RELIGIOUS AND MORAL EDUCATION: This is an interfaith body that began as a joint partnership between the Educational Institute of Scotland and the Church of Scotland to provide resources, training and support for the work of religious and moral education in schools. Mr Andrew Tomlinson, 121 George Street, Edinburgh EH2 4YN (0131 225 5722; atomlinson@churchofscotland. org.uk), and Mr Lachlan Bradley, 6 Clairmont Gardens, Glasgow G3 7LW (0141 353 3595).

SCRIPTURE UNION SCOTLAND: Scripture Union Scotland's vision is to see the children and young people of Scotland exploring the Bible and responding to the significance of Jesus. SU Scotland works in schools running SU groups and supporting Curriculum for Excellence. Its three activity centres, Lendrick Muir, Alltnacriche and Gowanbank, accommodate school groups and weekends away during term-time. During the school holidays it runs an extensive programme of events for school-age children – including residential holidays (some focused on disadvantaged children and young people), missions and church-based holiday clubs. In addition, it runs discipleship and training programmes for young people and is committed to promoting prayer for, and by, the young people of Scotland through a range of national prayer events and the *Pray for Schools Scotland* initiative. Scripture Union Scotland, 70 Milton Street, Glasgow G4 0HR (Tel: 0141 332 1162; Fax: 0141 352 7600; info@suscotland.org. uk; www.suscotland.org.uk).

STUDENT CHRISTIAN MOVEMENT: SCM is a student-led movement inspired by Jesus to act for justice and show God's love in the world. As a community we come together to pray, worship and explore faith in an open and non-judgemental environment. The movement is made up of a network of groups and individual members across Britain, as well as link churches and chaplaincies. As a national movement we come together at regional and national events to learn more about our faith and spend time as a community, and we take action on issues of social justice chosen by our members. SCM provides resources and training to student groups, churches and chaplaincies on student outreach and engagement, leadership and social action. Acting National Co-ordinator: Lisa Murphy, SCM, Grays Court, 3 Nursery Road, Edgbaston, Birmingham B15 3JX (0121 426 4918; scm@movement.org.uk; www.movement.org.uk).

WORLD DAY OF PRAYER: SCOTTISH COMMITTEE: Convener: Mrs Margaret Broster, Bryn a Glyn, 27b Braehead, Beith KA15 1EF (01505 503300; margaretbroster@hotmail. co.uk). Secretary: Marjorie Paton, Muldoanich, Stirling Street, Blackford, Auchterarder PH4 1QG (01764 682234; marjoriepaton.wdp@btinternet.com; www.wdpscotland.org.uk).

YMCA SCOTLAND: Offers support, training and guidance to churches seeking to reach out to love and serve young people's needs. Chief Executive – National General Secretary: Mrs Kerry Reilly, YMCA Scotland, 1 Chesser Avenue, Edinburgh EH14 1TB (0131 228 1464; kerry@ymcascotland.org; www.ymca.scot).

YOUTH FOR CHRIST: Youth for Christ is a national Christian charity committed to taking the Good News of Jesus Christ relevantly to every young person in Great Britain. In Scotland there are 5 locally governed, staffed and financed centres, communicating and demonstrating the Christian faith. Local Ministries Director: Lauren Fox (0121 502 9620; lauren.fox@yfc.co.uk; www.yfc.co.uk/local-centres/scotland).

2. CHURCH OF SCOTLAND SOCIETIES

CHURCH OF SCOTLAND ABSTAINERS' ASSOCIATION: Recognising that alcohol is a major – indeed a growing – problem within Scotland, the aim of the Church of Scotland Abstainers' Association, with its motto 'Abstinence makes sense', is to encourage more people to choose a healthy alcohol-free lifestyle. Further details are available from 'Blochairn', 17A Culduthel Road, Inverness IV24 4AG (jamwall@talktalk.net; www.kirkabstainers.org.uk).

The CHURCH OF SCOTLAND CHAPLAINS' ASSOCIATION: The Association consists of serving and retired chaplains to HM Forces. It holds an annual meeting and lunch on Shrove Tuesday, and organises the annual Service of Remembrance in St Giles' Cathedral on Chaplains' Day of the General Assembly. Hon. Secretary: Rev. Stephen A. Blakey BSc BD, Balduff House, Kilry, Blairgowrie PH11 8HS (01575 560226; SBlakey@churchofscotland.org.uk).

The CHURCH OF SCOTLAND RETIRED MINISTERS' ASSOCIATION: The Association meets in St. Andrew's and St. George's West Church, George St., Edinburgh, normally on the first Monday of the month, from October to April. The group is becoming increasingly ecumenical. Meetings include a talk, which can be on a wide variety of topics, which is followed by afternoon tea. Details of the programme from Hon. Secretary: Rev. Douglas A.O. Nicol, 1/2 North Werber Park, Edinburgh EH4 1SY (07811 437075; Douglas.Nicol@churchofscotland.org.uk).

The CHURCH SERVICE SOCIETY: Founded in 1865 to study the development of Christian worship through the ages and in the Reformed tradition, and to work towards renewal in contemporary worship. It has published since 1928, and continues to publish, a liturgical journal, archived on its website. Secretary: Rev. Dr Martin S. Ritchie (0131 447 4032; MRitchie@churchofscotland.org.uk; www.churchservicesociety.org).

FORUM OF GENERAL ASSEMBLY AND PRESBYTERY CLERKS: Secretary: Rev. Bryan Kerr, Greyfriars Manse, 3 Bellefield Way, Lanark ML11 7NW (01555 663363; lanark@churchofscotland.org.uk).

COVENANT FELLOWSHIP SCOTLAND (formerly FORWARD TOGETHER): An organisation for evangelicals within the Church of Scotland. Contact the Director, Mr Eric C. Smith (07715 665728; director@covenantfellowshipscotland.com), or the Chairman, Rev. Louis Kinsey (07787 145918; LKinsey@churchofscotland.org.uk; http://covenantfellowshipscotland.com).

The FRIENDS OF TABEETHA SCHOOL, JAFFA: The Friends seek to support the only school run by the Church of Scotland in the world. Based in Jaffa, Israel, it seeks to promote tolerance and understanding amongst pupils and staff alike. President: Irene Anderson. Hon. Secretary: Rev. David J. Smith, 1 Cawdor Drive, Glenrothes KY6 2HN (01592 611963; David.Smith@churchofscotland.org.uk).

The IRISH GATHERING: An informal annual meeting with a guest speaker; all those having a connection with or an interest in the Presbyterian Church in Ireland are very welcome. Secretary: Rev. William McLaren, 23 Shamrock Street, Dundee DD4 7AH (01382 459119; WMcLaren@churchofscotland.org.uk).

SCOTTISH CHURCH SOCIETY: Founded in 1892 to 'defend and advance Catholic doctrine as set forth in the Ancient Creeds and embodied in the Standards of the Church of Scotland', the Society meets for worship and discussion at All Saints' Tide, holds a Lenten Quiet Day, an AGM, and other meetings by arrangement; all are open to non members. The Society is also now working closely with the Church Service Society and is arranging meetings which are of joint interest. Secretary: Rev. W. Gerald Jones MA BD MTh, The Manse, Patna Road, Kirkmichael, Maybole KA19 7PJ (01655 750286; WJones@churchofscotland. org.uk).

SCOTTISH CHURCH THEOLOGY SOCIETY: The Society encourages theological exploration and discussion of the main issues confronting the Church in the twenty-first century. Rev. Alexander Shuttleworth, 62 Toll Road, Kincardine, Alloa FK10 4QZ (01259 731002; AShuttleworth@churchofscotland.org.uk).

SOCIETY OF FRIENDS OF ST ANDREW'S JERUSALEM: In co-operation with the World Mission Council, the Society seeks to provide support for the work of the Congregation of St Andrew's Scots Memorial Church, Jerusalem, and St Andrew's Guesthouse. Hon. Secretary and Membership Secretary: Walter T. Dunlop, c/o World Mission Council, 121 George Street, Edinburgh, EH2 4YN.

3. BIBLE SOCIETIES

The SCOTTISH BIBLE SOCIETY: Chief Executive: Elaine Duncan, 7 Hampton Terrace, Edinburgh EH12 5XU (0131 337 9701; info@scottishbiblesociety.org; https:// scottishbiblesociety.org).

WEST OF SCOTLAND BIBLE SOCIETY: Secretary: Rev. Finlay Mackenzie, 19 The Glebe, Kiltarlity, Inverness IV4 7BF (07817 680011; f.c.mack51@gmail.com; www. westofscotlandbiblesociety.com).

4. GENERAL

The BOYS' BRIGADE: A volunteer-led Christian youth organisation which was founded in Scotland in 1883 and now operates in many different countries around the world. Our vision is that children and young people experience life to the full (John 10:10). We provide opportunities for young people to learn, grow and discover in a safe, caring and fun environment. John Sharp, Director for Scotland, Scottish Headquarters, Carronvale House, Carronvale Road, Larbert FK5 3LH (01324 562008; scottishhq@boys-brigade.org.uk; www.boys-brigade.org.uk/Scotland). Scottish Chaplain for the Brigade: Rev Derek Gunn (scottishchaplain@boys-brigade.org.uk).

BROKEN RITES: Support group for divorced and separated clergy spouses. (01896 759254; eshirleydouglas@hotmail.co.uk; www.brokenrites.org).

CHRISTIAN AID SCOTLAND: Sally Foster-Fulton, Head of Christian Aid Scotland, Sycamore House, 290 Bath Street, Glasgow G2 4JR (0141 221 7475; glasgow@christian-aid.org; Edinburgh Office: 0131 220 1254; edinburgh@christian-aid.org; www.christianaid.org.uk/ get-involved-locally/scotland).

CHRISTIAN ENDEAVOUR IN SCOTLAND: Challenging and encouraging children and young people in the service of Christ and the Church, especially through the CE Award Scheme: 16 Queen Street, Alloa FK10 2AR (01259 215101; admin@cescotland.org; www. cescotland.org).

DAY ONE CHRISTIAN MINISTRIES: Day One has produced Christian literature for over 35 years. A variety of books are published for both adults and young people, as well as cards, bookmarks and stationery items. Ryelands Road, Leominster, Herefordshire HR6 8NZ. Contact Mark Roberts for further information (01568 613740; mark@dayone.co.uk; www. dayone.co.uk).

ECO-CONGREGATION SCOTLAND: Eco-Congregation Scotland is the largest movement of community-based environment groups in Scotland. We offer a programme to help congregations reduce their impact on climate change and live sustainably in a world of limited resources. 121 George Street, Edinburgh EH2 4YN (0131 240 2274; manager@ ecocongregationscotland.org; www.ecocongregationscotland.org).

GIRLGUIDING SCOTLAND: 16 Coates Crescent, Edinburgh EH3 7AH (Tel: 0131 226 4511; Fax: 0131 220 4828; administrator@girlguiding-scot.org.uk; www.girlguidingscotland.org.uk).

GIRLS' BRIGADE SCOTLAND: 11A Woodside Crescent, Glasgow G3 7UL (0141 332 1765; caroline.goodfellow@girls-brigade-scotland.org.uk; www.girls-brigade-scotland.org.uk).

The LEPROSY MISSION SCOTLAND: Working in over 30 countries, the Leprosy Mission is a global fellowship united by our Christian faith and commitment to seeing leprosy defeated and lives transformed. The Leprosy Mission Scotland, Suite 2, Earlsgate Lodge, Livilands Lane, Stirling FK8 2BG (01786 449266; contactus@leprosymission.scot; www. leprosymission.scot).

RELATIONSHIPS SCOTLAND: Scotland's largest provider of relationship counselling, family mediation and child contact centre services. Chief Executive: Mr Stuart Valentine, 18 York Place, Edinburgh EH1 3EP (Tel: 0345 119 2020; Fax: 0845 119 6089; enquiries@ relationships-scotland.org.uk; www.relationships-scotland.org.uk).

SCOTTISH CHURCH HISTORY SOCIETY: Promoting interest in the history of Christianity in Scotland. Secretary: Dr Laura Mair (schssec@outlook.com; www.schs.org.uk).

SCOTTISH EVANGELICAL THEOLOGY SOCIETY: Seeks to promote theology which serves the church, is faithful to Scripture, grounded in scholarship, informed by worship, sharpened in debate, catholic in scope, with a care for Scotland and its people. Secretary: Rev. M.G. Smith, 0/2, 2008 Maryhill Road, Glasgow G20 0AB (0141 570 8680; sets. secretary@gmail.com; www.s-e-t-s.org.uk).

The SCOTTISH REFORMATION SOCIETY: Exists to defend and promote the work of the Protestant Reformation in Scotland by organising meetings, publishing literature and running an essay competition. Chairman: Rev. Kenneth Macdonald. Vice-Chairman: Mr Allan McCulloch. Secretary: Rev. Dr Douglas Somerset. Treasurer: Rev. Andrew W.F. Coghill. The Magdalen Chapel, 41 Cowgate, Edinburgh EH1 1JR (0131 220 1450; info@ scottishreformationsociety.org; www.scottishreformationsociety.org).

SCOUTS SCOTLAND: Scottish Headquarters, Fordell Firs, Hillend, Dunfermline KY11 7HQ (01383 419073; hello@scouts.scot; www.scouts.scot).

TEARFUND: Helps communities overcome the worst effects of poverty and disasters, working alongside local churches and other locally-based organisations in over 50 countries. 100 Church Road, Teddington TW11 8QE (0208 977 9144). Director: Graeme McMeekin, Tearfund Scotland, Baltic Chambers, Suite 529, 50 Wellington Street, Glasgow G2 6HJ (0141 332 3621; scotland@tearfund.org; www.tearfund.org/scotland).

The WALDENSIAN MISSIONS AID SOCIETY FOR WORK IN ITALY: Supporting the outreach of the Waldensian Churches, including important work with immigrant communities in the *Mediterranean Hope* project. David A. Lamb SSC, 36 Liberton Drive, Edinburgh EH16 6NN (0131 664 3059; david@dlamb.co.uk; www.scottishwaldensian. org.uk).

YOUTH SCOTLAND: Balfour House, 19 Bonnington Grove, Edinburgh EH6 4BL (Tel: 0131 554 2561; Fax: 0131 454 3438; office@youthscotland.org.uk; www.youthscotland.org.uk).

THE YOUNG WOMEN'S MOVEMENT: Our vision is a world where every woman can shape her own life journey and fulfil her potential, where the voices of women are heard, respected and celebrated. We help to bring this about by creating empowering spaces for girls and young women to meet together in groups and clubs, activities and conversations. Director: Patrycja Kupiec, Office 5, 19 Smith's Place, Edinburgh EH6 8NT (0131 652 0248; hello@ ywcascotland.org; www.ywcascotland.org).

---

(9) TRUSTS AND FUNDS

ABERNETHY ADVENTURE CENTRES: Full board residential accommodation and adventure activities available for all Church groups, plus a range of Christian summer camps at our four centres across Scotland. 01479 818005; marketing@abernethy.org.uk; www.abernethy.org.uk).

The BAIRD TRUST: Assists in the building and repair of churches and halls, and generally assists the work of the Church of Scotland. Apply to Iain A.T. Mowat CA, 182 Bath Street, Glasgow G2 4HG (0141 332 0476; info@bairdtrust.org.uk; www.bairdtrust.org.uk).

The Rev. Alexander BARCLAY BEQUEST: Assists a family member of a deceased minister of the Church of Scotland who at the time of his/her death was acting as his/her housekeeper and who is in needy circumstances, and in certain circumstances assists Ministers, Deacons, Ministries Development Staff and their spouses facing financial hardship. Applications can only be submitted to the trustees by the Ministries Council Pastoral Support Team, 121 George Street, Edinburgh EH2 4YN (0131 225 5722; pastoralsupport@churchofscotland.org.uk).

BELLAHOUSTON BEQUEST FUND: Gives grants to Protestant denominations in the City of Glasgow and certain areas within five miles of the city boundary for building and repairing churches and halls and the promotion of religion. Apply to Mr Donald B. Reid, Mitchells

Roberton, 36 North Hanover Street, Glasgow G1 2AD (0141 552 3422; info@mitchells-roberton.co.uk).

BEQUEST FUND FOR MINISTERS: Provides financial assistance to ministers in outlying districts towards the cost of manse furnishings, pastoral efficiency aids, and personal and family medical or educational (including university) costs. Apply to A. Linda Parkhill CA, 60 Wellington Street, Glasgow G2 6HJ (0141 226 4994; mail@parkhillmackie.co.uk).

CARNEGIE TRUST FOR THE UNIVERSITIES OF SCOTLAND: The Carnegie Trust invites applications by students who have had at least two years education at a secondary school in Scotland (or can demonstrate evidence of a substantial link to Scotland), for Tuition Fee Grants towards tuition fee costs for a first undergraduate degree at a Scottish university. For more information and a link to the online application form visit the Trust's website (https://www.carnegie-trust.org/award-schemes/undergraduate-tuition-fee-grants/) or contact the Carnegie Trust for the Universities of Scotland, Andrew Carnegie House, Pittencrieff Street, Dunfermline KY12 8AW (01383 724990; admin@carnegie-trust.org; www.carnegie-trust.org).

CHURCH HYMNARY TRUST: The trust is 'formed for the advancement of the Christian Faith through the promotion and development of hymnody in Scotland with particular reference to the Church of Scotland by assisting in the development, promotion, provision and understanding of hymns, psalms and paraphrases suitable for use in public worship, and in the distribution and making available of the same in books, discs, electronically and in other media for use by the Church of Scotland ....' The trust wishes to encourage applications for projects or schemes which are consistent with its purposes. These can include training courses, provision of music and guides to music, but the trust is not limited to those activities. The trust usually meets annually in early February, though applications may be considered out of committee. Applications should be made to the secretary and treasurer Hugh Angus, 56-66 Frederick Street, Edinburgh EH2 1LS, hugh.angus@balfour-manson.co.uk.

CHURCH OF SCOTLAND INSURANCE SERVICES LTD: Insurance intermediary, authorised and regulated by the Financial Conduct Authority, which arranges and manages the facility providing insurance protection for Church of Scotland congregations, including their activities and assets. Cover can also be arranged for other religious groups, charities, and non-profitmaking organisations, and household insurance is available for members. Profits are distributed to the Church of Scotland through Gift Aid. Contact 121 George Street, Edinburgh EH2 4YN (Tel: 0131 220 4119; Fax: 0131 220 3113; b.clarkson@cosic.co.uk; www.cosic.co.uk).

CHURCH OF SCOTLAND MINISTRIES BENEVOLENT FUND: Makes grants to the following beneficiaries who are in need:
(a) any retired person who has been ordained or commissioned for the Ministry of the Church of Scotland;
(b) Minsters inducted or introduced to a charge or Ordained National Ministers appointed to posts under approval of Presbytery;
(c) Ministries Development Staff appointed to a Presbytery planned post (including Deacons);
(d) Ordained Local Minsters, Auxiliary Ministers or Deacons serving under the appointment of Presbytery;
(e) Readers set apart by Presbytery to carry out the work of the Church;
(f) any widow, widower and/or orphan of any person categorised in (a) to (e) above;
(g) any spouse or former spouse and/or child (natural or otherwise) of any person categorised by (a) to (e) above.

Apply to Ministries Council Pastoral Support Team, 121 George Street, Edinburgh EH2 4YN (0131 225 5722).

The CINTRA BEQUEST: See 'Tod Endowment Trust ...' entry below.

CLARK BURSARY: Awarded to accepted candidate(s) for the ministry of the Church of Scotland whose studies for the ministry are pursued at the University of Aberdeen. Applications or recommendations for the Bursary to the Clerk to the Presbytery of Aberdeen, Mastrick Church, Greenfern Road, Aberdeen AB16 6TR.

CRAIGCROOK MORTIFICATION: The Trust has power to award grants or pensions (1) to men and women of 60 years of age or over born in Scotland or who have resided in Scotland for not less than 10 years who appear to be in poor circumstances, and (2) to children of deceased persons who met those conditions at the time of death and who appear to require assistance. The Trust has made single payments but normally awards pensions of £1,030 payable biannually. Ministers are invited to notify the Clerk and Factor, Jennifer Law CA, Exchange Place 3, Semple Street, Edinburgh EH3 8BL (0131 473 3500; charity@scott-moncrieff.com) of deserving persons and should be prepared to act as a referee on the application form. Application process currently suspended.

The DRUMMOND TRUST: Makes grants towards the cost of publication of books of 'sound Christian doctrine and outreach'. The Trustees are also willing to receive grant requests towards the cost of audio-visual programme material, but not equipment, software but not hardware. Requests for application forms should be made to the Secretaries, Hill and Robb Limited, 3 Pitt Terrace, Stirling FK8 2EY (01786 450985; fleurmcintosh@hillandrobb.co.uk). Manuscripts should *not* be sent.

The DUNCAN McCLEMENTS TRUST FOR ECUMENICAL TRAINING: Makes grants towards the cost of attendance at ecumenical assemblies and conferences; gatherings of young people; short courses or conferences promoting ecumenical understanding. Also to enable schools to organise one-off events to promote better understanding among differing communities and cultures with different religious backgrounds. The Trust also helps towards the cost of resources and study materials. Enquiries to: Committee on Ecumenical Relations, Church of Scotland, 121 George Street, Edinburgh EH2 4YN (0131 240 2208; ecumenical@churchofscotland.org.uk).

The David DUNCAN TRUST: Makes grants annually to students for the ministry and students in training to become deacons in the Church of Scotland in the Faculties of Arts and Divinity. Preference is given to those born or educated within the bounds of the former Presbytery of Arbroath. Applications not later than 31 October to Thorntons Law LLP, Brothockbank House, Arbroath DD11 1NE (reference: Glyn Roberts (Trust Manager); 01382 346299; groberts@thorntons-law.co.uk).

ERSKINE CUNNINGHAM HILL TRUST: Donates its annual income to the central funds of the Church of Scotland and 50% to other charities. Individual donations are in the region of £1,000. Priority is given to charities administered by voluntary or honorary officials, in particular charities registered and operating in Scotland and relating to the elderly, young people, ex-service personnel or seafarers. Application forms from the Secretary, Alan Ritchie, 121 George Street, Edinburgh EH2 4YN (0131 240 2260; aritchie@churchofscotland.org.uk).

ESDAILE TRUST: Assists the education and advancement of daughters of ministers, missionaries and widowed deaconesses of the Church of Scotland between 12 and 25 years of age. Applications are to be lodged by 31 May in each year with the Clerk and Treasurer, Jennifer Law CA, Exchange Place 3, Semple Street, Edinburgh EH3 8BL (0131 473 3500; charity@ scott-moncrieff.com).

FERGUSON BEQUEST FUND: Assists with the building and repair of churches and halls and, more generally, with the work of the Church of Scotland. Priority is given to the Counties of Ayr, Kirkcudbright, Wigtown, Lanark, Dunbarton and Renfrew, and to Greenock, Glasgow, Falkirk and Ardrossan; applications are, however, accepted from across Scotland. Apply to Iain A.T. Mowat CA, 182 Bath Street, Glasgow G2 4HG (0141 332 0476; info@fergusonbequestfund. org.uk; www.fergusonbequestfund.org.uk).

James GILLAN'S BURSARY FUND: Bursaries are available for male or female students for the ministry who were born or whose parents or parent have resided and had their home for not less than three years continually in the old counties of Moray or Nairn. Apply to The Minister, St Leonard's Manse, Nelson Road, Forres IV36 IDR (01309 672380).

The GLASGOW SOCIETY OF THE SONS AND DAUGHTERS OF MINISTERS OF THE CHURCH OF SCOTLAND: The Society's primary purpose is to grant financial assistance to children (no matter what age) of deceased ministers of the Church of Scotland. Applications for first grants can be lodged at any time. Thereafter annual applications must be lodged by 31 December for consideration by Council in February. To the extent that funds are available, grants are also given for the children of ministers or retired ministers, although such grants are normally restricted to university and college students. These latter grants are considered in conjunction with the Edinburgh-based Societies. Limited funds are also available for individual application for special needs or projects. Applications are to be submitted by 31 May in each year. Emergency applications can be dealt with at any time when need arises. More information can be found at www.mansebairnsnetwork.org. Application forms may be obtained from the Secretary and Treasurer, Jennifer Law CA, Exchange Place 3, Semple Street, Edinburgh EH3 8BL (0131 473 3500; charity@scott-moncrieff.com).

HAMILTON BURSARY: Awarded, subject to the intention on graduation to serve overseas under the Church of Scotland World Mission Council or to serve with some other Overseas Mission Agency approved by the Council, to a student at the University of Aberdeen (failing which to Accepted Candidate(s) for the Ministry of the Church of Scotland whose studies for the Ministry are pursued at Aberdeen University). Applications or recommendations for the Bursary to the Clerk to the Presbytery of Aberdeen, Mastrick Church, Greenfern Road, Aberdeen AB16 6TR.

Martin HARCUS BEQUEST: Makes annual grants to candidates for the ministry resident within the Presbytery of Edinburgh and currently under the jurisdiction of the Presbytery. Applications to the Principal's Secretary, New College, Mound Place, Edinburgh EH1 2LX (NewCollege@ ed.ac.uk) by 15 October.

The HOPE TRUST: In terms of its new constitution, gives support to organisations that (1) advance the cause of temperance through the promotion of temperance work and the combatting of all forms of substance abuse and (2) promote Reformed theology and Reformed church life especially in Scotland and the social mission of charities with historical or contemporary links to the Reformed tradition, and includes a scholarship programme, the appointment of a part-time post-doctoral fellowship and support for students in full time training. Apply to the Secretary, Robert P. Miller, Glenorchy House, 20 Union Street, Edinburgh, EH1 3LR (Tel: 0131 226 5151; Fax: 0131 556 5354 or Email: hopetrust@drummondmiller.co.uk).

KEAY THOM TRUST: The principal purposes of the Keay Thom Trust are:
1.   To benefit the widows, daughters or other dependent female relatives of deceased ministers, or wives of ministers who are now divorced or separated, all of whom have supported the minister in the fulfilment of his duties and who, by reason of death, divorce or separation, have been required to leave the manse. The Trust can assist them in the purchase of a house or by providing financial or material assistance whether it be for the provision of accommodation or not.
2.   To assist in the education or training of the above female relatives or any other children of deceased ministers.
Further information and application forms are available from Miller Hendry, Solicitors, 10 Blackfriars Street, Perth PH1 5NS (01738 637311; johnthom@millerhendry.co.uk).

LADIES' GAELIC SCHOOLS AND HIGHLAND BURSARY ASSOCIATION: Distributes money to students, preferably with a Highland/Gaelic background, who are training to be ministers in the Church of Scotland. Apply by 15 October in each year to the Secretary, Mrs Marion McGill, 61 Ladysmith Road, Edinburgh EH9 3EY (0131 667 4243; marionmcgill61@gmail.com).

The LYALL BEQUEST (Scottish Charity Number SC005542): Offers grants to ministers:
1.   Grants to individual ministers, couples and families, for a holiday for a minimum of seven nights. No reapplication within a three-year period; and thereafter a 50 per cent grant to those reapplying.
2.   Grants towards sickness and convalescence costs so far as not covered by the National Health Service. Applications should be made to the Secretary and Clerk, The Church of Scotland Trust, 121 George Street, Edinburgh EH2 4YN (0131 240 2222; jhamilton@churchofscotland.org.uk).

REV DR MACINNES AND MRS MACINNES TRUST: Provides grants to (1) retired ministers who have spent part of their ministry in the Counties of Nairn, Ross & Cromarty or Argyll and are solely dependent upon their pensions and preaching fees and (2) widows or widowers of such ministers solely dependent on their pensions. Applications should be made to the Secretary and Clerk, The Church of Scotland Trust, 121 George Street, Edinburgh EH2 4YN (0131 240 2222; jhamilton@churchofscotland.org.uk).

Gillian MACLAINE BURSARY FUND: Open to candidates for the ministry of the Church of Scotland of Scottish or Canadian nationality. Preference is given to Gaelic-speakers. Application forms available from Mr W Stewart Shaw DL BSc, Clerk to the Presbytery of Argyll, 59 Barone Road, Rothesay, Isle of Bute PA20 0DZ (07470 520240; argyll@churchofscotland.org.uk). Closing date for receipt of applications is 31 October.

The E. McLAREN FUND: The persons intended to be benefited are widows and unmarried ladies, preference being given to ladies above 40 years of age in the following order:
(a) Widows and daughters of Officers in the Highland Regiment, and
(b) Widows and daughters of Scotsmen.
Further details from the Secretary, The E. McLaren Fund, Messrs Wright, Johnston & Mackenzie

LLP, Solicitors, 302 St Vincent Street, Glasgow G2 5RZ (Tel: 0141 248 3434; Fax: 0141 221 1226; rmd@wjm.co.uk).

THE MEIKLE AND PATON TRUST: Grants are available to Ministers, Missionaries and Christian Workers including staff of the CSC for rest and recuperation at the following hotels: Crieff Hydro; Murraypark Hotel, Crieff; Peebles Hydro; Park Hotel, Peebles; Ballachulish Hotel and Isle of Glencoe Hotel. Grants give a subsidy for overnight residence, such subsidy being decreed by the Trustees at any given time. Booking may be made by telephone or on line and applicants will be required to state their page in the Church of Scotland Year Book or their unique number from the CSC list to obtain Meikle Paton benefit. Chairman: Rev. Iain F. Paton (iain.f.paton@btinternet.com).

MORGAN BURSARY FUND: Makes grants to candidates for the Church of Scotland ministry studying at the University of Glasgow. Apply to the Clerk to the Presbytery of Glasgow, 260 Bath Street, Glasgow G2 4JP (0141 332 6606; glasgow@churchofscotland.org.uk). Closing date October 31.

NEW MINISTERS' FURNISHING LOAN FUND: Makes loans (of £1,000) to ministers in their first charge to assist with furnishing the manse. Apply to Elaine Macadie, Finance Manager, Ministries Council, 121 George Street, Edinburgh EH2 4YN.

NOVUM TRUST: Provides small short-term grants – typically between £200 and £2,500 – to initiate projects in Christian action and research which cannot readily be financed from other sources. Trustees welcome applications from projects that are essentially Scottish, are distinctively new, and are focused on the welfare of young people, on the training of lay people or on new ways of communicating the Christian faith. The Trust cannot support large building projects, staff salaries or individuals applying for maintenance during courses or training. Application forms and guidance notes from novumt@cofscotland.org.uk or Mrs Susan Masterton, Blair Cadell WS, The Bond House, 5 Breadalbane Street, Edinburgh EH6 5JH (0131 555 5800; www.novum.org.uk).

PARK MEMORIAL BURSARY FUND: Provides grants for the benefit of candidates for the ministry of the Church of Scotland from the Presbytery of Glasgow under full-time training. Apply to the Clerk to the Presbytery of Glasgow, 260 Bath Street, Glasgow G2 4JP (0141 332 6606; glasgow@churchofscotland.org.uk). Closing date November 15.

PATON TRUST: Assists ministers in ill health to have a recuperative holiday outwith, and free from the cares of, their parishes. Apply to Alan S. Cunningham CA, Alexander Sloan, Accountants and Business Advisors, 180 St Vincent Street, Glasgow G2 5SG (Tel: 0141 204 8989; Fax: 0141 248 9931; alan.cunningham@alexandersloan.co.uk).

PRESBYTERY OF ARGYLL BURSARY FUND: Open to students who have been accepted as candidates for the ministry and the readership of the Church of Scotland. Preference is given to applicants who are natives of the bounds of the Presbytery, or are resident within the bounds of the Presbytery, or who have a strong connection with the bounds of the Presbytery. Application forms available from Mr W Stewart Shaw DL BSc, Clerk to the Presbytery of Argyll, 59 Barone Road, Rothesay, Isle of Bute PA20 0DZ (07470 520240; argyll@churchofscotland.org.uk). Closing date for receipt of applications is 31 October.

Margaret and John ROSS TRAVELLING FUND: Offers grants to ministers and their spouses for travelling and other expenses for trips to the Holy Land where the purpose is recuperation or relaxation. Applications should be made to the Secretary and Clerk, The Church of Scotland Trust, 121 George Street, Edinburgh EH2 4YN (0131 240 2222; jhamilton@churchofscotland. org.uk).

SCOTLAND'S CHURCHES TRUST: Assists, through grants, with the preservation of the fabric of buildings in use for public worship by any denomination. Also supports the playing of church organs by grants for public concerts, and through tuition bursaries for suitably proficient piano or organ players wishing to improve skills or techniques. SCT promotes visitor interest in churches through the trust's Pilgrim Journeys covering Scotland. Criteria and how to apply at www.scotlandschurchestrust.org.uk. Scotland's Churches Trust, 15 North Bank Street, Edinburgh EH1 2LP (info@scotlandschurchestrust.org.uk).

SCOTTISH CHURCHES HOUSE LEGACY RESERVE: Aim – to enable Scotland's churches and Christian organisations to resource new ways of ecumenical working. Between 1960 and 2011, the former Scottish Churches House in Dunblane was a centre for ecumenical encounter, sharing, challenge and development – the Legacy Reserve aims to continue this ethos. Applications are invited for the funding of projects; completed application forms must be submitted no later than 5th January in any year. Property schemes (such as repairs or purchase) are not eligible. Further details and application forms are available from the Interim General Secretary, Action of Churches Together in Scotland, Jubilee House, Forthside Way, Stirling FK8 1QZ. (ianboa@acts-scotland.org).

SMIETON FUND: To assist ministers who would benefit from a holiday because of a recent pastoral need. Administered at the discretion of the pastoral staff, who will give priority in cases of need. Applications to the Recruitment and Support Secretary, Ministries Council, 121 George Street, Edinburgh EH2 4YN (pastoralsupport@churchofscotland.org.uk).

Mary Davidson SMITH CLERICAL AND EDUCATIONAL FUND FOR ABERDEENSHIRE: Assists ministers who have been ordained for five years or over and are in full charge of a congregation in Aberdeen, Aberdeenshire and the north, to purchase books, or to travel for educational purposes, and assists their children with scholarships for further education or vocational training. Apply to Alan J. Innes MA LLB, 100 Union Street, Aberdeen AB10 1QR (01224 428000).

The SOCIETY FOR THE BENEFIT OF THE SONS AND DAUGHTERS OF THE CLERGY OF THE CHURCH OF SCOTLAND: Annual grants are made to assist in the education of the children (normally between the ages of 12 and 25 years) of ministers of the Church of Scotland. The Society also gives grants to aged and infirm daughters of ministers and ministers' unmarried daughters and sisters who are in need. Applications are to be lodged by 31 May in each year with the Secretary and Treasurer, Jennifer Law CA, Exchange Place 3, Semple Street, Edinburgh EH3 8BL (0131 473 3500; charity@scott-moncrieff.com).

The SOCIETY IN SCOTLAND FOR PROPAGATING CHRISTIAN KNOWLEDGE: The SSPCK gives grants to: 1. Resourcing mission within Scotland; 2. The training and education of Christians in Commonwealth countries overseas, aimed to equip them for service in the mission and outreach of the Church; 3.The training of British young people volunteering for periods of service in Christian mission and education overseas; 4. The resourcing of new initiatives in worldwide Christian misson. Chairman: Rev. Michael W. Frew; Secretary: Rev. Ian W. Alexander, SSPCK, c/o World Mission, 121 George Street, Edinburgh EH2 4YN (0131 225 5722; SSPCK@ churchofscotland.org.uk; www.sspck.co.uk).

The Nan STEVENSON CHARITABLE TRUST FOR RETIRED MINISTERS: Provides houses, or loans to purchase houses, on similar terms to the Housing and Loan Fund, for any retired paid church worker with a North Ayrshire connection. Secretary and Treasurer: Mrs Christine Thomas, 18 Brisbane Street, Largs KA30 8QN (01475 338564; 07891 838778; cathomas54@gmail.com).

Miss M.E. SWINTON PATERSON'S CHARITABLE TRUST: The Trust can give modest grants to support smaller congregations in urban or rural areas who require to fund essential maintenance or improvement works at their buildings. Applications for grants should be made via the Trust's online application form available at www.swintonpaterson.org.uk.

SYNOD OF GRAMPIAN CHILDREN OF THE CLERGY FUND: Makes annual grants to children of deceased ministers. Apply to Rev. Iain U. Thomson, Clerk and Treasurer, 4 Keirhill Gardens, Westhill AB32 6AZ (01224 746743; iainuthomson@googlemail.com).

SYNOD OF GRAMPIAN WIDOWS' FUND: Makes annual grants (currently £300 p.a.) to widows or widowers of deceased ministers who have served in a charge in the former Synod. Apply to Rev. Iain U. Thomson, Clerk and Treasurer, 4 Keirhill Gardens, Westhill AB32 6AZ (01224 746743; iainuthomson@googlemail.com).

TOD ENDOWMENT TRUST; CINTRA BEQUEST; TOD ENDOWMENT SCOTLAND HOLIDAY FUND: The Trustees of the Cintra Bequest and of the Tod Endowment Scotland Holiday Fund can consider an application for a grant from the Tod Endowment funds from any ordained or commissioned minister or deacon in Scotland of at least two years' standing before the date of application, to assist with the cost of the beneficiary and his or her spouse or partner and dependants obtaining rest and recuperation in Scotland. The Trustees of the Tod Endowment Scotland Holiday Fund can also consider an application from an ordained or commissioned minister or deacon who has retired. Application forms are available from Mrs Jennifer Hamilton, Deputy Solicitor (for the Cintra Bequest), and from Ministries Council Pastoral Support Team (for the Tod Endowment Scotland Holiday Fund). The address in both cases is 121 George Street, Edinburgh EH2 4YN (0131 225 5722). (Attention is drawn to the separate entry above for the Church of Scotland Ministries' Benevolent Fund.)

STEPHEN WILLIAMSON & ALEX BALFOUR FUND: Offers grants to Ministers in Scotland, with first priority being given to Ministers in the Presbyteries of Angus and Dundee, followed by the Presbyteries in Fife, to assist with the cost of educational school/ college/university trips for sons and daughters of the Manse who are under 25 years and in full time education. Application for trips in any year will be considered by the Trustees in the January of that year, when the income of the previous financial year will be awarded in grants. The applications for trips in that calendar year must be submitted by 31 December of the preceding year. For applications from outwith the 5 priority Presbyteries the total cost of the trip must be in excess of £500, with the maximum grant which can be awarded being £200. The trustees will always give priority to new applicants. If funds still remain for distribution after the allocation of grants in January further applications for that year will be considered. Applications from the Presbyteries of Angus, Dundee, Dunfermline, Kirkcaldy and St Andrews will be considered at any time of year as the

Trustees have retained income for these grants. Applications should be made to the Secretary and Clerk, The Church of Scotland Trust, 121 George Street, Edinburgh EH2 4YN (0131 240 2222; jhamilton@churchofscotland.org.uk).

(10) LONG SERVICE CERTIFICATES

Long Service Certificates, signed by the Moderator, are available for presentation to elders and voluntary office bearers in respect of not less than thirty years of service. At the General Assembly of 2015, it was agreed that further certificates could be issued at intervals of ten years thereafter. It should be noted that the period is years of *service*, not (for example) years of ordination in the case of an elder. In the case of those volunteers engaged in children's and youth work, the qualifying period is twenty-one years of service. Certificates are not issued posthumously, nor is it possible to make exceptions to the rules, for example by recognising quality of service in order to reduce the qualifying period, or by reducing the qualifying period on compassionate grounds, such as serious illness. Applications for Long Service Certificates should be made in writing to the Principal Clerk at 121 George Street, Edinburgh EH2 4YN by the parish minister, or by the session clerk on behalf of the Kirk Session. Certificates are not issued from this office to the individual recipients, nor should individuals make application themselves. If a note of the award of the Certificate is to be inserted in *Life and Work* contact should be made with that publication direct.

(11) RECORDS OF THE CHURCH OF SCOTLAND

Church records more than fifty years old, unless still in use, should be sent or delivered to the Principal Clerk for onward transmission to the National Records of Scotland. Where ministers or session clerks are approached by a local repository seeking a transfer of their records, they should inform the Principal Clerk, who will take the matter up with the National Records of Scotland.

Where a temporary retransmission of records is sought, it is extremely helpful if notice can be given three months in advance so that appropriate procedures can be carried out satisfactorily.

SECTION 3

Church Procedure

A. THE MINISTER AND BAPTISM

See www.churchofscotland.org.uk > Resources > Yearbook > Section 3A

B. THE MINISTER AND MARRIAGE

See www.churchofscotland.org.uk > Resources > Yearbook > Section 3B

C. CONDUCT OF MARRIAGE SERVICES (CODE OF GOOD PRACTICE)

See www.churchofscotland.org.uk > Resources > Yearbook > Section 3C

D. MARRIAGE AND CIVIL PARTNERSHIP (SCOTLAND) ACT 2014

See www.churchofscotland.org.uk > Resources > Yearbook > Section 3D

E. CONDUCT OF FUNERAL SERVICES: FEES

See www.churchofscotland.org.uk > Resources > Yearbook > Section 3E

F. PULPIT SUPPLY FEES AND EXPENSES

See www.churchofscotland.org.uk > Resources > Yearbook > Section 3F

G. PROCEDURE IN A VACANCY

A full coverage can be found in two handbooks listed under *Interim Moderators and Nominating Committees* on the Ministries Resources pages on the Church of Scotland website, which also includes information on locum appointments:
www.churchofscotland.org.uk > Resources > Subjects > Ministries resources > Interim Moderators and Nominating Committees

SECTION 4

General Assembly 2019

OFFICE-BEARERS OF THE GENERAL ASSEMBLY

The Lord High Commissioner:	The Duke of Buccleuch and Queensberry KT KBE DL FSA FRSE
Moderator:	The Right Rev. Colin A.M. Sinclair
Chaplains to the Moderator:	Rev. Andrew F. Anderson Rev. Timothy D. Sinclair
Principal Clerk:	Rev. Dr George J. Whyte
Depute Clerk:	Ms Christine Paterson
Procurator:	Ms Laura Dunlop QC
Law Agent:	Miss Mary Macleod
Convener of the Business Committee:	Rev. Fiona E. Smith
Vice-Convener of the Business Committee:	Rev. Donald G.B. McCorkindale
Precentor:	Rev. Dr D. Douglas Galbraith
Chief Steward:	Mr Alexander F. Gemmill
Assembly Officer:	Mr William Mearns
Assistant Assembly Officer:	Mrs Karen McKay

THE MODERATOR

The Right Reverend Colin A.M. Sinclair BA BD

The invitation to Colin Sinclair to adopt the words of Jesus, "Follow me!", for the theme of his year as Moderator, was entirely appropriate. His life and ministry have been spent answering this call.

Colin was brought up in south Glasgow, attending Glasgow Academy, before going to read Economics at Stirling University. It was at the age of 12 that Colin became a Christian, following a chance encounter at school with a Scripture Union (SU) meeting, which led him to attend his first SU camp. Many other camps followed, and he was increasingly impressed with their range of activities, the warm and happy atmosphere, and, particularly, the evident Christian faith of the leaders. Colin's subsequent involvement with SU has been lifelong, and a very significant part of his ministry.

During his years at Stirling University, and now a member of George Philip's congregation at Sandyford Henderson Memorial Church in Glasgow, Colin sensed an increasingly strong call to the ordained ministry. He applied to the Church of Scotland to be a candidate and was accepted. But, before returning to university for a Divinity degree, he accepted an invitation from SU to go out to Zambia to work with students. He stayed for three years, an important and happy experience, giving him a taste of the world church, and laying a strong foundation for what was to come.

In the autumn of 1977 Colin started his Divinity degree at New College, University of Edinburgh, specialising in Church History, but also much involved in the wider life of the

College, including playing rugby for the College. He graduated with a first-class honours degree, and was widely regarded as one of the outstanding students of his generation. It was during this time in Edinburgh that Colin married Ruth. Their complementary gifts and personalities and their shared loves and concerns have equipped them to be a happy and fruitful partnership wherever they have been called to serve. Colin and Ruth have four children, Joanna, Timothy, Rachel and Bethany, and are now proud and doting grandparents to Finley, Mollie, Andrew and Levi.

After New College, Colin served his probationary period at Palmerston Place Church in Edinburgh, being ordained in 1981, to which he would later return as Minister. During his time there he developed a Bible teaching programme with the congregation, later published as The Hitch-Hikers Guide to the Bible.

In 1982 Colin moved to the west coast to accept a call from the congregation of Newton-on-Ayr, and was duly inducted to the parish ministry. It was work that he quickly came to appreciate and love deeply. He served there for six years before being persuaded to apply, successfully, to be the General Director of Scripture Union Scotland, moving with his family back to Glasgow. Thus began a fruitful period of leadership, travelling and speaking widely, much involved with his wife in running annual camps, and being introduced to Spring Harvest of which he went on to become chairman, and a regular speaker.

In 1996 Colin made the difficult but important decision to answer a call from Palmerston Place Church in Edinburgh. He has now been Minister there for over 20 years in a parish ministry that has flourished in many different directions. With its emphasis on good preaching and teaching, its strong pastoral concern, and outreach to young people, it has seen a significant number of candidates coming forward for Christian ministry. Colin has overseen all this work, as well as finding time with the central courts and committees of the church, serving as Moderator of the Presbytery of Edinburgh, and Convenor of the Mission and Discipleship Council.

Colin brings huge gifts and experience to the office of Moderator: his lifelong involvement with SU nationally and internationally, much experience in the central workings of the church, and deep involvement over many years in congregational and parish life. Above all, he brings his passion for the gospel of Jesus Christ, and his infectious and obvious enjoyment of following Jesus in the Christian life.

Andrew Anderson and Timothy Sinclair
Moderator's Chaplains

Report from the General Assembly 2019
Theme: Jesus said: Follow me, and I will make you fish for people!

Change was in the air from the outset of the 2019 General Assembly. It was evident in the words of His Grace Richard Scott, the Duke of Buccleuch and Queensberry, welcomed for his second year as Lord High Commissioner and who anticipated heart-searching and serious debates. Representing ecumenical visitors, the Moderator of the United Reformed Church in Britain raised the need to grasp "the Kairos moment" – that moment of decision or action which demands that we be "not in control but in counsel".

In fact, the Assembly of 2019 emerged as a necessary sequel to that of 2018, offering not only responses – mostly well received – to last year's frustrated cries for structural change but also a range of answers to 2018's final question, posed by members of the National Youth Assembly: What will Christian discipleship, now and in the future, look like?

Radical plans

Visions of discipleship would be filtered through the week's discussions (much as a notably wide variety of music was released from its traditional worship slots to bookend a number of sessions). However, the words dominating the opening days were: "radical action plan". In practice, this took the form of three deliberately complementary reports: from the Council of Assembly; the General Trustees; and a Special Commission on Structural Reform, for which the Council of Assembly itself had called, aware that its own place in the development of strategic priorities was in need of objective scrutiny, together with that of the other councils, committees and courts of the Church.

The Commission's closely defined remit was to review the governance structure of the Church of Scotland as a regulated charity. It argued that structures that have served the Church for the best part of four centuries can no longer respond with the speed and flexibility necessary to tackle today's challenges; nor are they sustainable by a membership that has halved over the last twenty years. The headline proposals were to establish a new trustee body (to replace the Council of Assembly and articulate a strategy for the Church); to slim down the Church's central organisations, including the General Assembly itself, making rapid budget savings of between 20 and 30 percent; and the devolution of responsibility to the regional level of the Church, requiring fewer and larger presbyteries. Not every proposal or detail was without precedent; rather, what felt new was the shared sense of urgency, such that commissioners tightened and firmed up even the brisk timescales recommended by the Commission, including for the consolidation of four of the Church's councils into two.

In particular, the principle of devolving responsibility was impressed upon commissioners. They were warned by Special Commission convener Professor David Fergusson that "without reform of presbyteries I doubt that we can succeed in what we're setting out to do". The same premise was carried through the 17 actions of the Council of Assembly's own plan, which emphasised consolidating and reordering the Church's finances, and enabling their distribution more transparently for local mission through new funds. Flexibility, collaboration and trust would be the watchwords to make this happen. Likewise, the General Trustees offered examples of presbyteries working together in order to establish criteria for which buildings should be retained for active, sustainable 21st century mission, and which won't usefully outlive their existing congregations. Urgently concerned by the number of buildings still expected to remain beyond the lifetime of present presbytery plans, the chairman stressed the need to "get real. . . to be fleeter of foot, not encumbered with buildings that take up energy that should be used for worship and mission." To that end, the Trustees brought to the Assembly a consultation document that will inform an overall plan for the Church's congregational land and buildings.

The new Moderator, the Right Revd Colin Sinclair, reminded the Assembly that "deciding is not doing". He described the Special Commission's work in particular as a "monumental act of service", adding: "We must be ambassadors for the words." Having overseen the passage of these detailed, far-reaching proposals, however, the immediate task facing Mr Sinclair was equally challenging – to get through the rest of the week's business, some of it inevitably squeezed by the weight of the week's earlier debates.

Adapting to the times

Presenting the report of the Mission and Discipleship Council, the Revd Norman Smith offered six characteristics of discipleship for congregations to grapple, pray and live with; meanwhile, the Joint Emerging Church Group proposed a goal of 100 new worshipping communities in Scotland over the next decade. Such encouragements for growth, and an evident desire for mission, were tempered by a pragmatism for which the Special Commission had paved the way. Recognising that mission cannot today be delivered as it was even a few decades ago (it is no longer "business as usual"), the Ministries Council is exploring "mixed modes" of learning for its ministry candidates, including distance learning options, and a reduction in the number of academic institutions used for training. Examples of local innovation were shared too, including from the Presbytery of Shetland, which appeared to be punching above its weight this year. Its uniting parishes are moving towards having a single kirk session to oversee all Shetland's congregations, with a plan that will redistribute consolidated funds in a ratio of 25 per cent for building maintenance and 75 per cent for mission.

Commissioners also questioned the ongoing viability of inducting parish ministers on an unrestricted basis. Arguing the need for increased flexibility, they instructed the Ministries Council to consider new legislation that would permit tenure "on a renewable basis of no more than seven years". Moreover, in response to the structural changes already agreed by the Assembly, commissioners also accepted the Revd Gordon Kennedy's request for a Special Commission to investigate the current effectiveness of Presbyterian Church government as a whole in supporting the mission of local congregations and developing leadership in the Church.

Proposals to end the National Youth Assembly met with resistance, but concerns that the Church is critically under-investing in the young people and under-40s it wishes to attract (and indeed that under-40s increasingly distrust any organisation run by millennials, the Church included) were countered with the stated intention of spreading engagement with young people across a broader age range and through a greater number of residential gatherings. With a view to extending the role of young people locally, the Legal Questions Committee has also been asked to consider the implications of reducing to 16 the age at which someone may become an Elder.

Climate challenges and the Church

Youth delegates have become ever more influential participants in Assembly debates since 1994, to the extent that their presence is perhaps sometimes taken for granted. This year, they led the way in what, like the tenure question, has become a recurring debate: whether or not the Church should disinvest from industries reliant on fossil fuels. It is a question on which conflicting approaches become evident between different central bodies of the Church as well amongst individual commissioners. The subject was raised in the context of a wider conversation about climate change – one made especially personal this year by the contribution of a delegate from Mozambique, who conveyed the trauma of his compatriots in the face of cyclones Idai and Kenneth: "a result of climate change", he said. Our relationship to the natural world was tackled over a number of issues – including a telling criticism of single-use plastic water bottles in the Assembly Hall itself. However, it was the question of how the Church's money is invested that permeated the week: raised on the opening day in relation to pension funds and, on the closing day, inspiring a musical climate change protest from the gallery at the opening of the Investors Trust report.

The Church and Society Council was instructed in 2018 to maintain dialogue with oil and gas companies, but this year some commissioners argued that such an approach is proving ineffectual, that the Church's moral credibility is being undermined, and that support for a net zero greenhouse gas emissions economy in Scotland by 2045 demands that the Church acts now. On the other hand, from the Investors Trust, there is a strong commitment to collaborating with other Christian investor organisations in the belief that, together, they can make a difference; and from more than one speaker a warning that we can't make the oil and gas companies change if we don't change our own consumer "addictions". An amendment that would have led to disinvestment fell by 40 votes; an appeal to the conscience of the institutional Church and individuals alike remained powerfully present.

The importance of presence

A sustained debate such as that on climate, fuel and investment can overshadow significant, ongoing work carried out by so-called "smaller committees": exploring new options for delivering the sacraments in worship, for instance, and proposing fixed-term membership of kirk sessions. Nevertheless, it reveals the Assembly at its most well-informed, and evidences the Church's sense of its place in society, both in Scotland and globally. From the work of 112 football chaplains across Scotland, hailed by one commissioner, to a call that Ministry of Defence records of the 1994 RAF Chinook helicopter disaster over the Mull of Kintyre be safely retained, the sharing of experience and information at the 2019 Assembly reaffirmed confidence in the Church's voice, even as it accepts the need for radical reforms in the face of tighter finances and smaller worshipping communities. Such confidence is rooted, for example, in the Church of Scotland's 150 years of formal social care, celebrated this year by CrossReach. Transformational stories, too, from the Church's partnerships worldwide lay behind the affirmation: "This modest Church of ours, on the edge of Northern Europe has made a difference" – to prospects for peace in war-torn South Sudan; by its initiation of Scottish Faiths Action for Refugees; and through its expenditure, not without its critics, on buildings as well as personnel in Israel-Palestine. Of Tabeetha School in Jaffa, one of the few schools in Israel where Christians, Jews and Muslims work and learn together, the World Mission Convener said: "It breaks down barriers and fosters positive relationships. . . between faiths that are too often separated and consequently suspicious of one another."

That point was echoed by Scotland's First Minister, Nicola Sturgeon MSP, addressing commissioners almost 20 years to the day after she made her maiden parliamentary speech in the Assembly Hall itself – then a temporary home to the fledgling Scottish Parliament. She noted that the Kirk's work on interfaith cooperation is especially vital at a time when intolerance and bigotry are on the rise in parts of the world, and offered a "thankyou" for the Church's valued contributions to Scotland and countries worldwide, "benefitting not just Christians but people of other faiths and none". Replying, the Moderator said: "The Church is not just a hobby for religious geeks" – it cares about Scotland and values opportunities to speak out on important issues, as much through the voice of the Assembly as through the active presence of flourishing congregations, working alongside partners as catalysts for change in local neighbourhoods.

Laurence Wareing
*(Laurence Wareing produced twice daily podcasts of the
proceedings of the 2019 General Assembly.)*

SECTION 5

Presbytery Lists

In each Presbytery list, the congregations ('charges') are listed in alphabetical order. In a linked charge, the names appear under the first-named congregation. Under the name of the congregation will be found the name of the minister and, where applicable, that of an associate minister, ordained local minister, auxiliary minister and member of the Diaconate. The years indicated after a name in the congregational section of each Presbytery list are the year of ordination (column 1) and the year of current appointment (column 2). Where only one date is given, it is both the year of ordination and the year of appointment. Where no other name is listed, the name of the session clerk(s) or interim moderator is given.

In the second section of each Presbytery list, the first part lists those ministers and deacons in other appointments, while the second part lists those demitted/retired. The first date is the year of ordination, and the following date is the year of appointment or retirement. If the person concerned is retired, then the appointment last held will be shown in brackets.

F   A charge with a Facebook page.
GD   A charge where it is desirable that the minister should have a knowledge of Gaelic.
GE   A charge where public worship must be regularly conducted in Gaelic.
H   A hearing aid loop system has been installed.
L   A chair lift or lift has been installed.
T   A charge with a Twitter account.
W   A charge with a website.

PRESBYTERY NUMBERS

1	Edinburgh	18	Dumbarton
2	West Lothian	19	Argyll
3	Lothian	20	
4	Melrose and Peebles	21	
5	Duns	22	Falkirk
6	Jedburgh	23	Stirling
7	Annandale and Eskdale	24	Dunfermline
8	Dumfries and Kirkcudbright	25	Kirkcaldy
9	Wigtown and Stranraer	26	St Andrews
10	Ayr	27	Dunkeld and Meigle
11	Irvine and Kilmarnock	28	Perth
12	Ardrossan	29	Dundee
13	Lanark	30	Angus
14	Greenock and Paisley	31	Aberdeen
15	Glasgow	32	Kincardine and Deeside
16	Glasgow	33	Gordon
17	Hamilton	34	Buchan
35	Moray		
36	Abernethy		
37	Inverness		
38	Lochaber		
39	Ross		
40	Sutherland		
41	Caithness		
42	Lochcarron – Skye		
43	Uist		
44	Lewis		
45	Orkney		
46	Shetland		
47	England		
48	International Charges		
49	Jerusalem		

(1) EDINBURGH (F W)

The Presbytery meets at Greyfriars Kirk, Edinburgh, on (2019) 5 November, 3 December (in the Moderator's church), and (2020) on 4 February, 31 March, 16 June, 8 September, 3 November and 1 December.

Clerk:	REV. MARJORY McPHERSON LLB BD MTh	10/1 Palmerston Place, Edinburgh EH12 5AA edinburgh@churchofscotland.org.uk		0131 225 9137
Depute Clerk:	HAZEL HASTIE MA CQSW PhD AIWS	10/1 Palmerston Place, Edinburgh EH12 5AA HHastie@churchofscotland.org.uk		07827 314374

1 Edinburgh: Albany Deaf Church of Edinburgh (F H) — 0131 444 2054

Albany Deaf Church is a Mission Initiative of Edinburgh: St Andrew's and St George's West

2 Edinburgh: Balerno (F H W)
Andre J. Groenewald BA BD MDiv DD   1994   2016
bpc-admin@balernochurch.org.uk — 0131 449 7245
3 Johnsburn Road, Balerno EH14 7DN — 0131 449 3830
AGroenewald@churchofscotland.org.uk

3 Edinburgh: Barclay Viewforth (F W)
Vacant
Interim Moderator: Ian A. MacDonald
admin@barclaychurch.org.uk — 0131 229 6810
113 Meadowspot, Edinburgh EH10 5UY — 0131 478 2376
Ian.Angus.MacDonald@churchofscotland.org.uk — 0131 281 6153

4 Edinburgh: Blackhall St Columba's (T W)
Vacant
Interim Moderator: G. Russell Barr
secretary@blackhallstcolumba.org.uk — 0131 332 4431
5 Blinkbonny Crescent, Edinburgh EH4 3NB — 0131 343 3708
GBarr@churchofscotland.org.uk — 0131 336 2036

5 Edinburgh: Bristo Memorial Craigmillar (F W)
Vacant
Interim Moderator: Donald H. Scott
72 Blackchapel Close, Edinburgh EH15 3SL — 0131 657 3266
Donald.Scott@churchofscotland.org.uk — 0131 468 1254

6 Edinburgh: Broughton St Mary's (F H L W)
Peter J. Macdonald BD DipMin   1986   2018
mail@bstmchurch.org.uk — 0131 556 4252
78 March Road, Edinburgh EH4 3SY — 0131 312 7440
PMacdonald@churchofscotland.org.uk — 07946 715166

7 Edinburgh: Canongate (F H T W)
Neil N. Gardner MA BD RNR   1991   2006
canongatekirk@btinternet.com — 0131 556 3515
The Manse of Canongate, Edinburgh EH8 8BR — 0131 556 3515
NGardner@churchofscotland.org.uk

8	**Edinburgh: Carrick Knowe (H W)** Fiona M. Mathieson (Mrs) BEd BD PGCommEd MTh	1988	2001	ckchurch@talktalk.net 21 Traquair Park West, Edinburgh EH12 7AN FMathieson@churchofscotland.org.uk	**0131 334 1505** 0131 334 9774
9	**Edinburgh: Colinton (F H W)** Rolf H. Billes BD	1996	2009	**church.office@colinton-parish.com** The Manse, Colinton, Edinburgh EH13 0JR RBilles@churchofscotland.org.uk	**0131 441 2232** 0131 466 8384
10	**Edinburgh: Corstorphine Craigsbank (H T W)** Vacant Session Clerks: Margaret G. Adair Elaine Thompson			17 Craigs Bank, Edinburgh EH12 8HD craigsbanksc@gmail.com craigsbanksc@gmail.com	**0131 334 6365** 0131 467 6826 0131 334 5117 0131 334 0202
11	**Edinburgh: Corstorphine Old (F H W)** Moira McDonald MA BD	1997	2005	corold@aol.com 23 Manse Road, Edinburgh EH12 7SW MMcDonald@churchofscotland.org.uk	**0131 334 7864** 0131 476 5893
12	**Edinburgh: Corstorphine St Anne's (F H L T W)** James J. Griggs BD MTh ALCM PGCE	2011	2013	**office@stannes.corstorphine.org.uk** 1/5 Morham Gait, Edinburgh EH10 5GH JGriggs@churchofscotland.org.uk	**0131 316 4740** 0131 466 3269
13	**Edinburgh: Corstorphine St Ninian's (F H W)** James D. Aitken BD	2002	2017	**office@st-ninians.co.uk** 17 Templeland Road, Edinburgh EH12 8RZ JAitken@churchofscotland.org.uk	**0131 539 6204** 0131 334 2978
14	**Edinburgh: Craiglockhart (F H T W)** Gordon Kennedy BSc BD MTh	1993	2012	**office@craiglockhartchurch.org** 20 Craiglockhart Quadrant, Edinburgh EH14 1HD GKennedy@churchofscotland.org.uk	**0131 455 8229** 0131 444 1615
15	**Edinburgh: Craigmillar Park (H W)** **linked with Edinburgh: Reid Memorial (F H W)** Alexander T. McAspurren BD MTh	2002	2019	**cpkirk@btinternet.com** **reid.memorial@btinternet.com** 14 Hallhead Road, Edinburgh EH16 5QJ AMcAspurren@churchofscotland.org.uk	**0131 667 5862** **0131 662 1203** 0131 667 1623
16	**Edinburgh: Cramond (F H T W)** G. Russell Barr BA BD MTh DMin	1979	1993	**cramond.kirk@blueyonder.co.uk** Manse of Cramond, Edinburgh EH4 6NS GBarr@churchofscotland.org.uk	**0131 336 2036** 0131 336 2036

17 **Edinburgh: Currie (F H W)**
V. Easter Smart BA MDiv DMin
1996   2015
currie_kirk@btconnect.com
43 Lanark Road West, Currie EH14 5JX
ESmart@churchofscotland.org.uk
0131 451 5141
0131 449 4719

18 **Edinburgh: Dalmeny (F W) linked with Edinburgh: Queensferry (F H W)**   **office@qpcweb.org**
David C. Cameron BD CertMin
1993   2009
1 Station Road, South Queensferry EH30 9HY
DavidCCameron@churchofscotland.org.uk
0131 331 1100
0131 331 1100

19 **Edinburgh: Davidson's Mains (F H W)**
Daniel Robertson BA BD
2009   2016
life@dmainschurch.plus.com
1 Hillpark Terrace, Edinburgh EH4 7SX
Daniel.Robertson@churchofscotland.org.uk
0131 312 6282
0131 336 3078
07909 840654

20 **Edinburgh: Drylaw (F W)**
Jenny M. Williams BSc CQSW BD
(Transition Minister)
1996   2017
drylawparishchurch@btinternet.com
15 House o' Hill Gardens, Edinburgh EH4 2AR
JWilliams@churchofscotland.org.uk
0131 332 6863
0131 332 0896

21 **Edinburgh: Duddingston (F H W)**
James A.P. Jack
BSc BArch BD DMin RIBA ARIAS
1989   2001
dodinskirk@aol.com
Manse of Duddingston, Old Church Lane, Edinburgh EH15 3PX
JJack@churchofscotland.org.uk
0131 661 4240
0131 661 4240

22 **Edinburgh: Fairmilehead (F H W)**
Cheryl McKellar-Young (Mrs)
BA BD MSc
2013   2018
office@fhpc.org.uk
14 Margaret Rose Drive, Edinburgh EH10 7ER
CMcKellarYoung@churchofscotland.org.uk
0131 445 2374
07590 230121

23 **Edinburgh: Gorgie Dalry Stenhouse (F H T W)**
Peter I. Barber MA BD
1984   1995
contactus@gdschurch.org.uk
90 Myreside Road, Edinburgh EH10 5BZ
PBarber@churchofscotland.org.uk
0131 337 7936
0131 337 2284

24 **Edinburgh: Gracemount (W) linked with Edinburgh: Liberton (F H T W)**
John N. Young MA BD PhD
1996
7 Kirk Park, Edinburgh EH16 6HZ
JYoung@churchofscotland.org.uk
0131 664 3067

25 **Edinburgh: Granton (F H T W)**
Norman A. Smith MA BD
1997   2005
8 Wardie Crescent, Edinburgh EH5 1AG
NSmith@churchofscotland.org.uk
0131 552 3033
0131 551 2159

26 **Edinburgh: Greenbank (F H W)**
Martin S. Ritchie MA BD PhD
2018
greenbankchurch@btconnect.com
112 Greenbank Crescent, Edinburgh EH10 5SZ
MRitchie@churchofscotland.org.uk
0131 447 9969
0131 447 4032

Tel/Fax

27 Edinburgh: Greenside (H W)
Guardianship of the Presbytery
Interim Moderator: Suzie Stark
80 Pilrig Street, Edinburgh EH6 5AS
SStark@churchofscotland.org.uk
0131 556 5588
0131 554 3277
0131 551 1381

28 Edinburgh: Greyfriars Kirk (F GE H T W)
Richard E. Frazer BA BD DMin   1986
enquiries@greyfriarskirk.com
12 Tantallon Place, Edinburgh EH9 1NZ
RFrazer@churchofscotland.org.uk
0131 225 1900
0131 667 6610

Kenneth L. Luscombe DipPhysEd TSTC   1982
BTh BD ThM (Associate Minister)
Greyfriars Kirk, Greyfriars Place, Edinburgh EH1 2QQ
KLuscombe@churchofscotland.org.uk
0131 225 1900

29 Edinburgh: High (St Giles') (F T W)
Calum I. MacLeod BA BD   1996
alison.wylie@stgilescathedral.org.uk
St Giles' Cathedral, High Street, Edinburgh EH1 1RE
Calum.MacLeod@churchofscotland.org.uk
0131 225 4363
0131 225 4363

30 Edinburgh: Holy Trinity (F H)
Ian A. MacDonald BD MTh   2005
5 Baberton Mains Terrace, Edinburgh EH14 3DG
Ian.Angus.MacDonald@churchofscotland.org.uk
0131 442 3304
0131 281 6153

Rita M. Welsh BA PhD   2017
(Ordained Local Minister)
19 Muir Wood Road, Currie EH14 5JW
RWelsh@churchofscotland.org.uk
0131 451 5943

31 Edinburgh: Inverleith St Serf's (F H W)
Joanne G. Foster (Mrs)   1996
DipTMus BD AdvDipCouns MBACP(Acc)
78 Pilrig Street, Edinburgh EH6 5AS
JFoster@churchofscotland.org.uk
0131 561 1392

32 Edinburgh: Juniper Green (F H W)
James S. Dewar MA BD   1983
jgpc@supanet.com
476 Lanark Road, Juniper Green, Edinburgh EH14 5BQ
JDewar@churchofscotland.org.uk
0131 458 5147
0131 453 3494

33 Edinburgh: Kirkliston (W)
Vacant
Interim Moderator: John A. Cowie
43 Main Street, Kirkliston EH29 9AF
JCowie@churchofscotland.org.uk
0131 333 3298
0131 557 6052
07506 104416

34 Edinburgh: Leith North (F H W)
Vacant
Interim Moderator: R. Russell McLarty
nlpc-office@btinternet.com
6 Craighall Gardens, Edinburgh EH6 4RJ
Russell.McLarty@churchofscotland.org.uk
0131 553 7378
0131 551 5252
01875 614496
07751 755986

35 Edinburgh: Leith St Andrew's (H W)
A. Robert A. Mackenzie LLB BD — 1993 — 2013
leithstandrews@yahoo.co.uk
30 Lochend Road, Edinburgh EH6 8BS
AMacKenzie@churchofscotland.org.uk
0131 553 8839
0131 553 2122

36 Edinburgh: Leith South (H W)
John S. (Iain) May BSc MBA BD — 2012
slpcoffice@gmail.com
37 Claremont Road, Edinburgh EH6 7NN
JMay@churchofscotland.org.uk
0131 554 2578
0131 555 0392

37 Edinburgh: Liberton See Edinburgh: Gracemount

38 Edinburgh: Liberton Northfield (F H W)
Vacant
Interim Moderator: Gordon Kennedy
9 Claverhouse Drive, Edinburgh EH16 6BR
GKennedy@churchofscotland.org.uk
0131 551 3847
0131 664 5490
0131 444 1615

39 Edinburgh: Marchmont St Giles' (F H T W)
Karen K. Campbell BD MTh DMin — 1997 — 2002
office@marchmontstgiles.org.uk
2 Trotter Haugh, Edinburgh EH9 2GZ
KKCampbell@churchofscotland.org.uk
0131 447 4359
0131 447 2834

40 Edinburgh: Mayfield Salisbury (F W)
Scott S. McKenna BA BD MTh MPhil PhD — 1994 — 2000
churchmanager@googlemail.com
26 Seton Place, Edinburgh EH9 2JT
SMcKenna@churchofscotland.org.uk
Kay McIntosh (Mrs) DCS — 1990 — 2018
(member of West Lothian Presbytery)
4 Jacklin Green, Livingston EH54 8PZ
kay@backedge.co.uk
0131 667 1522
0131 667 1286
01506 440543

41 Edinburgh: Meadowbank (F T W)
R. Russell McLarty MA BD — 1985 — 2017
(Transition Minister)
meadowbank@meadowbankchurch.com
9 Sanderson's Wynd, Tranent EH33 1DA
RussellMcLarty@churchofscotland.org.uk
01875 614496
07751 755986

42 Edinburgh: Morningside (F H W)
Derek Browning MA BD DMin — 1987 — 2001
office@morningsideparishchurch.org.uk
20 Braidburn Crescent, Edinburgh EH10 6EN
Derek.Browning@churchofscotland.org.uk
0131 447 6745
0131 447 1617

43 Edinburgh: Morningside United (H W)
Steven Manders LLB BD STB MTh — 2008 — 2015
churchoffice.muc@gmail.com
1 Midmar Avenue, Edinburgh EH10 6BS
stevenmanders@hotmail.com
0131 447 3152
0131 447 7943
07808 476733

Morningside United is a Local Ecumenical Partnership with the United Reformed Church

44 Edinburgh: Murrayfield (F H W)
Keith Edwin Graham MA PGDip BD MTh — 2008 — 2014
mpchurch@btconnect.com
45 Murrayfield Gardens, Edinburgh EH12 6DH
KEGraham@churchofscotland.org.uk
0131 337 1091
0131 337 1364

45 Edinburgh: Newhaven (F H W)
Peter B. Bluett BTh   1996   2007
158 Granton Road, Edinburgh   EH5 3RF
PBluett@churchofscotland.org.uk
0131 476 5212

46 Edinburgh: Old Kirk and Muirhouse (F H T W)
Stephen Ashley-Emery BD DPS   2006   2016
35 Silverknowes Road, Edinburgh   EH4 5LL
SEmery@churchofscotland.org.uk
0131 476 2580
07484 536297

47 Edinburgh: Palmerston Place (F H T W)
Colin A.M. Sinclair BA BD   1981   1996
admin@palmerstonplacechurch.com
30B Cluny Gardens, Edinburgh   EH10 6BJ
CSinclair@churchofscotland.org.uk
0131 220 1690
0131 447 9598
Fax   0131 225 3312

48 Edinburgh: Pilrig St Paul's (F W)
Mark M. Foster BSc BD   1998   2013
mail@pilrigstpauls.org.uk
78 Pilrig Street, Edinburgh   EH6 5AS
MFoster@churchofscotland.org.uk
0131 553 1876
0131 332 5736

49 Edinburgh: Polwarth (F H W)
Jack Holt BSc BD MTh   1985   2011
office@polwarth.org.uk
88 Craiglockhart Road, Edinburgh   EH14 1EP
JHolt@churchofscotland.org.uk
0131 346 2711
0131 441 6105

50 Edinburgh: Portobello and Joppa (F H W)
Stewart G. Weaver BA BD PhD   2003   2014
office@portyjoppachurch.org
6 St Mary's Place, Edinburgh   EH15 2QF
SWeaver@churchofscotland.org.uk
0131 657 3401
0131 669 2410

Lourens de Jager PgDip MDiv BTh   2013   2015
(Associate Minister)
1 Brunstane Road North, Edinburgh   EH15 2DL
LDeJager@churchofscotland.org.uk
07521 426644

51 Edinburgh: Priestfield (F H W)
Donald H. Scott BA BD   1983   2018
13 Lady Road, Edinburgh   EH16 5PA
Donald.Scott@churchofscotland.org.uk
0131 667 5644
0131 468 1254

52 Edinburgh: Queensferry See Edinburgh: Dalmeny

53 Edinburgh: Ratho (F W)
Ian J. Wells BD   1999
2 Freelands Road, Ratho, Newbridge   EH28 8NP
IWells@churchofscotland.org.uk
0131 333 1346

54 Edinburgh: Reid Memorial See Edinburgh: Craigmillar Park

No.	Charge / Minister	Dates	Address / Email	Telephone
55	**Edinburgh: Richmond Craigmillar (F H)** Elizabeth M. Henderson MA BD MTh	1985 1997	Manse of Duddingston, Old Church Lane, Edinburgh EH15 3PX EHenderson@churchofscotland.org.uk	**0131 661 6561** 0131 661 4240
56	**Edinburgh: St Andrew's and St George's West (F H L W)** Rosemary E. Magee MDiv DMin	2009 2019	info@stagw.org.uk 25 Comely Bank, Edinburgh EH4 1AJ RMagee@churchofscotland.org.uk	**0131 225 3847** 0131 332 5848
57	**Edinburgh: St Andrew's Clermiston (F)** Alistair H. Keil BD DipMin	1989	87 Drum Brae South, Edinburgh EH12 8TD AKeil@churchofscotland.org.uk	0131 339 4149
58	**Edinburgh: St Catherine's Argyle (H W)** Stuart D. Irvin BD	2013 2016	5 Palmerston Road, Edinburgh EH9 1TL SIrvin@churchofscotland.org.uk	**0131 667 7220** 0131 667 9344
59	**Edinburgh: St Cuthbert's (F H L T W)** Peter Sutton AKC BA BD MThCouns	2017	office@st-cuthberts.net St Cuthbert's Church, 5 Lothian Road, Edinburgh EH1 2EP PSutton@churchofscotland.org.uk	**0131 229 1142** 07718 311319
60	**Edinburgh: St David's Broomhouse (F H W)** Michael J. Mair BD	2014	33 Traquair Park West, Edinburgh EH12 7AN MMair@churchofscotland.org.uk	**0131 443 9851** 0131 334 1730
61	**Edinburgh: St John's Colinton Mains (F W)** Peter Nelson BSc BD	2015	2 Caiystane Terrace, Edinburgh EH10 6SR PNelson@churchofscotland.org.uk	07500 057889
62	**Edinburgh: St Margaret's (F H W)** Vacant Interim Moderator: Stewart G. Weaver	2003	stmpc@btconnect.com 43 Moira Terrace, Edinburgh EH7 6TD SWeaver@churchofscotland.org.uk	**0131 554 7400** 0131 669 7329 0131 669 2410
63	**Edinburgh: St Martin's (F W)** William M. Wishart BD	2017	1 Toll House Gardens, Tranent EH33 2QQ BWishart@churchofscotland.org.uk	01875 704071
64	**Edinburgh: St Michael's (H W)** Andrea E. Price (Mrs)	1997 2018	office@stmichaels-kirk.co.uk 13 Dovecot Park, Edinburgh EH14 2LN	**0131 478 9675** 0131 443 4355

65 Edinburgh: St Nicholas' Sighthill (F W)
Thomas M. Kisitu MTh PhD 1993 2015
122 Sighthill Loan, Edinburgh EH11 4NT
TMKisitu@churchofscotland.org.uk
0131 442 3978

66 Edinburgh: St Stephen's Comely Bank (F W)
George Vidits BD MTh 2000 2015
office@comelybankchurch.com
8 Blinkbonny Crescent, Edinburgh EH4 3NB
GVidits@churchofscotland.org.uk
0131 315 4616
0131 332 3364

67 Edinburgh: Slateford Longstone (F W)
Samuel A.R. Torrens BD 1995 2019
50 Kingsknowe Road South, Edinburgh EH14 2JW
STorrens@churchofscotland.org.uk
0131 466 5308

68 Edinburgh: Stockbridge (F H T W)
John A. Cowie BSc BD DMin 1983 2013
stockbridgechurch@btconnect.com
19 Eildon Street, Edinburgh EH3 5JU
JCowie@churchofscotland.org.uk
0131 332 0122
0131 557 6052
07506 104416

69 Edinburgh: Tron Kirk (Gilmerton and Moredun) (F)
Cameron Mackenzie BD 1997 2010
467 Gilmerton Road, Edinburgh EH17 7JG
Cammy.Mackenzie@churchofscotland.org.uk
0131 664 7538

Janet R. McKenzie (Mrs) 2016
(Ordained Local Minister)
80C Colinton Road, Edinburgh EH14 1DD
JMcKenzie@churchofscotland.org.uk
0131 444 2054
07980 884653

Liz Crocker DipComEd DCS 1985 2015
77c Craigcrook Road, Edinburgh EH4 3PH
ECrocker@churchofscotland.org.uk
0131 332 0227

70 Edinburgh: Wardie (H T W)
Ute Jaeger-Fleming MTh CPS 2008 2015
churchoffice@wardie.org.uk
35 Lomond Road, Edinburgh EH5 3JN
UJaeger-Fleming@churchofscotland.org.uk
0131 551 3847
0131 552 0190

71 Edinburgh: Willowbrae (F H W)
A. Malcolm Ramsay BA LLB DipMin 1986 2017
(Transition Minister)
office.willowbrae@gmail.com
19 Abercorn Road, Edinburgh EH8 7DP
MRamsay@churchofscotland.org.uk
0131 661 8259
0131 652 2938

In other appointments
Alexander, Ian W. BA BD STM 1990 2010
Secretary, World Mission Council
121 George Street, Edinburgh EH2 4YN
IAlexander@churchofscotland.org.uk
0131 225 5722

Name			Position	Address / Email	Telephone
Donald, Alistair P. MA PhD BD	1999	2009	Chaplain: Heriot-Watt University	The Chaplaincy, Heriot-Watt University, Edinburgh EH14 4AS a.p.donald@hw.ac.uk	0131 451 4508
Evans, Mark BSc MSc DCS	1988	2006	Head of Spiritual Care NHS Fife	13 Easter Drylaw Drive, Edinburgh EH4 2QA (Home) mark.evans59@nhs.net (Office)	0131 343 3089 01383 674136 0131 447 4022
Fergusson, David A.S. (Prof.) OBE MA BD DPhil DD FRSE FBA	1984	2000	University of Edinburgh: New College	23 Riselaw Crescent, Edinburgh EH10 6HN	07949 468341
Fraser, Liam J. LLB BD MTh PhD	2017		Campus Minister, University of Edinburgh	Edinburgh University Campus Ministry (EUCAM), 138–140 The Pleasance, Edinburgh EH8 9RR lfraser@churchofscotland.org.uk	
Hardman Moore, Susan (Prof.) MA MAR PhD	2013	2018	Principal, New College, University of Edinburgh (Ordained Local Minister)	New College, Mound Place, Edinburgh EH1 2LX SHardman-Moore@churchofscotland.org.uk	0131 650 8908 07811 345699
MacMurchie, F. Lynne LLB BD	1998	2003	Healthcare Chaplain	Royal Edinburgh Hospital, Community Mental Health, Astley Ainslie Hospital lynne.macmurchie@nhslothian.scot.nhs.uk	0131 537 6775
McPheat, Elspeth DCS	1985	2001	Deacon: CrossReach	53 Wood Street, Grangemouth FK3 8LS elspeth176@sky.com	01324 282406
McPherson, Marjory (Mrs) LLB BD MTh	1990	2017	Presbytery Clerk: Edinburgh	10/1 Palmerston Place, Edinburgh EH12 5AA MMcPherson@churchofscotland.org.uk	0131 225 9137
Mathieson, Angus R. MA BD	1988	2018	Secretary, Mission and Discipleship Council	21 Traquair Park West, Edinburgh EH12 7AN AMathieson@churchofscotland.org.uk	0131 334 9774
Orr, Sheena BA MSc MBA BD	2011	2018	Chaplaincy Adviser, Scottish Prison Service	Calton House, 5 Redheughs Rigg, South Gyle, Edinburgh EH12 9HW sheena.orr@sps.pnn.gov.uk	0131 330 3575 07922 649160
Pennykid, Gordon J. BD DCS	2015	2018	Chaplain, HMP Edinburgh	8 Glenfield, Livingston EH54 7BG GPennykid@churchofscotland.org.uk	07747 652652
Ridland, Alistair K. MA BD PGDip MRAeS MInstLM RAFAC	1982	2000	Chaplain: Western General Hospital	13 Stewart Place, Kirkliston EH29 0BQ (Home) alistair.ridland@nhslothian.scot.nhs.uk (Office)	0131 333 2711 0131 537 1400
Robertson, Pauline (Mrs) DCS BA CertTheol	2003	2016	Port Chaplain, Sailors' Society	6 Ashville Terrace, Edinburgh EH6 8DD probertson@sailors-society.org	0131 554 6564 07759 436303
Stark, Suzie BD	2013	2016	Hospice Chaplain	St Columba's Hospice, 15 Boswall Road, Edinburgh EH5 3RW SStark@churchofscotland.org.uk	0131 551 1381
Stewart, Lezley J. BD ThM MTh DMin	2000	2017	Ministries Council	121 George Street, Edinburgh EH2 4YN LStewart@churchofscotland.org.uk	0131 225 5722
Swan, David BVMS BD	2005	2018	Chaplain, HMP Edinburgh	159 Redhall Drive, Edinburgh EH13 2LR davidswan97@gmail.com	07944 598988
Tweedie, Fiona J. BSc PhD	2011	2014	Ordained Local Minister: Mission Statistics Co-ordinator	121 George Street, Edinburgh EH2 4YN FTweedie@churchofscotland.org.uk	0131 225 5722
Whyte, George J. BSc BD DMin	1981	2017	Principal Clerk	Church Offices, 121 George Street, Edinburgh EH2 4YN GWhyte@churchofscotland.org.uk	0131 240 2240
Demitted					
Alexander, Helen J.R. BD DipSW	1981	2019	(Assistant, Edinburgh: High (St Giles'))	7 Polwarth Place, Edinburgh EH11 1LG HAlexander@churchofscotland.org.uk	0131 346 0685
Armitage, William L. BSc BD	1976	2006	(Edinburgh: London Road)	Flat 7, 4 Papermill Wynd, Edinburgh EH7 4GJ bill@billarm.plus.com	0131 558 8534

Name			Charge/Role	Address	Tel
Baird, Kenneth S. MSc PhD BD MIMarEST			(Edinburgh: Leith North)	3 Maule Terrace, Gullane EH31 2DB	01620 843447
Bicket, Matthew S. BD	1998	2009	(Carnoustie: Panbride)	9/2 Connaught Place, Edinburgh EH6 4RQ	0131 552 8781
Blakey, Ronald S. MA BD MTh	1989	2017	(Assembly Council)	24 Kimmerghame Place, Edinburgh EH4 2GE kathleen.blakey@gmail.com	0131 343 6352
Booth, Jennifer (Mrs) BD	1962	2000	(Associate: Edinburgh: Leith South)	39 Lilyhill Terrace, Edinburgh EH8 7DR	0131 661 3813
Borthwick, Kenneth S. MA BD	1996	2004	(Edinburgh: Holy Trinity)	34 Rodger Crescent, Armadale EH48 3GR kennysamuel@aol.com	07735 749594
Boyd, Kenneth M. (Prof.) MA BD PhD FRCPE	1983	2016	(University of Edinburgh: Medical Ethics)	1 Doune Terrace, Edinburgh EH3 6DY k.boyd@ed.ac.uk	0131 225 6485
Brady, Ian D. BSc ARCST BD	1970	2004	(Edinburgh: Corstorphine Old)	28 Frankfield Crescent, Dalgety Bay, Dunfermline KY11 9LW bradye500@gmail.com	01383 825104
Brook, Stanley A. BD MTh	1967	2001	(Newport-on-Tay)	4 Scotstoun Green, South Queensferry EH30 9YA stan_brook@btinternet.com	0131 331 4237
Brown, William D. BD CQSW	1977	2016	(Edinburgh: Murrayfield)	79 Cambee Park, Edinburgh EH16 6GG wdb@talktalk.net	0131 261 7297
Cameron, John W.M. MA BD	1987	2013	(Edinburgh: Liberton)	10 Plewlands Gardens, Edinburgh EH10 5JP	0131 447 1277
Chalmers, Murray MA	1957	1996	(Hospital Chaplain)	8 Easter Warriston, Edinburgh EH7 4QX	0131 552 4211
Clark, Christine M. (Mrs) BA BD MTh	1965	2006	(Chaplain, Royal Hospital for Sick Children, Edinburgh)	40 Pentland Avenue, Edinburgh EH13 0HY CClark@churchofscotland.org.uk	07444 819237
Clinkenbeard, William W. BSc BD STM	2006	2019	(Edinburgh: Carrick Knowe)	3/17 Western Harbour Breakwater, Edinburgh EH6 6PA bjclinks@compuserve.com	0131 664 1358
Curran, Elizabeth M. (Miss) BD	1966	2000	(Aberlour)	Blackford Grange, 39/2 Blackford Avenue, Edinburgh EH9 3HN ecurran8@aol.com	
Cuthell, Tom C. MA BD MTh	1995	2008	(Edinburgh: St Cuthbert's)	Flat 10, 2 Kingsburgh Crescent, Waterfront, Edinburgh EH5 1JS	0131 476 3864
Davidson, D. Hugh MA	1965	2007	(Edinburgh: Inverleith)	Flat 1/2, 22 Summerside Place, Edinburgh EH6 4NZ hdavidson35@btinternet.com	0131 554 8420
Dawson, Michael S. BTech BD	1965	2009	(Associate: Edinburgh: Holy Trinity)	9 The Broich, Alva FK12 5NR mixpen.dawson@btinternet.com	01259 769309
Douglas, Alexander B. BD	1979	2005	(Edinburgh: Blackhall St Columba's)	15 Inchview Gardens, Dalgety Bay, Dunfermline KY11 9SA alexandjill@douglas.net	01383 791080
Dunn, W. Iain C. DA LTh	1979	2014	(Edinburgh: Pilrig and Dalmeny Street)	10 Fox Covert Avenue, Edinburgh EH12 6UQ	0131 334 1665
Embleton, Brian M. BD	1983	1998	(Edinburgh: Reid Memorial)	54 Edinburgh Road, Peebles EH45 8EB bmembleton@gmail.com	01721 602157
Embleton, Sara R. (Mrs) BA BD MTh	1976	2015	(Edinburgh: Leith St Serf's)	54 Edinburgh Road, Peebles EH45 8EB srembleton@gmail.com	01721 602157
Farquharson, Gordon MA BD DipEd	1988	2010	(Stonehaven: Dunnottar)	26 Learmonth Court, Edinburgh EH4 1PB gfarqu@talktalk.net	0131 343 1047
Forrester, Margaret R. (Mrs) MA BD DD	1998	2007	(Edinburgh: St Michael's)	25 Kingsbrough Road, Edinburgh EH12 6DZ margaret@rosskeen.org.uk	0131 337 5646
Fraser, Shirley A. (Miss) MA BD	1974	2003	(Scottish Field Director: Friends International)	6/50 Roseburn Drive, Edinburgh EH12 5NS	0131 347 1400
	1992	2008			

Frew, Michael W. BSc BD	1978	2017	(Edinburgh: Slateford Longstone)	37 Swanston Terrace, Edinburgh EH10 7DN	07712 162375
Gardner, John V.	1997	2003	(Glamis, Inverarity and Kinnettles)	75/1 Lockharton Avenue, Edinburgh EH14 1BD jvgardnerf66@googlemail.com	0131 443 7126
Gilmour, Ian Y. BD	1985	2018	(Edinburgh: St Andrew's and St George's West)	29/7 South Trinity Road, Edinburgh EH5 3PN ianyg@gmail.com	07794 149852
Gordon, Margaret (Mrs) DCS	1998	2012	(Deacon)	92 Lanark Road West, Currie EH14 5LA	0131 449 2554
Graham, W. Peter MA BD	1967	2008	(Presbytery Clerk: Edinburgh)	23/6 East Comiston, Edinburgh EH10 6RZ	0131 445 5763
Harkness, James CB OBE QHC MA DD	1961	1995	(Chaplain General: Army)	13 Saxe Coburg Place, Edinburgh EH3 5BR	0131 343 1297
Hay, Jared W. BA MTh DipMin DMin	1987	2017	(Edinburgh: Priestfield)	39 Netherbank, Edinburgh EH16 6YR jaredhay3110@gmail.com	07906 662515
Inglis, Ann (Mrs) LLB BD	1986	2015	(Langton and Lammermuir Kirk)	34 Echline View, South Queensferry EH30 9XL revainglis@gmail.com	0131 629 0233
Irving, William D. LTh	1985	2005	(Golspie)	122 Swanston Muir, Edinburgh EH10 7HY	0131 441 3384
Kingston, David V.F. BD DipPTh	1993	2015	(Chaplain: Army)	2 Cleuch Avenue, North Middleton, Gorebridge EH23 4RP	01875 822026
Lamont, Stewart J. BSc BD	1972	2015	(Arbirlot with Carmylie)	13/1 Grosvenor Crescent, Edinburgh EH12 5EL lamontsj@gmail.com	07557 532012
Lane, Margaret R. (Mrs) BA BD MTh	2009	2019	(Edinburgh: Kirkdistor)	6 Overhaven, Limekilns KY11 3JH MLane@churchofscotland.org.uk	01383 873328 07897 525692
Lawson, Kenneth C. MA BD	1963	1999	(Adviser in Adult Education)	56 Easter Drylaw View, Edinburgh EH4 2QP	0131 539 3311
Logan, Anne T. (Mrs) MA BD MTh DMin PhD	1981	2012	(Edinburgh: Stockbridge)	Sunnyside Cottage, 18 Upper Broomieknowe, Lasswade EH18 1LP annetlogan@sky.com	0131 663 9550
Macdonald, William J. BD	1976	2002	(Board of National Mission: New Charge Development)	1/13 North Werber Park, Edinburgh EH4 1SY	0131 332 0254
MacGregor, Margaret S. (Miss) MA BD DipEd	1985	1994	(Calcutta)	16 Learmonth Court, Edinburgh EH4 1PB	0131 332 1089
McGregor, Alistair G.C. QC BD	1987	2002	(Edinburgh: Leith North)	22 Primrose Bank Road, Edinburgh EH5 3JG	0131 551 2802
McGregor, T. Stewart MBE MA BD	1957	1998	(Chaplain: Edinburgh Royal Infirmary)	19 Lonsdale Terrace, Edinburgh EH3 9HL cetsm@uwclub.net	0131 229 5332
Mackenzie, James G. BA BD	1980	2005	(Jersey: St Columba's)	26 Drylaw Crescent, Edinburgh EH4 2AU jgmackenzie@jerseymail.co.uk	0131 332 3720
Maclean, Ailsa G. (Mrs) BD DipCE	1979	2017	(Chaplain: George Heriot's School)	28 Swan Spring Avenue, Edinburgh EH10 6NJ	0131 445 1320
Macmillan, Gilleasbuig I. KCVO MA BD DHrc DD FRSE HRSA FRCSEd	1969	2013	(Edinburgh: High (St Giles'))	207 Dalkeith Road, Edinburgh EH16 5DS gmacmillan1@btinternet.com	0131 667 5732
McPake, John M. LTh	2000	2013	(Edinburgh: Liberton Northfield)	9 Claverhouse Drive, Edinburgh EH16 6BR john_mcpake@yahoo.co.uk	0131 658 1754
Moir, Ian A. MA BD	1962	2000	(Adviser for Urban Priority Areas)	28/6 Comely Bank Avenue, Edinburgh EH4 1EL	0131 332 2748
Morrison, Mary B. (Mrs) MA BD DipEd	1978	2000	(Edinburgh: Stenhouse St Aidan's)	174 Craigcrook Road, Edinburgh EH4 3PP	0131 336 4706
Mulligan, Anne MA DCS	1974	2013	(Deacon: Hospital Chaplain)	27A Craigour Avenue, Edinburgh EH17 1NH mulliganne@aol.com	0131 664 3426
Munro, John P.L. MA BD PhD	1977	2008	(Kinross)	5 Marchmont Crescent, Edinburgh EH9 1HN jplmunro@yahoo.co.uk	0131 623 0198
Munro, John R. BD	1976	2018	(Edinburgh: Fairmilehead)	23 Braid Farm Road, Edinburgh EH10 6LE revjohnmunro@hotmail.com	0131 446 9363

Name	Dates	Role	Address / Email	Phone
Nicol, Douglas A.O. MA BD	1974 2018	(Hobkirk and Southdean with Ruberslaw)	1/2 North Werber Park, Edinburgh EH4 1SY Douglas.Nicol@churchofscotland.org.uk	07811 437075
Paterson, Douglas S. MA BD	1976 2010	(Edinburgh: St Colm's)	4 Ards Place, High Street, Aberlady EH32 0DB	01875 870192
Rennie, Agnes M. (Miss) DCS	1974 2012	(Deacon)	3/1 Craigmillar Court, Edinburgh EH16 4AD	0131 661 8475
Robertson, Charles LVO MA	1965 2005	(Edinburgh: Canongate)	3 Ross Gardens, Edinburgh EH9 3BS canongate1@aol.com	0131 662 9025
Ross, Keith W. MA BD	1984 2015	(Congregational Development Officer)	Easter Bavelaw House, Pentland Hills Regional Park, Balerno EH14 7JS keithwross@outlook.com	07855 163449
Scott, Jayne E. BA MEd MBA	1988 2019	(Secretary, Ministries Council)	52 Ravenscroft Gardens, Edinburgh EH17 8RP JScott@churchofscotland.org.uk	
Scott, Martin C. DipMusEd RSAM BD PhD	1986 2019	(Secretary, Council of Assembly)	52 Ravenscroft Gardens, Edinburgh EH17 8RP martin.scott14@sky.com	07856 165820
Smith, Angus MA LTh	1965 2006	(Chaplain to the Oil Industry)	3/7 West Powburn, West Savile Gait, Edinburgh EH9 3EW	0131 667 1761
Stephen, Donald M. TD MA BD ThM	1962 2001	(Edinburgh: Marchmont St Giles')	10 Hawkhead Crescent, Edinburgh EH16 6LR donaldmstephen@gmail.com	0131 658 1216
Stevenson, John MA BD PhD	1963 2001	(Department of Education)	12 Swanston Gardens, Edinburgh EH10 7DL	0131 445 3960
Tait, John M. BSc BD	1985 2012	(Edinburgh: Pilrig St Paul's)	82 Greenend Gardens, Edinburgh EH17 7QH johnmtait@me.com	0131 258 9105
Taylor, William R. MA BD MTh	1983 2018	(Chaplaincy Adviser, Scottish Prison Service)	33 Kingsknowe Drive EH14 2JY wlretl@outlook.com	0131 443 5590
Teague, Yvonne (Mrs) DCS	1965 2002	(Board of Ministry)	46 Craigcrook Avenue, Edinburgh EH4 3PX y.teague.1@blueyonder.co.uk	07447 258525
Thomson, Donald M. BD	1975 2013	(Tullibody: St Serf's)	50 Sighthill Road, Edinburgh EH11 4NY donniethomson@tiscali.co.uk	0131 336 3113
Torrance, Iain R. (Prof.) KCVO Kt DD FRSE	1982 2012	(President: Princeton Theological Seminary)	25 The Causeway, Duddingston Village, Edinburgh EH15 3QA irt@ptsem.edu	0131 661 3092
Watson, Nigel G. MA	1998 2012	(Associate: East Kilbride: Old/Stewartfield/West)	7 St Catherine's Place, Edinburgh EH9 1NU nigel.g.watson@gmail.com	0131 662 4191
Wigglesworth, J. Christopher MBE BSc PhD BD	1968 1999	(St Andrew's College, Selly Oak)	12 Leven Terrace, Edinburgh EH3 9LW wiggles@talk21.com	0131 228 6335
Wood, Peter J. MA BD	1993 2018	(Director of Mission, Diocese of Ely)	12 Duncan Street, Edinburgh EH9 1SZ pejo.wood@btinternet.com	07776 119901
Wynne, Alistair T.E. BA BD	1982 2009	(Nicosia Community Church, Cyprus)	Flat 6, 14 Burnbrae Drive, Edinburgh EH12 8AS awynne2@googlemail.com	0131 339 6462

EDINBURGH ADDRESSES

Albany	at St Andrew's and St George's West
Balerno	Johnsburn Road, Balerno
Barclay Viewforth	Barclay Place
Blackhall St Columba's	Queensferry Road
Bristo Memorial	Peffermill Road, Craigmillar
Broughton St Mary's	Bellevue Crescent
Canongate	Canongate
Carrick Knowe	North Saughton Road
Colinton	Dell Road
Corstorphine	
Craigsbank	Craigs Crescent
Old	Kirk Loan
St Anne's	Kaimes Road
St Ninian's	St John's Road
Craiglockhart	Craiglockhart Avenue
Craigmillar Park	Craigmillar Park
Cramond	Cramond Glebe Road
Currie	Kirkgate, Currie
Dalmeny	Main Street, Dalmeny
Davidson's Mains	Quality Street
Drylaw	Groathill Road North
Duddingston	Old Church Lane, Duddingston
Fairmilehead	Frogston Road West, Fairmilehead
Gorgie Dalry Stenhouse	Gorgie Road
Gracemount	Gracemount Primary School
Granton	Boswall Parkway
Greenbank	Braidburn Terrace
Greenside	Royal Terrace
Greyfriars Kirk	Greyfriars Place
High (St Giles')	High Street
Holy Trinity	Hailesland Place, Wester Hailes
Inverleith St Serf's	Ferry Road
Juniper Green	Lanark Road, Juniper Green
Kirkliston	The Square, Kirkliston
Leith	
North	Madeira Street off Ferry Road
St Andrew's	Easter Road
South	Kirkgate, Leith
Liberton	Kirkgate, Liberton
Northfield	Gilmerton Road, Liberton
Marchmont St Giles'	Kilgraston Road
Mayfield Salisbury	Mayfield Road x West Mayfield
Meadowbank	Dalziel Place x London Road
Morningside	Cluny Gardens
Morningside United	Bruntsfield Place x Chamberlain Rd
Murrayfield	Abinger Gardens
Newhaven	Craighall Road
Old Kirk and Murhouse	Pennywell Gardens
Palmerston Place	Palmerston Place
Pilrig St Paul's	Pilrig Street
Polwarth	Polwarth Terrace x Harrison Road
Portobello and Joppa	Abercorn Terrace
Priestfield	Dalkeith Road x Marchhall Place
Queensferry	The Loan, South Queensferry
Ratho	Baird Road, Ratho
Reid Memorial	West Savile Terrace
Richmond Craigmillar	Niddrie Mains Road
St Andrew's and St George's West	George Street
St Andrew's Clermiston	Clermiston View
St Catherine's Argyle	Grange Road x Chalmers Crescent
St Cuthbert's	Lothian Road
St David's Broomhouse	Broomhouse Crescent
St John's Colinton Mains	Oxgangs Road North
St Margaret's	Restalrig Road South
St Martin's	Magdalene Drive
St Michael's	Slateford Road
St Nicholas' Sighthill	Calder Road
St Stephen's Comely Bank	Comely Bank
Slateford Longstone	Kingsknowe Road North
Stockbridge	Saxe Coburg Street
Tron Kirk	Craigour Gardens and Ravenscroft Street
(Gilmerton and Moredun)	
Wardie	Primrosebank Road
Willowbrae	Willowbrae Road

(2) WEST LOTHIAN (F W)

Meets in the church of the incoming Moderator on the first Tuesday of September and in St John's Church Hall, Bathgate, on the first Tuesday of every other month, except June and December, when the meeting is on the second Tuesday, and January, April, July and August, when there is no meeting.

Clerk: REV. DUNCAN SHAW BD MTh   St John's Manse, Mid Street, Bathgate EH48 1QD   01506 653146
westlothian@churchofscotland.org.uk

Abercorn (H W) linked with Pardovan, Kingscavil (H) and Winchburgh (H W)
A. Scott Marshall DipComm BD   1984   1998   The Manse, Winchburgh, Broxburn EH52 6TT   01506 890919
SMarshall@churchofscotland.org.uk   07415 028678

Derek R. Henderson MA DipTP DipCS   2017   45 Priory Road, Linlithgow EH49 6BP   01506 844787
(Ordained Local Minister)   DHenderson@churchofscotland.org.uk   07968 491441

Armadale (H W)
Julia C. Wiley (Ms) MA(CE) MDiv   1998   2010   70 Mount Pleasant, Armadale, Bathgate EH48 3HB   01501 730358
JWiley@churchofscotland.org.uk

Margaret Corrie (Miss) DCS   1989   2013   44 Sunnyside Street, Camelon, Falkirk FK1 4BH   07955 633969
MCorrie@churchofscotland.org.uk

Avonbridge (H) linked with Torphichen (F H W)
Ann Lyall DCS   1980   2017   Manse Road, Torphichen, Bathgate EH48 4LT   01506 635957
(Interim Deacon)   ALyall@churchofscotland.org.uk

Bathgate: Boghall (F H W)
Christopher G. Galbraith BA LLB BD   2012   1 Manse Place, Ash Grove, Bathgate EH48 1NJ   01506 652715
CGalbraith@churchofscotland.org.uk

Bathgate: High (F H W)
Vacant   info@bathgatehigh.com   **01506 650217**
Session Clerk: John Macfarlane   john.macfarlane@gmx.com   01506 632283

Bathgate: St John's (H W)
Duncan Shaw BD MTh   1975   1978   St John's Manse, Mid Street, Bathgate EH48 1QD   01506 653146
westlothian@churchofscotland.org.uk

Blackburn and Seafield (F H W)
Sandra Boyd (Mrs) BEd BD — 2007 — 2019
The Manse, 5 MacDonald Gardens, Blackburn, Bathgate EH47 7RE
SBoyd@churchofscotland.org.uk — 01506 652825

Blackridge (H) linked with Harthill: St Andrew's (F H)
Vacant
Session Clerk, Blackridge: Jean Mowitt (Mrs)
East Main Street, Harthill, Shotts ML7 5QW
jean.mowitt@yahoo.com — 01501 751239 / 01501 750401 / 07590 901933 / 01501 752594
Session Clerk: Harthill: Alexander Kennedy
alex.kend@gmail.com

Breich Valley (F H)
Vacant
Session Clerk: Mary McKenzie (Mrs)
Breich Valley Manse, Stoneyburn, Bathgate EH47 8AU
mmckenzie889@hotmail.co.uk — 01501 763142 / 01506 635818

Broxburn (F H W)
Jacobus Boonzaaier BA BCom(OR) BD MDiv PhD — 1995 — 2015
2 Church Street, Broxburn EH52 5EL
JBoonzaaier@churchofscotland.org.uk — 01506 337560

Fauldhouse: St Andrew's (H)
Scott Raby LTh — 1991 — 2018
7 Glebe Court, Fauldhouse, Bathgate EH47 9DX
SRaby@churchofscotland.org.uk — 01501 771190

Harthill: St Andrew's See Blackridge

Kirknewton (H) and East Calder (F H W)
Alistair J. Cowper BSc BD — 2011 — 2018
8 Manse Court, East Calder, Livingston EH53 0HF
ACowper@churchofscotland.org.uk — 01506 357083 / 07791 524504
Brenda Robson PhD (Auxiliary Minister) — 2005 — 2014
22 Ratho Park Road, Ratho, Newbridge EH28 8NY
BRobson@churchofscotland.org.uk — 0131 281 9511

Kirk of Calder (F H W)
John M. Povey MA BD — 1981
19 Maryfield Park, Mid Calder, Livingston EH53 0SB
JPovey@churchofscotland.org.uk — 01506 882495

Linlithgow: St Michael's (F H W)
Vacant
info@stmichaels-parish.org.uk
St Michael's Manse, Kirkgate, Linlithgow EH49 7AL — 01506 842188
Thomas S. Riddell BSc CEng FIChemE (Auxiliary Minister) — 1993 — 1994
4 The Maltings, Linlithgow EH49 6DS
TRiddell@churchofscotland.org.uk — 01506 842195 / 01506 843251

Linlithgow: St Ninian's Craigmailen (H W)
W. Richard Houston BSc BD   1998   2004   29 Philip Avenue, Linlithgow EH49 7BH   01506 202246
                                                                                  WHouston@churchofscotland.org.uk

Livingston: Old (F H W)
Netu I. Balaj BD MA ThD   2010   2017   Manse of Livingston, Charlesfield Lane, Livingston EH54 7AJ   01506 411888
                                                                                  NBalaj@churchofscotland.org.uk

Livingston United (F W)
Vacant   2 Eastcroft Court, Livingston EH54 7ET   01506 467426
Stephanie Njeru BA   2015   13 Eastcroft Court, Livingston EH54 7ET   01506 464587
                                                                                  stephanie.njeru@methodist.org.uk

   Livingston United is a Local Ecumenical Partnership with the Scottish Episcopal, Methodist and United Reformed Churches

Pardovan, Kingscavil and Winchburgh See Abercorn

Polbeth Harwood (F W) linked with West Kirk of Calder (F H W)
Jonanda Groenewald BA BD MTh DD   2000   2014   3 Johnsburn Road, Balerno EH14 7DN   0131 261 7977
                                                                                  JGroenewald@churchofscotland.org.uk
Alison Quilter   2018   27 Northfield Meadows, Longridge, Bathgate EH47 8SA   07741 985597
(Ordained Local Minister)   AQuilter@churchofscotland.org.uk

Strathbrock (F H T W)
Vacant   1 Manse Park, Uphall, Broxburn EH52 6NX   **01506 856433**
Session Clerk: Lynne McEwen   lynnemcewen@hotmail.co.uk   01506 852550
                                                                                                                                   01506 855513

Torphichen See Avonbridge

Uphall: South (F H W)
Ian D. Maxwell MA BD PhD   1977   2013   8 Fernlea, Uphall, Broxburn EH52 6DF   01506 239840
                                                                                  IMaxwell@churchofscotland.org.uk

West Kirk of Calder (H) See Polbeth Harwood

Whitburn: Brucefield (F H W)
Alexander M. Roger BD PhD   1982   2014   **contact@brucefieldchurch.org.uk**   **01501 748666**
                                                                                  48 Gleneagles Court, Whitburn, Bathgate EH47 8PG   01501 229354
                                                                                  ARoger@churchofscotland.org.uk

Whitburn: South (H W)
Vacant
Session Clerk: James A.R. Brown

admin@whitburnsouthparishchurch.org.uk
5 Mansewood Crescent, Whitburn, Bathgate EH47 8HA
jim3059@gmail.com

01501 740333
01506 813914

In other appointments

Name	Appointment	Dates	Address / Email	Tel
Dunphy, Rhona B. (Mrs) BD DPTheol DrPhil	Ministries Council	2005 2016	92 The Vennel, Linlithgow EH49 7ET / RDunphy@churchofscotland.org.uk	07791 007158
McIntosh, Kay (Mrs) DCS	Deacon, Edinburgh: Mayfield Salisbury	1990 2018	4 Jacklin Green, Livingston EH54 8PZ / kay@backedge.co.uk	01506 440543
Nelson, Georgina MA BD PhD DipEd	Hospital Chaplain, NHS Lothian	1990 1995	63 Hawthorn Bank, Seafield, Bathgate EH47 7EB / georgina.nelson@nhslothian.scot.nhs.uk	

Demitted

Name		Dates	Address / Email	Tel
Black, David W. BSc BD	(Strathbrock)	1968 2008	66 Bridge Street, Newbridge EH28 8SH / dw.black66@yahoo.co.uk	0131 333 2609
Darroch, Richard J.G. BD MTh MA(CMS)	(Whitburn: Brucefield)	1993 2010	23 Barnes Green, Livingston EH54 8PP / richdarr@aol.com	01506 436648
Dunleavy, Suzanne BD DipEd	(Bridge of Weir: St Machar's Ranfurly)	1990 2016	44 Tantallon Gardens, Bellsquarry, Livingston EH54 9AT / suzanne.dunleavy@btinternet.com	
Greig, Ronald G. MA BD	(Livingston United)	1987 2018	47 Mallace Avenue, Armadale EH48 2QD / rgglep@gmail.com	01501 731969 / 07787 887427
Jamieson, Gordon D. MA BD	(Head of Stewardship)	1974 2012	41 Goldpark Place, Livingston EH54 6LW / gdj1949@talktalk.net	01506 412020
Kenton, Marc B. BTh MTh	(Strathbrock)	1997 2018	18 Taylor Green, Livingston EH54 8SY / marc@kentonfamily.co.uk	07790 012128
Kerr, Angus BD CertMin ThM DMin	(Whitburn: South)	1983 2019	27 Pelham Court, Jackton, East Kilbride G74 5PZ	01355 570962
Mackay, Kenneth J. MA BD	(Edinburgh: St Nicholas' Sighthill)	1971 2007	46 Chuckethall Road, Livingston EH54 8FB / knnth_mackay@yahoo.co.uk	01506 410884
Merrilees, Ann (Miss) DCS	(Deacon)	1994 2006	23 Cuthill Brae, West Calder EH55 8QE / mabmerrilees@gmail.com	01501 762909
Smith, Graham W. BA BD FSAScot	(Livingston: Old)	1995 2016	76 Bankton Park East, Livingston EH54 9BN / smithgraham824@gmail.com	01506 442917
Thomson, Phyllis (Miss) DCS	(Deacon)	2003 2010	63 Caroline Park, Mid Calder, Livingston EH53 0SJ	01506 883207
Trimble, Robert DCS	(Deacon)	1988 1998	5 Templar Rise, Dedridge, Livingston EH54 6PJ	01506 412504
Walker, Ian BD MEd DipMS	(Rutherglen: Wardlawhill)	1973 2007	92 Carseknowe, Linlithgow EH49 7LG / walk102822@aol.com	01506 844412

(3) LOTHIAN (W)

Meets at Musselburgh: St Andrew's High Parish Church at 7pm on the last Thursday in February, April, June and November, and in a different church on the last Thursday in September.

Clerk:	MR JOHN D. McCULLOCH DL	20 Tipperwell Way, Howgate, Penicuik EH26 8QP lothian@churchofscotland.org.uk	01968 676300
Depute Clerk:	REV MICHAEL D. WATSON	47 Crichton Terrace, Pathhead EH37 5QZ MWatson@churchofscotland.org.uk	01875 320043

Aberlady (F H W) linked with Gullane (F H W)
Brian C. Hilsley LLB BD   1990   2015   The Manse, Hummel Road, Gullane EH31 2BG   **01875 870777**
BHilsley@churchofscotland.org.uk   01620 843192

Athelstaneford (W) linked with Whitekirk and Tyninghame (W)
Vacant
Michael D. Watson   2013   2019   The Manse, Athelstaneford, North Berwick EH39 5BE   01620 880378
(Ordained Local Minister)   47 Crichton Terrace, Pathhead EH37 5QZ   01875 320043
MWatson@churchofscotland.org.uk

Belhaven (F H T W) linked with Spott (F W)
Neil H. Watson BD   2017   The Manse, Belhaven Road, Dunbar EH42 1NH   01368 860672
NWatson@churchofscotland.org.uk   07974 074549

Bilston linked with Glencorse (H) linked with Roslin (H)
John R. Wells BD DipMin   1991   2005   31A Manse Road, Roslin EH25 9LG   0131 440 2012
wellsjr3@aol.com

Bonnyrigg (F H)
Vacant
June E. Johnston BSc MEd BD   2013   2018   9 Viewbank View, Bonnyrigg EH14 2HU   01896 870754
(Ordained Local Minister)   21 Caberston Road, Walkerburn EH43 6AT   07754 448889
June.Johnston@churchofscotland.org.uk

Cockenzie and Port Seton: Chalmers Memorial (F H W)   contact@chalmerschurch.co.uk
Robin N. Allison BD DipMin   1994   2018   2 Links Road, Port Seton, Prestonpans EH32 0HA   01875 812225
RAllison@churchofscotland.org.uk

Cockenzie and Port Seton: Old (F H)
Guardianship of the Presbytery
Session Clerk: Eizabeth W. Malcolm (Miss)   malcolm771@btinternet.com   01875 813659

Cockpen and Carrington (F H W) linked with Lasswade (H) and Rosewell (H W)
Lorna M. Souter MA BD MSc   2016   11 Pendreich Terrace, Bonnyrigg EH19 2DT   0131 663 6392
LSouter@churchofscotland.org.uk   07889 566418

Elisabeth G.B. Spence BD DipEd   1995   2016   18 Castell Maynes Avenue, Bonnyrigg EH19 3RW   07432 528205
(Pioneer Minister, Hopefield Connections)   ESpence@churchofscotland.org.uk

Dalkeith: St John's and King's Park (F H W)   **sjkpdalkeith@gmail.com**
Keith L. Mack BD MTh DPS   2002   13 Weir Crescent, Dalkeith EH22 3JN   **0131 660 5871**
KMack@churchofscotland.org.uk   0131 454 0206

Dalkeith: St Nicholas Buccleuch (F H T W)
Alexander G. Horsburgh MA BD   1995   2004   1 Nungate Gardens, Haddington EH41 4EE   01620 824728
AHorsburgh@churchofscotland.org.uk

Dirleton (F H) linked with North Berwick: Abbey (F H W)   **abbeychurch@btconnect.com**
David J. Graham BSc BD PhD   1982   1998   Sydserff, Old Abbey Road, North Berwick EH39 4BP   **01620 892800**
DGraham@churchofscotland.org.uk   01620 890800

Dunbar (H W)
Gordon Stevenson BSc BD   2010   The Manse, 10 Bayswell Road, Dunbar EH42 1AB   01368 865482
revgstev@gmail.com

Dunglass (W)
Suzanne G. Fletcher (Mrs) BA MDiv MA   2001   2011   The Manse, Cockburnspath TD13 5XZ   01368 830713
SFletcher@churchofscotland.org.uk   07973 960544

Garvald and Morham (W) linked with Haddington: West (H W)   **hwcofs@hotmail.com**
John D. Vischer   1993   2011   15 West Road, Haddington EH41 3RD   01620 822213
JVischer@churchofscotland.org.uk

Gladsmuir linked with Longniddry (F H W)
Robin E. Hill LLB BD PhD   2004   The Manse, Elcho Road, Longniddry EH32 0LB   01875 853195
RHill@churchofscotland.org.uk

Glencorse (H) See Bilston

Gorebridge (F H W)
Mark S. Nicholas MA BD — 1999
office@gorepc.com
100 Hunterfield Road, Gorebridge EH23 4TT
MNicholas@churchofscotland.org.uk
01875 820387
01875 820387
07816 047493

Gullane See Aberlady

Haddington: St Mary's (F H T W)
Alison P. McDonald MA BD — 1991 2019
1 Nungate Gardens, Haddington EH41 4EE
Alison.McDonald@churchofscotland.org.uk
01620 823109

Haddington: West See Garvald and Morham

Humbie (F W) linked with Yester, Bolton and Saltoun (F W)
Anikó Schütz Bradwell MA BD — 2015
The Manse, Tweeddale Avenue, Gifford, Haddington EH41 4QN
ASchuetzBradwell@churchofscotland.org.uk
01620 811193

Lasswade and Rosewell See Cockpen and Carrington

Loanhead (F T W)
Graham L. Duffin BSc BD DipEd — 1989 2001
120 The Loan, Loanhead EH20 9AJ
GDuffin@churchofscotland.org.uk
0131 448 2459

Longniddry See Gladsmuir

Musselburgh: Northesk (F H W)
Vacant
16 New Street, Musselburgh EH21 6JP
0131 665 2128

Musselburgh: St Andrew's High (H W)
A. Leslie Milton MA BD PhD — 1996 2019
8 Ferguson Drive, Musselburgh EH21 6XA
LMilton@churchofscotland.org.uk
0131 665 7239
0131 665 1124

Musselburgh: St Clement's and St Ninian's
Guardianship of the Presbytery
Session Clerk: Ivor A. Highley
110 Inveresk Road, Musselburgh EH21 7AY
0131 665 5674

Musselburgh: St Michael's Inveresk (F W)
Malcolm M. Lyon BD — 2007 2017
5 Crookston Ct., Crookston Rd., Inveresk, Musselburgh EH21 7TR
MLyon@churchofscotland.org.uk
0131 653 2411

Newbattle (F H W)
Gayle J.A. Taylor MA BD PGDipCouns   1999   Parish Office, Mayfield and Easthouses Church, Bogwood Court, Easthouses EH22 5DG   **0131 663 3245**
(Transition Minister)
GTaylor@churchofscotland.org.uk   0131 663 3245

Malcolm T. Muir LTh   2001   2015   Mayfield and Easthouses Church, Bogwood Court, Mayfield, Dalkeith EH22 5DG   0131 663 3245
(Associate Minister)
MMuir@churchofscotland.org.uk   07920 855467

Newton
Guardianship of the Presbytery   2006   2013   5 Eskvale Court, Penicuik EH26 8HT   0131 663 3845
Andrew Don MBA
(Ordained Local Minister)
ADon@churchofscotland.org.uk   01968 675766

North Berwick: Abbey See Dirleton

North Berwick: St Andrew Blackadder (F H W)   admin@standrewblackadder.org.uk
Neil J. Dougall BD DipMin DMin   1991   2003   7 Marine Parade, North Berwick EH39 4LD   01620 892132
NDougall@churchofscotland.org.uk

Ormiston (W) linked with Pencaitland (F W)
David J. Torrance BD DipMin   1993   2009   The Manse, Pencaitland, Tranent EH34 5DL   01875 340963
DTorrance@churchofscotland.org.uk

Pencaitland See Ormiston

Penicuik: North (F H W)
Graham G. Astles BD MSc   2007   2019   35 Esk Bridge, Penicuik EH26 8QR   07906 290568
GAstles@churchofscotland.org.uk

Penicuik: St Mungo's (F H W)
John C.C. Urquhart MA MA BD   2010   2017   10 Fletcher Grove, Penicuik EH26 0JT   01968 382116
JCUrquhart@churchofscotland.org.uk   07392 069957

Penicuik: South and Howgate (H W)   admin@psah.church
Vacant
Session Clerk: Rosemary Townsley (Mrs)   15 Stevenson Road, Penicuik EH26 0LU   01968 679103
rosemarytownsley@icloud.com
New charge formed by the union of Howgate and Penicuik: South

Prestonpans: Prestongrange (F W)

Kenneth W Donald BA BD	1982	2014	The Manse, East Loan, Prestonpans EH32 9ED KDonald@churchofscotland.org.uk	01875 813643

Roslin See Bilston
Spott See Belhaven

Tranent (F W)

Erica M Wishart (Mrs) MA BD	2014	1 Toll House Gardens, Tranent EH33 2QQ EWishart@churchofscotland.org.uk	01875 704071 07503 170173

Traprain (W)

David D. Scott BSc BD	1981	2010	The Manse, Preston Road, East Linton EH40 3DS DDScott@churchofscotland.org.uk	01620 860227

Tyne Valley (F H W)

Dale K. London BTh FSAScot	2011	2018	Cranstoun Cottage, Ford, Pathhead EH37 5RE DLondon@churchofscotland.org.uk	01875 321329

Whitekirk and Tyninghame See Athelstaneford
Yester, Bolton and Saltoun See Humbie

In other appointments

Berry, Geoff T. BD BSc	2009	2011	Army Chaplain	4 Regiment RA, Alanbrooke Barracks, Topcliffe, Thirsk YO7 3EY	
Cobain, Alan R. BD	2000	2017	Army Chaplain	1 Yorks BHQ, Battlesbury Barracks, Woodcock Lane, Warminster BA12 9DT 1yorks-ai-bhq-padre@mod.gov.uk	
Frail, Nicola R. BLE MBA MDiv	2000	2012	Army Chaplain	32 Engineer Regiment, Marne Barracks, Catterick Garrison DL10 7NP nrfscot@hotmail.com	
Harrison, Frederick	2013		Ordained Local Minister	24 Comrie Avenue, Dunbar EH42 1ZN FHarrison@churchofscotland.org.uk	01368 860508 07703 527240
Kellock, Chris N. MA BD	1998	2012	Army Chaplain	HQ 12 Armoured Infantry Brigade, Ward Barracks, Bulford, Wiltshire SP4 9NA nicandchris@hotmail.co.uk	

Demitted

Allison, Ann BSc PhD BD	2000	2017	(Crail with Kingsbarns)	99 Coalgate Avenue, Tranent EH33 1JW revann@sky.com	01875 571778 07857 525439
Andrews, J. Edward MA BD DipCG FSAScot	1985	2005	(Armadale)	Dunnichen, 1B Cameron Road, Nairn IV12 5NS edward.andrews@btinternet.com	01667 459466 07808 720708

Name	Ord.	Ret.	Charge	Address / Email	Telephone
Atkins, Yvonne E.S. (Mrs) BD	1997	2018	(Musselburgh: St Andrew's High)	6 Robert de Quincy Place, Prestonpans EH32 9NS / yveatkins@yahoo.com	01875 819858
Brown, Ronald H.	1974	1998	(Musselburgh: Northesk)	6 Monktonhall Farm Cottages, Musselburgh EH21 6RZ	0131 653 2531
Buchanan, John DCS	1988		(Deacon)	19 Gillespie Crescent, Edinburgh EH10 4HU	0131 229 0794
Buchanan, Marion MA DCS	1983	2019	(Deacon)	40 Links View, Port Seton, Prestonpans EH32 0EZ	01875 814632
Burt, Thomas W. BD	1982	2013	(Carlops with Kirkurd and Newlands with West Linton: St Andrew's)	7 Arkwright Court, North Berwick EH39 4RT / tomburt@westlinton.com	01620 895494
Cairns, John B. KCVO LTh LLB LLD DD	1974	2009	(Aberlady with Gullane)	Bell House, Roxburghe Park, Dunbar EH42 1LR / johncairns@mail.com	01368 862501
Coltart, Ian O. CA BD	1988	2010	(Arbirlot with Carmyllie)	25 Bothwell Gardens, Dunbar EH42 1PZ	01368 860064
Dick, Andrew B. BD DipMin	1986	2015	(Musselburgh: St Michael's Inveresk)	4 Kirkhill Court, Gorebridge EH23 4TW / dixbit@aol.com	07540 099480
Duncan, Maureen M. (Mrs) BD	1996	2018	(Lochend and New Abbey)	2 Chalybeate, Haddington EH41 4NX / revmo43@gmail.com	01620 248559 / 07443 501738
Fraser, John W. MA BD	1974	2011	(Penicuik: North)	66 Camus Avenue, Edinburgh EH10 6QX / jijij2005@hotmail.co.uk	0131 623 0647
Glover, Robert L. BMus BD MTh ARCO	1971	2010	(Cockenzie and Port Seton: Chalmers Memorial)	12 Seton Wynd, Port Seton, Prestonpans EH32 0TY / rtglover@btinternet.com	01875 818759
Gordon, Thomas J. MA BD	1974	2009	(Chaplain, Marie Curie Hospice, Edinburgh)	22 Gosford Road, Port Seton, Prestonpans EH32 0HF / tom.swallowsnest@gmail.com	01875 812262
Jones, Anne M. (Mrs) BD	1998	2002	(Hospital Chaplain)	7 North Elphinstone Farm, Tranent EH33 2ND / revamjones@aol.com	01875 614442
Macaulay, Glendon D. BD	1999	2012	(Falkirk: Erskine)	43 Gavin's Lee, Tranent EH33 2AP / gd.macaulay@btinternet.com	01875 615851
Manson, James A. LTh	1981	2004	(Glencorse with Roslin)	31 Nursery Gardens, Kilmarnock KA1 3JA / jimamanson@gmail.com	01563 535430
Mitchell, John LTh CertMin	1991	2018	(Bonnyrigg)	28 Shiel Hall Crescent, Rosewell EH24 9DD / JMitchell@churchofscotland.org.uk	0131 448 2676
Pirie, Donald LTh	1975	2006	(Bolton and Saltoun with Humbie with Yester)	46 Caiystane Avenue, Edinburgh EH10 6SH	0131 445 2654
Scott, Ian G. BSc BD STM	1965	2006	(Edinburgh: Greenbank)	50 Forthview Walk, Tranent EH33 1FE / igscott50@btinternet.com	01875 612907
Simpson, Robert R. BA BD	1994	2014	(Callander)	10 Bellsmains, Gorebridge EH23 4QD / robert@pansmanse.co.uk	01875 820843
Steele, Marilynn J. (Mrs) BD DCS	1999	2012	(Deacon)	2 Northfield Gardens, Prestonpans EH32 9LQ / marilynnsteele@aol.com	01875 811497
Stein, Jock MA BD	1973	2008	(Tulliallan and Kincardine)	35 Dunbar Road, Haddington EH41 3PJ / jstein@handselpress.org.uk	01620 824896
Stein, Margaret E. (Mrs) DA BD DipRE	1984	2008	(Tulliallan and Kincardine)	35 Dunbar Road, Haddington EH41 3PJ / margaretestein@hotmail.com	01620 824896
Steven, Gordon R. BD DCS	1997	2012	(Deacon)	51 Nantwich Drive, Edinburgh EH7 6RB / grsteven@btinternet.com	0131 669 2054 / 07904 385256
Torrance, David W. MA BD	1955	1991	(Earlston)	38 Forth Street, North Berwick EH39 4JQ / torrance103@btinternet.com	01620 895109
Watson, James B. BSc	1969	2009	(Coldstream with Eccles)	20 Randolph Crescent, Dunbar EH42 1GL	01368 865045 / 07825 285660

(4) MELROSE AND PEEBLES (W)

Meets at Innerleithen on the first Tuesday of February, March, May, October, November and December, and on the fourth Tuesday of June, and in places to be appointed on the first Tuesday of September.

Clerk:	REV. VICTORIA LINFORD LLB BD	20 Wedale View, Stow, Galashiels TD1 2SJ melrosepeebles@churchofscotland.org.uk	01578 730237
Depute Clerk:	REV. JULIE M. RENNICK BTh	The Manse, High Street, Earlston TD4 6DE JRennick@churchofscotland.org.uk	01896 849236

Ashkirk (W) linked with Selkirk (F H W)

Margaret D.J. Steele (Miss) BSc BD	2000	2011	office@selkirkparish.church 1 Loanside, Selkirk TD7 4DJ MSteele@churchofscotland.org.uk	01750 **22078** 01750 23308

Bowden (H) and Melrose (F H W)

Rosemary Frew (Mrs) MA BD	1988	2017	bowden.melrosepc@btinternet.com The Manse, Tweedmount Road, Melrose TD6 9ST RFrew@churchofscotland.org.uk	01896 **823339** 01896 822217

Broughton, Glenholm and Kilbucho (F H W) linked with Skirling (F W) linked with Stobo and Drumelzier (F W) linked with Tweedsmuir (F H W)

Vacant			info@uppertweeddale.org.uk	
Secretary to the Upper Tweed Parishes: Isobel Hunter			The Manse, Broughton, Biggar ML12 6HQ isobel@skirlinghouse.com	01899 830331 01899 860274

Caddonfoot (H) linked with Galashiels: Trinity (H)

Elspeth S. Harley BA MTh	1991	2014	8 Mossilee Road, Galashiels TD1 1NF EHarley@churchofscotland.org.uk	01896 **752967** 01896 758485

Carlops (W) linked with Kirkurd and Newlands (F H) linked with West Linton: St Andrew's (F H W)

Stewart M. McPherson BD CertMin (Interim Minister)	1991	2018	The Manse, Main Street, West Linton EH46 7EE SMcPherson@churchofscotland.org.uk	01968 660221 07814 901429

Channelkirk and Lauder

Marion A. (Rae) Clark MA BD	2014		The Manse, Brownsmuir Park, Lauder TD2 6QD RClark@churchofscotland.org.uk	01578 718996

Earlston (F W)
Julie M. Rennick (Mrs) BTh 2005 2011 The Manse, High Street, Earlston TD4 6DE 01896 849236
JRennick@churchofscotland.org.uk

Eddleston (F H) linked with Peebles: Old (F H W)
Vacant admin@topcop.org.uk **01721 723986**
Pamela D. Strachan (Lady) MA (Cantab) 2015 7 Clement Gunn Square, Peebles EH45 8LW 01721 720568
(Ordained Local Minister) Glenhighton, Broughton, Biggar ML12 6JF 01899 830423
PStrachan@churchofscotland.org.uk 07837 873688
Session Clerk, Eddleston: Lorraine E. Lorajazz@aol.com 01721 730332
Mulholland (Mrs) 07708 414467
Session Clerk, Peebles: Old: Vivien Aitchison vivaitchison@btinternet.com 01721 722197

Ettrick and Yarrow (F W)
Vacant 01750 52349
Session Clerk: Nora Hunter nhunter.ettrickyarrow@btinternet.com

Galashiels: Old and St Paul's (H W) linked with Galashiels: St John's (H)
Vacant Woodlea, Abbotsview Drive, Galashiels TD1 3SL 01896 753029
Session Clerk, St John's: Andrew T. Bramhall andrewtbramhall@gmail.com 01896 755326

Galashiels: St John's See Galashiels: Old and St Paul's
Galashiels: Trinity See Caddonfoot

Innerleithen (H), Traquair and Walkerburn (W)
Vacant The Manse, 1 Millwell Park, Innerleithen, Peebles EH44 6JF 01896 830309
Session Clerk: Jim Borthwick james.borthwick@btinternet.com 01721 720483

Kirkurd and Newlands See Carlops

Lyne and Manor (W) linked with Peebles: St Andrew's Leckie (F H W) office@standrewsleckie.co.uk **01721 723121**
Malcolm S. Jefferson 2012 Mansefield, Innerleithen Road, Peebles EH45 8BE 01721 725148
MJefferson@churchofscotland.org.uk

Maxton and Mertoun (F W) linked with Newtown (F W) linked with St Boswells (F W) web4churches@gmail.com
Sheila W. Moir (Ms) MTheol 2008 7 Strae Brigs, St Boswells, Melrose TD6 0DH 01835 822255
SMoir@churchofscotland.org.uk

Newtown See Maxton and Mertoun
Peebles: Old See Eddleston

Peebles: St Andrew's Leckie See Lyne and Manor
St Boswells See Maxton and Mertoun
Selkirk See Ashkirk
Skirling See Broughton, Glenholm and Kilbucho
Stobo and Drumelzier See Broughton, Glenholm and Kilbucho

Stow: St Mary of Wedale and Heriot (W)
Victoria J. Linford (Mrs) LLB BD   2010   20 Wedale View, Stow, Galashiels TD1 2SJ   01578 730237
VLinford@churchofscotland.org.uk

Tweedsmuir See Broughton, Glenholm and Kilbucho
West Linton: St Andrew's See Carlops

Demitted

Name			(Role)	Address	Phone
Arnott, A. David K. MA BD	1971	2010	(St Andrews: Hope Park with Strathkinness)	53 Whitehaugh Park, Peebles EH45 9DB adka53@btinternet.com	01721 725979 07759 709205
Cashman, P. Hamilton BSc	1985	1998	(Dirleton with North Berwick: Abbey)	38 Abbotsford Road, Galashiels TD1 3HR mcashman@tiscali.co.uk	01896 752711
Devenny, Robert P.	2002	2017	(Head of Spiritual Care, NHS Borders)	Blakeburn Cottage, Wester Housebyres, Melrose TD6 9BW	01896 822350
Dick, J. Ronald BD	1973	2012	(Hospital Chaplain)	1 Viewfield Terrace, Leet Street, Coldstream TD12 4BL ron.dick180@yahoo.co.uk	01890 882206
Dobie, Rachel J.W. (Mrs) LTh	1991	2008	(Broughton, Glenholm and Kilbucho with Skirling with Stobo and Drumelzier with Tweedsmuir)	20 Moss Side Crescent, Biggar ML12 6GE revracheldobie@talktalk.net	01899 229244
Dodd, Marion E. (Miss) MA BD LRAM	1988	2010	(Kelso: Old and Sprouston)	Esdaile, Tweedmount Road, Melrose TD6 9ST mariondodd@btinternet.com	01896 822446
Donaldson, David MA BD DMin	1969	2018	(Manish-Scarista)	13 Rose Park, Peebles EH45 8HP davidandjeandonaldson@gmail.com	07817 479866
Faris, Janice M. (Mrs) BSc BD	1991	2018	(Innerleithen, Traquair and Walkerburn)	Overdale Cottage, Grange Park Road, Orton Grange, Carlisle CA5 6LT revjfaris@gmail.com	07427 371239
Hogg, Thomas M. BD	1986	2007	(Tranent)	22 Douglas Place, Galashiels TD1 3BT	01896 759381
Kellet, John M. MA	1962	1995	(Leith: South)	4 High Cottages, Walkerburn EH43 6AZ	01896 870351
Lawrie, Bruce B. BD	1974	2012	(Duffus, Spynie and Hopeman)	5 Thorncroft, Scotts Place, Selkirk TD7 4LN thorncroft54@gmail.com	01750 725427
Levison, Chris L. MA BD	1972	2010	(Health Care Chaplaincy Training and Development Officer)	Gardenfield, Nine Mile Burn, Penicuik EH26 9LT chrislevison@hotmail.com	01968 674566
Macdonald, Finlay A.J. MA BD PhD DD	1971	2010	(Principal Clerk)	8 St Ronan's Way, Innerleithen EH44 6RG finlay_macdonald@btinternet.com	01896 831631
Macdougall, Malcolm M. BD MTh DipCE	1981	2019	(Eddleston with Peebles: Old)	2 Woodlee, Broughton, Biggar ML12 6GB MMacdougall@churchofscotland.org.uk	

Milloy, A. Miller DPE LTh DipTrMan   1979   2012   (General Secretary: United Bible Societies)   18 Kittlegairy Crescent, Peebles EH45 9NJ   ammilloy@aol.com   01721 723380

Moore, W. Haisley MA   1966   1996   (Secretary: The Boys' Brigade)   1/2 Dovecot Court, Peebles EH45 8FG   jillandhaisley@outlook.com   01721 720837

Munson, Winnie (Ms) BD   1996   2006   (Delting with Northmavine)   6 St Cuthbert's Drive, St Boswells, Melrose TD6 0DF   wabsmith@btinternet.com   01835 823375

Norman, Nancy M. (Miss) BA MDiv MTh   1988   2012   (Lyne and Manor)   25 March Street, Peebles EH45 8EP   nancy.norman1@googlemail.com   01721 721699

Rae, Andrew W.   1951   1987   (Annan: St Andrew's Greenknowe Erskine)   Roseneuk, Tweedside Road, Newtown St Boswells TD6 0PQ   01835 823783

Rennie, John D. MA   1962   1996   (Broughton, Glenholm and Kilbucho with Skirling with Stobo and Drumelzier with Tweedsmuir)   29/1 Rosetta Road, Peebles EH45 8HJ   tworennies@talktalk.net   01721 720963

Riddell, John A. MA BD   1967   2006   (Jedburgh: Trinity)   Orchid Cottage, Gingham Row, Earlston TD4 6ET   01896 848784

Siroky, Samuel BA MTh   2003   2017   (Ettrick and Yarrow)   c/o Hopeview House, Yarrow, Selkirk TD7 5LB

Steele, Leslie M. MA BD   1973   2013   (Galashiels: Old and St Paul's)   25 Bardfield Road, Colchester CO2 8LW   lms@hotmail.co.uk   01206 621939   07786 797974

Taverner, Glyn R. MA BD   1957   1995   (Maxton and Mertoun with St Boswells)   Woodcot Cottage, Waverley Road, Innerleithen EH44 6QW   01896 830156

Wallace, James H. MA BD   1973   2011   (Peebles: St Andrew's Leckie)   52 Waverley Mills, Innerleithen EH44 6RH   jimwallace121@btinternet.com   01896 831637

(5) DUNS (W)

Meets at Duns, in the Parish Church hall at 7pm on the first Tuesday of September and of December; and at venues to be announced on the first Saturday of February, the first Tuesday of May and the last Tuesday of June. It also meets throughout the year for developmental activities.

Clerk: MR DAVID S. PHILP   Sea View, West Winds, Upper Burnmouth TD14 5SL   duns@churchofscotland.org.uk   01890 781568

Ayton (H) and District Churches
Norman R. Whyte BD MTh DipMin   1982   2006   The Manse, Beanburn, Ayton, Eyemouth TD14 5QY   NWhyte@churchofscotland.org.uk   01890 781333

Berwick-upon-Tweed: St Andrew's Wallace Green (H) and Lowick (F W)
Adam J.J. Hood MA BD DPhil   1989   2012   3 Meadow Grange, Berwick-upon-Tweed TD15 1NW   AHood@churchofscotland.org.uk   01289 332787

Chirnside (F) linked with Hutton and Fishwick and Paxton
Michael A. Taylor DipTh MPhil   2006   2018
The New Manse, The Glebe, Chirnside, Duns TD11 3XE
MTaylor@churchofscotland.org.uk
01890 819109
07479 985075

Coldingham and St Abbs (F W) linked with Eyemouth (F W)
Andrew N. Haddow BEng BD   2012
The Manse, Victoria Road, Eyemouth TD14 5JD
AHaddow@churchofscotland.org.uk
01890 750327

Coldstream and District Parishes (H) linked with Eccles and Leitholm
David J. Taverner MCIBS ACIS BD   1996   2011
36 Bennecourt Drive, Coldstream TD12 4BY
DTaverner@churchofscotland.org.uk
01890 883887

Duns and District Parishes (F W)
Andrew J. Robertson BD   2008   2019
admin@dunsanddistrict.org.uk
The Manse, Castle Street, Duns TD11 3DG
ARobertson@churchofscotland.org.uk
01361 884502
01361 883755

Eccles and Leitholm See Coldstream
Eyemouth See Coldingham and St Abbs

Fogo (F W)
H. Dane Sherrard BD DMin   1971   2019
(Non-Stipendiary)
Mount Pleasant Granary, Mount Pleasant Farm, Duns TD11 4HU
dane@mountpleasantgranary.net
01361 882254
07801 939138

Gordon: St Michael's linked with Greenlaw (H) linked with Legerwood linked with Westruther
Thomas S. Nicholson BD DPS   1982   1995
The Manse, Todholes, Greenlaw, Duns TD10 6XD
TNicholson@churchofscotland.org.uk
01361 810316

Greenlaw See Gordon: St Michael's
Hutton and Fishwick and Paxton See Chirnside
Legerwood See Gordon: St Michael's
Westruther See Gordon: St Michael's

Demitted
Cartwright, Alan C.D. BSc BD   1976 2016   (Fogo and Swinton with Ladykirk and Whitsome with Leitholm)   Drumgray, Edrom, Duns TD11 3PX
merse.minister@btinternet.com   01890 819191

Gaddes, Donald R.   1961 1994   (Kelso: North and Ednam)   2 Teindhill Green, Duns TD11 3DX
drgaddes@btinternet.com   01361 883172

Higham, Robert D. BD   1985 2002   (Tiree)   36 Low Greens, Berwick-upon-Tweed TD15 1LZ   01289 302392

Hope, Geraldine H. (Mrs) MA BD	1986 2007	(Foulden and Mordington with Hutton and Fishwick and Paxton)	4 Well Court, Chirnside, Duns TD11 3UD geraldine.hope@virgin.net	01890 818134
Landale, William S.	2005 2016	(Auxiliary Minister)	Green Hope Guest House, Ellemford, Duns TD11 3SG WLandale@churchofscotland.org.uk	01361 890242
Neill, Bruce F. MA BD	1966 2007	(Maxton and Mertoun with Newtown with St Boswells)	18 Brierydean, St Abbs, Eyemouth TD14 5PQ bneill@phonecoop.coop	01890 771569
Paterson, William BD	1977 2001	(Bonkyl and Preston with Chirnside with Edrom: Allanton)	Benachie, Gavinton, Duns TD11 3QT billdm.paterson@btinternet.com	01361 882727
Shields, John M. MBE LTh	1972 2007	(Channelkirk and Lauder)	12 Eden Park, Ednam, Kelso TD5 7RG john.shields118@btinternet.com	01573 229015
Walker, Kenneth D.F. MA BD PhD	1976 2008	(Athelstaneford with Whitekirk and Tyninghame)	Allanbank Kothi, Allanton, Duns TD11 3PY walkerkenneth49@gmail.com	01890 817102
Walker, Veronica (Mrs) BSc BD		(Licentiate)	Allanbank Kothi, Allanton, Duns TD11 3PY walkerkenneth49@gmail.com	01890 817102

(6) JEDBURGH

Meets at Denholm Church on the first Wednesday of February, March, May, September (this meeting in the out-going Moderator's church), October, November and December and on the last Wednesday of June.

Clerk	REV. LISA-JANE RANKIN BD CPS	4 Wilton Hill Terrace, Hawick TD9 8BE jedburgh@churchofscotland.org.uk	01450 370744

Ale and Teviot United (F H W)
Vacant
| Session Clerk: John Rogerson | 22 The Glebe, Ancrum, Jedburgh TD8 6UX B166ESS@yahoo.co.uk | 01835 830318 07813 367533 |

Cavers and Kirkton (W) linked with Hawick: Trinity (H W)
Vacant
| Interim Moderator: Alistair Cook | trinityhawick@outlook.com Trinity Manse, Howdenburn, Hawick TD9 8PH ACook@churchofscotland.org.uk | 01450 378248 01450 616352 |

Cheviot Churches (H W)
| Colin D. Johnston MA BD | 1986 2019 | CDJohnston@churchofscotland.org.uk | |

Hawick: Burnfoot (F T W)
Vacant
| Session Clerk: Marion Webb (Ms) | 29 Wilton Hill, Hawick TD9 8BA bpcsessionclerk@gmail.com | 01450 373181 07843 794247 |

Hawick: St Mary's and Old (F H W) linked with Hawick: Teviot (H) and Roberton (F W) info@smop-tero.org
Alistair W. Cook BSc CA BD   2008   2017
4 Heronhill Close, Hawick TD9 9RA
ACook@churchofscotland.org.uk
01450 378175
07802 616352

Hawick: Teviot and Roberton See Hawick: St Mary's and Old
Hawick: Trinity See Cavers and Kirkton

Hawick: Wilton linked with Teviothead
Lisa-Jane Rankin BD CPS   2003
4 Wilton Hill Terrace, Hawick TD9 8BE
LRankin@churchofscotland.org.uk
01450 370744

Hobkirk and Southdean (F W) linked with Ruberslaw (F W)
Rachel Wilson BA MTh   2018
The Manse, Leydens Road, Denholm, Hawick TD9 8NB
RWilson@churchofscotland.org.uk
01450 870874

Jedburgh: Old and Trinity (F W)
Stephen Manners MA BD   1989   2019
1 The Meadow, Stichill TD5 7TG
SManners@churchofscotland.org.uk

Kelso Country Churches (W)
Stephen Manners MA BD   1989   2019
1 The Meadow, Stichill TD5 7TG
SManners@churchofscotland.org.uk

Kelso: North (H) and Ednam (F H W) office@kelsonorthandednam.org.uk
Anna S. Rodwell BD DipMin   1998   2016
The Manse, 24 Forestfield, Kelso TD5 7BX
ARodwell@churchofscotland.org.uk
01573 224154
01573 224248
07765 169826

Kelso: Old and Sprouston (F)
Alexander W. Young BD DipMin   1988   2017
The Manse, Glebe Lane, Kelso TD5 7AU
AYoung@churchofscotland.org.uk
01573 348749

Oxnam
Guardianship of the Presbytery
Session Clerk: Morag McKeand (Mrs)
mh.mckeand@btinternet.com
01835 840284

Ruberslaw See Hobkirk and Southdean
Teviothead See Hawick: Wilton

Combe, Neil R. BSc MSc BD	1984	2015	(Hawick: St Mary's and Old with Hawick: Teviot and Roberton)	2 Abbotsview Gardens, Galashiels TD1 3ER neil.combe@btinternet.com	01896 755869
McNicol, Bruce	1967	2006	(Jedburgh: Old and Edgerston)	42 Dounehill, Jedburgh TD8 6LJ mcnicol942@gmail.com	01835 862991
Stewart, Una B. (Ms) BD DipEd	1995	2014	(Law)	10 Inch Park, Kelso TD5 7BQ rev.ubs@virgin.net	01573 219231

HAWICK ADDRESSES

Burnfoot	Fraser Avenue	St Mary's and Old	Kirk Wynd	Wilton	Princes Street
		Teviot	St George's Lane		
		Trinity	Central Square		

(7) ANNANDALE AND ESKDALE

Meets on the first Tuesday of September, October, December, February and June and the second Tuesday of April. The September meeting is held in the Moderator's charge. The other meetings are held in Dryfesdale Church Hall, Lockerbie, except for the June meeting, which is separately announced.

Clerk:	**VERY REV. WILLIAM HEWITT BD DipPS**	**Presbytery Office, Dryfesdale Parish Church, High Street, Lockerbie DG11 2AA** **annandaleeskdale@churchofscotland.org.uk**	**07769 625321**

Annan: Old (F H W) linked with Dornock (F) 1998 2018
David Whiteman BD	12 Plumdon Park Avenue, Annan DG12 6EY DWhiteman@churchofscotland.org.uk	01461 392048

Annan: St Andrew's (H W) linked with Brydekirk (W)
John G. Pickles BD MTh MSc	2011	1 Annerley Road, Annan DG12 6HE JPickles@churchofscotland.org.uk	01461 202626

Applegarth, Sibbaldbie (H) and Johnstone (F) linked with Lochmaben (H W)
Paul R. Read BSc MA(Th)	2000	2013	The Manse, Barrashead, Lochmaben, Lockerbie DG11 1QF PRead@churchofscotland.org.uk	01387 810640

Brydekirk See Annan: St Andrew's

Canonbie United (F H W) linked with Liddesdale (F H W)
Vacant
    churchoffice@liddesdalechurch.org.uk
    23 Langholm Street, Newcastleton TD9 0QX   01387 375242
Session Clerk, Canonbie United: Ruth Gilbert, Leoniek van Belzen
and Lois Lane   canonbiechurch@gmail.com
Session Clerk, Liddesdale:
    Glynis Cambridge (Mrs)   lpctreasurer1@gmail.com   01387 375488

    Canonbie United is a Local Ecumenical Partnership shared with the United Free Church

Dalton and Hightae (F) linked with St Mungo (F)
Vacant   The Manse, Hightae, Lockerbie DG11 1JL   01387 811499
Session Clerk, Dalton: Isobel Tinning (Mrs)   isobel.tinning@gmail.com   01387 269133
Session Clerk, St Mungo: Annie Hutchon (Mrs)   anniehutchon45@gmail.com   01576 510280

Dornock   See Annan: Old

Gretna: Old (H), Gretna: St Andrew's (H), Half Morton and Kirkpatrick Fleming
Vacant   The Manse, Gretna Green, Gretna DG16 5DU   01461 338313

Hoddom, Kirtle-Eaglesfield and Middlebie (F W)
Vacant   The Manse, Main Road, Ecclefechan, Lockerbie DG11 3BU   01576 300108
Session Clerk: Tom Owen   potstown@hotmail.com   01461 600246

Kirkpatrick Juxta (F) linked with Moffat: St Andrew's (F H W) linked with Wamphray (F)   standrewsmoffat@gmail.com
Vacant   The Manse, 1 Meadowbank, Moffat DG10 9LR   01683 220128
Session Clerk, Kirkpatrick Juxta: Mary Brown (Mrs)   marybrown591@gmail.com   01683 300451
Session Clerk, Moffat: Donald Walker   donaldann66@gmail.com   01683 220707
Session Clerk, Wamphray: Helen Braid (Mrs)   r.braid557@btinternet.com   01576 470637

Langholm Eskdalemuir Ewes and Westerkirk (W)
Vacant   leewparishchurch@outlook.com
Session Clerk: vacant   The Manse, Langholm DG13 0BL   01387 380252

Liddesdale   See Canonbie United
Lochmaben   See Applegarth, Sibbaldbie and Johnstone

Lockerbie: Dryfesdale, Hutton and Corrie (F W)
Vacant
Eric T. Dempster | 2016 | 2018 | Annanside, Wamphray, Moffat DG10 9LZ | 01576 470496
(Ordained Local Minister) | | | EDempster@churchofscotland.org.uk

Moffat: St Andrew's See Kirkpatrick Juxta
St Mungo See Dalton

The Border Kirk (F W)
David G. Pitkeathly LLB BD | 1996 | 2007 | **Chapel Street, Carlisle CA1 1JA** | **01228 591757**
| | | 95 Pinecroft, Carlisle CA3 0DB | 01228 593243
| | | DPitkeathly@churchofscotland.org.uk

Tundergarth
Guardianship of the Presbytery
Session Clerk: David Paterson | | | jilljoe@tiscali.co.uk | 07982 037029

Wamphray See Kirkpatrick Juxta

In other appointments
Brydson, Angela (Mrs) DCS | 2015 | 2014 | Deacon, Lochmaben, Moffat and Lockerbie Grouping | 52 Victoria Park, Lockerbie DG11 2AY | 07543 796820
| | | | ABrydson@churchofscotland.org.uk
Campbell, Neil G. MA BD | 1988 | 2018 | Chaplain, HM Prison Dumfries and HMP Greenock | 12 Charles Street, Annan DG12 5AJ
| | | | neil.campbell2@sps.pnn.gov.uk
Harvey, P. Ruth (Ms) MA BD | 2009 | 2016 | Director, Place for Hope | Croslands, Beacon Street, Penrith CA11 7TZ | 01768 840749
| | | | ruth.harvey@placeforhope.org.uk | 07403 638339
Macpherson, Duncan J. BSc BD | 1993 | 2002 | Chaplain: Army | MP413, Kentigern House, 65 Brown Street, Glasgow G2 8EX
Steenbergen, Pauline (Ms) MA BD | 1996 | 2018 | Locum Minister, Presbytery | The Vicarage, Townhead Road, Dalston, Cumbria CA5 7LF | 07743 927182
| | | | locum.ae@gmail.com

Demitted
Annand, James M. MA BD | 1955 | 1995 | (Lockerbie: Dryfesdale) | Dere Cottage, 48 Main Street, Newstead, Melrose TD6 9DX
Beveridge, S. Edwin P. BA | 1959 | 2004 | (Brydekirk with Hoddom) | 19 Rothesay Terrace, Edinburgh EH3 7RY | 0131 225 3393
Dawson, Morag A. BD MTh | 1999 | 2016 | (Dalton with Highrae with St Mungo) | 34 Kennedy Crescent, Tranent EH33 1DP
| | | | moragdawson@yahoo.co.uk
Gibb, J. Daniel M. BA LTh | 1994 | 2006 | (Aberfoyle with Port of Menteith) | 1 Beechfield, Newton Aycliffe DL5 7AX
| | | | dannygibb@hotmail.co.uk
Seaman, Ronald S. MA | 1967 | 2007 | (Dornock) | 1 Springfield Farm Court, Springfield, Gretna DG16 5EH | 01461 337228

(8) DUMFRIES AND KIRKCUDBRIGHT

Meets at Dumfries on the last Wednesday of February, April, June, September and November.

Clerk: REV. DONALD CAMPBELL   BD   St George's Church, 50 George Street, Dumfries   DG1 1EJ   **01387 252965**
dumfrieskirkcudbright@churchofscotland.org.uk

Balmaclellan, Kells (H) and Dalry (H) linked with Carsphairn (H)
David S. Bartholomew   BSc MSc PhD BD   1994   The Manse, Dalry, Castle Douglas   DG7 3PJ   01644 430380
DBartholomew@churchofscotland.org.uk

New charge formed by the union of Balmaclellan and Kells and Dalry

Caerlaverock (F) linked with Dumfries: St Mary's-Greyfriars' (F H W)
David D.J. Logan   MStJ BD MA   2009   2016   4 Georgetown Crescent, Dumfries   DG1 4EQ   01387 270128
DLogan@churchofscotland.org.uk   07793 542411

Carsphairn   See Balmaclellan, Kells and Dalry

Castle Douglas (H W) linked with The Bengairn Parishes (W)
Alison H. Burnside (Mrs)   MA BD   1990   2018   1 Castle View, Castle Douglas   DG7 1BG   01556 505983
ABurnside@churchofscotland.org.uk

Oonagh Dee   2014   2016   Kendoon, Merse Way, Kippford, Dalbeattie   DG5 4LL   01556 620001
(Ordained Local Minister)   ODee@churchofscotland.org.uk

Closeburn linked with Kirkmahoe
Vacant   The Manse, Kirkmahoe, Dumfries   DG1 1ST   01387 710572
Session Clerk, Closeburn: Jack Tait   jacktait1941@gmail.com   01848 331700
Session Clerk, Kirkmahoe: Alexander Fergusson   alexanderfergusson@btinternet.com   01387 253014

Colvend, Southwick and Kirkbean (W)
James F. Gatherer   BD   1984   2003   The Manse, Colvend, Dalbeattie   DG5 4QN   01556 630255
JGatherer@churchofscotland.org.uk

Corsock and Kirkpatrick Durham (W) linked with Crossmichael, Parton and Balmaghie (W)
Sally M.F. Russell   BTh MTh   2006   Knockdrocket, Clarebrand, Castle Douglas   DG7 3AH   01556 503645
SRussell@churchofscotland.org.uk

Crossmichael, Parton and Balmaghie See Corsock and Kirkpatrick Durham

Cummertrees, Mouswald and Ruthwell (H W)
Vacant
Interim Moderator: William Holland
The Manse, Ruthwell, Dumfries DG1 4NP
billholland55@btinternet.com
01387 870217
01387 256131

Dalbeattie and Kirkgunzeon (F H W) linked with Urr (H W)
Fiona A. Wilson (Mrs) BD   2008   2014
36 Mill Street, Dalbeattie DG5 4HE
FWilson@churchofscotland.org.uk
01556 610708

Dumfries: Maxwelltown West (H W)
Vacant
Session Clerk: Drew Crossan
Maxwelltown West Manse, 11 Laurieknowe, Dumfries DG2 7AH
andrew@ahrcrossan.co.uk
01387 255900
01387 247538
01387 255265

Dumfries: Northwest (F)
Vacant
Session Clerk: Clara Jackson
c/o Church Office, Dumfries Northwest Church, Lochside Road, Dumfries DG2 0DZ
sessionclerk.dumfriesnorthwest@gmail.com
01387 249964
01387 249964

Dumfries: St George's (F H W)
Donald Campbell BD   1997
office@saint-georges.org.uk
9 Nunholm Park, Dumfries DG1 1JP
DCampbell@churchofscotland.org.uk
01387 267072
01387 252965

Dumfries: St Mary's-Greyfriars' See Caerlaverock

Dumfries: St Michael's and South (W)
Vacant
secretary@troqueerparishchurch.com
39 Cardoness Street, Dumfries DG1 3AL
01387 253849

Dumfries: Troqueer (F H W)
John R. Notman BSc BD   1990   2015
secretary@troqueerparishchurch.com
Troqueer Manse, Troqueer Road, Dumfries DG2 7DF
JNotman@churchofscotland.org.uk
01387 253043

Dunscore (F W) linked with Glencairn and Moniaive (F W)
Vacant
Interim Moderator: J. Stuart Mill
Session Clerk, Dunscore: Colin Mitchell
Wallaceton, Auldgirth, Dumfries DG2 0TJ
JMill@churchofscotland.org.uk
c.mitchell50@btinternet.com
01387 820245
01848 331191
01387 820455

Durisdeer linked with Penpont, Keir and Tynron linked with Thornhill (H)
J. Stuart Mill MA MBA BD DipEd   1974   2013   The Manse, Manse Park, Thornhill DG3 5ER   01848 331191
JMill@churchofscotland.org.uk

Gatehouse and Borgue linked with Tarff and Twynholm
Valerie J. Ott (Mrs) BA BD   2002   The Manse, Planetree Park, Gatehouse of Fleet, Castle Douglas   01557 814233
DG7 2EQ
VOtt@churchofscotland.org.uk

Glencairn and Moniaive See Dunscore

Irongray, Lochrutton and Terregles
Gary J. Peacock MA BD MTh   2015   The Manse, Shawhead, Dumfries DG2 9SJ   01387 730759
GPeacock@churchofscotland.org.uk

Kirkconnel (H) linked with Sanquhar: St Bride's (F H)
Vacant   St Bride's Manse, Glasgow Road, Sanquhar DG6 6BZ   01659 50247
Session Clerk, Kirkconnel: Fay Rafferty   fayrafferty1957@gmail.com   01659 67650
Session Clerk, Sanquhar: Duncan Close   dunruth@btinternet.com   01659 50596

Kirkcudbright (H W)
Vacant   church@kirkcudbrightparishchurch.org.uk   01557 330489
Interim Moderator: David S. Bartholomew   6 Bourtree Avenue, Kirkcudbright DG6 4AU   01644 430380
DBartholomew@churchofscotland.org.uk

Kirkmahoe See Closeburn

Kirkmichael, Tinwald and Torthorwald (W)
Vacant   Manse of Tinwald, Tinwald, Dumfries DG1 3PL   01387 710246
Mhairi Wallace (Mrs)   2013   2017   5 Dee Road, Kirkcudbright DG 4HQ   07701 375064
(Ordained Local Minister)   MWallace@churchofscotland.org.uk

Lochend and New Abbey
Vacant   New Abbey Manse, 32 Main Street, New Abbey, Dumfries DG2 8BY   01387 850490
Elizabeth A. Mack (Miss) DipEd   1994   2018   24 Roberts Crescent, Dumfries DG2 7RS   01387 264847
(Auxiliary Minster)   mackliz@btinternet.com

Penpont, Keir and Tynron See Durisdeer

Sanquhar: St Bride's See Kirkconnel
Tarff and Twynholm See Gatehouse and Borgue
The Bengairn Parishes See Castle Douglas
Thornhill See Durisdeer
Urr See Dalbeattie and Kirkgunzeon

Demitted

Bond, Maurice S. MTh BA DipEd PhD	1983	2019	(Dumfries: St Michael's and South)	MBond@churchofscotland.org.uk	
Burns, John H. BSc BD	1985	2019	(Inch with Portpatrick with Stranraer: Trinity)		
Collard, John K. MA BD	1986	2019	(Interim Minister)	1 Nelson Terrace, East Kilbride G74 2EY / JCollard@churchofscotland.org.uk	01355 520093
du Plessis, Joachim J.H. BA BD MTh	1976	2019	(Dunscore with Glencairn and Moniaive)	Postnet Suite 283, Private Suite 283, Elardus Park, South Africa 0047	
Finch, Graham S. MA BD	1977	2015	(Cadder)	32a St Mary Street, Kirkcudbright DG6 4DN / gsf231@gmail.com	01557 620123
Hammond, Richard J. BA BD	1993	2007	(Kirkmahoe)	3 Marchfield Mount, Marchfield, Dumfries DG1 1SE / libby.hammond@virgin.net	07764 465783
Hogg, William T. MA BD	1979	2018	(Kirkconnel with Sanquhar St Bride's)	30 Castle Street, Kirkcudbright DG6 4JD / WHogg@churchofscotland.org.uk	
Holland, William MA	1967	2009	(Lochend and New Abbey)	Ardshean, 55 Georgetown Road, Dumfries DG1 4DD / billholland55@btinternet.com	01387 256131 / 07766 531732
Irving, Douglas R. LLB BD WS	1984	2016	(Kirkcudbright)	17 Galla Crescent, Dalbeattie DG5 4JY / douglas.irving@outlook.com	01556 610156
Kelly, William W. BSc BD	1994	2014	(Dumfries: Troqueer)	6 Vitality Way, Craigie, Perth, WA 6025, Australia / ww.kelly@yahoo.com	
McKay, David M. MA BD	1979	2007	(Kirkpatrick Juxta with Moffat: St Andrew's with Wamphray)	20 Auld Brig View, Auldgirth, Dumfries DG2 0XE / davidmckay20@tiscali.co.uk	01387 740013
McKenzie, William M. DA	1958	1993	(Dumfries: Troqueer)	41 Kingholm Road, Dumfries DG1 4SR / mckenzie.dumfries@btinternet.com	01387 253688
McLauchlan, Mary C. (Mrs) LTh	1997	2013	(Mochrum)	3 Ayr Street, Moniaive, Thornhill DG3 4HP / mary@revmother.co.uk	01848 200786
Owen, John J.C. LTh	1967	2001	(Applegarth and Sibbaldbie with Lochmaben)	5 Galla Avenue, Dalbeattie DG5 4JZ / jj.owen@onetel.net	01556 612125
Sutherland, Colin A. LTh	1995	2007	(Blantyre: Livingstone Memorial)	71 Caulstran Road, Dumfries DG2 9FJ / colin.csutherland@btinternet.com	01387 279954
Wotherspoon, Robert C. LTh	1976	1998	(Corsock and Kirkpatrick Durham with Crossmichael and Parton)	5 Goddards Green Cottages, Goddards Green, Beneden, Cranbrook TN17 4AW	01580 243091

DUMFRIES ADDRESSES

Maxwelltown West	Laurieknowe		
	Northwest	Lochside Road	St Michael's and South	St Michael's Street
	St George's	George Street	Troqueer	Troqueer Road
	St Mary's-Greyfriars	St Mary's Street		

(9) WIGTOWN AND STRANRAER

Meets at Glenluce, in the church hall, on the first Tuesday of March, October and December for ordinary business; on the first Tuesday of September for formal business followed by meetings of committees; on the first Tuesday of November, February and May for worship followed by meetings of committees; and at a church designated by the Moderator on the first Tuesday of June for Holy Communion followed by ordinary business.

Clerk: MR SAM SCOBIE   40 Clenoch Parks Road, Stranraer DG9 7QT   01776 703975
wigtownstranraer@churchofscotland.org.uk

Ervie Kirkcolm (H W) linked with Leswalt (W)
Guardianship of the Presbytery
Session Clerk, Ervie Kirkcolm:
Jennifer Comery (Mrs)   Skellies Knowe West, Leswalt, Stranraer DH9 0RY   01776 854277
Session Clerk, Leswalt: Fiona McColm (Mrs)   sessionclerk@leswaltparishchurch.org.uk   01776 870555

Glasserton and Isle of Whithorn linked with Whithorn: St Ninian's Priory (F W)
Alexander I. Currie BD CPS   1990   The Manse, Whithorn, Newton Stewart DG8 8PT   01988 500267
ACurrie@churchofscotland.org.uk

Inch linked with Portpatrick linked with Stranraer: Trinity (H W)
Vacant   Bayview Road, Stranraer DG9 8BE   01776 702383
Pamela A. Bellis BA   2014   2018   Mayfield, Dunragit, Stranraer DG9 8PG   01581 400378
(Ordained Local Minister)   PBellis@churchofscotland.org.uk   07751 379249

Kirkcowan (H) linked with Wigtown (F H W)
Eric Boyle BA MTh   2006   Seaview Manse, Church Lane, Wigtown, Newton Stewart DG8 9HT   01988 402314
EBoyle@churchofscotland.org.uk

Kirkinner linked with Mochrum linked with Sorbie (H)
Jeffrey M. Mead BD   1978   1986   The Manse, Kirkinner, Newton Stewart DG8 9AL   01988 840643
JMead@churchofscotland.org.uk

Kirkmabreck (W) linked with Monigaff (H W)
Stuart Farmes   2011   2014   Creebridge, Newton Stewart DG8 6NR   01671 403361
SFarmes@churchofscotland.org.uk

Kirkmaiden (F H W) linked with Stoneykirk
Christopher Wallace BD DipMin   1988   2016   Church Road, Sandhead, Stranraer DG9 9JJ   01776 830757
Christopher.Wallace@churchofscotland.org.uk

Leswalt See Ervie Kirkcolm

Luce Valley (F W)
Stephen Ogston MPhys MSc BD   2009   2017   Ladyburn Manse, Main Street, Glenluce, Newton Stewart DG8 0PU   01581 300316
SOgston@churchofscotland.org.uk

Mochrum See Kirkinner
Monigaff See Kirkmabreck

Penninghame (F H)
Edward D. Lyons BD MTh   2007   The Manse, 1A Corvisel Road, Newton Stewart DG8 6LW   01671 404425
ELyons@churchofscotland.org.uk

Portpatrick See Inch
Sorbie See Kirkinner
Stoneykirk See Kirkmaiden

Stranraer: High Kirk (H)
Vacant   Stoneleigh, Whitehouse Road, Stranraer DG9 0JB   01776 700616

Stranraer: Trinity See Inch
Whithorn: St Ninian's Priory See Glasserton and Isle of Whithorn
Wigtown See Kirkcowan

Demitted

Baker, Carolyn M. (Mrs) BD   1997 2008   (Ochiltree with Stair)   Clanary, 1 Maxwell Drive, Newton Stewart DG8 6EL
cncbaker@btinternet.com

Cairns, Alexander B. MA   1957 2009   (Turin)   Beechwood, Main Street, Sandhead, Stranraer DG9 9JG   01776 830389
dorothycairns@aol.com

Sheppard, Michael J. BD   1977 2016   (Ervie Kirkcolm with Leswalt)   4 Mill Street, Drummore, Stranraer DG9 9PS   01776 840369
michaelsheppard00@gmail.com

(10) AYR

Meets in the Carrick Centre, Maybole (except as shown), on the first Tuesday of September, the fourth Tuesday of October (at a designated location), the first Tuesday of December, the first Tuesday of March, the first Tuesday of May, and the third Tuesday of June (in the Moderator's church). A conference is held in January.

Clerk: REV. KENNETH C. ELLIOTT BD BA CertMin
68 St Quivox Road, Prestwick KA9 1JF
ayr@churchofscotland.org.uk   **01292 478788**

Presbytery Office: Prestwick South Parish Church, 50 Main Street,
Prestwick KA9 1NX
ayroffice@cofscotland.org.uk   **01292 678556**

Alloway (F H W)
Neil A. McNaught BD MA   1987   1999
secretary.allowaypc@gmail.com   **01292 442083**
1A Parkview, Alloway, Ayr KA7 4QG   01292 441252
NMcNaught@churchofscotland.org.uk

Annbank (H W) linked with Tarbolton (F W)
Vacant
Session Clerk, Annbank: Audrey Brown (Mrs)
Session Clerk, Tarbolton: Maureen McNae (Mrs)
The Manse, Tarbolton, Mauchline KA5 5QJ   01292 540969
thebroonsat53@aol.com
maureen@mcnae.net

Auchinleck (F H) linked with Catrine (F)
Stephen F. Clipston MA BD   1982   2006
28 Mauchline Road, Auchinleck KA18 2BN   01290 424776
SClipston@churchofscotland.org.uk

Ayr: Auld Kirk of Ayr (St John the Baptist) (H L W)
David R. Gemmell MA BD   1991   1999
auldkirkayr@hotmail.co.uk   **01292 262938**
20 Seafield Drive, Ayr KA7 4BQ   01292 864140   Tel/Fax
DGemmell@churchofscotland.org.uk

Ayr: Castlehill (F H W)
Vacant
Session Clerk: Douglas Owens
office@castlehillchurch.org   **01292 267520**
3 Old Hillfoot Road, Ayr KA7 3LW
jdoayr@aol.com

Ayr: Newton Wallacetown (F H W)
Vacant
Session Clerk: John Bell
9 Nursery Grove, Ayr KA7 3PH   **01292 611371**
johnbell31@gmail.com   01292 264251

Ayr: St Andrew's (F H W)
Vacant
Session Clerk: Ian Lamberton

info@standrewsayr.org.uk
ian.lamberton@outlook.com

Ayr: St Columba (F H W)
Vacant
Session Clerk: Robert Bartholomew

irene@ayrstcolumba.co.uk
3 Upper Crofts, Alloway, Ayr KA7 4QX
sessionclerk@ayrstcolumba.co.uk

01292 **269524**
01292 443747

Ayr: St James' (F H W)
Barbara V. Suchanek-Seitz CertMin DTh   2016

admin@stjamesayr.plus.com
1 Prestwick Road, Ayr KA8 8LD
BSuchanek-Seitz@churchofscotland.org.uk

01292 **266993**
01292 262420

Ayr: St Leonard's (F H W) linked with Dalrymple (F)
Brian R. Hendrie BD   1992   2015

st_leonards@btinternet.com
25 Roman Road, Ayr KA7 3SZ
BHendrie@churchofscotland.org.uk

01292 **611117**
01292 283825

Ayr: St Quivox (F H W)
Vacant
Session Clerk: David McMahon

11 Springfield Avenue, Prestwick KA9 2HA
mcmahon728@gmail.com

01292 478306

Ballantrae (H W) linked with St Colmon (Arnsheen Barrhill and Colmonell) (W)
Theodore Corney BA MTh GDipTh   2006   2019

The Manse, 1 The Vennel, Ballantrae, Girvan KA26 0NH
TCorney@churchofscotland.org.uk

01465 831252

Barr linked with Dailly linked with Girvan: South
Vacant

30 Henrietta Street, Girvan KA26 9AL

01465 713370

Catrine See Auchinleck

Coylton (F W) linked with Drongan: The Schaw Kirk (W)
Alwyn Landman BTh MDiv MTh DMin   2005   2019

4 Hamilton Place, Coylton, Ayr KA6 6JQ
ALandman@churchofscotland.org.uk

01292 571442

Craigie Symington (W) linked with Prestwick South (H W)
Kenneth C. Elliott BD BA Cert Min   1989

office@pwksouth.plus.com
68 St Quivox Road, Prestwick KA9 1JF
KElliott@churchofscotland.org.uk

01292 **678556**
01292 478788

Tom McLeod   2014   2015
(Ordained Local Minister)

3 Martnaham Drive, Coylton KA6 6JE
TMcleod@churchofscotland.org.uk

01292 570100

Crosshill (H) linked with Maybole (F W)   1984   2018
Robert G.D.W. Pickles BD MPhil PhD
74A Culzean Road, Maybole KA19 8AH   01655   889454
RPickles@churchofscotland.org.uk

Dailly See Barr

Dalmellington (F) linked with Patna Waterside (F)
Vacant
Interim Moderator: Bill Mackie
4 Carsphairn Road, Dalmellington, Ayr KA6 7RE   01292   551503
bill.ayr1304@outlook.com   01292   281163

Dalrymple See Ayr: St Leonard's
Drongan: The Schaw Kirk See Coylton

Dundonald (H W)   2019
Lynsey J. Brennan BA
64 Main Street, Dundonald, Kilmarnock KA2 9HG   01563   850243
LBrennan@churchofscotland.org.uk

Fisherton (H) linked with Kirkoswald (H W)   1990   2016
Ian R. Stirling BSc BD MTh MSc DPT
The Manse, Kirkoswald, Maybole KA19 8HZ   01655   760532
IStirling@churchofscotland.org.uk

Girvan: North (F H W)
Vacant
Interim Moderator: Ian R. Stirling
churchoffice12@btconnect.com   **01465   712672**
38 The Avenue, Girvan KA26 9DS   01465   713203
IStirling@churchofscotland.org.uk   01655   760532

Girvan: South See Barr

Kirkmichael linked with Straiton: St Cuthbert's   1984   1985
W. Gerald Jones MA BD MTh
The Manse, Patna Road, Kirkmichael, Maybole KA19 7PJ   01655   750286
WJones@churchofscotland.org.uk

Kirkoswald See Fisherton

Lugar linked with Old Cumnock: Old (H)   1994
John W. Paterson BSc BD DipEd
33 Barrhill Road, Cumnock KA18 1PJ   01290   420769
JPaterson@churchofscotland.org.uk

Mauchline (H W) linked with Sorn   1991   2011   mauchlineparish@yahoo.com
David A. Albon BA MCS   4 Westside Gardens, Mauchline KA5 5DJ   01290 518528
                                                                             DAlbon@churchofscotland.org.uk

Maybole See Crosshill

Monkton and Prestwick: North (F H T W)   2010   office@mpnchurch.org.uk   **01292 678810**
David Clarkson BSc BA MTh   40 Monkton Road, Prestwick KA9 1AR   01292 471379
                                                                             DClarkson@churchofscotland.org.uk

Muirkirk (H W) linked with Old Cumnock: Trinity (F W)
Vacant   46 Ayr Road, Cumnock KA18 1DW   01290 422145
Session Clerk, Muirkirk: Sylvia McGlynn (Miss)   hiddendepths@hotmail.com
Session Clerk, Trinity: Kay Mitchell (Mrs)   kaymitch14@sky.com

New Cumnock (F H W)   2009   37 Castle, New Cumnock, Cumnock KA18 4AG   01290 338296
Helen E. Cuthbert MA MSc BD   HCuthbert@churchofscotland.org.uk

Ochiltree (W) linked with Stair (F W)   2011   2017   10 Mauchline Road, Ochiltree, Cumnock KA18 2PZ   01290 700365
Morag Garrett (Mrs) BD   MGarrett@churchofscotland.org.uk

Old Cumnock: Old See Lugar
Old Cumnock: Trinity See Muirkirk
Patna Waterside See Dalmellington

Prestwick: Kingcase (F H W)   1993   2015   office@kingcase.freeserve.co.uk   01292 479571
Ian Wiseman BTh DipHSW   15 Bellrock Avenue, Prestwick KA9 1SQ
                                                                             IWiseman@churchofscotland.org.uk

Prestwick: St Nicholas' (H W)   office@stnicholasprestwick.org.uk   **01292 671547**
Vacant   3 Bellevue Road, Prestwick KA9 1NW   01292 477613
Session Clerk: Margaret McIntosh   mwmcin@mwmcin6woodlea.plus.com

Prestwick: South See Craigie Symington
St Colmon (Arnsheen Barrhill and Colmonell) See Ballantrae
Sorn See Mauchline
Stair See Ochiltree

Straiton: St Cuthbert's See Kirkmichael
Tarbolton See Annbank

Troon: Old (F H W)
David B. Prentice-Hyers BA MDiv   2003   2013
office@troonold.org.uk   01292 313520
85 Bentinck Drive, Troon KA10 6HZ   01292 313644
DPrentice-Hyers@churchofscotland.org.uk

Troon: Portland (F H W)
Vacant
Session Clerk: John Reid
office@troonportlandchurch.org.uk   01292 317929
89 South Beach, Troon KA10 6HX   01292 318929
session@troonportlandchurch.org.uk

Troon: St Meddan's (F H T W)
Derek A. Peat BA BD MTh   2013
stmeddanschurch@gmail.com   01292 317750
27 Bentinck Drive, Troon KA10 6HX   01292 319163
DPeat@churchofscotland.org.uk

In other appointments

Blackshaw, Christopher J. BA(Theol)   2015   2017   Pioneer Minister, Farming Community   Livestock Auction Mart, Whitefordhill, Ayr KA6 5JW   01292 262241 / 07989 100818
Chris Blackshaw is a Methodist Minister   CBlackshaw@churchofscotland.org.uk

Crossan, Morag BA   2016   Ordained Local Minister   1A Church Hill, Dalmellington KA26 9AN   MCrossan@churchofscotland.org.uk   07861 736071

Crumlish, Elizabeth A. BD   1995   2015   Path of Renewal Co-ordinator   53 Ayr Road, Prestwick KA9 1SY   ECrumlish@churchofscotland.org.uk   07464 675434

Hogg, James   2018   Ordained Local Minister   35 Auchentrae Crescent, Ayr KA7 4BD   JHogg@churchofscotland.org.uk   01292 262034

Jackson, Nancy   2009   Auxiliary Minister   nancyjaxon@btinternet.com

Moore, Douglas T.   2003   Auxiliary Minister   9 Midton Avenue, Prestwick KA9 1PU   DMoore@churchofscotland.org.uk   01292 671352

Demitted

Aitken, Fraser R. MA BD   1978   2019   (Ayr: St Columba)   Sandringham, 38 Coylebank, Prestwick KA9 2DH   FAitken@churchofscotland.org.uk   01292 225087

Anderson, Robert A. MA BD DPhil   1984   2017   (Blackburn and Seafield)   Aiona, 8 Old Auchans View, Dundonald KA2 9EX   robertanderson307@btinternet.com   01563 850554 / 07484 206190

Birse, G. Stewart CA BD BSc   1980   2013   (Ayr: Newton Wallacetown)   9 Calvinston Road, Prestwick KA9 2EL   stewart.birse@gmail.com   01292 474556

Blyth, James G.S. BSc BD   1963   1986   (Glenmuick)   40 Robsland Avenue, Ayr KA7 2RW   01292 261276

Bogle, Thomas C. BD   1983   2003   (Fisherton with Maybole: West)   38 McEwan Crescent, Mossblown, Ayr KA6 5DR   01292 521215

Brown, Jack M. BSc BD   1977   2012   (Applegarth, Sibbaldbie and Johnstone with Lochmaben)   69 Berelands Road, Prestwick KA9 1ER   jackm.brown@tiscali.co.uk   01292 477151

Name			(Charge)	Address / email	Tel
Crichton, James MA BD MTh	1969	2010	(Crosshill with Dalrymple)	60 Kyle Court, Ayr KA7 3AW crichton.james@btinternet.com	01292 618512
Dickie, Michael M. BSc	1955	1993	(Ayr: Castlehill)	8 Noltmire Road, Ayr KA8 9ES	07925 004062
Fiddes, George R. BD	1979	2019	(Prestwick: St Nicholas')	14 Crawford Avenue, Prestwick KA9 2BN fidkid@hotmail.co.uk	
Geddes, Alexander J. MA BD	1960	1998	(Stewarton: St Columba's)	2 Gregory Street, Mauchline KA5 6BY sandy270736@gmail.com	01290 518597
Glencross, William M. LTh	1968	1999	(Bellshill: Macdonald Memorial)	1 Lochay Place, Troon KA10 7HH	01292 317097
Guthrie, James A.	1969	2005	(Corsock and Kirkpatrick Durham with Crossmichael and Parton)	2 Barrhill Road, Pinwherry, Girvan KA26 0QE p.h.n.guthrie@btinternet.com	01465 841236
Hannah, William BD MCAM MIPR	1987	2001	(Muirkirk)	8 Dovecote View, Kirkintilloch, Glasgow G66 3HY carrickhill34@outlook.com	0141 776 1337
Harper, David L. BSc BD	1972	2012	(Troon: St Meddan's)	19 Calder Avenue, Troon KA10 7JT d.l.harper@btinternet.com	01292 312626
Keating, Glenda K. (Mrs) MTh	1996	2015	(Craigie Symington)	8 Wardlaw Gardens, Irvine KA11 2EW kirkglen@btinternet.com	01294 218820
Laing, Iain A. MA BD	1971	2009	(Bishopbriggs: Kenmuir)	9 Annfield Road, Prestwick KA9 1PP iandrlaing@yahoo.co.uk	01292 471732
Lennox, Lawrie I. MA BD DipEd	1991	2006	(Cromar)	7 Carwinshoch View, Ayr KA7 4AY lennox127@btinternet.com	01292 288658
Lochrie, John S. BSc BD MTh PhD	1967	2008	(St Colmon)	Cosyglen, Kilkerran, Maybole KA19 8LS	01465 811262
McGurk, Andrew F. BD	1983	2011	(Largs: St John's)	15 Fraser Avenue, Troon KA10 6XF afmcg.largs@talk21.com	01292 676008
McLachlan, Ian K. MA BD	1999	2019	(Barr with Dailly with Girvan: South)	22 Beeches Road, Blairgowrie PH10 6PN iankmclachlanyetiville53@gmail.com	
McNidder, Roderick H. BD	1987	2007	(Chaplain: NHS Ayrshire and Arran Trust)	6 Hollow Park, Alloway, Ayr KA7 4SR roddymcnidder@sky.com	01292 442554
McPhail, Andrew M. BA	1968	2002	(Ayr: Wallacetown)	25 Maybole Road, Ayr KA7 2QA	01292 282108
MacPherson, Gordon C. MA BD MTh	1963	1988	(Associate, Kilmarnock: Henderson)	6 Crosbie Place, Troon KA10 6EY ggmacpherson@btinternet.com	01292 679146
Matthews, John C. MA BD OBE	1992	2010	(Glasgow: Ruchill Kelvinside)	12 Arrol Drive, Ayr KA7 4AF mejohnmatthews@gmail.com	01292 264382
Mayes, Robert BD	1982	2017	(Dundonald)	Garfield Cottage, Sorn Road, Mauchline KA5 6HQ bobmayes3@gmail.com	01290 519869
Morrison, Alistair H. BTh DipYCS	1985	2004	(Paisley: St Mark's Oldhall)	92 St Leonard's Road, Ayr KA7 2PU alistairmorrison@gmail.com	01292 266021
Ness, David T. LTh	1972	2008	(Ayr: St Quivox)	17 Winston Avenue, Prestwick KA9 2EZ dtness@gmail.com	01292 471625
Ogston, Edgar J. BSc BD	1976	2017	(North West Lochaber)	14 North Park Avenue, Girvan KA26 9DH edgar.ogston@macfish.com	01465 713081
Paterson, John L. MA BD STM	1964	2003	(Linlithgow: St Michael's)	9 The Pines, Murdoch's Lane, Alloway, Ayr KA7 4WD lpaterson38@btinternet.com	01292 443615
Rae, Scott M. MBE BD CPS	1976	2016	(Muirkirk with Old Cumnock: Trinity)	2 Primrose Place, Kilmarnock KA1 2RR scottrae1@btopenworld.com	01563 532711

Russell, Paul R. MA BD	1984	2019	(Hospital Chaplain, NHS Ayrshire and Arran)	23 Nursery Wynd, Ayr KA7 3NZ russellpr@btinternet.com	01292 618020
Sanderson, Alastair M. BA LTh	1971	2007	(Craigie with Symington)	26 Main Street, Monkton, Prestwick KA9 2QL alel@sanderson29.fsnet.co.uk	01292 475819
Simpson, Edward V. BSc BD	1972	2009	(Glasgow: Giffnock South)	8 Paddock View, Thorntoun, Crosshouse, Kilmarnock KA2 0BH eddie.simpson3@talktalk.net	01563 522841
Symington, Alastair H. MA BD	1972	2012	(Troon: Old)	1 Cavendish Place, Troon KA10 6JG revdahs@virginmedia.com	01292 312556
Young, Rona M. (Mrs) BD DipEd	1991	2015	(Ayr: St Quivox)	16 Macintyre Road, Prestwick KA9 1BE revronyoung@hotmail.com	01292 471982
Yorke, Kenneth B.	1982	2009	(Dalmellington with Patna Waterside)	13 Annfield Terrace, Prestwick KA9 1PS kenyorke@yahoo.com	01292 670476

AYR ADDRESSES

Ayr

Auld Kirk	Kirkport (116 High Street)
Castlehill	Castlehill Road x Hillfoot Road
Newton Wallacetown	Main Street
St Andrew's	Park Circus
St Columba	Midton Road x Carrick Park
St James'	Prestwick Road x Falkland Park Road
St Leonard's	St Leonard's Road x Monument Road

Girvan

North	Montgomerie Street
South	Stair Park

Prestwick

Kingcase	Waterloo Road
Monkton and Prestwick North	Monkton Road
St Nicholas	Main Street
South	Main Street

Troon

Old	Ayr Street
Portland	St Meddan's Street
St Meddan's	St Meddan's Street

(11) IRVINE AND KILMARNOCK (W)

The Presbytery meets at 7:00pm in the Howard Centre, Portland Road, Kilmarnock, on the first Tuesday in September, December and March and on the fourth Tuesday in June for ordinary business, and at different locations on the first Tuesday in October, November, February and May for mission. The September meeting commences with the celebration of Holy Communion.

Clerk:	REV. H. TAYLOR BROWN BD CertMin	14 McLelland Drive, Kilmarnock KA1 1SE	01563 529920 (Home)
		HBrown@churchofscotland.org.uk	
Presbytery Office:		Howard Centre, 5 Portland Road, Kilmarnock KA1 2BT	01563 526295 (Office)
		irvinekilmarnock@churchofscotland.org.uk	

The Presbytery office is staffed each Tuesday, Wednesday and Thursday from 9am until 12:30pm.

Ayrshire Mission to the Deaf
Richard C. Durno DSW CQSW   1989   2013   31 Springfield Road, Bishopbriggs,   (Voice/Text/Fax) 0141 772 1052
Glasgow G64 1PJ   (Voice/Text/Voicemail) (Mbl) 07748 607721
richard.durno@btinternet.com

Caldwell (F) linked with Dunlop (W)
Alison McBrier MA BD   2011   2017   4 Dampark, Dunlop, Kilmarnock KA3 4BZ   01560 673686
AMcBrier@churchofscotland.org.uk

Crosshouse (F H W)
T. Edward Marshall BD   1987   2007   27 Kilmarnock Road, Crosshouse, Kilmarnock KA2 0EZ   01563 524089
TMarshall@churchofscotland.org.uk

Darvel (F W)
Vacant   46 West Main Street, Darvel KA17 0AQ   **01560 322924**
Interim Moderator: Margaret A. Hamilton (Mrs)   mahamilton1@outlook.com   01560 322924
01563 534431

Dreghorn and Springside (T W)
Vacant   01294 273741
Interim Moderator: Neil Urquhart   NUrquhart@churchofscotland.org.uk

Dunlop See Caldwell

Fenwick (F H W) linked with Kilmarnock: Riccarton (F H W)
Colin A. Strong BSc BD   1989   2007   2 Jasmine Road, Kilmarnock KA1 2HD   01563 549490
CStrong@churchofscotland.org.uk

Galston (F H W)
Kristina I. Hine BS MDiv — 2011 2016 — 19 Manse Gardens, Galston KA4 8DX
KHine@churchofscotland.org.uk — **01563 820136**

Hurlford (F H W)
Ada V. MacLeod MA BD PGCE — 2013 2018 — 12 Main Road, Crookedholm, Kilmarnock KA3 6JT
AVMacLeod@churchofscotland.org.uk — 01563 539739

Irvine: Fullarton (F H T W)
Neil Urquhart BD DipMin — 1989 — secretary@fullartonchurch.co.uk
48 Waterside, Irvine KA12 8QJ
NUrquhart@churchofscotland.org.uk — **01294 273741**
01294 279909

Irvine: Girdle Toll (F H) linked with Irvine: St Andrew's (H)
Ian W. Benzie BD — 1999 2008 — St Andrew's Manse, 206 Bank Street, Irvine KA12 0YD
Ian.Benzie@churchofscotland.org.uk — **01294 276051**
01294 216139

Irvine: Mure (F H)
Vacant — 9 West Road, Irvine KA12 8RE — 01294 279916

Irvine: Old (F H)
Vacant
Interim Moderator: Kim Watt — 22 Kirk Vennel, Irvine KA12 0DQ
KWatt@churchofscotland.org.uk — **01294 273503**
01294 279265
01560 482267

Irvine: Relief Bourtreehill (F H W)
Vacant
Interim Moderator: Colin A. Strong — 4 Kames Court, Irvine KA11 1RT
CStrong@churchofscotland.org.uk — 01294 216939
01563 549490

Irvine: St Andrew's (H) See Irvine: Girdle Toll

Kilmarnock: Kay Park (F H W)
Fiona E. Maxwell BA BD — 2004 2018 — 1 Glebe Court, Kilmarnock KA1 3BD
FMaxwell@churchofscotland.org.uk — **01563 574106**
01563 521762

Kilmarnock: New Laigh Kirk (F H W)
David S. Cameron BD — 2001 2009 — 1 Holmes Farm Road, Kilmarnock KA1 1TP
David.Cameron@churchofscotland.org.uk — 01563 525416

Kilmarnock: Riccarton See Fenwick

Kilmarnock: St Andrew's and St Marnock's (F W) 1983
James McNaughton BD DipMin
35 South Gargieston Drive, Kilmarnock KA1 1TB
JMcNaughtan@churchofscotland.org.uk
01563 521665

Kilmarnock: St John's Onthank (F H W) 2015 2017
Allison E. Becker BA MDiv
84 Wardneuk Drive, Kilmarnock KA3 2EX
ABecker@churchofscotland.org.uk
07716 162380

Kilmarnock: St Kentigern's (F W)
Vacant
Interim Moderator: Anne McAllister
stkentigern@hotmail.co.uk
1 Thirdpart Place, Kilmarnock KA1 1UL
AMcAllister@churchofscotland.org.uk
01563 571280
01560 483191

Kilmarnock: South (F H) 1997 2002
H. Taylor Brown BD CertMin
14 McLelland Drive, Kilmarnock KA1 1SE
HBrown@churchofscotland.org.uk
01563 529920

Kilmaurs: St Maur's Glencairn (H) 1993
John A. Urquhart BD
9 Standalane, Kilmaurs, Kilmarnock KA3 2NB
John.Urquhart@churchofscotland.org.uk
01563 538289

Newmilns: Loudoun (F H T W)
Vacant
Interim Moderator: James McNaughtan
Loudoun Manse, 116A Loudoun Road, Newmilns KA16 9HH
JMcNaughtan@churchofscotland.org.uk
01560 320174
01563 521665

Stewarton: John Knox (F T W) 2010
Gavin A. Niven BSc MSc BD
getconnected@johnknox.org.uk
27 Avenue Street, Stewarton, Kilmarnock KA3 5AP
GNiven@churchofscotland.org.uk
01560 484560
01560 482418

Stewarton: St Columba's (H W)
Vacant
Interim Moderator: T. Edward Marshall
1 Kirk Glebe, Stewarton, Kilmarnock KA3 5BJ
TMarshall@churchofscotland.org.uk
01560 485113
01563 524089

In other appointments

Clancy, P. Jill (Mrs) BD DipMin 2000 2017
Prison Chaplain, HMP Barlinnie and HMP Kilmarnock
27 Cross Street, Galston KA4 8AA
jgibson@totalise.co.uk
07956 557087

Name			Position	Address / Contact	Tel.
Huggett, Judith A. (Miss) BA BD	1990	1998	Lead Chaplain, NHS Ayrshire and Arran	4 Westmoor Crescent, Kilmarnock KA1 1TX judith.huggett@aapct.scot.nhs.uk	01560 482267
Watt, Kim	2015		Ordained Local Minister, Presbytery	Reddans Park Gate, The Crescent, Stewarton, Kilmarnock KA3 5AY KWatt@churchofscotland.org.uk	

Demitted

Name			Position	Address / Contact	Tel.
Brockie, Colin G.F. BSc(Eng) BD SOSc	1967	2007	(Presbytery Clerk, Irvine and Kilmarnock)	36 Braehead Court, Kilmarnock KA3 7AB colin@brockie.org.uk	01563 559960
Burgess, Paul C.J. MA	1970	2003	(World Mission Partner, Gujranwala Theological Seminary, Pakistan)	Springvale, Halket Road, Lugton, Kilmarnock KA4 3EE paulandcathie@gmail.com	01505 850254
Cant, Thomas M. MA BD	1964	2004	(Paisley: Laigh Kirk)	3 Meikle Cutstraw, Stewarton, Kilmarnock KA3 5HU revtmcant@aol.com	01560 480566
Christie, Robert S. MA BD ThM	1964	2000	(Kilmarnock: West High)	24 Homeroyal House, 2 Chalmers Crescent, Edinburgh EH9 1TP	
Davidson, James BD DipAFH	1989	2002	(Wishaw: Old)	13 Redburn Place, Irvine KA12 9BQ	01294 312515
Garrity, T. Alan W. BSc BD MTh	1969	2008	(Bermuda)	17 Solomon's View, Dunlop, Kilmarnock KA3 4ES alangarrity@btinternet.com	01560 486879
Gillon, C. Blair BD	1975	2007	(Glasgow: Ibrox)	East Muirshiel Farmhouse, Dunlop, Kilmarnock KA3 4EJ charlesgillon21@gmail.com	01560 483778
Godfrey, Linda BSc BD	2012	2014	(Ayr: St Leonard's with Dalrymple)	9 Taybank Drive, Ayr KA7 4RL godfreykayak@aol.com	07825 663866
Hall, William M. BD	1972	2010	(Kilmarnock: Old High Kirk)	33 Cairns Terrace, Kilmarnock KA1 2JG revwillie@talktalk.net	01563 525080
Hewitt, William C. BD DipPS	1977	2017	(Presbytery Clerk: Glasgow)	6 Woodlands Grove, Kilmarnock KA3 1TZ WHewitt@churchofscotland.org.uk	01563 533312
Horsburgh, Gary E. BA	1977	2015	(Dreghorn and Springside)	1 Woodlands Grove, Kilmarnock KA3 1TY garyhorsburgh@hotmail.co.uk	01563 624508
Lacy, David BA BD Dlitt DL	1976	2017	(Kilmarnock: Kay Park)	4 Cairns Terrace, Kilmarnock KA1 2JG DLacy@churchofscotland.org.uk	01563 624034 07974 760272
Lamarti, Samuel H. BD MTh PhD	1979	2006	(Stewarton: John Knox)	7 Dalwhinnie Crescent, Kilmarnock KA3 1QS samlamar@pobroadband.co.uk	01563 529632
Lind, George K. BD MCIBS	1998	2017	(Stewarton: St. Columba's)	Endrig, 98 Loudoun Road, Newmilns KA16 9HQ gklind@talktalk.net	01560 428732
McAllister, Anne C. BSc DipEd CCS	2013	2016	(Ordained Local Minister)	39 Bowes Rigg, Stewarton, Kilmarnock KA3 5EN AMcAllister@churchofscotland.org.uk	01560 483191
McCulloch, James D. BD MIOP MIP3 FSAScot	1996	2016	(Hurlford)	18 Edradour Place, Dunsmuir Park, Kilmarnock KA3 1US mccullochmanse1@btinternet.com	01563 535833
MacLeod, Malcolm (Calum) BA BD	1979	2018	(Rutherglen: Old)	12 Main Road, Crookedholm, Kilmarnock KA3 6JT	01563 539739
Scott, Thomas T.	1968	1989	(Kilmarnock: St Marnock's)	6 North Hamilton Place, Kilmarnock KA1 2QN tomtscott@btinternet.com	01563 531415
Shaw, Catherine A.M. MA	1998	2006	(Auxiliary Minister)	40 Merrygreen Place, Stewarton, Kilmarnock KA3 5EP catherine.shaw@tesco.net	01560 483352

Urquhart, Barbara (Mrs) DCS	1986 2017	(Deacon)	9 Standalane, Kilmaurs, Kilmarnock KA3 2NB barbaraurquhart1@gmail.com	01563 538289
Wark, Alexander C. MA BD STM	1982 2017	(Mid Deeside)	43 Mure Avenue, Kilmarnock KA 3 1TT alecwark@yahoo.co.uk	01563 559581
Welsh, Alex M. MA BD	1979	(Hospital Chaplain, NHS Ayrshire and Arran)	8 Greenside Avenue, Prestwick KA9 2HB alexandevelyn@hotmail.com	01292 475341

IRVINE and KILMARNOCK ADDRESSES

Irvine

Dreghorn and Springside		Relief Bourtreehill	Crofthead, Bourtreehill
Fullarton	Townfoot x Station Brae	St Andrew's	Caldon Road x Oaklands Ave
Girdle Toll	Marress Road x Church Street		
Mure	Bryce Knox Court		
Old	West Road		
	Kirkgate		

Riccarton — Old Street

Kilmarnock		St Andrew's and St Marnock's — St Marnock Street
Ayrshire Mission to the Deaf	10 Clark Street	St John's Onthank — 84 Wardneuk Street
Kay Park	London Road	St Kentigern's — Dunbar Drive
New Laigh Kirk	John Dickie Street	South — Whatrigs Road

(12) ARDROSSAN (F W)

Meets at Ardrossan and Saltcoats: Kirkgate, on the first Tuesday of February, March, May, September, October, November and December; and on the second Tuesday of June.

Clerk:	MRS JEAN C. Q. HUNTER BD		The Manse, Shiskine, Isle of Arran KA27 8EP ardrossan@churchofscotland.org.uk	01770 860380 07961 299907

Ardrossan: Park (W)

Tanya J. Webster BCom DipAcc BD	2011	35 Ardneil Court, Ardrossan KA22 7NQ TWebster@churchofscotland.org.uk	01294 463711 01294 538903

Ardrossan and Saltcoats: Kirkgate (F H W)

Vacant

Session Clerk: Vivien Bruce (Mrs)	10 Seafield Drive, Ardrossan KA22 8NU andrew_bruce2@sky.com	01294 472001 01294 463571

Beith (F H W)

Roderick I.T. MacDonald BD CertMin	1992 2005	2 Glebe Court, Beith KA15 1ET RMacDonald@churchofscotland.org.uk	beithchurch@btinternet.com 01505 502686 01505 503858
Fiona Blair DCS	1994 2015	9 Powgree Crescent, Beith KA15 1ES FBlair@churchofscotland.org.uk	07495 673428

Brodick (W) linked with Corrie linked with Lochranza and Pirnmill (W) linked with Shiskine (F H W)
brodickchurch@gmail.com;
info@lochranzachurch.org.uk; stmolios@gmail.com **01770 870228**

R. Angus Adamson BD 2006 Otterburn, Corriecravie, Isle of Arran KA27 8EP
RAdamson@churchofscotland.org.uk 01770 870228

Corrie See Brodick

Cumbrae (F W) linked with Largs: St John's (F H W) Cumbrae: **01475 531198** St John's: **01475 674468**
Jonathan C. Fleming MA BD 2012 2017 1 Newhaven Grove, Largs KA30 8NS
JFleming@churchofscotland.org.uk 01475 329933

Dalry: St Margaret's (F W) stmargaret@talktalk.net **01294 832264**
Vacant
Marion L.K. Howie (Mrs) MA ARCS 1992 2016 51 High Road, Stevenston KA20 3DY
(Auxiliary Minister) MHowie@churchofscotland.org.uk 01294 466571

Dalry: Trinity (F H W)
Martin Thomson BSc DipEd BD 1988 2004 Trinity Manse, West Kilbride Road, Dalry KA24 5DX
MThomson@churchofscotland.org.uk 01294 832363

Fairlie (F H W) linked with Largs: St Columba's (F W) **01475 68212**
Graham McWilliams BSc BD DMin 2005 2019 14 Fairliebume Gardens, Fairlie, Largs KA29 0ER
GMcWilliams@churchofscotland.org.uk 01475 568515

Kilbirnie: Auld Kirk (F H)
Vacant
Session Clerk: Archie Currie 49 Holmhead, Kilbirnie KA25 6BS 01505 682342
archiecurrie@yahoo.co.uk 01505 681474

Kilbirnie: St Columba's (H W) **01505 685239**
Fiona C. Ross (Miss) BD DipMin 1996 2004 Manse of St Columba's, Dipple Road, Kilbirnie KA25 7JU
FRoss@churchofscotland.org.uk 01505 683342

Kilmory (F W) linked with Lamlash (W)
Lily F. McKinnon (Mrs) MA BD PGCE 1993 2015 The Manse, Lamlash, Isle of Arran KA27 8LE
LMcKinnon@churchofscotland.org.uk 01770 600074

Kilwinning: Mansefield Trinity (F W)
Hilary Beresford BD | 2000 | 2018 | Mansefield Trinity Church, West Doura Way, Kilwinning KA13 6DY
HBeresford@churchofscotland.org.uk | 01294 **550746**
01294 550746

Kilwinning: Old (W)
Vacant | 2014 | 2016 | 54 Dalry Road, Kilwinning KA13 7HE
Isobel Beck BD DCS | | | 16 Patrick Avenue, Stevenston KA20 4AW
IBeck@churchofscotland.org.uk | 01294 **552606**
01294 552606
07919 193425

Lamlash See Kilmory

Largs: Clark Memorial (H W)
T. David Watson BSc BD | 1988 | 2014 | 31 Douglas Street, Largs KA30 8PT
DWatson@churchofscotland.org.uk | 01475 **675186**
01475 672370

Largs: St Columba's See Fairlie
Largs: St John's See Cumbrae
Lochranza and Pirnmill See Brodick

Saltcoats: North (W)
Alexander B. Noble MA BD ThM | 1982 | 2003 | 25 Longfield Avenue, Saltcoats KA21 6DR
ANoble@churchofscotland.org.uk | 01294 **464679**
01294 604923

Saltcoats: St Cuthbert's (H W)
Sarah E.C. Nicol (Mrs) BSc BD MTh | 1985 | 2018 | 10 Kennedy Road, Saltcoats KA21 5SF
SNicol@churchofscotland.org.uk | 01294 696030

Shiskine See Brodick

Stevenston: Ardeer (F W) linked with Stevenston: Livingstone (F H W)
David A. Sutherland BD | 2001 | 2017 | 27 Cuninghame Drive, Stevenston KA20 4AB
DSutherland@churchofscotland.org.uk | 01294 608993

Stevenston: High (F H W)
M. Scott Cameron MA BD | 2002 | Glencairn Street, Stevenston KA20 3DL
Scott.Cameron@churchofscotland.org.uk | 01294 463356

Stevenston: Livingstone See Stevenston: Ardeer

West Kilbride (F T H W)
James J. McNay MA BD   2008

office@westkilbrideparishchurch.org.uk
The Manse, Goldenberry Avenue, West Kilbride KA23 9LJ
JMcNay@churchofscotland.org.uk

01294 829902
01294 823186

Whiting Bay and Kildonan
Elizabeth R.L. Watson (Miss) BA BD   1981 1982

The Manse, Whiting Bay, Brodick, Isle of Arran KA27 8RE
EWatson@churchofscotland.org.uk

01770 700289

In other appointments

Ralph, Mandy R. RGN   2013   Ordained Local Minister

Lagnaleon, 4 Wilson Street, Largs KA30 9AQ
MRalph@churchofscotland.org.uk

01475 675347
07743 760792

Demitted

Black, Andrew R. BD   1987 2018   (Irvine: Relief Bourtreehill)

4 Nursery Wynd, Kilwinning KA13 6ER
andrewblack@tiscali.co.uk

01294 673090

Cruickshank, Norman BA BD   1983 2006   (West Kilbride: Overton)

24D Faulds Wynd, Seamill, West Kilbride KA23 9FA

01294 822239

Davidson, Amelia (Mrs) BD   2004 2011   (Coatbridge: Calder)

11 St Mary's Place, Saltcoats KA21 5NY

Drysdale, James H. LTh   1987 2006   (Blackbraes and Shieldhill)

10 John Clark Street, Largs KA30 9AH

01475 674870

Falconer, Alan D. MA BD DLitt DD   1972 2011   (Aberdeen: St Machar's Cathedral)

18 North Crescent Road, Ardrossan KA22 8NA
alanfalconer@gmx.com

01294 472991

Finlay, William P. MA BD   1969 2000   (Glasgow: Townhead Blochairn)

High Corrie, Brodick, Isle of Arran KA27 8JB

01770 810689

Ford, Alan A. BD   1977 2013   (Glasgow: Springburn)

14 Corsankell Wynd, Saltcoats KA21 6HY
alan.andy@btinternet.com

01294 465740

Gordon, David C.   1953 1988   (Gigha and Cara)

Hebenton, David J. MA BD   1958 2002   (Ayton and Burnmouth with Grantshouse and Houndwood and Reston)

South Beach House, South Crescent Road, Ardrossan KA22 8DU

McCallum, Alexander D. BD   1987 2005   (Saltcoats: New Trinity)

22B Faulds Wynd, Seamill, West Kilbride KA23 9FA
59 Woodcroft Avenue, Largs KA30 9EW
sandyandjose@madasafish.com

01294 829228
01475 670133

McCance, Andrew M. BSc   1986 1995   (Coatbridge: Middle)

6A Douglas Place, Largs KA30 8PU

01475 673303

Mackay, Marjory H. (Mrs) BD DipEd CCE   1998 2008   (Cumbrae)

4 Golf Road, Millport, Isle of Cumbrae KA28 0HB
marjory.mackay@gmail.com

01475 530388

MacKinnon, Ronald M. DCS   1996 2012   (Deacon)

32 Strathclyde House, Shore Road, Skelmorlie PA17 5AN
ronnie@ronniemac.plus.com

01475 521333
07594 427960

MacLeod, Ian LTh BA MTh PhD   1969 2006   (Brodick with Corrie)

Cromla Cottage, Corrie, Isle of Arran KA27 8JB
i.macleod829@btinternet.com

01770 810237

Mitchell, D. Ross BA BD   1972 2007   (West Kilbride: St Andrew's)

11 Dunbar Gardens, Saltcoats KA21 6GJ
ross.mitchell@virgin.net

Paterson, John H. BD   1977 2000   (Kirkintilloch: St David's Memorial Park)

Creag Bhan, Golf Course Road, Whiting Bay, Isle of Arran KA27 8QT

01770 700569

Roy, Iain M. MA BD	1960	1997	(Stevenson: Livingstone)	2 The Fieldings, Dunlop, Kilmarnock KA3 4AU	01560 483072
Taylor, Andrew S. BTh FPhS	1959	1992	(Greenock: The Union)	9 Raillies Avenue, Largs KA30 8QY andrew.taylor_123@btinternet.com	01475 674709
Travers, Robert BA BD	1993	2015	(Irvine Old)	74 Caledonian Road, Stevenston KA20 3LF roberttravers@live.co.uk	01294 279265
Ward, Alan H. MA BD	1978	2015	(Interim Minister)	47 Meadowfoot Road, West Kilbride KA23 9BU	01475 822244 07709 906130
Whitecross, Jeanette BD	2002	2019	(Kilwinning: Old)	4 Fir Bank, Ayr KA7 3SX jeanettewx@yahoo.com	01292 225922

(13) LANARK (W)

Meets on the first Tuesday of February, March, May, September, October, November and December, and on the third Tuesday of June.

Presbytery Office: Greyfriars Parish Church, Bloomgate, Lanark ML11 9ET
administrator@lanarkpresbytery.org — 01555 437050

Clerk: REV. BRYAN KERR BA BD — Greyfriars Manse, 3 Bellefield Way, Lanark ML11 7NW
lanark@churchofscotland.org.uk — 01555 437050 / 01555 663363

Depute Clerk: REV. GEORGE C. SHAND MA BD — 16 Abington Road, Symington, Biggar ML12 6JX
George.Shand@churchofscotland.org.uk — 01899 309400

Biggar (F H W) linked with Black Mount
Mike D. Fucella BD MTh — 1997 2013 — biggarkirk09@gmail.com
'Candlemas', 6C Leafield Road, Biggar ML12 6AY
MFucella@churchofscotland.org.uk — 01889 229291 / 01899 229291

Black Mount See Biggar

Cairngryffe (F W) linked with Libberton and Quothquan (F H W) linked with Symington (F W) (The Tinto Parishes)
contactus@symingtonkirk.com
George C. Shand MA BD — 1981 2014 — 16 Abington Road, Symington, Biggar ML12 6JX
George.Shand@churchofscotland.org.uk — 01899 309400

Carluke: Kirkton (H W)
Iain D. Cunningham MA BD — 1979 1987 — kirktonchurch@btconnect.com
9 Station Road, Carluke ML8 5AA
ICunningham@churchofscotland.org.uk — 01555 750778 / 01555 771262

Carluke: St Andrew's (H W)
Helen E. Jamieson (Mrs) BD DipEd

1989

standrewscarluke@btinternet.com
120 Clyde Street, Carluke ML8 5BG
HJamieson@churchofscotland.org.uk

01555 771218

Carluke: St John's (F H W)
Elijah O. Obinna BA MTh PhD

2002   2016

18 Old Bridgend, Carluke ML8 4HN
EObinna@churchofscotland.org.uk

01555 751730
01555 752389

Carnwath (H) linked with Carstairs (W)
Vacant
Session Clerk, Carnwath: Betty McLeod
Session Clerk, Carstairs: Ruth Campbell

11 Range View, Cleghorn, Carstairs, Lanark ML11 8TF
williemcleod913@btinternet.com
ruth25c@aol.com

01555 840736
01555 870441

Carstairs See Carnwath

Coalburn and Lesmahagow: Old (F H W)
Vacant
Session Clerk: Douglas Walsh

lopc@btinternet.com
9 Elm Bank, Lesmahagow, Lanark ML11 0EA
dougandwilma1@btinternet.com

01555 892425
01555 892848

Crossford (H) linked with Kirkfieldbank
Steven Reid BAcc CA BD

1989   1997

74 Lanark Road, Crossford, Carluke ML8 5RE
SReid@churchofscotland.org.uk

01555 860415

Douglas Valley (F W)
Vacant
Session Clerk: Andy Robinson

office.tdvc@yahoo.co.uk
The Manse, Douglas, Lanark ML11 0RB
gavdrewandjoe@aol.com

01555 850000
01555 851246

Forth: St Paul's (F H W)
Elspeth J. MacLean (Mrs) BVMS BD

2011   2016

22 Lea Rig, Forth, Lanark ML11 8EA
EMacLean@churchofscotland.org.uk

01555 728837

Kirkfieldbank See Crossford

Kirkmuirhill (F H W)
Andrew D. Rooney BSc BD

2019

kirkmuirhillchurch@btinternet.com
The Manse, 82 Vere Road, Kirkmuirhill, Lanark ML11 9RP
ARooney@churchofscotland.org.uk

01555 895593
01555 892409

Lanark: Greyfriars (F H T W)
Bryan Kerr BA BD
2002   2007
office@lanarkgreyfriars.com
Greyfriars Manse, 3 Bellefield Way, Lanark ML11 7NW
BKerr@churchofscotland.org.uk
01555 437050
01555 663363

Lanark: St Nicholas' (F H W)
Louise E. Mackay BSc BD
2017
lanarkstnicholas@outlook.com
2 Kairnhill Court, Lanark ML11 9HU
01555 666220
01555 661936

Law (F W)
Paul G.R. Grant BD MTh UKBHC
2003   2018
info@lawparishchurch.org
3 Shawgill Court, Law, Carluke ML8 5SJ
PGrant@churchofscotland.org.uk
01698 373180

Lesmahagow: Abbeygreen (W)
David S. Carmichael
1982
information@abbeygreen.org.uk
Abbeygreen Manse, Lesmahagow, Lanark ML11 0DB
David.Carmichael@churchofscotland.org.uk
01555 893384

Libberton and Quothquan See Cairngryffe
Symington See Cairngryffe

Upper Clyde (F W)
Nikki M. Macdonald BD MTh PhD
2014
31 Carlisle Road, Crawford, Biggar ML12 6TP
NMacdonald@churchofscotland.org.uk
01864 502139

In other appointments

Clelland, Elizabeth B. (Mrs) BD   2002 2012   Resident Chaplain, Divine Healing   Braehead House Christian Healing and Retreat Centre, Braidwood Road, 01555 860716
Fellowship (Scotland)   Crossford, Carluke ML8 5NQ
liz_clelland@yahoo.co.uk

Demitted

Buchan, William BD DipTheol   1987 2001   (Kilwinning: Abbey)   9 Leafield Road, Biggar ML12 6AY   01899 229253
billbuchan3@btinternet.com

Cowan, James S.A. BD DipMin   1986 2019   (Barrhead: St Andrew's)   30 Redding Road, Falkirk FK2 9XJ   01555 665509
Cowell, Susan G. (Miss) BA BD   1986 1998   (Budapest)   3 Gavel Lane, Regency Gardens, Lanark ML11 9FB   01721 723950
Cutler, James S.H.   1986 2011   (Black Mount with Culter with   12 Kittlegairy Place, Peebles EH45 9LW
BD CEng MIStructE   Libberton and Quothquan)   revjimc@outlook.com
Findlay, Henry J.W. MA BD   1965 2005   (Wishaw: St Mark's)   2 Alba Gardens, Carluke ML8 5US   01555 759995
henryfindlay@btinternet.com

Houston, Graham R.   1978 2011   (Cairngryffe with Symington)   3 Alder Lane, Beechtrees, Lanark ML11 9FT   01555 678004
BSc BD MTh PhD   gandih6156@btinternet.com

Webster, Peter BD   1977 2014   (Edinburgh: Portobello St James')   51 Kempock Street, Gourock PA19 1NF   01555 893357
Young, David A.   1972 2003   (Kirkmuirhill)   110 Carlisle Road, Blackwood, Lanark ML11 9RT
                                                                            youngdavid@aol.com

(14) GREENOCK AND PAISLEY (W)

Meets on the second Tuesday of September, November, December, February, March and May, and on the third Tuesday of June.

Clerk:	REV. PETER McENHILL BD PhD	The Presbytery Office (see below) greenockpaisley@churchofscotland.org.uk	
Depute Clerk:	REV. ALISTAIR N. SHAW MA BD MTh PhD		
Presbytery Office:		'Homelea', Faith Avenue, Quarrier's Village, Bridge of Weir PA11 3SX	Tel 01505 615033 Fax 01505 615088

Barrhead: Bourock (F H W)   2006   2014   14 Maxton Avenue, Barrhead, Glasgow G78 1DY   **0141 881 9813**
Pamela Gordon BD   PGordon@churchofscotland.org.uk   0141 881 8736

Barrhead: St Andrew's (F H W)   10 Arthurlie Avenue, Barrhead, Glasgow G78 2BU   **0141 881 8442**
Vacant   0141 881 3457

Bishopton (F H W)   2017   office@bishoptonkirk.org.uk   **01505 862583**
Yvonne Smith BSc BD   The Manse, Newton Road, Bishopton PA7 5JP   01505 862161
                                                          YSmith@churchofscotland.org.uk

Bridge of Weir: Freeland (F H W)   1988   15 Lawmarnock Crescent, Bridge of Weir PA11 3AS   **01505 612610**
Kenneth N. Gray BA BD   aandkgray@btinternet.com   01505 690918

Bridge of Weir: St Machar's Ranfurly (F W)   2017   9 St Andrew's Drive, Bridge of Weir PA11 3SH   **01505 612975**
Hanneke Marshall (Mrs) MTh MA PGCE   Hanneke.Marshall@churchofscotland.org.uk   01505 612975
CertMin

Elderslie Kirk (F H W)
G. Gray Fletcher BSc BD   1989   2019   282 Main Road, Elderslie, Johnstone PA5 9EF
GFletcher@churchofscotland.org.uk
01505 323348
01505 321767

Erskine (F W)
Vacant
Interim Moderator: David Stewart   The Manse, 7 Leven Place, Linburn, Erskine PA8 6AS
revdavidst@aol.com
0141 812 4620
0141 570 8103
01475 675159

Gourock: Old Gourock and Ashton (H W)
David W.G. Burt BD DipMin   1989   2014   331 Eldon Street, Gourock PA16 7QN
DBurt@churchofscotland.org.uk
01475 633914

Gourock: St John's (F H T W)
Teri C. Peterson MDiv BMus   2006   2018   **office@stjohns-gourock.org.uk**
6 Barrhill Road, Gourock PA19 1JX
TPeterson@churchofscotland.org.uk
01475 632143

Greenock: East End (F) linked with Greenock: Mount Kirk (F W)
Francis E. Murphy BEng DipDSE BD   2006   **info@themountkirk.org.uk**
76 Finnart Street, Greenock PA16 8HJ
FMurphy@churchofscotland.org.uk
01475 722338

Greenock: Lyle Kirk (F T W)
Vacant   **office@lylekirk.org**
39 Fox Street, Greenock PA16 8PD
01475 727694
01475 717229

Greenock: Mount Kirk See Greenock: East End

Greenock: St Margaret's (F W)
Vacant
01475 781953

Greenock: St Ninian's
Vacant
Interim Moderator: Karen Harbison   5 Auchmead Road, Greenock PA16 0PY
KHarbison@churchofscotland.org.uk
01475 631878
01475 721048

Greenock: Wellpark Mid Kirk (F)
Alan K. Sorensen DL BD MTh
DipMin FSAScot   1983   2000   101 Brisbane Street, Greenock PA16 8PA
ASorensen@churchofscotland.org.uk
01475 721741

Greenock: Westburn (F W) Karen E. Harbison (Mrs) MA BD	1991	2014	50 Ardgowan Street, Greenock PA16 8EP KHarbison@churchofscotland.org.uk	**01475 720257** 01475 721048
Houston and Killellan (F H W) Gary D. Noonan BA	2018		The Manse of Houston, Main Street, Houston, Johnstone PA6 7EL GNoonan@churchofscotland.org.uk	01505 612569
Howwood (W) Guardianship of the Presbytery Interim Moderator: Alistair N. Shaw			Alistair.Shaw@churchofscotland.org.uk	01505 320060
Inchinnan (F H W) Ann Knox BD Cert.Healthc.Chap	2017		51 Old Greenock Road, Inchinnan, Renfrew PA4 9PH AKnox@churchofscotland.org.uk	**0141 812 1263** 0141 389 1724 07534 900065
Inverkip (H W) linked with Skelmorlie and Wemyss Bay (W) Archibald Speirs BD	1995	2013	**admin@inverkip.org.uk** 3a Montgomery Terrace, Skelmorlie PA17 5DT ASpeirs@churchofscotland.org.uk	01475 529320
Johnstone: High (F H W) Ann C. McCool (Mrs) BD DSD IPA ALCM	1989	2001	76 North Road, Johnstone PA5 8NF AMcCool@churchofscotland.org.uk	**01505 336303** 01505 320006
Johnstone: St Andrew's Trinity Charles M. Cameron BA BD PhD	1980	2013	45 Woodlands Crescent, Johnstone PA5 0AZ Charles.Cameron@churchofscotland.org.uk	**01505 337827** 01505 672908
Johnstone: St Paul's (F H W) Alistair N. Shaw MA BD MTh PhD	1982	2003	9 Stanley Drive, Brookfield, Johnstone PA5 8UF Alistair.Shaw@churchofscotland.org.uk	**01505 321632** 01505 320060
Kilbarchan (F T W) Stephen J. Smith BSc BD	1993	2015	The Manse, Church Street, Kilbarchan, Johnstone PA10 2JQ SSmith@churchofscotland.org.uk	01505 702621

Kilmacolm: Old (F H W)   1992   2007   The Old Kirk Manse, Glencairn Road, Kilmacolm PA13 4NJ   **01505 873911**
Peter McEnhill BD PhD   PMcEnhill@churchofscotland.org.uk   01505 873174

Kilmacolm: St Columba (F H)   1986   1992   6 Churchill Road, Kilmacolm PA13 4LH   01505 873271
R. Douglas Cranston MA BD   RCranston@churchofscotland.org.uk

Langbank (F T W) linked with Port Glasgow: St Andrew's (F H W)   **info@langbankparishchurch.co.uk**
Vacant   St Andrew's Manse, Barr's Brae, Port Glasgow PA14 5QA   01475 741486
Interim Moderator: Jack McHugh (Mr)   jackmchugh1@btinternet.com   01505 612789

Linwood (F H)   2005   2008   1 John Neilson Avenue, Paisley PA1 2SX   **01505 328802**
Eileen M. Ross (Mrs) BD MTh   ERoss@churchofscotland.org.uk   0141 887 2801

Lochwinnoch (F W)
Guardianship of the Presbytery
Interim Moderator: Hanneke Marshall   Hanneke.Marshall@churchofscotland.org.uk   01505 612975

Neilston (F W)   **0141 881 9445**
Vacant   The Manse, Neilston Road, Neilston, Glasgow G78 3NP   0141 258 0805
Interim Moderator: Maureen Leitch   maureen.leitch@ntl.world   0141 580 2927

Paisley: Abbey (F H W)   1979   1988   **info@paisleyabbey.org.uk**   0141 889 7654; Fax **0141 887 3929**
Alan D. Birss MA BD   15 Main Road, Castlehead, Paisley PA2 6AJ   0141 889 3587
                                                     ABirss@churchofscotland.org.uk

Paisley: Glenburn (F T W)   **0141 884 2602**
Vacant   10 Hawick Avenue, Paisley PA2 9LD   0141 884 4903
Interim Moderator: Maureen Leitch   maureen.leitch@ntl.world   0141 580 2927

Paisley: Lylesland (F H W)   **0141 561 7139**
Vacant   36 Potterhill Avenue, Paisley PA2 8BA   0141 561 9277
Interim Moderator: John Murning   JMurning@churchofscotland.org.uk   0141 316 2678

Paisley: Martyrs' Sandyford   **0141 889 6603**
Vacant   27 Acer Crescent, Paisley PA2 9LR   0141 884 7400
Interim Moderator: Philip Wallace   PWallace@churchofscotland.org.uk   0141 570 3502

Paisley: Oakshaw Trinity (F H W)   **0141 887 4647; Fax 0141 848 5139**
Gordon B. Armstrong BD FIAB BRC CertCS   1998   2012   The Manse, 52 Balgonie Drive, Paisley PA2 9LP   0141 587 3124
                                                        GArmstrong@churchofscotland.org.uk

Oakshaw Trinity is a Local Ecumenical Partnership with the United Reformed Church

Paisley: St Columba Foxbar (H)   **01505 812377**
Vacant   13 Corsebar Drive, Paisley PA2 9QD   0141 884 5826
Interim Moderator: Gordon Armstrong   GArmstrong@churchofscotland.org.uk   0141 587 3124

Paisley: St Luke's (F H W)
Vacant   31 Southfield Avenue, Paisley PA2 8BX   0141 884 6215
Interim Moderator: Pamela Gordon   PGordon@churchofscotland.org.uk   0141 881 8736

Paisley: St Mark's Oldhall (F H W)   **0141 882 2755**
Vacant   **office@stmarksoldhall.org.uk**   0141 889 4279
Interim Moderator: Ian Bell   36 Newtyle Road, Paisley PA1 3JX   01475 529312
                                                    ianbell@gmail.com

Paisley: St Ninian's Ferguslie (F T W)   **0141 887 9436**
Guardianship of the Presbytery
Stuart Stevenson   2011   2017   143 Springfield Park, Johnstone PA5 8JT   0141 886 2131
(Ordained Local Minister)   SStevenson@churchofscotland.org.uk

Paisley: Sherwood Greenlaw (F H W)   **0141 889 7060**
John Murning BD   1988   2014   5 Greenlaw Drive, Paisley PA1 3RX   0141 316 2678
                                                    JMurning@churchofscotland.org.uk

Paisley: Stow Brae Kirk (F W)   **0141 889 4335**
Vacant   **stowbraekirk@gmail.com**   0141 576 1710
                                                    290 Glasgow Road, Paisley PA1 3DP   0141 812 1425
Mhairi Breingan   2011   2019   6 Park Road, Inchinnan, Renfrew PA4 4QJ
(Ordained Local Minister)   mhairi.b@btinternet.com

Paisley: Wallneuk North (F W)   **0141 889 9265**
Peter G. Gill MA BA   2008   **wallneuknorthchurch@gmail.com**   0141 884 4429
                                                    5 Glenville Crescent, Paisley PA2 8TW
                                                    PGill@churchofscotland.org.uk

Port Glasgow: Hamilton Bardrainney (F) linked with Port Glasgow: St. Martin's
Vacant   80 Bardrainney Avenue, Port Glasgow PA14 6HD   01475 701213
Interim Moderator: Francis Murphy   FMurphy@churchofscotland.org.uk   01475 722338

Port Glasgow: St Andrew's See Langbank

Port Glasgow: St Martin's See Port Glasgow: Hamilton Bardrainney

Renfrew: North (F T W)
Philip D. Wallace BSc BTh DTS 1998 2018 contact@renfrewnorth.org.uk **0141 530 1308**
1 Alexandra Drive, Renfrew PA4 8UB 0141 570 3502
PWallace@churchofscotland.org.uk

Renfrew: Trinity (F H W)
Stuart C. Steell BD CertMin 1992 2015 25 Paisley Road, Renfrew PA4 8JH **0141 885 2129**
SSteell@churchofscotland.org.uk 0141 387 2464

Skelmorlie and Wemyss Bay See Inverkip

In other appointments

Davidson, Stuart BD	2008	2017	Pioneer Minister, Paisley North End	25H Cross Road, Paisley PA2 9QJ SDavidson@churchofscotland.org.uk	07717 503059
Geddes, Elizabeth (Mrs)	2013		Ordained Local Minister	9 Shillingworth Place, Bridge of Weir PA11 3DY EGeddes@churchofscotland.org.uk	01505 612639
Manson, Eileen (Mrs) DipCE	1994		Auxiliary Minister	1 Cambridge Avenue, Gourock PA19 1XT EManson@churchofscotland.org.uk	01475 632401

Demitted

Armstrong, William R. BD	1979	2008	(Skelmorlie and Wemyss Bay)	25A The Lane, Skelmorlie PA17 5AR warmstrong17@tiscali.co.uk	01475 520891
Bell, Ian W. LTh	1990	2011	(Erskine)	40 Brueacre Drive, Wemyss Bay PA18 6HA revianbell@gmail.com	01475 529312
Bell, May (Mrs) LTh	1998	2012	(Johnstone: St Andrew's Trinity)	40 Brueacre Drive, Wemyss Bay PA18 6HA revmaybell22@gmail.com	01475 529312
Black, Janette M.K. (Mrs) BD	1993	2006	(Assistant: Paisley: Oakshaw Trinity)	5 Craigiehall Avenue, Erskine PA8 7DB	0141 812 0794
Coull, Morris C. BD	1974	2018	(Greenock St Margaret's)	14 Kelvin Gardens, Largs KA30 8SY	
Currie, Ian S. MBE BD	1975	2010	(The United Church of Bute)	26 Old Bridge of Weir, Houston PA6 7EB ianscurrie@tiscali.co.uk	07764 254300
Easton, Lilly C. (Mrs)	1999	2012	(Renfrew: Old)	Flat 0/2, 90 Beith Street, Glasgow G11 6DG revlillyeaston@hotmail.co.uk	0141 586 7628
Fraser, Ian C. BA BD	1982	2008	(Glasgow: St Luke's and St Andrew's)	62 Kingston Avenue, Neilston, Glasgow G78 3JG ianandlindafraser@gmail.com	0141 563 6794
Gray, Greta (Miss) DCS	1992	2014	(Deacon)	67 Crags Avenue, Paisley PA3 6SG greta.gray@ntlworld.com	0141 884 6178

Hood, E. Loma OBE MA BD DD	1978	2016	(Renfrew: North)	4 Thornly Park Drive, Paisley PA2 7RR revlomahood@gmail.com	0141 384 9516
Kay, David BA BD MTh	1974	2008	(Paisley: Sandyford: Thread Street)	36 Donaldswood Park, Paisley PA2 8RS david.kay500@o2.co.uk	0141 884 2080
Leitch, Maureen (Mrs) BA BD	1995	2011	(Barrhead: Bourock)	Rockfield, 92 Paisley Road, Barrhead G78 1NW maureen.leitch@ntlworld.com	0141 580 2927
MacColl, James C. BSc BD	1966	2002	(Johnstone: St Andrew's Trinity)	20 Dunrobin Avenue, Johnstone PA5 9NW hamishmaccoll@gmail.com	01505 227439
Macdonald, Alexander MA BD	1966	2006	(Neilston)	35 Lochore Avenue, Paisley PA3 4BY alexsmacdonald42@aol.com	0141 889 0066
McFarlane, Robert G. BD	2001	2018	(Paisley St Mark's Oldhall)	990 Crookston Road, Glasgow G53 7DY	01475 723235
Mayne, Kenneth A.L. BA MSc CertEd	1976	2018	(Paisley Martyrs' Sandyford)	300 Glasgow Road, Paisley PA1 3DP	07957 642709
Nicol, Joyce M. (Mrs) BA DCS	1974	2006	(Deacon)	93 Brisbane Street, Greenock PA16 8NY joycenicol@hotmail.co.uk	07795 972560
Ramsden, Iain R. MStJ BTh	1999	2013	(Killearnan with Knockbain)	Flat 1/1, 15 Cardon Square, Renfrew PA4 8BY s4rev@sky.com	0141 887 2801
Ross, Duncan DCS	1996	2015	(Deacon)	1 John Neilson Avenue, Paisley PA1 2SX ssomacnud@hotmail.com	01475 520582
Simpson, James H. BD LLB	1964	2004	(Greenock: Mount Kirk)	82 Harbourside, Inverkip, Greenock PA16 0BF jameshsimpson@yahoo.co.uk	0141 812 7030
Smillie, Andrew M. LTh	1990	2005	(Langbank)	7 Turnbull Avenue, West Freeland, Erskine PA8 7DL andrewsmillie@talktalk.net	01475 675159
Stewart, David MA DipEd BD MTh	1977	2013	(Howwood)	72 Glen Avenue, Largs KA30 8QQ revdavidst@aol.com	01475 726102
Watson, Valerie G.C. MA BD STM	1987	2018	(North and West Islay)	Flat 0/1, 38 Brougham Street, Greenock PA16 8AH vgcwatson@btinternet.com	01505 229611
Whiteford, Alexander LTh	1996	2013	(Ardersier with Petty)	Cumbrae, 17 Netherburn Gardens, Houston, Johnstone PA6 7NG alex.whiteford@hotmail.co.uk	0141 881 4942
Whyte, Margaret A. (Mrs) BA BD	1988	2011	(Glasgow: Pollokshaws)	4 Springhill Road, Barrhead G78 2AA mawhyte@hotmail.co.uk	

GREENOCK AND PAISLEY ADDRESSES

Gourock

Old Gourock and Ashton	41 Royal Street
St John's	Bath Street x St John's Road

Greenock

East End	Crawfurdsburn Community Centre
Lyle Kirk	Newark Street x Bentinck Street
Mount Kirk	Dempster Street at Murdieston Park
St Margaret's	Finch Road x Kestrel Crescent
St Ninian's	Warwick Road, Larkfield
Wellpark Mid Kirk	Cathcart Square
Westburn	9 Nelson Street

Paisley

Abbey	Town Centre
Glenburn	Nethercraigs Drive off Glenburn Road
Lylesland	Rowan Street off Neilston Road
Martyrs'	King Street
Sandyford	Churchill
Oakshaw Trinity	Montgomery Road
St Columba Foxbar	Amochrie Road, Foxbar
St Luke's	Neilston Road
St Mark's Oldhall	Glasgow Road, Ralston
St Ninian's Ferguslie	Blackstoun Road
Sherwood Greenlaw	Glasgow Road
Stow Brae Kirk	Causeyside Street
Wallneuk North	off Renfrew Road

Port Glasgow

Hamilton Bardrainney	Bardrainney Avenue x Auchenbothie Road
St Andrew's	Princes Street
St Martin's	Mansion Avenue

(16) GLASGOW (F W)

Meets at 7pm on the second Tuesday of every month apart from June when it is the third Tuesday and July, August and January when it does not meet. Details of the venue are displayed on the Presbytery website.

Clerk: REV. GEORGE S. COWIE BSc BD   260 Bath Street, Glasgow G2 4JP   0141 332 6606
Treasurer: MRS ALISON WHITELAW   glasgow@churchofscotland.org.uk   Fax 0141 352 6646
                                                treasurer@presbyteryofglasgow.org.uk

1 **Banton (F W) linked with Twechar (W)**
   Guardianship of the Presbytery
   Session Clerk, Banton: Mary Dixon (Mrs)   magicmaria67@gmail.com   01236 822055
   Session Clerk, Twechar: Gena Whyte (Mrs)   whyteg@live.co.uk   0141 777 7704

2 **Bishopbriggs: Kenmure (F W)**   1999   2010   100 Kenmure Avenue, Bishopbriggs, Glasgow G64 2DB   **0141 762 4242**
   James Gemmell BD MTh   JGemmell@churchofscotland.org.uk   0141 390 3598

3 **Bishopbriggs: Springfield Cambridge (F W)** 1995 2006 **springfieldcamb@btconnect.com**   **0141 772 1596**
   Ian Taylor BD ThM   64 Miller Drive, Bishopbriggs, Glasgow G64 1FB   0141 772 1540
                                                ITaylor@churchofscotland.org.uk

4 **Broom (W)**   1992   2007   **office@broomchurch.org.uk**   **0141 639 3528**   Tel
   James A.S. Boag BD CertMin   3 Laigh Road, Newton Mearns, Glasgow G77 5EX   0141 639 2916
   JBoag@churchofscotland.org.uk   0141 639 3528   Fax

5 **Burnside Blairbeth (F W)**   1999   2006   **theoffice@burnsideblairbeth.church**   **0141 634 7383**
   William T.S. Wilson BSc BD   59 Blairbeth Road, Burnside, Glasgow G73 4JD   0141 583 6470
                                WWilson@churchofscotland.org.uk

6 **Busby (F W)**   1995   1998   17A Carmunnock Road, Busby, Glasgow G76 8SZ   **0141 644 2073**
   Jeremy C. Eve BSc BD   JEve@churchofscotland.org.uk   0141 644 3670

7	**Cadder (W)**			
	John B. MacGregor BD	1999 2017	231 Kirkintilloch Road, Bishopbriggs, Glasgow G64 2JB JMacGregor@churchofscotland.org.uk	**0141 772 7436** 0141 576 7127
8	**Cambuslang (F W)**		**JMacGregor@churchofscotland.org.uk**	**0141 642 9271**
	Vacant		74 Stewarton Drive, Cambuslang, Glasgow G72 8DG	0141 641 2028
	Karen M. Hamilton (Mrs) DCS	1995 2014	6 Beckfield Gate, Glasgow G33 1SW	0141 558 3195
			KHamilton@churchofscotland.org.uk	07514 402612
	Session Clerk: Janet Stewart (Miss)		office@cambuslangparishchurch.org.uk	01555 860095
9	**Cambuslang: Flemington Hallside (F W)**			
	Ian A. Cathcart BSc BD	1994 2018	59 Hay Crescent, Cambuslang, Glasgow G72 6QA ICathcart@churchofscotland.org.uk	0141 641 1049 07758 441895
10	**Campsie (F W)**		**campsieparishchurch@hotmail.com**	**01360 310939**
	Jane M. Denniston MA BD MTh DPT	2002 2016	Campsie Parish Church, 130 Main Street, Lennoxtown, Glasgow G66 7DA Jane.Denniston@churchofscotland.org.uk	07738 123101
11	**Chryston (H T W)**		**chrystonchurch@hotmail.com**	**0141 779 4188**
	Mark Malcolm MA BD	1999 2008	The Manse, 109 Main Street, Chryston, Glasgow G69 9LA MMalcolm@churchofscotland.org.uk	0141 779 1436 07731 737377
	Mark W.J. McKeown MEng MDiv (Associate Minister)	2013 2014	6 Glenapp Place, Moodiesburn, Glasgow G69 0HS MMcKeown@churchofscotland.org.uk	01236 263406
12	**Eaglesham (F W)**		**office@eagleshamparishchurch.co.uk**	**01355 302087**
	Vacant		The Manse, Cheapside Street, Eaglesham, Glasgow G76 0NS	01355 303495
13	**Fernhill and Cathkin (F W)**			
	Aquila R. Singh BA PGCE BD	2017	20 Glenlyon Place, Rutherglen, Glasgow G73 5PL ASingh@churchofscotland.org.uk	0141 389 3599
14	**Gartcosh (F H T W) linked with Glenboig (F T W)**			Gartcosh: **01236 872274**
	David G. Slater BSc BA DipThRS	2011	26 Inchnock Avenue, Gartcosh, Glasgow G69 8EA DSlater@churchofscotland.org.uk	07722 876616

15 Giffnock: Orchardhill (F W)
S. Grant Barclay LLB DipLP BD MSc PhD 1995 2016
23 Huntly Avenue, Giffnock, Glasgow G46 6LW
GBarclay@churchofscotland.org.uk
0141 638 3604
0141 387 8254

16 Giffnock: South (F W)
Catherine J. Beattie (Mrs) BD 2008 2011
164 Ayr Road, Newton Mearns, Glasgow G77 6EE
CBeattie@churchofscotland.org.uk
0141 638 2599
0141 258 7804

17 Giffnock: The Park (F W)
Calum D. Macdonald BD 1993 2001
contact@parkchurch.org.uk
41 Rouken Glen Road, Thornliebank, Glasgow G46 7JD
CMacdonald@churchofscotland.org.uk
0141 620 2204
0141 638 3023

18 Glenboig See Gartcosh

19 Greenbank (F H W)
Jeanne N. Roddick BD 2003
greenbankoffice@tiscali.co.uk
Greenbank Manse, 38 Eaglesham Road, Clarkston,
Glasgow G76 7DJ
JRoddick@churchofscotland.org.uk
0141 644 1841
0141 644 1395

20 Kilsyth: Anderson (F T W)
Allan S. Vint BSc BD MTh 1989 2013
Anderson Manse, 1 Kingston Road, Kilsyth, Glasgow G65 0HR
AVint@churchofscotland.org.uk
01236 822345
07795 483070

21 Kilsyth: Burns and Old (F W)
Robert Johnston BD MSc FSAScot 2017
boldchurch@hotmail.com
The Grange, 17 Glasgow Road, Kilsyth G65 9AE
RJohnston@churchofscotland.org.uk
01236 899901
07810 377582

22 Kirkintilloch: Hillhead (W)
Guardianship of the Presbytery
Bill H Finnie BA PgDipSW CertCRS 2015
(Ordained Local Minister)
hillheadparish@gmail.com
27 Hallside Crescent, Cambuslang, Glasgow G72 7DY
BFinnie@churchofscotland.org.uk
07518 357138

23 Kirkintilloch: St Columba's (H W)
Philip A. Wright BSc MSc PhD BTh 2017
6 Glenwood Road, Lenzie, Glasgow G66 4DS
PWright@churchofscotland.org.uk
0141 578 0016
07427 623393

24 Kirkintilloch: St David's Memorial Park (F H W)
Adam J. Dillon BD ThM 2003 2018
sdmp2@outlook.com
2 Roman Road, Kirkintilloch, Glasgow G66 1EA
ADillon@churchofscotland.org.uk
0141 776 4989
0141 588 3570

25 Kirkintilloch: St Mary's (W)
Vacant
Session Clerk: Gordon Morrison
St Mary's Manse, 60 Union Street, Kirkintilloch, Glasgow G66 1DH
office.stmarys@btconnect.com
0141 775 1166
0141 775 1166

26 Lenzie: Old (H W)
Louise J.E. McClements BD   2008
41 Kirkintilloch Road, Lenzie, Glasgow G66 4LB
LMcClements@churchofscotland.org.uk
0141 573 5006

27 Lenzie: Union (F H W)
Daniel J.M. Carmichael MA BD   1994   2003
office@lenzieunion.org
1 Larch Avenue, Lenzie, Glasgow G66 4HX
DCarmichael@churchofscotland.org.uk
0141 776 1046
0141 776 3831

28 Maxwell Mearns Castle (W)
Scott R.M. Kirkland BD MAR DMin   1996   2011
office@maxwellmearns.org.uk
122 Broomfield Avenue, Newton Mearns, Glasgow G77 5JR
SKirkland@churchofscotland.org.uk
Tel/Fax **0141 639 5169**
0141 560 5603

29 Mearns (F H W)
Joseph A. Kavanagh BD DipPTh MTh   1992   1998
office@mearnskirk.church
11 Belford Grove, Newton Mearns, Glasgow G77 5FB
JKavanagh@churchofscotland.org.uk
0141 639 6555
0141 384 2218

30 Milton of Campsie (F H W)
Julie H.C. Moody BA BD PGCE   2006
16 Cannerton Park, Milton of Campsie, Glasgow G66 8HR
JMoody@churchofscotland.org.uk
01360 310548

31 Netherlee (F H W) linked with Stamperland (F H W)
Scott Blythe BSc BD MBA   1997   2017
office@netherleechurch.org.uk
stamperland@tiscali.org.uk
25 Ormonde Avenue, Netherlee, Glasgow G44 3QY
SBlythe@churchofscotland.org.uk
0141 637 2503
0141 637 4999
0141 533 7147
07706 203786

32 Newton Mearns (F H W)
Stuart J. Crawford BD MTh   2017
office@churchatthecross.org.uk
28 Waterside Avenue, Newton Mearns, Glasgow G77 6TJ
SCrawford@churchofscotland.org.uk
0141 639 7373
07912 534280

33 Rutherglen: Old (F H T W)
Vacant
Session Clerk: Hugh Millar
31 Highburgh Drive, Rutherglen, Glasgow G73 3RR
sessionclerk@rutherglenold.com
0141 534 7477
0141 634 4355

34 Rutherglen: Stonelaw (F T W)
Alistair S. May LLB BD PhD   2002
info@stonelawchurch.org
80 Blairbeth Road, Rutherglen, Glasgow G73 4JA
AMay@churchofscotland.org.uk
0141 647 5113
0141 583 0157

35 Rutherglen: West and Wardlawhill (F W) 1984 2017
Malcolm Cuthbertson BA BD
info@westandwardlawhill.org
12 Albert Drive, Rutherglen, Glasgow G73 3RT
MCuthbertson@churchofscotland.org.uk
0844 736 1470
07864 820612

36 Stamperland See Netherlee

37 Stepps (F H W) 1985 2014
Gordon MacRae BD MTh
112 Jackson Drive, Crowwood Grange, Stepps, Glasgow G33 6GF
GMacRae@churchofscotland.org.uk
0141 779 5742

38 Thornliebank (F H W) 2008 2014
Mike R. Gargrave BD
12 Parkholm Quadrant, Thornliebank, Glasgow G53 7ZH
MGargrave@churchofscotland.org.uk
0141 880 5532

39 Torrance 1991
Nigel L. Barge BSc BD
1 Atholl Avenue, Torrance, Glasgow G64 4JA
NBarge@churchofscotland.org.uk
01360 620970
01360 622379

40 Twechar See Banton

41 Williamwood (F W) 2003 2015
Janet S. Mathieson MA BD
125 Greenwood Road, Clarkston, Glasgow G76 7LL
JMathieson@churchofscotland.org.uk
0141 638 2091
0141 579 9997

42 Glasgow: Baillieston Mure Memorial (F W) linked with Glasgow: Baillieston St Andrew's (F W) 1988 2019
Sandra Black BSc BD
(Interim Minister)
Mure Memorial: **0141 773 1216**
36 Glencairn Drive, Glasgow G41 4PW
SBlack@churchofscotland.org.uk
07703 822057

43 Glasgow: Baillieston St Andrew's See Glasgow: Baillieston Mure Memorial

44 Glasgow: Balshagray Victoria Park (W) 1982 2001
Campbell Mackinnon BSc BD
20 St Kilda Drive, Glasgow G14 9JN
CMackinnon@churchofscotland.org.uk
0141 954 9780

45 Glasgow: Barlanark Greyfriars (W)
Willem J. Bezuidenhout BA BD MHEd MEd   1977   2016
enquiries@barlanark-greyfriars.co.uk
4 Rhindmuir Grove, Baillieston, Glasgow   G69 6NE
WBezuidenhout@churchofscotland.org.uk
0141 771 6477
0141 771 7103

46 Glasgow: Blawarthill (F T W)
G. Melvyn Wood MA BD   1982   2009
46 Earlbank Avenue, Glasgow G14 9HL
GMelvynWood@churchofscotland.org.uk
0141 579 6521

47 Glasgow: Bridgeton St Francis in the East (F H L W)
Howard R. Hudson MA BD   1982   1984
bridgetonstfrancis@gmail.com   **0141 556 2830** (Church House)
10 Albany Drive, Rutherglen, Glasgow G73 3QN
HHudson@churchofscotland.org.uk
0141 554 8045)
0141 587 8667

48 Glasgow: Broomhill Hyndland (F W)
George C. Mackay
BD CertMin CertEd DipPC   1994   2014
info@broomhillhyndlandchurch.org
27 St Kilda Drive, Glasgow G14 9LN
GMackay@churchofscotland.org.uk
0141 334 2540
0141 959 8697
07711 569127

49 Glasgow: Calton Parkhead
Alison E.S. Davidge MA BD   1990   2008
98 Drumover Drive, Glasgow G31 5RP
ADavidge@churchofscotland.org.uk
0141 554 3866
07843 625059

50 Glasgow: Cardonald (F W)
Gavin McFadyen BEng BD   2006   2018
133 Newtyle Road, Paisley PA1 3LB
GMcFadyen@churchofscotland.org.uk
0141 882 6264
0141 576 6818
07960 212106

51 Glasgow: Carmunnock
Vacant
The Manse, 161 Waterside Road, Carmunnock,
Glasgow G76 9AJ
Tel/Fax **0141 644 0655**
0141 644 1578

Session Clerk: Helen Thomson
HBBThomson@aol.com
0141 239 6071

52 Glasgow: Carmyle (W) linked with Glasgow: Kenmuir Mount Vernon (F W)
Murdo MacLean BD CertMin   1997   1999
3 Meryon Road, Glasgow G32 9NW
Murdo.MacLean@churchofscotland.org.uk
0141 778 2625

Roland Hunt BSc PhD CertEd   2016
(Ordained Local Minister)
4 Flora Gardens, Bishopbriggs, Glasgow G64 1DS
RHunt@churchofscotland.org.uk
0141 563 3257

53 Glasgow: Carntyne
Joan Ross BSc BD PhD   1999   2016
163 Lethamhill Road, Glasgow G33 2SQ
JRoss@churchofscotland.org.uk
0141 778 4186
0141 770 9247

No.	Charge / Minister	Ord.	Ind.	Address / Email	Tel
54	**Glasgow: Carnwadric (F L W)** Vacant Mary S. Gargrave (Mrs) DCS	1989	2007	62 Loganswell Road, Thornliebank, Glasgow G46 8AX 12 Parkholm Quadrant, Thornliebank, Glasgow G53 7ZH Mary.Gargrave@churchofscotland.org.uk	**0141 638 5884** 0141 880 5532 07896 866618
55	**Glasgow: Castlemilk (F H W)** Sarah A. Brown (Ms) MA BD ThM DipYW/Theol PDCCE John Paul Cathcart DCS	2012 2000	 2017	156 Old Castle Road, Glasgow G44 5TW Sarah.Brown@churchofscotland.org.uk 9 Glen More, East Kilbride, Glasgow G74 2AP Paul.Cathcart@churchofscotland.org.uk	**0141 634 7113** 0141 637 5451 01355 243970 07708 396074
56	**Glasgow: Cathcart Old (F)** Neil W. Galbraith BD CertMin	1987	1996	21 Courthill Avenue, Cathcart, Glasgow G44 5AA NGalbraith@churchofscotland.org.uk	**0141 637 4168** 0141 633 5248 Tel/Fax
57	**Glasgow: Cathcart Trinity (F H W)** Alasdair MacMillan LLB BD	2015		**office@cathcarttrinity.org.uk** 21 Muirhill Avenue, Glasgow G44 3HP Alasdair.MacMillan@churchofscotland.org.uk	**0141 637 6658** 0141 391 9102
58	**Glasgow: Cathedral (High or St Mungo's) (F W)** Mark E. Johnstone DL MA BD	1993	2019	41 Springfield Road, Bishopbriggs, Glasgow G64 1PL Mark.Johnstone@churchofscotland.org.uk	**0141 552 8198** 07515 285374
59	**Glasgow: Causeway (Tollcross) (F)** Monica Michelin-Salomon BD	1999	2007	228 Hamilton Road, Glasgow G32 9QU MMichelin-Salomon@churchofscotland.org.uk	0141 778 2413
60	**Glasgow: Clincarthill (F H W)** Stuart Love BA MTh	2016		90 Mount Annan Drive, Glasgow G44 4RZ SLove@churchofscotland.org.uk	**0141 632 4206** 0141 632 2985
61	**Glasgow: Colston Milton** Christopher J. Rowe BA BD	2008		118 Birsay Road, Milton, Glasgow G22 7QP CRowe@churchofscotland.org.uk	**0141 772 1922** 0141 564 1138
62	**Glasgow: Colston Wellpark (F H W)** Guardianship of the Presbytery Leslie E.T. Grieve BSc BA (Ordained Local Minister)	2014		23 Hertford Avenue, Kelvindale, Glasgow G12 0LG LGrieve@churchofscotland.org.uk	**0141 772 8672** 07813 255052

63	**Glasgow: Cranhill (F H W)** Muriel B. Pearson (Ms) MA BD PGCE	2004		31 Lethamhill Crescent, Glasgow G33 2SH MPearson@churchofscotland.org.uk	**0141 774 3344** 0141 770 6873 07951 888860
64	**Glasgow: Croftfoot (F H W)** Robert M. Silver BA BD	1995	2011	4 Inchmurrin Gardens, High Burnside, Rutherglen, Glasgow G73 5RU RSilver@churchofscotland.org.uk	**0141 637 3913** 0141 258 7268
65	**Glasgow: Dennistoun New (F H W)** Ian M.S. McInnes BD DipMin	1995	2008	31 Pencaitland Drive, Glasgow G32 8RL IMcInnes@churchofscotland.org.uk	**0141 554 1350** 0141 564 6498
66	**Glasgow: Drumchapel St Andrew's (F W)** John S. Purves LLB BD	1983	1984	6 Firdon Crescent, Old Drumchapel, Glasgow G15 6QQ	**0141 944 3758** 0141 944 4566
67	**Glasgow: Drumchapel St Mark's (F)** Audrey J. Jamieson BD MTh	2004	2007	146 Garscadden Road, Glasgow G15 6PR AJamieson@churchofscotland.org.uk	0141 944 5440
68	**Glasgow: Easterhouse (F W)** Derek W. Hughes BSc BD DipEd	1990	2018	3 Barony Gardens, Springhill, Glasgow G69 6TS DHughes@churchofscotland.org.uk	**0141 771 8810** 07984 019903
69	**Glasgow: Eastwood (F W)** James R. Teasdale BA BD	2009	2016	54 Mansewood Road, Eastwood, Glasgow G43 1TL JTeasdale@churchofscotland.org.uk	0141 571 7648
70	**Glasgow: Gairbraid (F H W)** Donald Michael MacInnes BD	2002	2011	4 Blackhill Gardens, Summerston, Glasgow G23 5NE DMacInnes@churchofscotland.org.uk	0141 946 0604
71	**Glasgow: Gallowgate** Peter L.V. Davidge BD MTh	2003	2009	98 Drumover Drive, Glasgow G31 5RP	07765 096599

72 Glasgow: Garthamlock and Craigend East (F W)
I. Scott McCarthy BD
2010   2018
9 Craigievar Court, Garthamlock, Glasgow G33 5DJ
ISMcCarthy@churchofscotland.org.uk
07725 037394

73 Glasgow: Gorbals
Ian F. Galloway BA BD
1977   1996
6 Stirlingfauld Place, Gorbals, Glasgow G5 9QF
IGalloway@churchofscotland.org.uk
07753 686603

74 Glasgow: Govan and Linthouse (F T W)
Eleanor J. McMahon BEd BD
(Interim Minister)
1994   2017
glpcglasgow@googlemail.com
81 Moorpark Square, Renfrew PA4 8DB
EMcMahon@churchofscotland.org.uk
0141 445 2010
07974 116539

75 Glasgow: Hillington Park (F H W)
Robert Craig BA BD DipRS
2008   2019
81 Raeswood Road, Glasgow G53 7HH
RCraig@churchofscotland.org.uk
0141 463 3203

76 Glasgow: Ibrox (F H W)
Tara P. Granados (Ms) BA MDiv
2018
ibroxparishchurch@gmail.com
59 Langhaul Road, Glasgow G53 7SE
TGranados@churchofscotland.org.uk
07380   830030
07475 128128

77 Glasgow: John Ross Memorial Church for Deaf People (W)
Richard C. Durno DSW CQSW
1989   1998
31 Springfield Road, Bishopbriggs,
Glasgow G64 1PJ
RDurno@churchofscotland.org.uk
Voice/Text 0141 420 1391; Fax 0141 420 3778
0141 772 1052   Voice/Text/Fax
07748 607721   Voice/Text/Voicemail

78 Glasgow: Jordanhill (F W)
Bruce H Sinclair BA BD
2009   2015
12 Priorwood Gardens, Academy Park, Glasgow G13 1GD
BSinclair@churchofscotland.org.uk
0141 959 2496
0141 959 1310

79 Glasgow: Kelvinbridge (F W)
Gordon Kirkwood BSc BD MTh MPhil PGCE
1987   2003
Flat 2/2, 94 Hyndland Road, Glasgow G12 9PZ
GKirkwood@churchofscotland.org.uk
0141 339 1750
0141 334 5352

80 Glasgow: Kelvinside Hillhead (F W)
Vacant
Roger D. Sturrock (Prof.) BD MD FCRP
(Ordained Local Minister)
2014
36 Thomson Drive, Bearsden, Glasgow G61 3PA
RSturrock@churchofscotland.org.uk
0141 334 2788
0141 942 7412

81 Glasgow: Kenmuir Mount Vernon See Glasgow: Carmyle

82 Glasgow: King's Park (F H W)
Vacant
office@kingspark.church.co.uk
1101 Aikenhead Road, Glasgow G44 5SL
0141 636 8688

83 Glasgow: Kinning Park (W)
Margaret H. Johnston BD   1988   2000
168 Arbroath Avenue, Cardonald, Glasgow G52 3HH
MHJohnston@churchofscotland.org.uk
0141 810 3782

84 Glasgow: Knightswood St Margaret's (H W)
Alexander M. Fraser BD DipMin   1985   2009
26 Airthrey Avenue, Glasgow G14 9LJ
AFraser@churchofscotland.org.uk
0141 959 7075

85 Glasgow: Langside (F T W)
David N. McLachlan BD   1985   2004
langsidechurch@gmail.com
36 Madison Avenue, Glasgow G44 5AQ
DMcLachlan@churchofscotland.org.uk
0141 632 7520
0141 637 0797

86 Glasgow: Maryhill (F H W)
Stuart C. Matthews BD MA   2006   2010
251 Milngavie Road, Bearsden, Glasgow G61 3DQ
SMatthews@churchofscotland.org.uk
0141 946 3512
0141 942 0804

James Hamilton DCS   1997   2000
6 Beckfield Gate, Glasgow G33 1SW
James.Hamilton@churchofscotland.org.uk
0141 558 3195
07584 137314

87 Glasgow: Merrylea (F W)
Vacant
Session Clerk: Ralph P. Boettche
4 Pilmuir Avenue, Glasgow G44 3HX
merryleasessionclerk@outlook.com
0141 637 2009
07806 453724

88 Glasgow: Newlands South (H T W)
R. Stuart M. Fulton BA BD   1991   2017
secretary@newlandschurch.org.uk
24 Monreith Road, Glasgow G43 2NY
SFulton@churchofscotland.org.uk
0141 632 3055
0141 632 2588

89 Glasgow: Partick South (F H W)
James Andrew McIntyre BD   2010
3 Branklyn Crescent, Glasgow G13 1GJ
Andy.McIntyre@churchofscotland.org.uk
0141 339 8816
0141 959 3732

90 Glasgow: Partick Trinity (F H T W)
Timothy D. Sinclair MA MDiv   2018
enquiry@particktrinity.org.uk
99 Balshagray Avenue, Glasgow G11 7EQ
TSinclair@churchofscotland.org.uk
0141 563 6424

91	**Glasgow: Pollokshaws (F)** Roy J.M. Henderson MA BD DipMin	1987		33 Mannering Road, Glasgow G41 3SW RHenderson@churchofscotland.org.uk	**0141 649 1879** 0141 632 8768
92	**Glasgow: Pollokshields (F H T W)** David R. Black MA BD	1986	1997	36 Glencairn Drive, Glasgow G41 4PW DBlack@churchofscotland.org.uk	0141 423 4000
93	**Glasgow: Possilpark** Rosalind (Linda) E. Pollock (Miss) BD ThM ThM	2001	2014	108 Erradale Street, Lambhill, Glasgow G22 6PT RPollock@churchofscotland.org.uk	**0141 336 8028** 0141 384 5793
94	**Glasgow: Queen's Park Govanhill (F W)** Vacant Session Clerk: Jonathan Gibb			**officeQPG@btinternet.com** 32 Queen Mary Avenue, Crosshill, Glasgow G42 8DT jelgibb@aol.com	**0141 423 3654** 0141 638 5768 07522 997748
95	**Glasgow: Robroyston (F W)** Jonathan A. Keefe BSc BD	2009		**info@robroystonchurch.org.uk** 7 Beckfield Drive, Glasgow G33 1SR JKeefe@churchofscotland.org.uk	**0141 558 8414** 0141 558 2952
96	**Glasgow: Ruchazie (F)** Guardianship of the Presbytery Session Clerk: Margaret Dott				**0141 774 2759** 0141 572 0451
97	**Glasgow: Ruchill Kelvinside (W)** Mark Lowey BD DipTh	2012	2013	**ruchill.kelvinside@gmail.com** 41 Mitre Road, Glasgow G14 9LE MLowey@churchofscotland.org.uk	**0141 533 2731** 0141 959 6718
98	**Glasgow: St Andrew and St Nicholas (F W)** Lyn M. Peden (Mrs) BD	2010	2015	80 Tweedsmuir Road, Glasgow G52 2RX LPeden@churchofscotland.org.uk	**0141 882 3601** 0141 883 9873
99	**Glasgow: St Andrew's East (F W)** Vacant Session Clerk: Elizabeth McIvor			43 Broompark Drive, Glasgow G31 2JB emcivor@talktalk.net	**0141 554 1485** 0141 556 4838

100 Glasgow: St Andrew's West (F W)   **Tel: 0141 332 4293; Fax: 0141 332 8482**
Vacant   info@rsschurch.org.uk   0141 353 0349
Session Clerk: Kenneth Rogers   101 Hill Street, Glasgow G3 6TY   0141 954 3854
k.rogers@robertson.co.uk
New charge formed by the union of Glasgow: Anderston Kelvingrove and Glasgow: Renfield St Stephen's

101 Glasgow: St Christopher's Priesthill and Nitshill (W) 1987 1996   **0141 881 6541**
Douglas M. Nicol BD CA   36 Springkell Drive, Glasgow G41 4EZ   0141 427 7877
DNicol@churchofscotland.org.uk

102 Glasgow: St Columba (F GE W)   **0141 221 3305**
Vacant
Session Clerk: Duncan Mitchell   dpm@addapt.org.uk   0141 339 9679

103 Glasgow: St David's Knightswood (F) 1988 1999   **0141 954 1081**
Graham M. Thain LLB BD   60 Southbrae Drive, Glasgow G13 1QD   0141 959 2904
GThain@churchofscotland.org.uk

104 Glasgow: St Enoch's Hogganfield (F H W) 1985   **Tel 0141 770 5694; Fax 08702 840084**
Elaine H. MacRae (Mrs) BD   church@st-enoch.org.uk   0141 779 5742
112 Jackson Drive, Crowwood Grange, Stepps, Glasgow G33 6GF   07834 269487
EMacRae@churchofscotland.org.uk

105 Glasgow: St George's Tron (F W) 1989 2013   **0141 229 5746**
Alastair S. Duncan MA BD   info@sgt.church   07968 852083
(Transition Minister)   29 Hertford Avenue, Glasgow G12 0LG
ADuncan@churchofscotland.org.uk

106 Glasgow: St James' (Pollok)   **0141 882 4984**
Vacant   30 Ralston Avenue, Glasgow G52 3NA
Session Clerk: David T. Arbuckle   davidtarbuckle@outlook.com   07469 878303

107 Glasgow: St John's Renfield (W) 1985 2018   **0141 334 0782**
D. Stewart Gillan BSc MDiv PhD   secretary@sjrchurch.plus.com   0141 339 4637
26 Leicester Avenue, Glasgow G12 0LU
SGillan@churchofscotland.org.uk

108 Glasgow: St Paul's (F T W) 2010 2014   **0141 770 8559**
Daniel Manastireanu BA MTh   38 Lochview Drive, Glasgow G33 1QF   0141 770 1561
DManastireanu@churchofscotland.org.uk

109 Glasgow: St Rollox (F W)
Jane M. Howitt MA BD   1996   2016
(Transition Minister)
inbox@strollox.co.uk
42 Melville Gardens, Bishopbriggs, Glasgow   G64 3DE
JHowitt@churchofscotland.org.uk
0141 558 1809
0141 581 0050

110 Glasgow: Sandyford Henderson Memorial (F H L T W)
Vacant
Session Clerk: Noel Peacock (Prof.)
enquiries@sandyfordhenderson.net
66 Woodend Drive, Glasgow   G13 1TG
noel.peacock@glasgow.ac.uk
0141 226 3696
0141 954 9013
0141 334 1611

111 Glasgow: Sandyhills (W)
Norman A. Afrin BA   2018
60 Wester Road, Glasgow   G32 9JJ
NAfrin@churchofscotland.org.uk
0141 778 3415
07846 368895

112 Glasgow: Scotstoun (W)
Richard Cameron BD DipMin   2000
15 Northland Drive, Glasgow   G14 9BE
RCameron@churchofscotland.org.uk
0141 959 4637

113 Glasgow: Shawlands Trinity (F)
Valerie J. Duff (Miss) DMin   1993   2014
29 St Ronan's Drive, Glasgow   G41 3SQ
VDuff@churchofscotland.org.uk
0141 258 6782

114 Glasgow: Sherbrooke Mosspark (F H W)
Thomas L. Pollock   1982   2003
BA BD MTh FSAScot JP
114 Springkell Avenue, Glasgow   G41 4EW
TPollock@churchofscotland.org.uk
0141 427 1968
0141 427 2094

115 Glasgow: Shettleston New (F W)
W. Louis T. Reddick MA BD   2017
211 Sandyhills Road, Glasgow   G32 9NB
LReddick@churchofscotland.org.uk
0141 778 4769
0141 230 7365
07843 083548

116 Glasgow: Springburn (F H T W)
Brian M. Casey MA BD   2014
springburnparishchurch@btconnect.com
c/o Springburn Parish Church, 180 Springburn Way,
Glasgow G21 1TU
BCasey@churchofscotland.org.uk
0141 557 2345
07703 166772

117 Glasgow: Temple Anniesland (F W)
Fiona M.E. Gardner (Mrs) BD MA MLitt   1997   2011
info@tachurch.org.uk
76 Victoria Park Drive North, Glasgow   G14 9PJ
FGardner@churchofscotland.org.uk
0141 530 9745
0141 959 5647

Ruth Forsythe (Mrs) MCS   2017   2018
(Ordained Local Minister)
Flat 1/2, 41 Bellwood Street, Glasgow   G41 3EX
RForsythe@churchofscotland.org.uk
07824 641212

118 Glasgow: Toryglen (F H T W)
Vacant
Session Clerk: Ina Cole (Mrs)

toryglenparish@gmail.com — **07587 207981**
toryglensession@gmail.com — 0141 562 4807

119 Glasgow: Trinity Possil and Henry Drummond (W)   1990   1995
Richard G. Buckley BD MTh DMin

tphdcofs@yahoo.com — 0141 339 2870
50 Highfield Drive, Glasgow G12 0HL
RBuckley@churchofscotland.org.uk

120 Glasgow: Tron St Mary's (F)   2015
Rhona E. Graham BA BD

30 Louden Hill Road, Robroyston, Glasgow G33 1GA — **0141 558 1011**
RGraham@churchofscotland.org.uk — 0141 389 8816

121 Glasgow: Wallacewell (New Charge Development) (F T W)   1984   2011
Daniel L. Frank BA MDiv DMin

info@wallacewell.org — **0141 558 4466**
8 Streamfield Gate, Glasgow G33 1SJ — 0141 585 0283
DFrank@churchofscotland.org.uk

122 Glasgow: Wellington (F H T W)
Vacant
Roger D. Sturrock (Prof.) BD MD FCRP   2014
(Ordained Local Minister)

wellingtonchurch@btinternet.com — **0141 339 0454**
31 Hughenden Gardens, Glasgow G12 9YH — 0141 334 2343
36 Thomson Drive, Bearsden, Glasgow G61 3PA — 0141 942 7412
RSturrock@churchofscotland.org.uk

123 Glasgow: Whiteinch (F W)   1993   2000
Alan McWilliam BD MTh

65 Victoria Park Drive South, Glasgow G14 9NX — **0141 959 9317**
AMcWilliam@churchofscotland.org.uk — 0141 576 9020

124 Glasgow: Yoker (F T)   2005
Karen E. Hendry BSc BD

15 Coldingham Avenue, Glasgow G14 0PX — 0141 952 3620
KHendry@churchofscotland.org.uk

In other appointments

Bell, John L. MA BD FRSCM DUniv   1978   1988   Iona Community
Cowie, George S. BSc BD   1991   2017   Presbytery Clerk: Glasgow
148 West Princes Street, Glasgow G4 9DA — 0141 387 7628
260 Bath Street, Glasgow G2 4JP — 0141 332 6066
GCowie@churchofscotland.org.uk

Denniston, David W. BD DipMin   1981   2016   Interim Minister
c/o Campsie Parish Church, 130 Main Street, Lennoxtown,
Glasgow G66 7DA — 07903 926727
DDenniston@churchofscotland.org.uk

Forrest, Martin R. BA MA BD	Prison Chaplain	1988	2012	4/1, 7 Blochairn Place, Glasgow G21 2EB martinrforrest@gmail.com	0141 552 1132
Forsyth, Sandy O. LLB BD DipLP MTh PhD	University of Edinburgh, Lecturer, New College	2009	2018	48 Kerr Street, Kirkintilloch, Glasgow G66 1JZ AForsyth@churchofscotland.org.uk	0141 777 8194 07739 639037
Foster-Fulton, Sally BA BD	Head of Christian Aid Scotland	1999	2016	24 Monreith Road, Glasgow G43 2NY sallyfulton01@gmail.com	07850 937226
Gardner, Peter M. MA BD	Pioneer Minister, Glasgow Arts Community	1988	2016	Flat 3/2, 10 Haggswood Avenue, Glasgow G41 4RE PGardner@churchofscotland.org.uk	07743 539654
Gay, Douglas C. MA BD PhD	University of Glasgow: Trinity College	1998	2005	39 Athole Gardens, Glasgow G12 9BQ douggay@mac.com	0141 330 2073 07971 321452
Hood, David P. BD CertMin DipIOB(Scot)	Chaplain: Marie Curie Hospice	1997	2019	Flat 1/2, 32 Giffnock Park Avenue, Giffnock G46 6AY DHood@churchofscotland.org.uk	0141 636 5819
Johnstone, H. Martin J. MA BD MTh PhD	Secretary: Church and Society Council	1989	2015	3/1, 952 Pollokshaws Road, Glasgow G41 2ET MJohnstone@churchofscotland.org.uk	0141 429 7281
Love, Joanna (Ms) BSc DCS	Iona Community: Wild Goose Resource Group	1992	2009	92 Everard Drive, Glasgow G21 1XQ (Office) jo@wildgoose.scot	
MacDonald, Anne (Miss) BA DCS	Healthcare Chaplain	1980	2002	Chaplaincy Office, Glasgow Royal Infirmary G4 0SF	0141 211 4661
McDougall, Hilary N. (Mrs) MA PGCE BD	Congregational Facilitator: Presbytery of Glasgow	2004	2013	16 Central Court, Central Avenue, Cambuslang G72 8DJ hmcdougall@churchofscotland.org.uk	0141 641 8574 07539 321832
MacLeod, Iain A.	Ordained Local Minister	2012		6 Hallydown Drive, Glasgow G13 1UF IMacLeod@churchofscotland.org.uk	07795 014889
McPake, John L. BA BD PhD	Ecumenical Officer, Church of Scotland	1987	2017	121 George Street, Edinburgh EH2 4YN JMcPake@churchofscotland.org.uk	0131 240 2208
MacQuarrie, Stuart JP BD BSc MBA	Chaplain: University of Glasgow	1984	2001	The Chaplaincy Centre, University of Glasgow, Glasgow G12 8QQ	0141 330 5419
Maxwell, David	Ordained Local Minister	2014		248 Old Castle Road, Glasgow G44 5EZ DMaxwell@churchofscotland.org.uk	0141 569 6379 07561 427802
Walker, Linda	Auxiliary Minister, Presbytery	2008	2013	18 Valeview Terrace, Glasgow G42 9LA LWalker@churchofscotland.org.uk	0141 649 1340

Demitted

Alexander, Eric J. MA BD	(Glasgow: St George's Tron)	1958	1997	77 Norwood Park, Bearsden, Glasgow G61 2RZ	0141 942 4404
Alston, William G.	(Glasgow: North Kelvinside)	1961	2009	Flat 0/2, 5 Knightswood Court, Glasgow G13 2XN williamalston@hotmail.com	0141 959 3113
Beaton, Margaret S. (Miss) DCS	(Deacon)	1989	2015	64 Gardenside Grove, Carmyle, Glasgow G32 8EZ margaretbeaton54@hotmail.com	0141 646 2297 07796 642382
Birch, James PgDip FRSA FIOC	(Auxiliary Minister)	2001	2007	1 Kirkhill Grove, Cambuslang, Glasgow G72 8EH	0141 583 1722
Black, William B. MA BD	(Stornoway: High)	1970	2011	33 Tankerland Road, Glasgow G44 4EN revwillieblack@gmail.com	0141 637 4717
Blount, A. Sheila (Mrs) BD BA	(Cupar: St John's and Dairsie United)	1978	2010	28 Alcaig Road, Mosspark, Glasgow G52 1NH asheilablount@gmail.com	0141 419 0746
Blount, Graham K. LLB BD PhD	(Presbytery Clerk: Glasgow)	1976	2017	28 Alcaig Road, Mosspark, Glasgow G52 1NH Graham.Blount@churchofscotland.org.uk	0141 419 0746

Name	Ordained/Inducted	Role	Address	Phone
Brice, Dennis G. BSc BD	1981 1996	(Taiwan)	8 Parkwood Close, Broxbourne, Herts EN10 7PF / dbrice1@comcast.net	01702 555333
Campbell, A. Iain MA DipEd	1961 1997	(Busby)	430 Clarkston Road, Glasgow G44 3QF / iaingillian@talktalk.net	0141 637 7460
Campbell, John MA BA BSc	1973 2009	(Caldwell)	96 Boghead Road, Lenzie, Glasgow G66 4EN / johncampbell.lenzie@gmail.com	0141 776 0874
Carruth, Patricia A. (Mrs) BD	1998 2012	(Coatbridge: Blairhill Dundyvan)	38 Springhill Farm Road, Baillieston, Glasgow G69 6GW	0141 771 3758
Cartlidge, Graham R.G. MA BD STM	1977 2015	(Glasgow: Eastwood)	5 Briar Grove, Newlands, Glasgow G43 2TG	0141 637 3228
Cherry, Alastair J. BA BD FPLD	1982 2009	(Glasgow: Penilee St Andrew's)	8 Coruisk Drive, Clarkston, Glasgow G76 7NG / ajcherry133@gmail.com	0141 571 6052
Clark, Douglas W. LTh	1993 2015	(Lenzie: Old)	2 Poplar Drive, Lenzie, Glasgow G66 4DN / douglaswclark@hotmail.com	0141 776 1298
Cowie, Marian (Mrs) MA BD MTh	1990 2012	(Aberdeen: Midstocket)	120e Southbrae Drive, Glasgow G12 1TZ / mcowieou@aol.com	07740 174969
Cunningham, Alexander MA BD	1961 2002	(Presbytery Clerk: Glasgow)	18 Lady Jane Gate, Bothwell, Glasgow G71 8BW	01698 811051
Cunningham, James S.A. MA BD BLitt PhD	1992 2000	(Glasgow: Barlanark Greyfriars)	'Kirkland', 5 Inveresk Place, Coatbridge ML5 2DA	01236 421541
Drummond, John W. MA BD	1971 2011	(Rutherglen: West and Wardlawhill)	25 Kingsburn Drive, Rutherglen, Glasgow G73 2AN	0141 571 6002
Duff, T. Malcolm F. MA BD	1985 2009	(Glasgow: Queen's Park)	54 Hawkhead Road, Paisley PA1 3NB	0141 570 0614 / 07846 926584
Dunsmore, Barry W. MA BD	1982 2019	(Aberdeen: St Machar's Cathedral)	25H Hughenden Gardens, Hyndland, Glasgow G12 9XZ / barrydunsmore@gmail.com	07951 588912
Dutch, Morris M. BD BA Dip BTI	1998 2013	(Costa del Sol)	41 Baronald Drive, Glasgow G12 OHN / mmdutch@yahoo.co.uk	0141 357 2286
Easton, David J.C. MA BD	1965 2005	(Burnside Blairbeth)	6 Peveril Court, Burnside, Glasgow G73 4RE / deaston@btinternet.com	0141 634 9775
Farrington, Alexandra LTh	2003 2015	(Campsie)	'Glenburn', High Banton, Kilsyth G65 0RA / revsfarrington@aol.co.uk	01236 824516
Ferguson, James B. LTh	1972 2002	(Lenzie: Union)	3 Bridgeway Place, Kirkintilloch, Glasgow G66 3HW	0141 588 5868
Fleming, Alexander F. MA BD	1966 1995	(Strathblane)	11 Bankwood Drive, Kilsyth, Glasgow G65 0GZ	01236 821461
Haley, Derek BD DPS	1960 1999	(Chaplain: Gartnavel Royal)	9 Kinnaird Crescent, Bearsden, Glasgow G61 2BN	0141 942 9281
Hope, Evelyn P. (Miss) BA BD	1990 1998	(Wishaw: Thornlie)	Flat 0/1, 48 Moss Side Road, Glasgow G41 3UA	0141 649 1522
Hughes, Helen (Miss) DCS	1977 2008	(Deacon)	2/2, 43 Burnbank Terrace, Glasgow G20 6UQ / helhug35@gmail.com	0141 333 9459 / 07752 604817
Hunter, Alastair G. MSc BD	1976 2010	(University of Glasgow)	13 Kilmardinny Crescent, Bearsden, Glasgow G61 3NP	0141 931 5862
Johnston, Robert W.M. MA BD STM	1964 1999	(Glasgow: Temple Anniesland)	Flat 1/2, 17 Overdale Street, Glasgow G42 9PZ	0141 649 2714
Kelly, Ewan R. MB ChB PhD	1994 2019	(Associate, Glasgow: Queen's Park Govanhill)		
Lang, I. Pat (Miss) BSc	1996 2003	(Dunoon: The High Kirk)	37 Crawford Drive, Glasgow G15 6TW	0141 944 2240
Lloyd, John M. BD CertMin	1984 2009	(Glasgow: Croftfoot)	17 Acacia Way, Cambuslang, Glasgow G72 7ZY	07879 812816
Luman, David W. MA BD DUniv DLitt DD	1970 2009	(Presbytery Clerk: Glasgow)	30 Mill Road, Banton, Glasgow G65 0RD	01236 824110

Name	Year	Year	Role / Charge	Address	Telephone
MacDonald, Kenneth MA BA	2001	2006	(Auxiliary Minister)	5 Henderland Road, Bearsden, Glasgow G61 1AH	0141 943 1103
MacFadyen, Anne M. (Mrs) BSc BD FSAScot	1995	2003	(Auxiliary Minister)	295 Mearns Road, Glasgow G77 5LT	0141 639 3605
Mackenzie, Gordon R. BSc-Agr BD	1977	2014	(Chapelhall)	16 Crowhill Road, Bishopbriggs, Glasgow G64 1QY rev.g.mackenzie@btopenworld.com	0141 772 6052
MacKinnon, Charles M. BD	1989	2009	(Kilsyth: Anderson)	36 Hilton Terrace, Bishopbriggs, Glasgow G64 3HB cm.ccmackinnon@gmail.com	0141 772 3811
McLachlan, Eric BD MTh	1978	2005	(Glasgow: Cardonald)	16 Kinpurnie Road, Paisley PA1 3HH eric.janis@btinternet.com	0141 810 5789
McLachlan, T. Alastair BSc	1972	2009	(Craignish with Kilbrandon and Kilchattan with Kilninver and Kilmelford)	9 Alder Road, Milton of Campsie, Glasgow G66 8HH talastair@btinternet.com	01360 319861
McLaren, D. Muir MA BD MTh PhD	1971	2001	(Glasgow: Mosspark)	House 44, 145 Shawhill Road, Glasgow G43 1SX muir44@yahoo.co.uk	07931 155779
McLaughlin, Cathie H. (Mrs)	2014	2018	(Ordained Local Minister)	8 Lamlash Place, Glasgow G33 3XH	0141 774 2483
Macleod, Donald BD LRAM DRSAM	1987	2008	(Blairgowrie)	9 Millersneuk Avenue, Lenzie G66 5HJ donmac2@sky.com	0141 776 6235
McLellan, Margaret DCS	1986	2018	(Deacon)	18 Broom Road East, Newton Mearns, Glasgow G77 5SD margaretdmclellan@outlook.com	0141 639 6853
Miller, Elsie M. (Miss) DCS	1974	2001	(Deacon)	30 Swinton Avenue, Rowansbank, Baillieston, Glasgow G69 6JR	0141 771 0857
Miller, John D. BA BD DD	1971	2007	(Glasgow: Castlemilk East)	98 Kirkcaldy Road, Glasgow G41 4LD rev.john.miller@btinternet.com	0141 423 0221
Moffat, Thomas BSc BD	1976	2008	(Culross and Torryburn)	Flat 8/1, 8 Cranston Street, Glasgow G3 8GG tom@gallus.org.uk	0141 248 1886
Nelson, Thomas BSc BD	1992	2002	(Netherlee)	11a Crosshill Drive, Rutherglen, Glasgow G73 3QU	0141 534 7834
Ninian, Esther J. (Miss) MA BD	1993	2015	(Newton Mearns)	21 St Ronan's Drive, Burnside, Rutherglen G73 3SR estherninian5914@btinternet.com	0141 647 9720
Pacitti, Stephen A. MA	1963	2003	(Black Mount with Culter with Libberton and Quothquan)	157 Nithsdale Road, Glasgow G41 5RD	0141 423 5792
Pearson, Wilma (Mrs) BD	2004	2018	(Associate, Glasgow: Cathcart Trinity)	16 Newlands Road, Glasgow G43 2JR WPearson@churchofscotland.org.uk	0141 632 2491
Raeburn, Alan C. MA BD	1971	2010	(Glasgow: Battlefield East)	3 Orchard Gardens, Strathaven ML10 6UN acraeburn@hotmail.com	01357 522924
Ramsay, W.G.	1967	1999	(Glasgow: Springburn)	53 Kelvinvale, Kirkintilloch, Glasgow G66 1RD billram@btopenworld.com	0141 776 2915
Reid, Iain M.A. BD CQSW	1990	2017	(Paisley Glenburn)	16 Walker Court, Glasgow G16 6QP ireid@churchofscotland.org.uk	0141 577 1200
Ross, Donald M. MA	1953	1993	(Industrial Mission Organiser)	14 Cartsbridge Road, Busby, Glasgow G76 8DH	0141 644 2220
Shackleton, William	1960	1996	(Greenock: Wellpark West)	3 Tynwald Avenue, Burnside, Glasgow G73 4RN	0141 569 9407
Smith, G. Stewart MA BD STM	1966	2006	(Glasgow: King's Park)	33 Brent Road, Stewartfield, East Kilbride, Glasgow G74 4RA stewartandmary@googlemail.com	01355 226718 Tel/Fax
Spencer, John MA BD	1962	2001	(Dumfries: Lincluden with Holywood)	10 Kinkell Gardens, Kirkintilloch, Glasgow G66 2HJ	0141 777 8935
Stewart, Diane E. BD	1988	2006	(Milton of Campsie)	4 Miller Gardens, Bishopbriggs, Glasgow G64 1FG destewart@givemail.co.uk	0141 762 1358

Stewart, Norma D. (Miss) MA MEd BD MTh	1977	2000	(Glasgow: Strathbungo Queen's Park)	127 Nether Auldhouse Road, Glasgow G43 2YS	0141 637 6956
Thomson, Andrew BA	1976	2007	(Airdrie: Broomknoll)	3 Laurel Wynd, Drumsagard Village, Cambuslang, Glasgow G72 7BH AThomson@churchofscotland.org.uk	0141 641 2936 07772 502774
Tuton, Robert M. MA	1957	1995	(Glasgow: Shettleston Old)	6 Holmwood Gardens, Uddingston, Glasgow G71 7BH	01698 321108
Walton, Ainslie MA MEd	1954	1995	(University of Aberdeen)	Flat 26, 7 Eastwood Crescent, Thornliebank, Glasgow G46 8NS revainslie@aol.com	0141 638 1548
White, C. Peter BVMS BD MRCVS	1974	2011	(Glasgow: Sandyford Henderson Memorial)	2 Hawthorn Place, Torrance, Glasgow G64 4EA revcpw@gmail.com	01360 622680
White, David M. BA BD DMin	1988	2016	(Kirkintilloch St Columba's)	9 Lapwing Avenue, Lenzie, Glasgow G66 3DJ drdavidmwhite@btinternet.com	0141 578 4357
Whiteford, John D. MA BD	1989	2016	(Glasgow: Newlands South)	42 Maxwell Drive, East Kilbride, Glasgow G74 4HJ JWhiteford@churchofscotland.org.uk	07809 290806
Whyte, James BD	1981	2011	(Fairlie)	32 Torburn Avenue, Giffnock, Glasgow G46 7RB jameswhyte89@btinternet.com	0141 620 3043
Wilson, Phyllis M. (Mrs) DipCom DipRE	1985	2006	(Motherwell: South Dalziel)	Glasgow thomas.wilson38@btinternet.com	
Younger, Adah (Mrs) BD	1978	2004	(Glasgow: Dennistoun Central)	7 Gartocher Terrace, Glasgow G32 0HE	0141 774 6475

GLASGOW ADDRESSES

Congregation	Sub-name	Address
Banton		Kelvinhead Road, Banton
Bishopbriggs	Kenmure	Viewfield Road, Bishopbriggs
	Springfield Cambridge	The Leys, off Springfield Road Mearns Road, Newton Mearns
Broom		Mearns Road, Newton Mearns
Burnside Blairbeth		Church Avenue, Burnside Kirknggs Avenue, Blairbeth
Busby		Church Road, Busby
Cadder		Cadder Road, Bishopbriggs
Cambuslang		Arnot Way
Flemington Hallside		Hutchinson Place
Campsie		Main Street, Lennoxtown
Chryston		Main Street, Chryston 20 Blackwoods Crescent, Moodiesburn
Eaglesham		Montgomery Street, Eaglesham
Fernhill and Cathkin		Neilvaig Drive
Gartcosh		113 Lochend Road, Gartcosh

Congregation	Sub-name	Address
Giffnock	Orchardhill	Church Road
	South	Eastwood Toll
	The Park	Ravenscliffe Drive
Glenboig		Main Street, Glenboig
Greenbank		Eaglesham Road, Clarkston
Kilsyth	Anderson	Kingston Road, Kilsyth
	Burns and Old	Church Street, Kilsyth
Kirkintilloch	Hillhead	Newdyke Road, Kirkintilloch
	St Columba's	Waterside Road nr Auld Aisle Road
	St David's Mem Pk	Alexandra Street
	St Mary's	Cowgate
Lenzie	Old	Kirkintilloch Road x Garngaber Ave
	Union	65 Kirkintilloch Road

Congregation	Sub-name	Address
Maxwell		Waterfoot Road
Mearns Castle		Mearns Road, Newton Mearns
Mearns		Locheil Drive, Milton of Campsie
Milton of Campsie		
Netherlee		Ormonde Drive x Ormonde Avenue
Newton Mearns		Ayr Road, Newton Mearns
Rutherglen	Old	Main Street at Queen Street
	Stonelaw	Stonelaw Road x Dryburgh Avenue
	West and Wardlawhill	3 Western Avenue
Stamperland		Stamperland Gardens, Clarkston
Stepps		Whitehill Avenue
Thornliebank		61 Spiersbridge Road
Torrance		School Road, Torrance
Twechar		Main Street, Twechar
Williamwood		4 Vardar Avenue, Clarkston

Glasgow

Baillieston	
Mure Memorial	Maxwell Drive, Garrowhill
St Andrew's	Bredisholm Road
Balshagray Victoria Pk	218–230 Broomhill Drive
Barlanark Greyfriars	Edinburgh Rd x Hallhill Rd (365)
Blawarthill	Millbrix Avenue
Bridgeton St Francis in the East	26 Queen Mary Street
Broomhill Hyndland	64–66 Randolph Rd (x Marlborough Ave)
Calton Parkhead	122 Helenvale Street
Cardonald	2155 Paisley Road West
Carmunnock	Kirk Road, Carmunnock
Carmyle	155 Carmyle Avenue
Carntyne	358 Carntynehall Road
Carnwadric	556 Boydstone Road, Thornliebank
Castlemilk	1 Dougrie Road
Cathcart Old	119 Carmunnock Road
Cathcart Trinity	90 Clarkston Road
Cathedral	Cathedral Square, 2 Castle Street
Causeway, Tollcross	1134 Tollcross Road
Clincarthill	1216 Cathcart Road
Colston Milton	Egilsay Crescent
Colston Wellpark	1378 Springburn Road
Cranhill	109 Bellrock St (at Bellrock Cr)
Croftfoot	Croftpark Ave x Crofthill Road
Dennistoun New	9 Armadale Street
Drumchapel	
St Andrew's	153 Garscadden Road
St Mark's	281 Kinfauns Drive
Easterhouse	Boyndie Street
Eastwood	Mansewood Road
Gairbraid	1517 Maryhill Road
Gallowgate	Calton Parkhead halls, 122 Helenvale Street
Garthamlock and Craigend East	46 Porchester Street
Gorbals	1 Errol Gardens
Govan and Linthouse	Govan Cross
Hillington Park	24 Berryknowes Road
Ibrox	Carillon Road x Clifford Street
John Ross Memorial	100 Norfolk Street
Jordanhill	28 Woodend Drive (x Munro Road)
Kelvinbridge	Belmont Street at Belmont Bridge
Kelvinside Hillhead	Observatory Road
Kenmuir Mount Vernon	2405 London Road, Mount Vernon
King's Park	242 Castlemilk Road
Kinning Park	Eaglesham Place
Knightswood St Margaret's	2000 Great Western Road
Langside	167–169 Ledard Road (x Lochleven Road)
Maryhill	1990 Maryhill Road
Merrylea	78 Merrylee Road
Newlands South	Riverside Road x Langside Drive
Partick	
South	259 Dumbarton Road
Trinity	20 Lawrence Street x Elie Street
Pollokshaws	223 Shawbridge Street
Pollokshields	Albert Drive x Shields Road
Possilpark	124 Saracen Street
Queen's Park Govanhill	170 Queen's Drive
Robroyston	34 Saughs Road
Ruchazie	4 Elibank Street (x Milncroft Road)
Ruchill Kelvinside	Shakespeare Street nr Maryhill Rd
St Andrew and St Nicholas	224 Hartlaw Crescent
St Andrew's East	681 Alexandra Parade
St Andrew's West	260 Bath Street
St Christopher's Priesthill and Nitshill	
Priesthill building	100 Priesthill Rd (x Muirshiel Cr)
Nitshill building	36 Dove Street
St Columba	300 St Vincent Street
St David's Knightswood	66 Boreland Drive (nr Lincoln Avenue)
St Enoch's Hogganfield	860 Cumbernauld Road
St George's Tron	163 Buchanan Street
St James' (Pollok)	Lyoncross Road x Byrebush Road
St John's Renfield	22 Beaconsfield Road
St Paul's	30 Langdale St (x Greenrig St)
St Rollox	70 Fountainwell Road
Sandyford Henderson Memorial	Kelvinhaugh Street at Argyle Street
Sandyhills	28 Baillieston Rd nr Sandyhills Rd
Scotstoun	Earlbank Ave x Ormiston Ave
Shawlands Trinity	Shawlands Cross (1114 Pollokshaws Road)
Sherbrooke Mosspark	Nithsdale Rd x Sherbrooke Avenue
Shettleston New	679 Old Shettleston Road
Springburn	180 Springburn Way
Temple Anniesland	869 Crow Road
Torglen	Glenmore Ave nr Prospecthill Road
Trinity Possil and Henry Drummond	2 Crowhill Street (x Broadholm Street)
Tron St Mary's	128 Red Road
Wallacewell	57 Northgate Rd., Balornock
Wellington	University Ave x Southpark Ave
Whiteinch	1a Northinch Court
Yoker	10 Hawick Street

(17) HAMILTON (F W)

Meets at Motherwell: Dalziel St Andrew's Parish Church on the first Tuesday of February, March, May, September, October, November and December, and on the third Tuesday of June.

Presbytery Office:	Rex House, 103 Bothwell Road, Hamilton ML3 0DW hamilton@churchofscotland.org.uk	01698 285672
Clerk: REV. GORDON A. McCRACKEN BD CertMin DMin	c/o The Presbytery Office	
Depute Clerk: Vacant		
Presbytery Treasurer: MR DAVID J. WATT BAcc CA CPFA	c/o The Presbytery Office david.j.watt@btinternet.com	01698 285672

1 **Airdrie: Cairnlea (F H W) linked with Calderbank (F T)**
Peter H. Donald MA PhD BD   1991   2018
31 Victoria Place, Airdrie ML6 9BU
PDonald@churchofscotland.org.uk
Cairnlea: 01236 762101
01236 753159

2 **Airdrie: Clarkston (F W)**
Hanna I. Rankine BA BD   2018
66 Wellhall Road, Hamilton ML3 9BY
HRankine@churchofscotland.org.uk
01236 756862

3 **Airdrie: High (W) linked with Caldercruix and Longriggend (H)**
Ian R.W. McDonald BSc BD PhD   2007
17 Etive Drive, Airdrie ML6 9QL
IMcDonald@churchofscotland.org.uk
High: 01236 779620
01236 760023

4 **Airdrie: Jackson (W)**
Kay Gilchrist (Miss) BD   1996   2008
48 Dunrobin Road, Airdrie ML6 8LR
KGilchrist@churchofscotland.org.uk
01236 760154

5 **Airdrie: New Monkland (F H W) linked with Greengairs (F W)**
William Jackson BD CertMin   1994   2015
3 Dykehead Crescent, Airdrie ML6 6PU
WJackson@churchofscotland.org.uk
01236 761723

6 **Airdrie: St Columba's**
Margaret F. Currie BEd BD   1980   1987
52 Kennedy Drive, Airdrie ML6 9AW
MCurrie@churchofscotland.org.uk
01236 763173

7 **Airdrie: The New Wellwynd (W)**
Robert A. Hamilton BA BD   1995   2001
20 Arthur Avenue, Airdrie ML6 9EZ
RHamilton@churchofscotland.org.uk
01236 748646
01236 763022

8   Bargeddie (H W)
Vacant
The Manse, Manse Road, Bargeddie, Baillieston, Glasgow G69 6UB   0141 771 1322

9   Bellshill: Central (F T W)
Kevin M. de Beer BTh   1995   2016
32 Adamson Street, Bellshill ML4 1DT   01698 841176
KdeBeer@churchofscotland.org.uk   07555 265609

10   Bellshill: West (F H W)
Calum Stark LLB BD   2011   2015
16 Croftpark Street, Bellshill ML4 1EY   **01698 747581**
CStark@churchofscotland.org.uk   01698 842877

11   Blantyre: Livingstone Memorial (F W) linked with Blantyre St Andrew's (F)   info@livingstonechurch.org.uk
Murdo C. Macdonald MA BD   2002   2017
332 Glasgow Road, Blantyre, Glasgow G72 9LQ   01698 769699
Murdo.Macdonald@churchofscotland.org.uk

12   Blantyre: Old (F H T W)
Sarah L. Ross (Mrs) BD MTh PGDip   2004   2013
The Manse, Craigmuir Road, High Blantyre, Glasgow G72 9UA   01698 769046
SRoss@churchofscotland.org.uk

13   Blantyre: St Andrew's See Blantyre: Livingstone Memorial

14   Bothwell (F H W)
Vacant   **bothwellparishchurch@yahoo.com**
Manse Avenue, Bothwell, Glasgow G71 8PQ   Tel   **01698 854903**
01698 853189
Fax   01698 854903
01698 854998
Session Clerk: David Craig
craigdavid241@gmail.com

15   Calderbank See Airdrie: Cairnlea

16   Caldercruix and Longriggend See Airdrie: High

17   Chapelhall (F H W) linked with Kirk o' Shotts (F H W)
Vacant
Session Clerk, Chapelhall: Elizabeth Millar (Mrs)
The Manse, Russell Street, Chapelhall, Airdrie ML6 8SG   01236 763439
millarelizabeth@btconnect.com   01698 870205

18   Cleland (F H) linked with Wishaw: St Mark's (F)
Graham Austin BD   1997   2008
3 Laburnum Crescent, Wishaw ML2 7EH   01698 384596
GAustin@churchofscotland.org.uk

19   Coatbridge: Blairhill Dundyvan (H W) linked with Coatbridge: Middle (W)   Blairhill Dundyvan: 01236 435198
Vacant
1 Nelson Terrace, East Kilbride, Glasgow G74 2EY   01355 520093
Session Clerk, Blairhill Dundyvan: Myra Fraser   01236 421728
myrafraser@hotmail.co.uk

20 Coatbridge: Calder (F H W) linked with Coatbridge: Old Monkland (F W)
Vacant
26 Bute Street, Coatbridge ML5 4HF
01236 421516

21 Coatbridge: Middle See Coatbridge: Blairhill Dundyvan

22 Coatbridge: New St Andrew's (W)
Fiona M. Nicolson BA BD   1996   2005
77 Eglinton Street, Coatbridge ML5 3JF
FNicolson@churchofscotland.org.uk
01236 437271

23 Coatbridge: Old Monkland See Coatbridge: Calder

24 Coatbridge: Townhead (F H)
Ecilo Selemani LTh MTh   1993   2004
Crinan Crescent, Coatbridge ML5 2LH
ESelemani@churchofscotland.org.uk
01236 702914

25 Dalserf (F H)
Vacant
Session Clerk: Joan Pollok
Manse Brae, Dalserf, Larkhall ML9 3BN
joan.pollok@btinternet.com
01698 882195
07728 337212

26 East Kilbride: Claremont (F H W)
Gordon R. Palmer MA BD STM   1986   2003
office@claremontparishchurch.co.uk
17 Deveron Road, East Kilbride, Glasgow G74 2HR
GPalmer@churchofscotland.org.uk
01355 238088
01355 248526

27 East Kilbride: Greenhills
John Brewster MA BD DipEd   1988
21 Turnberry Place, East Kilbride, Glasgow G75 8TB
JBrewster@churchofscotland.org.uk
01355 221746
01355 242564

28 East Kilbride: Moncreiff (F H W)
Vacant
Session Clerk: William McDougall MBE
theoffice@moncreiffparishchurch.co.uk
16 Almond Drive, East Kilbride, Glasgow G74 2HX
mcdougall204@btinternet.com
01355 223328
01355 238639
01355 238075
07715 369757

29 East Kilbride: Mossneuk (F)
Vacant
Jim Murphy   2014   2017
(Ordained Local Minister)
30 Eden Grove, Mossneuk, East Kilbride, Glasgow G75 8XU
10 Hillview Crescent, Bellshill ML4 1NX
JMurphy@churchofscotland.org.uk
01355 260954
01355 234196
01698 740189

30 East Kilbride: Old (H W)
Anne S. Paton BA BD
2001
ekopc.office@btconnect.com
40 Maxwell Drive, East Kilbride, Glasgow G74 4HJ
APaton@churchofscotland.org.uk
01355 279004
01355 220732

31 East Kilbride: South (F H W)
Terry Ann Taylor BA MTh
2005   2017
7 Clamps Wood, St Leonard's, East Kilbride, Glasgow G74 2HB
TTaylor@churchofscotland.org.uk
01355 902758

32 East Kilbride: Stewartfield (New Charge Development) (W)
Douglas W. Wallace MA BD
1981   2001
8 Thistle Place, Stewartfield, East Kilbride, Glasgow G74 4RH
DWallace@churchofscotland.org.uk
01355 260879

33 East Kilbride: West (F H W)
Mahboob Masih BA MDiv MTh
1999   2008
4 East Milton Grove, East Kilbride, Glasgow G75 8FN
MMasih@churchofscotland.org.uk
01355 224469

34 East Kilbride: Westwood (H W)
Kevin Mackenzie BD DPS
1989   1996
16 Inglewood Crescent, East Kilbride, Glasgow G75 8QD
Kevin.MacKenzie@churchofscotland.org.uk
01355 245657
01355 223992

35 Greengairs See Airdrie: New Monkland

36 Hamilton: Cadzow (F H W)
W. John Carswell BS MDiv DPT
1996   2009
contact@cadzowchurch.org.uk
3 Carlisle Road, Hamilton ML3 7BZ
JCarswell@churchofscotland.org.uk
01698 428695
01698 426682

37 Hamilton: Gilmour and Whitehill (H W) linked with Hamilton: West (H W)
Vacant
Session Clerk, Gilmour: Ann Paul
Session Clerk, West: Ian Hindle
annepaul.gandw@gmail.com
ianmarilyn.hindle@googlemail.com
West: **01698 284670**
01698 284670
01698 421697
01698 429080

38 Hamilton: Hillhouse (F W)
Christopher A. Rankine MA MTh PgDE
2016
66 Wellhall Road, Hamilton ML3 9BY
CRankine@churchofscotland.org.uk
01698 327579

39 Hamilton: Old (F H W)
I. Ross Blackman BSc MBA BD
2015
office@hamiltonold.co.uk
1 Chateau Grove, Hamilton ML3 7DS
RBlackman@churchofscotland.org.uk
01698 281905
01698 640185

40 **Hamilton: St John's (H W)**
Joanne C. Hood (Miss) MA BD   2003   2012
9 Shearer Avenue, Ferniegair, Hamilton ML3 7FX
JHood@churchofscotland.org.uk
01698 **283492**
01698 425002

41 **Hamilton: South (F H) linked with Quarter (F)** South: 01698 **281014**
Vacant   01698 424511
Session Clerk, South: Joanne Kennedy   07828 504176
Session Clerk, Quarter: Louise Ross   01698 424458
The Manse, Limekilnburn Road, Quarter, Hamilton ML3 7XA
hamiltonsouthchurch@outlook.com
louise.ross7@btinternet.com

42 **Hamilton: Trinity**
S. Lindsay A. Turnbull BSc BD   2014
69 Buchan Street, Hamilton ML3 8JY
Lindsay.Turnbull@churchofscotland.org.uk
01698 **284254**
01698 284919

43 **Hamilton: West** See Hamilton: Gilmour and Whitehill

44 **Holytown (W) linked with New Stevenston: Wrangholm Kirk (W)**
Caryl A.E. Kyle (Mrs) BD DipEd   2008
The Manse, 260 Edinburgh Road, Holytown, Motherwell ML1 5RU
CKyle@churchofscotland.org.uk
01698 832622

45 **Kirk o' Shotts (H)** See Chapelhall

46 **Larkhall: Chalmers (F H)**
Vacant
Session Clerk: Christine Buck
Quarry Road, Larkhall ML9 1HH
chalmerscos@gmail.com
01698 882238
07518 510664

47 **Larkhall: St Machan's (F H W)**
Alastair McKillop BD DipMin   1995   2004
2 Orchard Gate, Larkhall ML9 1HG
AMcKillop@churchofscotland.org.uk
01698 321976

48 **Larkhall: Trinity**
Vacant
Session Clerk: Wilma Gilmour (Miss)
13 Machan Avenue, Larkhall ML9 2HE
gilmourgilmour@btinternet.com
01698 881401
01698 883002

49 **Motherwell: Crosshill (F H W) linked with Motherwell: St Margaret's (F W)**
Vacant
15 Orchard Street, Motherwell ML1 3JE
01698 263410

50 Motherwell: Dalziel St Andrew's (F H T W)
Vacant
Session Clerk: Helen Lawson
4 Pollock Street, Motherwell ML1 1LP
office@dlsa.org.uk
01698 264097
01698 263414
01698 264297

51 Motherwell: North (F W) linked with Wishaw: Craigneuk and Belhaven (H)
Derek H.N. Pope BD   1987   1995
35 Birrens Road, Motherwell ML1 3NS
DPope@churchofscotland.org.uk
01698 266716

52 Motherwell: St Margaret's See Motherwell: Crosshill

53 Motherwell: St Mary's (H T W)
Bryce Calder MA BD   1995   2017
office@stmarysmotherwell.org.uk
19 Orchard Street, Motherwell ML1 3JE
BCalder@churchofscotland.org.uk
01698 268554
07986 144834

54 Motherwell: South (F H T)
Alan W. Gibson BA BD   2001   2016
62 Manse Road, Motherwell ML1 2PT
Alan.Gibson@churchofscotland.org.uk
01698 239279

55 Newarthill and Carfin (F W)
Elaine W. McKinnon MA BD   1988   2014
Church Street, Newarthill, Motherwell ML1 5HS
EMcKinnon@churchofscotland.org.uk
01698 296850

56 Newmains: Bonkle (F H W) linked with Newmains: Coltness Memorial (F H W)
Graham Raeburn MTh   2004
5 Kirkgate, Newmains, Wishaw ML2 9BT
GRaeburn@churchofscotland.org.uk
01698 344001
01698 383858

57 Newmains: Coltness Memorial See Newmains: Bonkle

58 New Stevenston: Wrangholm Kirk See Holytown

59 Overtown (F W)
Lorna I. MacDougall MA DipGC BD   2003   2017
The Manse, 146 Main Street, Overtown, Wishaw ML2 0QP
LMacDougall@churchofscotland.org.uk
01698 358727
01698 352090

60 Quarter See Hamilton: South

61 Shotts: Calderhead Erskine
Vacant
Session Clerk: Liam T. Haggart SSC
The Manse, 9 Kirk Road, Shotts ML7 5ET
a2lth@hotmail.com
01501 823304
07896 557687

62 Stonehouse: St Ninian's (F H T W)
Stewart J. Cutler BA Msc DipHE   2017
4 Hamilton Way, Stonehouse, Larkhall ML9 3PU
revstewartcutler@gmail.com
01698 791508

Stonehouse: St Ninian's is a Local Ecumenical Partnership with the United Reformed Church

63 Strathaven: Avendale Old and Drumclog (F H W)   1983 2010
Alan B. Telfer BA BD
avendale_office@btconnect.com
4 Fortrose Gardens, Strathaven ML10 6SH
ATelfer@churchofscotland.org.uk
01357 529748
01357 523031

64 Strathaven: Trinity (F H W)   1991
Shaw J. Paterson BSc BD MSc
15 Lethame Road, Strathaven ML10 6AD
SPaterson@churchofscotland.org.uk
Tel 01357 520019
Fax 01357 529316

65 Uddingston: Burnhead (F H W)   2010
Les N. Brunger BD
90 Laburnum Road, Uddingston, Glasgow G71 5DB
LBrunger@churchofscotland.org.uk
01698 813716

66 Uddingston: Old (F H W)   2011
Fiona L.J. McKibbin (Mrs) MA BD
1 Belmont Avenue, Uddingston, Glasgow G71 7AX
FMcKibbin@churchofscotland.org.uk
01698 814015
01698 814757

67 Uddingston: Viewpark (F H W)   1993 2001
Michael G. Lyall BD
14 Holmbrae Road, Uddingston, Glasgow G71 6AP
MLyall@churchofscotland.org.uk
01698 810478
01698 813113

68 Wishaw: Cambusnethan North (F H W)   1989
Mhorag Macdonald (Ms) MA BD
350 Kirk Road, Wishaw ML2 8LH
Mhorag.Macdonald@churchofscotland.org.uk
01698 381305

69 Wishaw: Cambusnethan Old and Morningside (W)
Vacant
Session Clerk: Graeme Vincent
22 Coronation Street, Wishaw ML2 8LF
gvincent@theiet.org
01698 384235
01555 752166

70 Wishaw: Craigneuk and Belhaven See Motherwell North

71 Wishaw: Old (F H)
Vacant
Session Clerk: Thomas W. Donaldson   130 Glen Road, Wishaw ML2 7NP   **01698 376080**
tomdonaldson@talktalk.net   01698 375134
01698 357605

72 Wishaw: St Mark's See Cleland

73 Wishaw: South Wishaw (F H W)
Terence C. Moran BD CertMin   1995   2015   **southwishaw@tiscali.co.uk**   **01698 375306**
3 Walter Street, Wishaw ML2 8LQ   01698 767459
TMoran@churchofscotland.org.uk

In other appointments

Buck, Maxine	2007	2015	Auxiliary Minister, Presbytery	Brownlee House, Mauldslie Road, Carluke ML8 5HW MBuck@churchofscotland.org.uk	01555 759063
Gilroy, Lorraine (Mrs) DCS	1988		Deacon	68 Clement Drive, Airdrie ML16 7FB lorraine.gilroy@sky.com	07923 540602
McCracken, Gordon A. BD CertMin DMin	1988	2015	Presbytery Clerk: Hamilton	1 Kenilworth Road, Lanark ML11 7BL	07918 600720
Pandian, Ali R. BA BD PGCertHC	2017		Healthcare Chaplain: University Hospital Wishaw	50 Netherton Street, Wishaw ML2 0DP APandian@churchofscotland.org.uk	01698 366779 07966 368344

Demitted

Barrie, Arthur P. LTh	1973	2007	(Hamilton: Cadzow)	30 Airbles Crescent, Motherwell ML1 3AR elizabethbarrie@ymail.com	01698 261147
Baxendale, Georgina M. DipEd BD DMin	1981	2014	(Motherwell: South)	32 Meadowhead Road, Plains, Airdrie ML6 7HG georgiebaxendale@btinternet.com	01236 842752
Buchanan, Neil BD	1991	2019	(East Kilbride: Moncrieff)	40 Links View, Port Seton, Prestonpans EH32 0EZ NBuchanan@churchofscotland.org.uk	01875 814632
Colvin, Sharon E.F. (Mrs) BD LRAM LTCL	1985	2008	(Airdrie: Jackson)	25 Balblair Road, Airdrie ML6 6GQ dibleycol@hotmail.com	01236 590796
Cook, J. Stanley BD Dip PSS	1974	2001	(Hamilton: West)	Mansend, 137A Old Manse Road, Netherton, Wishaw ML2 0EW stancook@blueyonder.co.uk	01698 299600
Donaldson, George M. MA BD	1984	2015	(Caldercruix and Longriggend)	4 Toul Gardens, Motherwell ML1 2FE g.donaldson505@btinternet.com	01698 239477
Doyle, David W. MA BD	1977	2015	(Motherwell: St Mary's)	76 Kethers Street, Motherwell ML1 3HN	01698 263472

Name			Charge	Address / Contact	Tel
Fuller, Agnes A. (Mrs) BD	1987	2014	(Bellshill: West)	14 Croftpark Street, Bellshill ML14 1EY revamoore2@tiscali.co.uk	01698 748244
Gibson, James M. TD LTh LRAM	1978	2019	(Bothwell)	22 Kirklands Crescent, Bothwell, Glasgow G71 8HU JGibson@churchofscotland.org.uk	01698 854907
Gordon, Alasdair B. BD LLB EdD	1970	1980	(Aberdeen: Summerhill)	Flat 1, 13 Auchingramont Road, Hamilton ML3 6JP alasdairbgordon@hotmail.com	01698 200561 07768 897843
Grier, James BD	1991	2005	(Coatbridge: Middle)	14 Love Drive, Bellshill ML4 1BY	01698 742545
Jessamine, Alistair L. MA BD	1979	2011	(Dunfermline: Abbey)	11 Gallowhill Farm Cottages, Strathaven ML10 6BZ	01357 520934
Jones, Robert BSc BD	1990	2017	(Rosskeen)	3 Grantown Avenue, Airdrie ML6 8HH rob2jones@btinternet.com	07761 782714
Kent, Robert M. MA BD	1973	2011	(Hamilton: St John's)	48 Fyne Crescent, Larkhall ML9 2UX robertmkent@talktalk.net	01698 769244
McDonald, John A. MA BD	1978	1997	(Cumbernauld: Condorrat)	17 Thomson Drive, Bellshill ML4 3ND	
McKee, Norman B. BD	1987	2010	(Uddingston: Old)	148 Station Road, Blantyre, Glasgow G72 9BW normanmckee946@btinternet.com	01698 827358
MacKenzie, Ian C. MA BD	1970	2011	(Interim Minister)	21 Wilson Street, Motherwell ML1 1NP iancmac@blueyonder.co.uk	01698 301230
Munton, James G. BA	1969	2002	(Coatbridge: Old Monkland)	2 Moorcroft Drive, Airdrie ML6 8ES revjgm1@gmail.com	01236 754848
Murdoch, Iain C. MA LLB DipEd BD	1995	2017	(Wishaw: Cambusnethan Old and Morningside)	2 Pegasus Avenue, Carluke ML8 5TN iaincmurdoch@btopenworld.com	01555 773891
Ogilvie, Colin BA DCS	1998	2015	(Deacon)	21 Neilsland Drive, Motherwell ML1 3DZ colinogilvie2@gmail.com	01698 321836 07837 287804
Price, Peter O. CBE QHC BA FPhS	1960	1996	(Blantyre: Old)	22 Old Bothwell Road, Bothwell, Glasgow G71 8AW peteroprice@sky.com	01698 854032
Salmond, James S. BA BD MTh ThD	1979	2003	(Holytown)	165 Torbothie Road, Shotts ML7 5NE	01698 817582
Stevenson, John LTh	1998	2006	(Cambuslang: St Andrew's)	20 Knowehead Gardens, Uddingston, Glasgow G71 7PY therev20@sky.com	
Stewart, William T. BD	1980	2018	(Glassford with Strathaven East)	8 Cot Castle Grove, Stonehouse ML9 3RQ	01698 793979
Tait, Agnes (Mrs) DCS	1995		(Deacon)	10 Carnoustie Crescent, Greenhills, East Kilbride, Glasgow G75 8TE	01355 243095
Thomson, John M.A. TD JP BD ThM	1978	2014	(Hamilton: Old)	8 Skylands Place, Hamilton ML3 8SB jt@john1949.plus.com	01698 422511
Waddell, Elizabeth A. (Mrs) BD	1999	2014	(Hamilton: West)	114 Branchalfield, Wishaw ML2 8QD elizabethwaddell@tiscali.co.uk	01698 382909
Wilson, James H. LTh	1970	1996	(Cleland)	21 Austine Drive, Hamilton ML3 7YE wilsonjh@blueyonder.co.uk	01698 457042
Wyllie, Hugh R. MA DD FCIBS	1962	2000	(Hamilton: Old)	18 Chantinghall Road, Hamilton ML3 8NP	01698 420002
Zambonini, James LIADip	1997	2015	(Auxiliary Minister)	100 Old Manse Road, Netherton, Wishaw ML2 0EP	01698 350889

HAMILTON ADDRESSES

Airdrie
Cairnlea	89 Graham Street
Clarkston	Forrest Street
High	North Bridge Street
Jackson	Glen Road
New Monkland	Glenmavis
St Columba's	Thrashbush Road
The New Wellwynd	Wellwynd

Coatbridge
Blairhill Dundyvan	Blairhill Street
Calder	Calder Street
Middle	Bank Street
New St Andrew's	Church Street
Old Monkland	Woodside Street
Townhead	Crinan Crescent

East Kilbride
Claremont	High Common Road, St Leonard's
Greenhills	Greenhills Centre

Moncreiff	Calderwood Road
Mossneuk	Eden Drive
Old	Montgomery Street
South	Baird Hill, Murray
Stewartfield	Stewartfield Community Centre
West	Kittoch Street
Westwood	Belmont Drive, Westwood

Hamilton
Cadzow	Woodside Walk
Gilmour and Whitehill	Glasgow Road, Burnbank
Hillhouse	Clerkwell Road
Old	Leechlee Road
St John's	Duke Street
South	Strathaven Road
Trinity	Neilsland Square off Neilsland Road
West	Burnbank Road

Motherwell
Crosshill	Windmillhill Street x
	Airbles Street

Dalziel St Andrew's	
North	Merry Street and Muir Street
St Margaret's	Chesters Crescent
St Mary's	Shields Road
South	Avon Street
	Gavin Street

Uddingston
Burnhead	Laburnum Road
Old	Old Glasgow Road
Viewpark	Old Edinburgh Road

Wishaw
Cambusnethan North	Kirk Road
Old	Kirk Road
Craigneuk and Belhaven	Craigneuk Street
Old	Main Street
St Mark's	Coltness Road
South Wishaw	East Academy Street

(18) DUMBARTON (W)

Meets at Dumbarton, in Riverside Church Halls, on the first Tuesday of September, October, November, December 2019 and February, March, May 2020, the date of the June meeting to be arranged.

Clerk:	**VERY REV. JOHN C. CHRISTIE** **BSc BD MSB CBiol MRSB**	**10 Cumberland Avenue, Helensburgh G84 8QG** **dumbarton@churchofscotland.org.uk**	**01436 674078** **07711 336392**

Alexandria (W)
Vacant
Session Clerk: Linda Cust (Miss)   32 Ledrish Avenue, Balloch, Alexandria G83 8JB   01389 751933
lindaccust@btinternet.com   01389 754502

Arrochar (F W) linked with Luss (F W)

Louis C. Bezuidenhout BA MA BD DD (Transition Minister)	1978	2018	3 Havoc Road, Dumbarton G82 4JW LBezuidenhout@churchofscotland.org.uk	01389 763317

Baldernock (H) linked with Milngavie: St Paul's (F H W)
Fergus C. Buchanan MA BD MTh   1982   1988
stpauls@btconnect.com
8 Buchanan Street, Milngavie, Glasgow   G62 8DD   **0141 956 4405**
Fergus.Buchanan@churchofscotland.org.uk   0141 956 1043

David M. White BA BD DMin   1988   2018
(Associate Minister)
9 Lapwing Avenue, Lenzie, Glasgow   G66 3DJ
drdavidmwhite@btinternet.com   0141 578 4357

Bearsden: Baljaffray (F H W)
Ian K. McEwan BSc PhD BD FRSE   2008
5 Fintry Gardens, Bearsden, Glasgow   G61 4RJ   **0141 942 5304**
IMcEwan@churchofscotland.org.uk   0141 942 0366

Bearsden: Cross (F H W)
Graeme R. Wilson MCIBS BD ThM DMin   2006   2013
secretary@bearsdencross.org
61 Drymen Road, Bearsden, Glasgow   G61 2SU   **0141 942 0507**
GWilson@churchofscotland.org.uk   0141 942 0507

Bearsden: Killermont (F H W)
Alan J. Hamilton LLB BD PhD   2003
8 Clathic Avenue, Bearsden, Glasgow   G61 2HF
AHamilton@churchofscotland.org.uk   0141 942 0021

Bearsden: New Kilpatrick (F H W)
Roderick G. Hamilton MA BD   1992   2011
mail@nkchurch.org.uk
51 Manse Road, Bearsden, Glasgow   G61 3PN   **0141 942 2827**
Roddy.Hamilton@churchofscotland.org.uk   0141 942 0035

Bearsden: Westerton Fairlie Memorial (H W)
Christine M. Goldie LLB BD MTh DMin   1984   2008
westertonchurch@talktalk.net
3 Canniesburn Road, Bearsden, Glasgow   G61 1PW   **0141 942 6960**
CGoldie@churchofscotland.org.uk   0141 942 2672

Bonhill (H W) linked with Renton: Trinity (H)
Barbara A. O'Donnell BD PGSE   2007   2016
bonhillchurchoffice@gmail.com
Ashbank, 258 Main Street, Alexandria   G83 0NU   **Bonhill: 01389 756516**
BODonnell@churchofscotland.org.uk   01389 752356
07889 251912

Cardross (F H W)
Margaret McArthur BD DipMin   1995   2015
16 Bainfield Road, Cardross   G82 5JQ   **01389 841322**
MMcArthur@churchofscotland.org.uk   01389 849329
07799 556367

Clydebank: Faifley (F W)
Gregor McIntyre BSc BD   1991
Kirklea, Cochno Road, Hardgate, Clydebank   G81 6PT
Gregor.McIntyre@churchofscotland.org.uk   01389 876836

Clydebank: Kilbowie St Andrew's linked (F) with Clydebank: Radnor Park (H)
Vacant
Session Clerk, Kilbowie St Andrew's: Derek W. Smith   11 Tiree Gardens, Old Kilpatrick, Glasgow G60 5AT   01389 875599
ann.smith@live.co.uk   0141 952 8425

Session Clerk, Radnor Park: Mabel Baillie (Mrs)   r.baillie1@ntlworld.com   07703 185423
0141 579 5957

Clydebank: Radnor Park See Clydebank: Kilbowie St Andrew's

Clydebank: Waterfront (F W) linked with Dalmuir: Barclay (F W)   **Dalmuir Barclay: 0141 941 3988**
Ruth H.B. Morrison MA BD PhD   2009   2014   16 Parkhall Road, Dalmuir, Clydebank G81 3RJ   0141 941 3317
RMorrison@churchofscotland.org.uk

Craigrownie (F W) linked with Garelochhead (F W) linked with Rosneath: St Modan's (F H W)   **Garelochhead: 01436 810589**
Christine M. Murdoch BD   1999   2015   The Manse, Argyll Road, Kilcreggan, Helensburgh G84 0JW   01436 842274
CMurdoch@churchofscotland.org.uk   07973 331890

Ann J. Cameron (Mrs) CertCS DCE TEFL   2005   2017   Water's Edge, Ferry Road, Rosneath, Helensburgh G84 0RS   01436 831800
(Auxiliary Minister)   ACameron@churchofscotland.org.uk

Dalmuir: Barclay See Clydebank: Waterfront

Dumbarton: Riverside (F H W) linked with Dumbarton: St Andrew's (H W) linked with Dumbarton: West Kirk (F H W)   **Riverside: 01389 742551**
office@dumbartonriverside.org.uk
administration@standrewsdumbarton.co.uk
C. Ian W. Johnson MA BD   1997   2014   18 Castle Road, Dumbarton G82 1JF   01389 726685
CJohnson@churchofscotland.org.uk

Dumbarton: St Andrew's See Dumbarton: Riverside
Dumbarton: West Kirk See Dumbarton: Riverside

Duntocher: Trinity (F H L T W)   info@duntochertrinitychurch.co.uk
Vacant
Session Clerk: Colin G. Dow   The Manse, Roman Road, Duntocher, Clydebank G81 6BT   01389 380038
colin.g.dow@ntlworld.com

Garelochhead See Craigrownie

Helensburgh (F W) linked with Rhu and Shandon (F W)

| | | | | Helensburgh: 01436 **676880** |
| | | | | Rhu and Shandon: 01436 **820605** |

hello@helensburghcos.org

David T. Young BA BD MTh	2007	2015	35 East Argyle Street, Helensburgh G84 8UP — DYoung@churchofscotland.org.uk	01436 673365
Tina Kemp MA (Auxiliary Minister)	2005	2017	12 Oaktree Gardens, Dumbarton G82 1EU — TKemp@churchofscotland.org.uk	07508 628133 / 01389 730477

Jamestown (H)
Vacant
Session Clerk: Robert M. Kinloch — 26 Kessog's Gardens, Balloch, Alexandria G83 8QJ — rkinloch@blueyonder.co.uk — 01389 756447 / 07760 276505

Kilmaronock Gartocharn
Guardianship of the Presbytery
Session Clerk: Mark Smith — kilgartoch@gmail.com — 01389 830785 / 07796 938318

Luss See Arrochar

Milngavie: Cairns (H W) — 1987 / 1994
office@cairnschurch.org.uk
Andrew Frater BA BD MTh — 4 Cairns Drive, Milngavie, Glasgow G62 8AJ — AFrater@churchofscotland.org.uk — 0141 956 4868 / 0141 956 1717

Milngavie: St Luke's (W) — 1990 / 1997
Ramsay B. Shields BA BD — 70 Hunter Road, Milngavie, Glasgow G62 7BY — RShields@churchofscotland.org.uk — Tel 0141 956 4226 / 0141 577 9171 — Fax 0141 577 9181

Milngavie: St Paul's See Baldernock

Old Kilpatrick Bowling — 2015 / 2018
Scott McCrum BD — The Manse, Old Kilpatrick, Glasgow G60 5JQ — SMcCrum@churchofscotland.org.uk — 08005 668242

Renton: Trinity See Bonhill
Rhu and Shandon See Helensburgh
Rosneath: St Modan's See Craigrownie

In other appointments

Dalton, Mark BD DipMin RN	2002	Chaplain: Royal Navy	Royal Naval Air Station Culdrose, Helston, Cornwall TR12 7RH mark.dalton242@mod.gov.uk	
McCutcheon, John BA BD(Min)	2014	Ordained Local Minister	Flat 2/6 Parkview, Milton Brae, Milton, Dumbarton G82 2TT JMcCutcheon@churchofscotland.org.uk	01389 739034
Nutter, Margaret A.E.	2014 2019	Ordained Local Minister	Kilmorich, 14 Balloch Road, Balloch, Alexandria G83 8SR Presbytery-wide MNutter@churchofscotland.org.uk	01389 754505

Demitted

Booth, Frederick M. LTh	1970 2005	(Helensburgh: St Columba)	Achnashie Coach House, Clynder, Helensburgh G84 0QD boothef@btinternet.com	01436 831858
Campbell, Donald BD	1998 2016	(Houston and Killellan)	15 Garshake Road, Dumbarton G82 3LH	01389 739353
Christie, John C. BSc BD CBiol MRSB	1990 2012	(Interim Minister)	10 Cumberland Avenue, Helensburgh G84 8QG JChristie@churchofscotland.org.uk	01436 674078 07711 336392
Clark, David W. MA BD	1975 2014	(Helensburgh: St Andrew's Kirk with Rhu and Shandon)	3 Ritchie Avenue, Cardross, Dumbarton G82 5LL clarkdw@talktalk.net	01389 849319
Hamilton, David G. MA BD	1971 2004	(Braes of Rannoch with Foss and Rannoch)	79 Finlay Rise, Milngavie, Glasgow G62 6QL davidhamilton40@googlemail.com	0141 956 4202
Harris, John W.F. MA	1967 2012	(Bearsden: Cross)	68 Mitre Road, Glasgow G14 9LL jwfh@sky.com	0141 321 1061
Houston, Elizabeth W. MA BD DipEd	1985 2018	(Alexandria)	Croftengea, 25 Honeysuckle Lane, Jamestown, Alexandria G83 8PL Cleric2@hotmail.com	01389 721165
Lees, Andrew P. BD	1984 2017	(Baldernock)	58 Lindores Drive, Stepps G33 6PD andrew.lees@yahoo.co.uk	0141 389 5840
McIntyre, J. Ainslie MA BD	1963 1984	(University of Glasgow)	60 Bonnaughton Road, Bearsden, Glasgow G61 4DB jamcintyre@hotmail.com	0141 942 5143 07826 013266
Miller, Ian H. BA BD	1975 2012	(Bonhill)	Derand, Queen Street, Alexandria G83 0AS revianmiller@btinternet.com	01389 753039
Moore, Norma MA BD	1995 2017	(Jamestown)	25 Miller Street, Dumbarton G82 2JA norma-moore@sky.com	
Ramage, Alastair E. MA BA ADB CertEd	1996 2016	(Auxiliary Minister)	16 Claremont Gardens, Milngavie, Glasgow G62 6PG sueandalastairramage@btinternet.com	0141 956 2897
Robertson, Ishbel A. R. MA BD	2013 2018	(Ordained Local Minister)	Oakdene, 81 Bonhill Road, Dumbarton G82 2DU	01389 763436
Steven, Harold A.M. MStJ LTh FSA Scot	1970 2001	(Baldernock)	9 Cairnhill Road, Bearsden, Glasgow G61 1AT harold.allison.steven@gmail.com	0141 942 1598
Taylor, Jane C. BD DipMin	1990 2013	(Insch-Leslie-Premnay-Oyne)	Timbers, Argyll Road, Kilcreggan G84 0JW jane.c.taylor@btinternet.com	01436 842336
Wilson, John BD	1985 2010	(Glasgow: Temple Anniesland)	4 Carron Crescent, Bearsden, Glasgow G61 1HJ revjwilson@btinternet.com	0141 931 5609
Wright, Malcolm LTh	1970 2003	(Craigrownie with Rosneath: St Modan's)	30 Clairinsh, Drumkinnon Gate, Balloch, Alexandria G83 8SE malcolmcatherine@msn.com	01389 720338
Yule, Margaret J.B. BD	1992 2019	(Clydebank: Kilbowie St Andrew's with Radnor Park)	4 Overtoun Road, Clydebank G81 3QY	

DUMBARTON ADDRESSES

Bearsden
Baljaffray — Grampian Way
Cross — Drymen Road
Killermont — Rannoch Drive
New Kilpatrick — Manse Road
Westerton — Crarae Avenue

Clydebank
Faifley — Faifley Road
Kilbowie St Andrew's — Kilbowie Road
Radnor Park — Radnor Street
Waterfront — Town Centre

Dumbarton
Riverside — High Street
St Andrew's — Aitkenbar Circle
West Kirk — West Bridgend

Helensburgh — Colquhoun Square

Milngavie
Cairns — Buchanan Street
St Luke's — Kirk Street
St Paul's — Strathblane Road

(19) ARGYLL (F W)

Meets in the Village Hall, Tarbert, Loch Fyne, Argyll on the first Tuesday or Wednesday of March, June, September and December. For details, contact the Presbytery Clerk.

Clerk: MR W. STEWART SHAW DL BSC
59 Barone Road, Rothesay, Isle of Bute PA20 0DZ   07470 520240
argyll@churchofscotland.org.uk

Treasurer: REV. DAVID CARRUTHERS BD
The Manse, Park Road, Ardrishaig, Lochgilphead PA30 8HE   01546 603269
DCarruthers@churchofscotland.org.uk

Appin (F) linked with Lismore   1976   2015
Iain C. Barclay MBE TD MA BD MTh MPhil PhD FRSA
An Mansa, Appin, Argyll PA38 4DS
ICBarclay@churchofscotland.org.uk
Appin 01631 730143
Lismore 01631 760077

Ardchattan (H W) linked with Coll (W) linked with Connel (W)
Vacant
Session Clerk: Ardchattan: Catherine T. Robb (Miss)   catherinerobb02@btinternet.com
Session Clerk, Connel: Marion Fisher   marion.fisher46@gmail.com
Coll 01879 230366
01631 720335
01631 710589

Ardrishaig (H) linked with South Knapdale   1998
David Carruthers BD
The Manse, Park Road, Ardrishaig, Lochgilphead PA30 8HE
DCarruthers@churchofscotland.org.uk
01546 603269

Barra (GD) linked with South Uist (GD)   1995   2016
Lindsay Schluter ThE CertMin PhD
The Manse, Cuithir, Isle of Barra HS9 5XU
LSchluter@churchofscotland.org.uk
01871 810230
07835 913963

Bute, United Church of (F W)
John Owain Jones MA BD FSAScot   1981   2011   10 Bishop Terrace, Rothesay, Isle of Bute PA20 9HF   01700 504502
JJones@churchofscotland.org.uk

Campbeltown: Highland (H)
Vacant
Interim Moderator: David Carruthers   DCarruthers@churchofscotland.org.uk   01546 603269

Campbeltown: Lorne and Lowland (F H)
Vacant   Lorne and Lowland Manse, Castlehill, Campbeltown PA28 6AN   01586 552468
William Crossan   2014   2018   Gowanbank, Kilkerran Road, Campbeltown PA28 6JL   01586 553543
(Ordained Local Minister)

Coll See Ardchattan

Colonsay and Oronsay (W)
Guardianship of the Presbytery
Session Clerk: Kevin Bryne   colonsaybryne@gmail.com   01950 200320

Connel See Ardchattan

Craignish linked with Kilbrandon and Kilchattan linked with Kilninver and Kilmelford (Netherlorn FW)
Vacant   The Manse, Kilmelford, Oban PA34 4XA
Session Clerk, Kilbrandon and Kilchattan: Jean Alexander   jandjalex@gmail.com   01852 200565
Session Clerk, Kilninver and Kilmelford: Sally Inglis   sallyinglis12@gmail.com   01852 314242
01852 316271

Cumlodden, Lochfyneside and Lochgair linked with Glenaray and Inveraray (West Lochfyneside FW)
Vacant   01546 606914
Interim Moderator: Margaret Jacobsen   07833 177862

Dunoon: St John's linked with Kirn and Sandbank (H W) (Central Cowal)
Vacant   The Manse, 13 Dhailling Park, Hunter Street, Kirn, Dunoon   01369 702256
PA23 8FB
Glenda M. McLaren (Ms) DCS   1990   2006   Glenda.McLaren@churchofscotland.org.uk   01369 704168
Session Clerk, Kirn and Sandbank: James Anderson   j_anderson@btinternet.com   01369 705104
07725 186379

Dunoon: The High Kirk (H W) linked with Innellan (H) linked with Toward (H W) (South-East Cowal)
Vacant   7A Mathieson Lane, Innellan, Dunoon PA23 7SH   01369 830276
Ruth I. Griffiths (Mrs)   2004   Kirkwood, Mathieson Lane, Innellan, Dunoon PA23 7TA   01369 830145
(Auxiliary Minister)   RGriffiths@churchofscotland.org.uk

Gigha and Cara (H) (GD) linked with Kilcalmonell linked with Killean and Kilchenzie (H)
Scott E. Burton BD DipMin   1999   2019   The Manse, Muasdale, Tarbert, Argyll PA29 6XD   01583 421432
SBurton@churchofscotland.org.uk

Glassary, Kilmartin and Ford linked with North Knapdale (W)
Vacant   The Manse, Kilmichael Glassary, Lochgilphead PA31 8QA   01546 606926
Session Clerk, Glassary, Kilmartin and Ford: Linda Tighe   chalin@tiscali.co.uk   01546 600330
Session Clerk, North Knapdale: David Logue   sessionclerk@northknapdale.org   01546 870647

Glenaray and Inveraray See Cumlodden, Lochfyneside and Lochgair

Glenorchy and Innishael (W) linked with Strathfillan (W)
Vacant
Session Clerk, Strathfillan: Mary Anderson   m.anderson53@btinternet.com   01838 300253

Innellan See Dunoon: The High Kirk

Iona (W) linked with Kilfinichen and Kilvickeon and the Ross of Mull (W)
Jenny Earl MA BD   2007   2018   1 The Steadings, Achavaich, Isle of Iona PA76 6SW   07769 994680
JEarl@churchofscotland.org.uk

Jura (GD) linked with Kilarrow (H W) linked with Kildalton and Oa (GD H)
Vacant   uisdean001@gmail.com   01496 810658
Session Clerk, Kilarrow: Hugh Smith   dorothydennis792@btinternet.com   01496 302440
Session Clerk, Kildalton and Oa: Dorothy Dennis (Dr)

Kilarrow See Jura
Kilbrandon and Kilchattan See Craignish
Kilcalmonell See Gigha and Cara

Kilchrenan and Dalavich (W) linked with Muckairn (W)
Thomas W. Telfer BA MDiv   2008   2018   Muckairn Manse, Taynuilt PA35 1HW   01866 822204
TTelfer@churchofscotland.org.uk

Kildalton and Oa See Jura

Kilfinan linked with Kilmodan and Colintraive linked with Kyles (H) (West Cowal)
David Mitchell BD DipP'Theol MSc   1988   2006   West Cowal Manse, Kames, Tighnabruaich PA21 2AD   01700 811045
DMitchell@churchofscotland.org.uk

Kilfinichen and Kilvickeon and the Ross of Mull See Iona
Killean and Kilchenzie See Gigha and Cara
Kilmodan and Colintraive See Kilfinan

Kilmore and Oban (GD W)
Dugald J. Cameron BD DipMin MTh   1990   2007   **obancofs@btinternet.com**   **01631 562405**
Kilmore and Oban Manse, Ganavan Road, Oban PA34 5TU   01631 566253
Dugald.Cameron@churchofscotland.org.uk

Kilmun, Strone and Ardentinny: The Shore Kirk (H)
Vacant
Session Clerk: James Ritchie
The Manse, Blairmore, Dunoon PA23 8TE   01369 840313
jamesgibbritchie@gmail.com   01369 706949

Kilninian and Kilmore linked with Salen (H) and Ulva linked with Tobermory (F GD H)
linked with Torosay (H) and Kinlochspelvie (North Mull W)
Vacant
Contact: Elizabeth Gibson
The New Manse, Gruline Road, Salen, Aros, Isle of Mull PA72 6JF   01680 812541
egibson@churchofscotland.org.uk

Kilninver and Kilmelford See Craignish
Kirn and Sandbank See Dunoon: St John's
Kyles See Kilfinan
Lismore See Appin

Lochgilphead (F W)
Hilda C. Smith (Miss) MA BD MSc   1992   2005   Parish Church Manse, Manse Brae, Lochgilphead PA31 8QZ   01546 602238
HSmith@churchofscotland.org.uk

Lochgoilhead (H) and Kilmorich linked with Strachur and Strathlachlan (Upper Cowal)
Robert K. Mackenzie MA BD PhD   1976   1998   The Manse, Strachur, Cairndow PA27 8DG   01369 860246
RKMackenzie@churchofscotland.org.uk

Muckairn See Kilchrenan and Dalavich

North and West Islay (GD)
Vacant
Session Clerk: Marsali Thomson
The Manse, Port Charlotte, Isle of Islay PA48 7TW   01496 850241
marsalithomson@outlook.com   01496 810236

North Knapdale See Glassary, Kilmartin and Ford

Rothesay: Trinity (H W)
Sibyl A. Tchaikovsky BA BD MLitt   2018   12 Crichton Road, Rothesay, Isle of Bute PA20 9JR   01700   504047
                                                         STchaikovsky@churchofscotland.org.uk

Saddell and Carradale (H) linked with Southend (F H)
Stephen Fulcher BA MA   1993   2012   St Blaan's Manse, Southend, Campbeltown PA28 6RQ   01586   830504
                                                      SFulcher@churchofscotland.org.uk

Salen and Ulva See Kilninian and Kilmore

Skipness (F) linked with Tarbert, Loch Fyne and Kilberry (F H W)
Vacant   The Manse, Campbeltown Road, Tarbert, Argyll PA29 6SX   01880   821012
Session Clerk, Tarbert, Loch Fyne and Kilberry: Janne Leckie (Ms)   Janne.Leckie@argyll-bute.gov.uk   01880   820481

Southend See Saddell and Carradale
South Knapdale See Ardrishaig
South Uist See Barra
Strachur and Strathlachlan See Lochgoilhead and Kilmorich
Strathfillan See Glenorchy and Innishael
Tarbert, Loch Fyne and Kilberry See Skipness

Tiree (GD)
Vacant   The Manse, Scarinish, Isle of Tiree PA77 6TN   01879   220377
Interim Moderator: Douglas Allan   douglas.allan423@gmail.com   01700   502331
                                                                                                             07478   134946

Tobermory See Kilninian and Kilmore
Torosay and Kinlochspelvie See Kilninian and Kilmore
Toward See Dunoon: The High Kirk

In other appointments

Fulcher, Christine P. BEd   2012   2018   Ordained Local Minister: Presbytery   St Blaan's Manse, Southend, Campbeltown PA28 6SX   01586   830504
                                                  Ministries Co-ordinator, South Argyll   CFulcher@churchofscotland.org.uk

Gibson, Elizabeth A. (Mrs)   2003   2013   Locum Minister, North Mull   Mo Dhachaidh, Lochdon, Isle of Mull PA64 6AP   01680   812541
MA MLitt BD   egibson@churchofscotland.org.uk

Ross, Kenneth R. OBE BA BD PhD   1982   2019   Theological Educator, Africa   Zomba Theological College, PO Box 130, Zomba, Malawi
                                                                                      kross@thinkingmission.org

Demitted

Name	Ord.	Dem.	(Charge)	Address	Tel
Acklam, Clifford R. BD MTh	1997	2018	(Glassary, Kilmartin and Ford with North Knapdale)	4 Knoll View Terrace, Westtown, New York 10998, United States of America	07596 164112
Beautyman, Paul H. MA BD	1993	2019	(Youth Adviser, Argyll Presbytery)	130b John Street, Dunoon PA23 7BN PBeautyman@churchofscotland.org.uk	
Bell, Douglas W. MA LLB BD	1975	1993	(Alexandria: North)		
Campbell, Roderick D.M. OStJ TD BD DMin FSAScot	1975	2019	(Cumlodden, Lochfyneside and Lochgair with Glenaray and Inveraray)	3 Cairnbaan Lea, Cairnbaan, Lochgilphead PA31 8BA Roderick.Campbell@churchofscotland.org.uk	01546 606815
Cringles, George G. BD	1981	2017	(Coll with Connel)	The Moorings, Ganavan Road, Oban PA34 5TU george.cringles@gmail.com	01631 564215
Dunlop, Alistair J. MA	1965	2004	(Saddell and Carradale)	8 Pipers Road, Cairnbaan, Lochgilphead PA31 8UF dunrevn@btinternet.com	01546 600316
Gray, William LTh	1971	2006	(Kilberry with Tarbert)	Lochnagar, Longsdale Road, Oban PA34 5DZ gray98@hotmail.com	01631 567471
Henderson, Grahame McL. BD	1974	2008	(Kirn)	6 Gerhallow, Bullwood Road, Dunoon PA23 7QB ghende5884@aol.com	01369 702433
Hood, H. Stanley C. MA BD	1966	2000	(London: Crown Court)	10 Dalriada Place, Kilmichael Glassary, Lochgilphead PA31 8QA	01546 606168
Lamont, Archibald MA	1952	1992	(Kilcalmonell with Skipness)	22 Bonnyton Drive, Eaglesham, Glasgow G76 0LU	01349 865932
Lind, Michael J. LLB BD	1984	2012	(Campbeltown: Highland)	Maybank, Station Road, Conon Bridge, Dingwall IV7 8BJ mijylind@gmail.com	
Macfarlane, James PhD	1991	2011	(Lochgoilhead and Kilmorich)	'Lindores', 11 Bullwood Road, Dunoon PA23 7QJ mac.farlane@btinternet.com	01369 710626
McIvor, Anne (Miss) SRD BD	1996	2013	(Gigha and Cara)	20 Albyn Avenue, Campbeltown PA28 6LY annemcivor@btinternet.com	07901 964825
MacLeod, Roderick MBE MA BD PhD(Edin) PhD(Open)	1966	2011	(Cumlodden, Lochfyneside and Lochgair)	Creag-nam-Barnach, Furnace, Inveraray PA32 8XU mail@revroddy.co.uk	01499 500629
Marshall, Freda (Mrs) BD FCII	1993	2005	(Colonsay and Oronsay with Kilbrandon and Kilchattan)	Allt Mhaluidh, Glenview, Dalmally PA33 1BE mail@freda.org.uk	01838 200693
Mill, David GCSJ MA BD	1978	2018	(Kilmun, Strone and Ardentinny: The Shore Kirk)	The Hebrides, 107 Bullwood Road, Dunoon PA23 7QN revandevmill@aol.com	01369 707544
Millar, Margaret R.M. (Miss) BTh	1977	2008	(Kilchrenan and Dalavich with Muckairn)	Fearnoch Cottage, Fearnoch, Taynuilt PA35 1JB macoje@aol.com	01866 822416
Morrison, Angus W. MA BD	1959	1999	(Kildalton and Oa)	1 Livingstone Way, Port Ellen, Isle of Islay PA42 7EP	01496 300043
Park, Peter B. BD MCIBS	1997	2014	(Fraserburgh: Old)	Hillview, 24 McKelvie Road, Oban PA34 4GB peterpark9@btinternet.com	01631 565849
Ritchie, Walter M.	1973	1999	(Uphall: South)	Hazel Cottage, Barr Mor View, Kilmartin, Lochgilphead PA31 8UN	01546 510343
Scott, Randolph MA BD	1991	2013	(Jersey: St Columba's)	18 Lochan Avenue, Kim, Dunoon PA23 8HT rev.rs@hotmail.com	01369 703175
Stewart, Joseph LTh	1979	2011	(Dunoon: St John's with Sandbank)	7 Glenmorag Avenue, Dunoon PA23 7LG	01369 703438
Taylor, Alan T. BD	1980	2005	(Isle of Mull Parishes)	25 Munro Gate, Bridge of Allan FK9 4DJ	01688 302496
Wilkinson, W. Brian MA BD	1968	2007	(Glenaray and Inveraray)	3 Achlonan, Taynuilt PA35 1JJ williambrian35@btinternet.com	01866 822036

(22) FALKIRK (W)

Meets at Falkirk Trinity Parish Church on the first Tuesday of September, December, March and May, on the fourth Tuesday of October and January and on the third Tuesday of June.

Clerk:	REV. ANDREW SARLE BSc BD	114 High Station Road, Falkirk FK1 5LN falkirk@churchofscotland.org.uk	07565 362074
Depute Clerk and Treasurer:	MR CHRISTOPHER DUNN	3b Afton Road, Cumbernauld G67 2DS depclerk@falkirkpresbytery.org.uk	01236 720874 07799 478880

Airth (F H)

James F. Todd BD CPS	1984	2012	The Manse, Airth, Falkirk FK2 8LS JTodd@churchofscotland.org.uk	01324 831120

Blackbraes and Shieldhill (W) linked with Muiravonside (F W)

Vacant

Interim Moderator: Jean Gallacher	81 Stevenson Avenue, Polmont, Falkirk FK2 0GU JGallacher@churchofscotland.org.uk	01324 717757 01324 824540

Bo'ness: Old (F H T W)

Amanda J. MacQuarrie MA PGCE MTh	2014	2016	10 Dundas Street, Bo'ness EH51 0DG AMacQuarrie@churchofscotland.org.uk	01506 204585

Bo'ness: St Andrew's (F W)

Vacant

Interim Moderator: David Wandrum	St Andrew's Manse, 11 Erngath Road, Bo'ness EH51 9DP DWandrum@churchofscotland.org.uk	01506 **825803** 01506 822195 01236 723288

Bonnybridge: St Helen's (H W)

George MacDonald BTh	1996	2009	The Manse, 32 Reilly Gardens, High Bonnybridge FK4 2BB GMacDonald@churchofscotland.org.uk	01324 874807

Bothkennar and Carronshore (W)

Andrew J. Moore BSc BD	2007	11 Hunter Place, Greenmount Park, Carronshore, Falkirk FK2 8QS AMoore@churchofscotland.org.uk	01324 570525

Brightons (F H T W)

Scott W. Burton BA BA	2018	info@brightonschurch.org.uk The Manse, Maddiston Road, Brightons, Falkirk FK2 0JP Scott.Burton@churchofscotland.org.uk	01324 **713855** 01324 712062

Carriden (H W)
Vacant
David C. Wandrum | 1993 | 2017 | The Spires, Foredale Terrace, Carriden, Bo'ness EH51 9LW | 01506 822141
(Auxiliary Minister) | | | 5 Cawder View, Carrickstone Meadows, Cumbernauld, Glasgow G68 0BN | 01236 723288
DWandrum@churchofscotland.org.uk

Cumbernauld: Abronhill (H W)
Joyce A. Keyes (Mrs) BD | 1996 | 2003 | 26 Ash Road, Cumbernauld, Glasgow G67 3ED | 01236 723833
JKeyes@churchofscotland.org.uk

Cumbernauld: Condorrat (H W)
Grace I.M. Saunders BSc BTh | 2007 | 2011 | 11 Rosehill Drive, Cumbernauld, Glasgow G67 4EQ | 01236 452090
GSaunders@churchofscotland.org.uk

Cumbernauld: Kildrum (H W) linked with Cumbernauld St Mungo's (W)
Vacant
David Nicholson DCS | 1994 | 1993 | 18 Fergusson Road, Balloch, Cumbernauld, Glasgow G67 1LS | 01236 721513
| | | 2D Doonside, Kildrum, Cumbernauld, Glasgow G67 2HX | 01236 732260
DNicholson@churchofscotland.org.uk

Cumbernauld: Old (H W)
Elspeth M McKay LLB LLM PGCert BD | 2014 | 2017 | The Manse, 23 Baronhill, Cumbernauld, Glasgow G67 2SD | 01236 728853
EMckay@churchofscotland.org.uk
Valerie S. Cuthbertson (Miss) DipTMus DCS | 2003 | | 105 Bellshill Road, Motherwell ML1 3SJ | 01698 259001
VCuthbertson@churchofscotland.org.uk

Cumbernauld: St Mungo's See Cumbernauld: Kildrum

Denny: Old (W) linked with Haggs (H W)
Vacant
Interim Moderator: Aftab Gohar | | | 31 Duke Street, Denny FK6 6NR | 01324 824508
AGohar@churchofscotland.org.uk | | | | 01324 482109

Denny: Westpark (F H W)
D. I. Kipchumba Too BTh MTh MSc | 2017 | | 13 Baxter Crescent, Denny FK6 5EZ | 01324 882220
KToo@churchofscotland.org.uk | | | | 07340 868067

Dunipace (F H)
Jean W. Gallacher (Mrs) | 1989 | | The Manse, 239 Stirling Street, Dunipace, Denny FK6 6QJ | 01324 824540
BD CMin CTheol DMin
JGallacher@churchofscotland.org.uk

Falkirk: Bainsford (F H W)
Vacant
Andrew Sarle BSc BD   2013
(Ordained Local Minister)
1 Valleyview Place, Newcarron Village, Falkirk FK2 7JB
114 High Station Road, Falkirk FK1 5LN   01324 621648
ASarle@churchofscotland.org.uk

Falkirk: Camelon (F W)
Vacant
G.F. (Erick) du Toit BTh   2016   2018
(Associate Minister)
30 Cotland Drive, Falkirk FK2 7GE   01324 870011
30 Cotland Drive, Falkirk FK2 7GE   01324 623631
EduToit@churchofscotland.org.uk   01324 623631

Falkirk: Grahamston United (F H T W)
Ian Wilkie BD PGCE   2001   2007
Anne White BA DipTh   2018
(Ordained Local Minister)
16 Cromwell Road, Falkirk FK1 1SF   01324 624461
IWilkie@churchofscotland.org.uk   07877 803280 (Mbl)
94 Craigleith Road, Grangemouth FK3 0BA   01324 880864
AnneWhite@churchofscotland.org.uk

New charge formed by the union of Falkirk: Grahamston United and Falkirk: St James'
Grahamston United is a Local Ecumenical Partnership with the Methodist and United Reformed Churches

Falkirk: Laurieston (W) linked with Redding and Westquarter (W)
J. Mary Henderson MA BD DipEd PhD   1990   2009
11 Polmont Road, Laurieston, Falkirk FK2 9QQ   01324 621196
JMary.Henderson@churchofscotland.org.uk

Falkirk: St Andrew's West (H W)
Alastair M. Horne BSc BD   1989   1997
1 Maggiewood's Loan, Falkirk FK1 5SJ   01324 622091
AHorne@churchofscotland.org.uk   01324 623308

Falkirk: Trinity (F H T W)
Robert S.T. Allan LLB DipLP BD   1991   2003
office@falkirktrinity.org.uk
9 Major's Loan, Falkirk FK1 5QF   01324 611017
RAllan@churchofscotland.org.uk   01324 625124

Grangemouth: Abbotsgrange (F T W)
Aftab Gohar MA MDiv PgDip   1996   2010
8 Naismith Court, Grangemouth FK3 9BQ   01324 482109
AGohar@churchofscotland.org.uk   07528 143784

Grangemouth: Kirk of the Holy Rood (W)
Vacant
Session Clerk: Helen Scott
The Manse, Bowhouse Road, Grangemouth FK3 0EX   01324 471595
sessionclerk.khr@gmail.com   01324 486780

Grangemouth: Zetland (F H W)
Alison A. Meikle (Mrs) BD — 1999 — Ronaldshay Crescent, Grangemouth   FK3 9JH
AMeikle@churchofscotland.org.uk — 01324 336729

Haggs   See Denny: Old

Larbert: East (F W)
Melville D. Crosthwaite   BD DipEd DipMin — 1984 — 1 Cortachy Avenue, Carron, Falkirk   FK2 8DH
MCrosthwaite@churchofscotland.org.uk — 01324 562402

Larbert: Old (F H)
Guardianship of the Presbytery — The Manse, 38 South Broomage Avenue, Larbert   FK5 3ED — 01324 872760
Session Clerk: Eric Appelbe — larbertoldcontact@gmail.com — 01324 556551

Larbert: West (H W)
Vacant — 27 Drysdale Avenue, Kinnaird, Larbert   FK2 8RE — 01324 554874
Session Clerk: Carol Sergeant — sessionclerk.larbertwest@gmail.com

Muiravonside   See Blackbraes and Shieldhill

Polmont: Old (F W)
Deborah L. van Welie (Ms) MTheol — 2015 — 3 Orchard Grove, Polmont, Falkirk   FK2 0XE — **01324 715995**
DLVanWelie@churchofscotland.org.uk — 01324 713427

Redding and Westquarter   See Falkirk: Laurieston

Sanctuary First (F T W)
Albert O. Bogle BD MTh — 1981 — 49a Kenilworth Road, Bridge of Allan   FK9 4RS — 07715 374557
(Pioneer Minister) — AlbertBogle@churchofscotland.org.uk
Sanctuary First is a Presbytery Mission Initiative

Slamannan
Vacant
Monica MacDonald (Mrs) — 2014 — 32 Reilly Gardens, High Bonnybridge, Bonnybridge   FK4 2BB — 01324 874807
(Ordained Local Minister) — Monica.MacDonald@churchofscotland.org.uk

Stenhouse and Carron (F H W)

William Thomson BD	2001	2007	The Manse, 21 Tipperary Place, Stenhousemuir, Larbert FK5 4SX WThomson@churchofscotland.org.uk	01324 416628

In other appointments

Christie, Helen F. (Mrs) BD	1998	2015	Chaplain: Hospital (part-time)	4B Glencairn Road, Cumbernauld G67 2EN andychristie747@yahoo.com	01236 611583
Goodison, Michael J. BSc BD	2013		Chaplain: Army	40 Comyn Drive, Wallacestone, Falkirk FK2 7FH	07833 028256
McPherson, William BD DipEd	1994	2003	Chief Executive, The Vine Trust	83 Laburnum Road, Port Seton, Prestonpans EH32 0UD	01875 812252

Demitted

Black, Ian W. MA BD	1976	2013	(Grangemouth: Zetland)	Flat 1R, 2 Carrickvale Court, Carrickstone, Cumbernauld, Glasgow G68 0LA iwblack@hotmail.com	01236 453370
Brown, Kathryn L. (Mrs)	2014	2019	(Ordained Local Minister)	1 Callendar Park Walk, Callendar Grange, Falkirk FK1 1TA kaybrown1cpw@talktalk.net	01324 617352
Brown, T. John MA BD	1995	2006	(Tullibody: St Serf's)	1 Callendar Park Walk, Callendar Grange, Falkirk FK1 1TA johnbrown1cpw@talktalk.net	01324 617352
Campbell-Jack, W.C. BD MTh PhD	1979	2011	(Glasgow: Possilpark)	35 Castle Avenue, Airth, Falkirk FK2 8GA c.c-j@homecall.co.uk	01324 832011
Chalmers, George A. MA BD MLitt	1962	2002	(Catrine with Sorn)	3 Cricket Place, Brightons, Falkirk FK2 0HZ	01324 712030
Gunn, F. Derek BD	1986	2017	(Airdrie: Clarkston)	6 Yardley Place, Falkirk FK2 7FH	01324 624938
Job, Anne J. BSc BD	1993	2010	(Kirkcaldy: Viewforth with Thornton)	5 Carse View, Airth, Falkirk FK2 8NY aj@ajjob.co.uk	01324 832094
McCallum, John	1962	1998	(Falkirk: Irving Camelon)	11 Burnbrae Gardens, Falkirk FK1 5SB	01324 619766
McDowall, Ronald J. BD	1980	2001	(Falkirk: Laurieston with Redding and Westquarter)	'Kailas', Windsor Road, Falkirk FK1 5EJ	01324 871947
Mathers, Alexena (Sandra)	2015	2018	(Ordained Local Minister)	10 Ercall Road, Brightons, Falkirk FK2 0RS SMathers@churchofscotland.org.uk	01324 872253
Morrison, Iain C. BA BD	1990	2003	(Linlithgow: St Ninian's Craigmailen)	Whaligoe, 53 Eastcroft Drive, Polmont, Falkirk FK2 0SU iain@kirkweb.org	01324 713249
Ross, Evan J. LTh	1986	1998	(Cowdenbeath: West with Mossgreen and Crossgates)	5 Arneil Place, Brightons, Falkirk FK2 0NJ	01324 719936
Smith, Richard BD	1976	2002	(Denny: Old)	Easter Wayside, 46 Kennedy Way, Airth, Falkirk FK2 8GB richards@uklinux.net	01324 831386

FALKIRK ADDRESSES

Blackbraes and Shieldhill	Main St x Anderson Cr
Bo'ness:	
Old	Panbrae Road
St Andrew's	Grahamsdyke Avenue
Carriden	Carriden Brae
Cumbernauld:	
Abronhill	Larch Road
Condorrat	Main Road
Kildrum	Clouden Road
Old	Baronhill
St Mungo's	St Mungo's Road
Denny:	
Old	Denny Cross
Westpark	Duke Street
Dunipace	Stirling Street
Falkirk:	
Bainsford	Hendry Street, Bainsford
Camelon	Dorrator Road
Grahamston United	Bute Street
Laurieston	Polmont Road
St Andrew's West	Newmarket Street
Trinity	Kirk Wynd
Grangemouth:	
Abbotsgrange	Abbot's Road
Kirk of the Holy Rood	Bowhouse Road
Zetland	Ronaldshay Crescent
	Glasgow Road
Haggs	Kirk Avenue
Larbert:	
East	Denny Road x Stirling Road
Old	Main Street
West	off Vellore Road
Muiravonside	Kirk Entry/Bo'ness Road
Polmont: Old	Main Street
Redding and Westquarter	opposite Manse Place
Slamannan	Church Street
Stenhouse and Carron	

(23) STIRLING (F W)

Meets at the Moderator's church on the first Thursday of September, and at Bridge of Allan Parish Church on the first Thursday of February, March, April, May, June, October, November and December.

Clerk:	**REV. ALAN F. MILLER** **BA MA BD**	7 Windsor Place, Stirling FK8 2HY AMiller@churchofscotland.org.uk	01786 465166
Depute Clerk:	**MR EDWARD MORTON**	22 Torry Drive, Alva FK12 5LN edmort@aol.com	01259 760861
Treasurer:	**MR MARTIN DUNSMORE**	60 Brookfield Place, Alva FK12 5AT m.dunsmore53@btinternet.com	07525 005028 01259 762262
Presbytery Office:		St Columba's Church, Park Terrace, Stirling FK8 2NA stirling@churchofscotland.org.uk	01786 447575

Aberfoyle (H) linked with Port of Menteith (H)

Vacant			
Interim Moderator: Dan Gunn		The Manse, Lochard Road, Aberfoyle, Stirling FK8 3SZ degunn@hotmail.co.uk	01877 382391 01786 823798

Alloa: Ludgate (F W)

Vacant			
Interim Moderator: Dorothy U. Anderson		28 Alloa Park Drive, Alloa FK10 1QY DAnderson@churchofscotland.org.uk	01259 212709 01786 841706

Alloa: St Mungo's (F H T W)

Sang Y. Cha BD MTh	2011	contact@alloastmungos.org 37A Claremont, Alloa FK10 2DG SCha@churchofscotland.org.uk	**01259 723004** 01259 213872

Alva (F W)
James N.R. McNeil BSc BD — 1990 1997
alvaparishchurch@gmail.com
34 Ochil Road, Alva FK12 5JT
JMcNeil@churchofscotland.org.uk
01259 760262

Anne F. Shearer BA DipEd (Auxilliary Minister) — 2010 2018
10 Colsnaur, Menstrie FK11 7HG
AShearer@churchofscotland.org.uk
01259 769176

Balfron (F W) linked with Fintry (F H W)
Sigrid Marten — 1997 2013
admin@balfronchurch.org.uk
7 Station Road, Balfron, Glasgow G63 0SX
SMarten@churchofscotland.org.uk
01360 440285

Balquhidder linked with Killin and Ardeonaig (H W)
Russel Moffat BD MTh PhD — 1986 2016
The Manse, Killin FK21 8TN
Russel.Moffat@churchofscotland.org.uk
01567 820247

Bannockburn: Allan (F H T W) linked with Cowie and Plean (H T)
Vacant
Interim Moderator: Ian McVean
hiya@allanchurch.org
The Manse, Bogend Road, Bannockburn, Stirling FK7 8NP
ianmcvean@yahoo.co.uk
01786 814692
01360 440016

Bannockburn: Ladywell (F H W)
Elizabeth M.D. Robertson (Miss) BD CertMin — 1997
57 The Firs, Bannockburn FK7 0EG
ERobertson@churchofscotland.org.uk
01786 812467

Bridge of Allan (F H W)
Daniel (Dan) J. Harper BSc BD — 2016
office@bridgeofallanparishchurch.org.uk
29 Keir Street, Bridge of Allan, Stirling FK9 4QJ
DHarper@churchofscotland.org.uk
01786 834155
01786 832753

Buchanan linked with Drymen (W)
Alexander J. MacPherson BD — 1986 1997
Buchanan Manse, Drymen, Glasgow G63 0AQ
AMacPherson@churchofscotland.org.uk
01360 660370
01360 870212

Buchlyvie (H W) linked with Gartmore (H W)
Scott J. Brown CBE BD — 1993 2019
The Manse, 8 Culbowie Crescent, Buchlyvie FK8 3NH
SJBrown@churchofscotland.org.uk

Callander (F H W)
Jeffrey A. McCormick BD — 1984 2018
3 Aveland Park Road, Callander FK17 8FD
JMcCormick@churchofscotland.org.uk
Tel/Fax: **01877 331409**
01877 330097

Cambusbarron: The Bruce Memorial (F H W) 2006 2012
Graham P. Nash MA BD   14 Woodside Court, Cambusbarron, Stirling FK7 9PH   01786 442068
GPNash@churchofscotland.org.uk

Clackmannan (H W)
Vacant
Interim Moderator: James N.R. McNeil
office@clackmannankirk.org.uk   **01786 214238**
The Manse, Port Street, Clackmannan FK10 4JH   01259 211255
JMcNeil@churchofscotland.org.uk   01259 760262

Cowie and Plean See Bannockburn: Allan

Dollar (H W) linked with Glendevon linked with Muckhart (W)
Vacant
Session Clerk, Dollar: Catherine Gladwin (Mrs)   2 Princes Crescent East, Dollar FK14 7BU   01259 743593
Session Clerk, Muckhart: Sheena Anderson (Dr)   sessionclerk@dollarparishchurch.org.uk   01259 573476
sheena.c.anderson@btinternet.com   01259 781391

Drymen See Buchanan

Dunblane: Cathedral (F H T W)
Colin C. Renwick BMus BD   1989   2014   **office@dunblanecathedral.org.uk**   **01786 825388**
Cathedral Manse, The Cross, Dunblane FK15 0AQ   01786 822205
CRenwick@churchofscotland.org.uk

Dorothy U. Anderson (Mrs) LLB DipPL BD   2006   2017   Inverteith, Stirling Road, Doune FK16 6AA   01786 841706
(Associate Minister)   DAnderson@churchofscotland.org.uk

Dunblane: St Blane's (F H W) linked with Lecropt (F H W)
Gary J. Caldwell BSc BD   2007   2015   46 Kellie Wynd, Dunblane FK15 0NR   01786 825324
GCaldwell@churchofscotland.org.uk

Fallin (F W)
Vacant   **info@fallinchurch.com**   01786 818413
5 Fincastle Place, Cowie, Stirling FK7 7DS

Fintry See Balfron

Gargunnock (W) linked with Kilmadock (W) linked with Kincardine-in-Menteith (W)
Vacant
Lynne Mack (Mrs)   2013   2014   36 Middleton, Menstrie FK11 7HD   01259 761465
(Ordained Local Minister)   LMack@churchofscotland.org.uk

Gartmore See Buchlyvie

Glendevon See Dollar

Killearn (F H W)
Stuart W. Sharp MTheol DipPA — 2001 2018 — 2 The Oaks, Killearn G63 9SF
SSharp@churchofscotland.org.uk — 01360 550101

Killin and Ardeonaig See Balquhidder
Kilmadock See Gargunnock
Kincardine-in-Menteith See Gargunnock

Kippen (H W) linked with Norrieston (W)
Ellen M. Larson Davidson BA MDiv — 2007 2015 — The Manse, Main Street, Kippen, Stirling FK8 3DN
ELarsonDavidson@churchofscotland.org.uk — 01786 871249

Lecropt See Dunblane: St Blane's

Logie (F H W)
Ruth D. Halley BEd BD PGCM — 2012 2017 — 21 Craiglea, Causewayhead, Stirling FK9 5EE
RHalley@churchofscotland.org.uk — 01786 463060
07530 307413

Menstrie (F H T W)
Vacant
Interim Moderator: Drew Barrie — DBarrie@churchofscotland.org.uk — 01259 213326

Muckhart See Dollar
Norrieston See Kippen
Port of Menteith See Aberfoyle

Sauchie and Coalsnaughton (F)
Margaret Shuttleworth MA BD — 2013 — 62 Toll Road, Kincardine, Alloa FK10 4QZ
MShuttleworth@churchofscotland.org.uk — 01259 731002

Stirling: Allan Park South (F H T W)
Guardianship of the Presbytery
Interim Moderator: Stuart W. Sharp — **office@apschurch@gmail.com** — **01786 471998**
SSharp@churchofscotland.org.uk — 01360 550101

Stirling: Church of the Holy Rude (F H W) linked with Stirling: Viewfield Erskine (H)   holyrude@holyrude.org
Alan F. Miller BA MA BD   2000   2010
7 Windsor Place, Stirling FK8 2HY
AMiller@churchofscotland.org.uk   01786 465166

Stirling: North (F H W)   info@stirlingnorth.org
Scott McInnes MEng BD   2016
18 Shirras Brae Road, Stirling FK7 0BA
SMcInnes@churchofscotland.org.uk   01786 463376 / 01786 446116

Stirling: St Columba's (H W)   stcolumbasstirling@gmail.com
Vacant
St Columba's Manse, 5 Clifford Road, Stirling FK8 2AQ
Interim Moderator: Gary J. McIntyre
GMcIntyre@churchofscotland.org.uk   01786 449516 / 01786 469979 / 01786 474421

Stirling: St Mark's (T W)   stmarksstirling1@gmail.com
Barry J. Hughes MA BA   2011   2018
10 Laidlaw Street, Stirling FK8 1ZS
BHughes@churchofscotland.org.uk   01786 470733 / 07597 386762

Jean T. Porter (Mrs) BD DCS   2006   2008
3 Cochrie Place, Tullibody FK10 2RR
JPorter@churchofscotland.org.uk   07729 316321

Stirling: St Ninians Old (F H W)
Gary J. McIntyre BD DipMin   1993   1998
7 Randolph Road, Stirling FK8 2AJ
GMcIntyre@churchofscotland.org.uk   01786 474421

Stirling: Viewfield Erskine See Stirling: Church of the Holy Rude

Strathblane (F H T W)   strathblanekirk@gmail.com
Murdo M. Campbell BD DipMin   1997   2017
2 Campsie Road, Strathblane, Glasgow G63 9AB
MCampbell@churchofscotland.org.uk   01360 770418 / 01360 770226

Tillicoultry (F H W)
Alison E.P. Britchfield (Mrs) MA BD   1987   2013
The Manse, 17 Dollar Road, Tillicoultry FK13 6PD
ABritchfield@churchofscotland.org.uk   01259 750340

Tullibody: St Serf's (H W)
Drew Barrie BSc BD   1984   2016
16 Menstrie Road, Tullibody, Alloa FK10 2RG
DBarrie@churchofscotland.org.uk   01259 213326

In other appointments

Allen, Valerie L. (Ms) BMus MDiv DMin	1990	2015	Presbytery Chaplain	16 Pine Court, Doune FK16 6JE VL2allen@btinternet.com	01786 842577 07801 291538
Begg, Richard MA BD	2008	2016	Army Chaplain	12 Whiteyetts Drive, Sauchie FK10 3GE rbegg711@aol.com	
Boyd, Ronald M.H. BD DipTheol	1993	2010	Chaplain, Queen Victoria School	6 Victoria Green, Queen Victoria School, Dunblane FK15 0JY ron.boyd@qvs.org.uk	07766 004292
Cook, Helen (Mrs) BD	1974	2012	Hospital Chaplain	60 Pelstream Avenue, Stirling FK7 0BG revhcook@btinternet.com	01786 464128
Foggie, Janet P. MA BD PhD	2003	2016	Pioneer Minister, Stirling University	Pioneer Office, Logie Kirk Halls, 15–17 Alloa Road, Stirling FK9 5LH JFoggie@churchofscotland.org.uk	07899 349246
Jack, Alison M. MA BD PhD	1998	2001	Assistant Principal and Lecturer, New College, Edinburgh	5 Murdoch Terrace, Dunblane FK15 9JE alisonjack809@btinternet.com	01786 826953
Millar, Jennifer M. (Mrs) BD DipMin	1986	1988	Teacher: Religious and Moral Education	17 Mapledene Road, Scone, Perth PH2 6NX ajrmillar@blueyonder.co.uk	01738 550270
Russell, Kenneth G. BD CCE	1986	2013	Prison Chaplain	Chaplaincy Centre, HM Prison Perth, 3 Edinburgh Road, Perth PH2 7JH kenneth.russell@sps.pnn.gov.uk	01738 458216

Demitted

Barr, John BSc PhD BD	1958	1979	(Kilmacolm: Old)	6 Ferry Court, Stirling FK9 5GJ kilbrandon@btinternet.com	01786 472286
Brown, James H. BD	1977	2005	(Helensburgh: Park)	14 Gullipen View, Callander FK17 8HN revjimhbrown@yahoo.co.uk	01877 339425
Campbell, Andrew B. BD DPS MTh	1979	2018	(Gargunnock with Kilmadock with Kincardine-in-Menteith)	Seahaven, Ganavan, Oban PA34 5TU	
Cloggie, June (Mrs)	1997	2006	(Auxiliary Minister)	11A Tulipan Crescent, Callander FK17 8AR david.cloggie@hotmail.co.uk	01877 331021
Cochrane, James P.N. LTh	1994	2012	(Tillicoultry)	12 Sandpiper Meadow, Alloa Park, Alloa FK10 1QU jamescochrane@pobroadband.co.uk	01259 218883
Dunnett, Alan L. LLB BD	1994	2016	(Cowie and Plean with Fallin)	9 Tulipan Crescent, Callander FK17 8AR alan.dunnett@sky.com	01877 339640
Dunnett, Linda (Mrs) BA DCS	1976	2016	(Deacon)	9 Tulipan Crescent, Callander FK17 8AR lindadunnett@sky.com	01877 339640 07838 041683
Gaston, A. Ray C. MA BD	1969	2002	(Leuchars: St Athernase)	'Hamewith', 13 Manse Road, Dollar FK14 7AL gaston.arthur@yahoo.co.uk	01259 743202
Gilmour, William M. MA BD	1969	2008	(Lecropt)	14 Pine Court, Doune FK16 6JE	01786 842928
Goring, Iain M. BSc BD	1976	2015	(Interim Minister)	4 Argyle Grove, Dunblane FK15 9DU imgoring@gmail.com	01786 821688
Izett, William A.F.	1968	2000	(Law)	1 Duke Street, Clackmannan FK10 4EF william.izett@talktalk.net	01259 724203

Landels, James BD CertMin	1990	2015	(Bannockburn: Allan)	11 Ardgay Drive, Bonnybridge, Falkirk FK4 2FH revjimlandels@icloud.com	01324 810685 07860 944266
MacCormick, Moira G. BA LTh	1986	2003	(Buchlyvie with Gartmore)	12 Rankine Wynd, Tullibody, Alloa FK10 2UW mgmaccormick@o2.co.uk	01259 724619
McIntosh, Hamish N.M. MA	1949	1987	(Fintry)	9 Abbeyfield House, 17 Allan Park, Stirling FK8 2QG	01786 479294
McKenzie, Alan BSc BD	1988	2013	(Bellshill: Macdonald Memorial with Bellshill: Orbiston)	89 Drip Road, Stirling FK8 1RN rev.a.mckenzie@btopenworld.com	01786 430450
Malloch, Philip R.M. LLB BD	1970	2009	(Killearn)	8 Michael McParland Drive, Torrance, Glasgow G64 4EE pmalloch@mac.com	01360 620089
Mathew, J. Gordon MA BD	1973	2011	(Buckie: North)	45 Westhaugh Road, Stirling FK9 5GF jg.matthew@btinternet.com	01786 445951
Millar, Alexander M. MA BD MBA	1980	2018	(Stirling: St Columba's)	17 Mapledene Road, Scone, Perth PH2 6NX alexmillar0406@gmail.com	01738 550270
Millar, Jennifer M. (Mrs) BD DipMin	1986	1995	Teacher: Religious and Moral Education	25 Beechwood Gardens, Stirling FK8 2AX ajrmillar@blueyonder.co.uk	01786 469979
Ogilvie, Catriona (Mrs)	1999	2015	(Cumbernauld: Old)	Seberham Flat, 1A Bridge Street, Dollar FK14 7DF catriona.ogilvie1@btinternet.com	01259 742155
Ovens, Samuel B. BD	1982	1992	(Slamannan)	21 Bevan Drive, Alva FK12 5PD	01259 763456
Pryde, W. Kenneth DA BD	1994	2012	(Foveran)	Corrie, 7 Alloa Road, Woodside, Cambus FK10 2NT wkpryde@hotmail.com	01259 721562
Rose, Dennis S. LTh	1996	2016	(Arbuthnott, Bervie and Kinneff)	69 Blackthorn Grove, Menstrie FK11 7DX dennis2327@aol.com	01259 692451
Scott, James F.	1957	1997	(Dyce)	5 Gullipen View, Callander FK17 8HN	01877 330565
Sewell, Paul M.N. MA BD	1970	2010	(Berwick-upon-Tweed: St Andrew's Wallace Green and Lowick)	7 Bohun Court, Stirling FK7 7UT paulmsewell@btinternet.com	01786 489969
Sinclair, James H. MA BD DipMin	1966	2004	(Auchencairn and Rerrick with Buittle and Kelton)	16 Delaney Court, Alloa FK10 1RB	01259 729001
Thomson, Raymond BD DipMin	1992	2013	(Slamannan)	8 Rhodders Grove, Alva FK12 5ER	01259 769083
Wilson, Hazel MA BD DMS	1991	2015	(Dundee: Lochee)	2 Boe Court, Springfield Terrace, Dunblane FK15 9LU hmwilson704@gmail.com	01786 825850

STIRLING ADDRESSES

Allan Park South	Dumbarton Road	St Columba's	Park Terrace	Viewfield Erskine	Barnton Street
Holy Rude	St John Street	St Mark's	Drip Road		
North	Springfield Road	St Ninians Old	Kirk Wynd, St Ninians		

(24) DUNFERMLINE (F W)

Meets at Dunfermline in St Andrew's Erskine Church, Robertson Road, on the first Thursday of each month, except January, April, July, August and October when there is no meeting, and June when it meets on the last Thursday.

Clerk:	REV. IAIN M. GREENSHIELDS BD DipRS ACMA MSc MTh DD		38 Garvock Hill, Dunfermline KY12 7UU dunfermline@churchofscotland.org.uk	Office 01383 741495 Home 07427 477575

Aberdour: St Fillan's (H W)
Peter S. Gerbrandy-Baird
MA BD MSc FRSA FRGS
2004
St Fillan's Manse, 36 Bellhouse Road, Aberdour, Fife KY3 0TL
PGerbrandy-Baird@churchofscotland.org.uk
01383 861522

Beath and Cowdenbeath: North (H W)
Deborah J. Dobby (Mrs)
BA BD PGCE RGN RSCN
2014   2018
42 Woodside Avenue, Rosyth KY11 2LA
DDobby@churchofscotland.org.uk
01383 325520

Cairneyhill (H W) linked with Limekilns (H W)
Norman M. Grant BD
1990
Cairneyhill: 01383 882352 Limekilns: 01383 873337
The Manse, 10 Church Street, Limekilns, Dunfermline KY11 3HT
NGrant@churchofscotland.org.uk
01383 872341

Carnock and Oakley (H W)
Charles M.D. Lines BA
2010   2017
The Manse, Main Street, Carnock, Dunfermline KY12 9JG
CLines@churchofscotland.org.uk
01383 247209
07909 762257

Cowdenbeath: Trinity (H W)
Vacant
Interim Moderator: Monika R.W. Redman
2 Glenfield Road, Cowdenbeath KY4 9EL
MRedman@churchofscotland.org.uk
01383 510696
01383 300092

Culross and Torryburn (H)
Elizabeth A. Fisk BD
1996   2019
30 Masterton Road, Dunfermline KY11 8RB
EFisk@churchofscotland.org.uk
01383 730039

Dalgety (H W)
Christine M. Sime (Miss) BSc BD
1994   2012
office@dalgety-church.co.uk
9 St Colme Drive, Dalgety Bay, Dunfermline KY11 9LQ
CSime@churchofscotland.org.uk
01383 824092
01383 822316

Dunfermline: Abbey (F H T W)
MaryAnn R. Rennie (Mrs) BD MTh   1998   2012
dunfermline.abbey.church@gmail.com   01383 **724586**
3 Perdieus Mount, Dunfermline KY12 7XE   01383 727311
MARennie@churchofscotland.org.uk

Dunfermline: East (F W)
Andrew A. Morrice MA BD   1999   2010
71 Swift Street, Dunfermline KY11 8SN   01383 223144
AMorrice@churchofscotland.org.uk   07815 719301

Dunfermline: Gillespie Memorial (F H W)
Michael A. W. Weaver BSc BD   2017
office@gillespiechurch.org   01383 **621253**
4 Killin Court, Dunfermline KY12 7XF   01383 724347
MWeaver@churchofscotland.org.uk   07980 492299

Dunfermline: North
Ian G. Thom BSc PhD BD   1990   2007
13 Barbour Grove, Dunfermline KY12 9YB   01383 733471
IThom@churchofscotland.org.uk

Dunfermline: St Andrew's Erskine (W)
Muriel F. Willoughby (Mrs) MA BD   2006   2013
info@standrewserskine.org.uk   01383 **841660**
71A Townhill Road, Dunfermline KY12 0BN   01383 738487
MWilloughby@churchofscotland.org.uk

Dunfermline: St Leonard's (F W)
Monika R. W. Redman BA BD   2003   2014
office@slpc.org   01383 **620106**
12 Torvean Place, Dunfermline KY11 4YY   01383 300092
MRedman@churchofscotland.org.uk

Margaret Mateos   2018
(Ordained Local Minister)
43 South Street, Lochgelly KY5 9LJ   01592 780073
MMateos@churchofscotland.org.uk

Dunfermline: St Margaret's (F W)
Iain M. Greenshields   1984   2007
BD DipRS ACMA MSc MTh DD
38 Garvock Hill, Dunfermline KY12 7UU   01383 723955
IGreenshields@churchofscotland.org.uk   07427 477575

Dunfermline: St Ninian's (F W)
Carolann Erskine BD DipPSRP   2009   2018
51 St John's Drive, Dunfermline KY12 7TL   01383 271548
CErskine@churchofscotland.org.uk

Dunfermline: Townhill and Kingseat (F H W)
Jean A. Kirkwood BSc PhD BD   2015
info@townhillandkingseatchurchofscotland.org   01383 723691
7 Lochwood Park, Kingseat, Dunfermline KY12 0UX
JKirkwood@churchofscotland.org.uk

Inverkeithing (F W) linked with North Queensferry (W)
Colin M. Alston BMus BD BN RN   1975 2012
1 Dover Way, Dunfermline KY11 8HR
CAlston@churchofscotland.org.uk   01383 621050

Kelty (W)
Hugh D. Steele LTh DipMin   1994 2013
15 Artick Road, Kelty KY4 0BH
HSteele@churchofscotland.org.uk   01383 831362

Limekilns See Cairneyhill

Lochgelly and Benarty: St Serf's (F W)
Vacant
Pamela Scott (Mrs) DCS   2017
82 Main Street, Lochgelly KY5 9AA   01592 780435
177 Primrose Avenue, Rosyth KY11 2TZ   01383 410530
PScott@churchofscotland.org.uk   07548 819334

North Queensferry See Inverkeithing

Rosyth (F W)
D. Brian Dobby MA BA   1999 2018
rpc@cos8za.plus.com   **01383 412534**
42 Woodside Avenue, Rosyth KY11 2LA   01383 412776
BDobby@churchofscotland.org.uk
Morag Crawford (Miss) MSc DCS   1977 1998
118 Wester Drylaw Place, Edinburgh EH4 2TG   0131 332 2253
MCrawford@churchofscotland.org.uk   07970 982563

Saline and Blairingone (W) linked with Tulliallan and Kincardine (F)
Alexander J. Shuttleworth MA BD   2004 2013
62 Toll Road, Kincardine, Alloa FK10 4QZ   01259 731002
AShuttleworth@churchofscotland.org.uk

Tulliallan and Kincardine See Saline and Blairingone

In other appointments

Kenny, Elizabeth S.S. BD RGN SCM   1989 2011   Chaplain: HM Prison Glenochil
5 Cobden Court, Crossgates, Cowdenbeath KY4 8AU   07831 763494
esskenny@btinternet.com

Paterson, Andrew E. JP   1994 2016   Auxiliary Minister, Presbytery
6 The Willows, Kelty KY4 0FQ   01383 830998
APaterson@churchofscotland.org.uk

Demitted

Bjarnason, Sven S. CandTheol	1973	2011	(Tomintoul, Glenlivet and Inveraven)	14 Edward Street, Dunfermline KY12 0JW sven@bjarnason.org.uk	01383 724625
Boyle, Robert P. LTh	1990	2010	(Saline and Blairingone)	23 Farnell Way, Dunfermline KY12 0SR boab.boyle@btinternet.com	01383 729568
Brown, Peter MA BD FRAScot	1953	1987	(Holm)	24 Inchmickery Avenue, Dalgety Bay, Dunfermline KY11 5NF	01383 822456
Chalmers, John P. BD CPS DD	1979	2017	(Principal Clerk)	10 Liggars Place, Dunfermline KY12 7XZ	01383 739130
Christie, Arthur A. BD	1997	2018	(Anstruther and Cellardyke: St Ayle with Kilrenny)	194 Foulford Road, Cowdenbeath KY4 9AX revacc@btinternet.com	01383 511326
Farquhar, William E. BA BD	1987	2006	(Dunfermline: Townhill and Kingseat)	29 Queens Drive, Middlewich, Cheshire CW10 0DG	01606 835097
Jenkins, Gordon F.C. MA BD PhD	1968	2006	(Dunfermline: North)	2 Balrymonth Court, St Andrews KY16 8XT jenkinsgordon1@sky.com	01335 477194
Johnston, Thomas N. LTh	1972	2008	(Edinburgh: Priestfield)	71 Main Street, Newmills, Dunfermline KY12 8ST tomjohnston@blueyonder.co.uk	01383 889240
Laidlaw, Victor W.N. BD	1975	2008	(Edinburgh: St Catherine's Argyle)	9 Tern Road, Dunfermline KY11 8GA	01383 620134
Leith, D. Graham MA BD	1974	2012	(Tyne Valley)	9 St Margaret Wynd, Dunfermline KY12 0UT dgrahamleitch@gmail.com	01383 249245
McCulloch, William B BD	1997	2016	(Rome: St Andrew's)	81 Meldrum Court, Dunfermline KY11 4XR revwbmcculloch@hotmail.com	01383 730305
McDonald, Tom BD	1994	2015	(Kelso: North ar'd Ednam)	12 Woodmill Grove, Dunfermline KY11 4JR revtomparadise12@gmail.com	01383 695365
McKay, Violet C.C. BD	1988	2017	(Rosyth)	87 McDonald Street, Dunfermline KY11 8NG vcmckay@btinternet.com	01383 731410
McLellan, Andrew R.C. CBE MA BD STM DD	1970	2009	(HM Chief Inspector of Prisons for Scotland)	4 Liggars Place, Dunfermline KY12 7XZ	01383 725959
Redmayne, David W. BSc BD	2001	2017	(Beath and Cowdenbeath: North)	10 Hawthorn Park, Dunfermline KY12 0DY	01383 738137
Reid, A. Gordon BSc BD	1982	2008	(Dunfermline: Gillespie Memorial)	7 Arkleston Crescent, Paisley PA3 4TG reid501@fsmail.net	0141 842 1542 07773 300989
Reid, David MSc LTh FSAScot	1961	1992	(St Monans wit Largoward)	North Lethans, Saline, Dunfermline KY12 9TE	01383 733144
Watt, Robert J. BD	1994	2009	(Dumbarton: Riverside)	101 Birrell Drive, Dunfermline KY11 8FA robertwatt101@gmail.com	01383 735417 07753 683717
Whyte, Iain A. BA BD STM PhD	1968	2005	(Community Mental Health Chaplain)	14 Carlingnose Point, North Queensferry, Inverkeithing KY11 1ER iainisabelwhyte@gmail.com	01383 410732
Whyte, Isabel H. (Mrs) BD	1993	2006	(Chaplain: Queen Margaret Hospital, Dunfermline)	14 Carlingnose Point, North Queensferry, Inverkeithing KY11 1ER iainisabelwhyte@gmail.com	01383 410732
Williamson, James BA BD	1986	2009	(Cummertrees with Mouswald with Ruthwell)	12 Mulberry Drive, Dunfermline KY11 8BZ jimwill@rcmkirk.fsnet.co.uk	01383 734872

(25) KIRKCALDY (W)

Meets at Kirkcaldy, in the St Bryce Kirk Centre, on the first Tuesday of March, September, December and June. It meets also on the first Tuesday of November for Holy Communion at the church of the Moderator.

Clerk: REV. ALAN W.D. KIMMITT BSc BD   40 Liberton Drive, Glenrothes KY6 3PB   **01592 742233**
kirkcaldy@churchofscotland.org.uk

Depute Clerk: MRS. LAUREN JONES   57b Salisbury Street, Kirkcaldy KY2 5HP   **07913 611018**
kirkcaldy@churchofscotland.org.uk

Auchterderran Kinglassie (F W)
Donald R. Lawrie MA BD DipCouns   1991   2018   7 Woodend Road, Cardenden, Lochgelly KY5 0NE   01592 720508
DLawrie@churchofscotland.org.uk

Auchtertool (W) linked with Kirkcaldy: Linktown (F H W)
Catriona M. Morrison MA BD   1995   2000   16 Raith Crescent, Kirkcaldy KY2 5NN   **01592 641080** / 01592 265536
CMorrison@churchofscotland.org.uk
Marc A. Prowe   2000   2008   16 Raith Crescent, Kirkcaldy KY2 5NN   01592 265536
MProwe@churchofscotland.org.uk

Buckhaven and Wemyss
Vacant   **01592 715577**
Jacqueline Thomson (Mrs) MTh DCS   2004   2008   16 Aitken Place, Coaltown of Wemyss, Kirkcaldy KY1 4PA   07806 776560
Jacqueline.Thomson@churchofscotland.org.uk

Burntisland (F H W)
Vacant   01592 873567
Session Clerk: William Sweenie   21 Ramsay Crescent, Burntisland KY3 9JL
billsweenie01@gmail.com

Dysart: St Clair (H W)
Lynn Brady BD DipMin   1996   2017   42 Craigfoot Walk, Kirkcaldy KY1 1GA   01592 561967
(Interim Minister)   LBrady@churchofscotland.org.uk

Glenrothes: Christ's Kirk (H W)
Andrew Gardner BSc BD PhD   1997   2019   **christskirkglenrothes@yahoo.com**   **01592 745938** / 07411 989344
(Interim Minister)   Christ's Kirk, Pitcoudie Avenue, Glenrothes KY7 6SU
AGardner@churchofscotland.org.uk

Glenrothes: St Columba's (Rothes Trinity Parish Grouping) (F W)   2013   info@st-columbas.com
Alan W.D. Kimmitt BSc BD
40 Liberton Drive, Glenrothes KY6 3PB
Alan.Kimmitt@churchofscotland.org.uk
01592 752539
01592 742233

Glenrothes: St Margaret's (F H)   2014
Eileen Miller BD MBACP (Snr. Accred.)
DipCouns DipComEd
office@stmargaretschurch.org.uk
8 Alburne Park, Glenrothes KY7 5RB
EMiller@churchofscotland.org.uk
01592 328162
01592 752241

Glenrothes: St Ninian's (Rothes Trinity Parish Grouping) (F H W)   1992   2017
David J. Smith BD DipMin
office@stninians.co.uk
1 Cawdor Drive, Glenrothes KY6 2HN
David.Smith@churchofscotland.org.uk
01592 610560
01592 611963

Kennoway, Windygates and Balgonie: St Kenneth's (F W)   2018
Allan Morton MA BD PGDip
stkennethsparish@gmail.com
2 Fernhill Gardens, Windygates, Leven KY8 5DZ
AMorton@churchofscotland.org.uk
01333 351372
01333 350240

Kinghorn (F W)   1985   1997
James Reid BD
17 Myre Crescent, Kinghorn, Burntisland KY3 9UB
JReid@churchofscotland.org.uk
01592 890269

Kirkcaldy: Abbotshall (F H T W)   2018
Justin W. Taylor BTh MTh MTh
83 Milton Road, Kirkcaldy KY1 1TP
JTaylor@churchofscotland.org.uk
01592 267915

Kirkcaldy: Bennochy (F W)   1988   2011
Robin J. McAlpine BDS BD MTh
25 Bennochy Avenue, Kirkcaldy KY2 5QE
RMcAlpine@churchofscotland.org.uk
01592 201723
01592 643518

Kirkcaldy: Linktown See Auchtertool

Kirkcaldy: Pathhead (F H W)   1992   2005
Andrew C. Donald BD DPS
pathheadchurch@btconnect.com
73 Loughborough Road, Kirkcaldy KY1 3DB
ADonald@churchofscotland.org.uk
01592 204635
01592 652215

Kirkcaldy: St Bryce Kirk (F H T W)   1979
J. Kenneth (Ken) Froude MA BD
office@stbrycekirk.org.uk
6 East Fergus Place, Kirkcaldy KY1 1XT
JFroude@churchofscotland.org.uk
01592 640016
01592 264480

Kirkcaldy: Templehall (H)
Vacant
Session Clerk: George Thomson — 35 Appin Crescent, Kirkcaldy KY2 6EJ — georget1955@live.co.uk — 01592 260156 / 01592 203178

Kirkcaldy: Torbain (F W)
Ian J. Elston BD MTh — 1999 — 91 Sauchenbush Road, Kirkcaldy KY2 5RN — IElston@churchofscotland.org.uk — 01592 263015

Brian Porteous BSc DipCS (Ordained Local Minister) — 2018 — Kildene, Westfield Road, Cupar KY15 5DS — BPorteous@churchofscotland.org.uk — 01334 653561

Leslie: Trinity (Rothes Trinity Parish Grouping)
Guardianship of the Presbytery
Session Clerk: Alec Redpath — sessionclerk@leslietrinitychurch.co.uk — 01592 742636

Leven (F)
Gilbert C. Nisbet CA BD — 1993 2007 — levenparish@tiscali.co.uk — 5 Forman Road, Leven KY8 4HH — GNisbet@churchofscotland.org.uk — 01333 423969 / 01333 303339

Markinch and Thornton (F W)
Vacant
Session Clerk: Bryan Gould — 7 Guthrie Crescent, Markinch, Glenrothes KY7 6AY — monsieurgould@hotmail.com — 01592 758264

Methil: Wellesley (F H)
Gillian Paterson (Mrs) BD — 2010 — 10 Vettriano Vale, Leven KY8 4GD — GPaterson@churchofscotland.org.uk — 01333 423147

Methilhill and Denbeath (F)
Elisabeth F. Cranfield (Ms) MA BD — 1988 — 9 Chemiss Road, Methilhill, Leven KY8 2BS — ECranfield@churchofscotland.org.uk — 01592 713142

In other appointments
Wright, Lynda BEd DCS — 1979 2016 — Community Chaplaincy Listening Co-ordinator, NHS Fife — 71a Broomhill Avenue, Burntisland KY3 0BP — lyndawright20@gmail.com — 07835 303395

Demitted

Name	Ord	Dem	(Congregation)	Address / Contact	Tel
Adams, David G. BD	1991	2011	(Cowdenbeath Trinity)	13 Fernhill Gardens, Windygates, Leven KY8 5DZ adams.69@btinternet.com	01333 351214
Campbell, Reginald F. BSc BD DipChEd	1979	2015	(Daviot and Dunlichity with Moy, Dalarossie and Tomatin)	12 Alloway Drive, Kirkcaldy KY2 6DX campbell578@talktalk.net	01592 742915
Collins, Mitchell BD CPS	1996	2005	(Creich, Flisk and Kilmany with Monimail)	6 Netherby Park, Glenrothes KY6 3PL collinsmit@aol.com	
Deans, Graham D.S. MA BD MTh MLitt DMin	1978	2017	(Aberdeen: Queen Street)	38 Sir Thomas Elder Way, Kirkcaldy KY2 6ZS graham.deans@btopenworld.com	01592 641429
Dick, James S. MA BTh	1988	1997	(Glasgow Ruchazie)	20 Church Street, Kirkcaldy KY1 2AD jdick63@yahoo.com	01592 369239
Elston, Peter K.	1963	1999	(Dalgety)	6 Cairngorm Crescent, Kirkcaldy KY2 5RF peterkelston@btinternet.com	01592 205622
Ferguson, David J.	1966	2001	(Bellie with Speymouth)	4 Russell Gardens, Ladybank, Cupar KY15 7LT	01337 831406
Forrester, Ian L. MA	1964	1996	(Friockheim Kinnell with Inverkeilor and Lunan)	8 Bennochy Avenue, Kirkcaldy KY2 5QE	01592 260251
Forsyth, Alexander R. TD BA MTh	1973	2014	(Markinch)	49 Scaraben Crescent, Formonthills, Glenrothes KY6 3HL alex@arforsyth.com	01592 749049 07483 232581
Fowler, Anthony J.R. BSc BD	1982	2018	(Kirkcaldy Templehall)	1 Ratho Place, Kirkcaldy KY2 6XL	01592 372053
Galbraith, D. Douglas MA BD BMus MPhil ARSCM PhD	1965	2005	(Office for Worship, Doctrine and Artistic Matters)	34 Balbirnie Street, Markinch, Glenrothes KY7 6DA dgalbraith@churchofscotland.org.uk	01592 752403
Gordon, Ian D. LTh	1972	2001	(Markinch)	2 Somerville Way, Glenrothes KY7 5GE	01592 742487
McDonald, Ian J.M. MA BD	1984	2018	(Lausanne: The Scots Kirk)	11 James Grove, Kirkcaldy KY1 1TN IanJMMcdonald@churchofscotland.org.uk	07421 775644
McLeod, Alistair G.	1988	2005	(Glenrothes: St Columba's)	13 Greenmantle Way, Glenrothes KY6 3QG alistairmcleod1936@gmail.com	01592 744558
McNaught, Samuel M. MA BD MTh	1968	2002	(Kirkcaldy: St John's)	6 Munro Court, Glenrothes KY7 5GD sjmcnaught@btinternet.com	01592 742352
Munro, Andrew MA BD PhD	1972	2000	(Glencaple with Lowther)	7 Dunvegan Avenue, Kirkcaldy KY2 5SG am.smm@blueyonder.co.uk	01592 566129
Nicol, George G. BD DPhil	1982	2013	(Falkland with Freuchie)	48 Fidra Avenue, Burntisland KY3 0AZ ggnicol@totalise.co.uk	01592 873258
Paterson, Maureen (Mrs) BSc	1992	2010	(Auxiliary Minister)	91 Dalmahoy Crescent, Kirkcaldy KY2 6TA m.e.paterson@blueyonder.co.uk	01592 262300
Roy, Allistair BD DipSW PgDip	2007	2016	(Glenrothes: St Ninian's)	39 Ravenswood Drive, Glenrothes KY6 2PA minister@revroy.co.uk	
Sharp, Alan BSc BD	1980	2019	(Burntisland)	29 Cromwell Road, Burntisland KY3 9EH alansharp03@aol.com	
Templeton, James L. BSc BD	1975	2012	(Innerleven: East)	29 Coldstream Avenue, Leven KY8 5TN jamietempleton@btinternet.com	01333 427102
Thomson, John D. BD	1985	2005	(Kirkcaldy: Pathhead)	3 Tottenham Court, Hill Street, Dysart, Kirkcaldy KY1 2XY j.thomson10@sky.com	01592 655313 07885 414979

| Tomlinson, Bryan L. TD | 1969 | 2003 | (Kirkcaldy: Abbotshall) | 2 Duddingston Drive, Kirkcaldy KY2 6JP
abbkirk@blueyonder.co.uk | 01592 564843 |
| Wilson, Tilly (Miss) MTh | 1990 | 2012 | (Dysart) | 6 Citron Glebe, Kirkcaldy KY1 2NF
tillywilson1@sky.com | 01592 263134 |

KIRKCALDY ADDRESSES

Abbotshall	Abbotshall Road	
Bennochy	Elgin Street	Beauly Place
Linktown	Nicol Street x High Street	Carron Place
Pathhead	Harriet Street x Church Street	Viewforth Street x Viewforth
St Bryce Kirk	St Brycedale Avenue x Kirk Wynd	Terrace
Templehall		
Torbain		
Viewforth		
(Dysart St Clair)		

(26) ST ANDREWS (W)

Meets on the first Wednesday of February, May, September, October and December and on the last Wednesday of June. Locations to be announced.

| Clerk: | REV. NIGEL J. ROBB FCP MA BD ThM MTh | Presbytery Office, The Basement, 1 Howard Place, St Andrews KY16 9HL
standrews@churchofscotland.org.uk | 01334 461300 |

Anstruther and Cellardyke: St Ayle (H W) linked with Crail (F)

Vacant			16 Taeping Close, Cellardyke, Anstruther KY10 3YL	01333 313917
Session Clerk, St Ayle: Eleanor Blair			eleanor_blair@btinternet.com	01333 310438
Session Clerk, Crail: Helen Armitage (Mrs)			helenkarmitage@btinternet.com	01333 450516

Balmerino (H W) linked with Wormit (F H W)

| James Connolly | 1982 | 2004 | 5 Westwater Place, Newport-on-Tay DD6 8NS | 01382 542626 |
| DipTh CertMin MA(Theol) DMin | | | JConnolly@churchofscotland.org.uk | |

Boarhills and Dunino linked with St Andrews: Holy Trinity (W)

		holytrinitystandrews@gmail.com	01334 478317
Guardianship of the Presbytery			
Session Clerk, Boarhills and Dunino: Michael Foote		michaelfoote54@gmail.com	01334 880787
Session Clerk, Holy Trinity: Michael Stewart (Dr)		htsessionclerk@gmail.com	01334 461270

Cameron (F W) linked with St Andrews: St Leonard's (F H W)

| | 1993 | 2017 | stlencam@btconnect.com | 01334 478702 |
| Graeme W. Beebee BD | | | 1 Cairnhill Gardens, St Andrews KY16 8QY
GBeebee@churchofscotland.org.uk | 01334 472293 |

Carnbee linked with Pittenweem
Margaret E.S. Rose BD — 2007 — 29 Milton Road, Pittenweem, Anstruther KY10 2LN — MRose@churchofscotland.org.uk — 01333 312838

Ceres, Kemback and Springfield (W)
James W. Campbell BD — 1995 2010 — Almbank, Gladney, Ceres, Cupar KY15 5LT — James.Campbell@churchofscotland.org.uk — 01334 829350

Crail See Anstruther and Cellardyke: St Ayle

Creich, Flisk and Kilmany (W)
Guardianship of the Presbytery
Session Clerk: Sheena Fowler (Mrs) — sheena.fowler@btinternet.com — 01337 870216

Cupar: Old (H) and St Michael of Tarvit linked with Monimail
Jeffrey A. Martin BA MDiv — 1991 2016 — 76 Hogarth Drive, Cupar KY15 5YU — JMartin@churchofscotland.org.uk — 01334 656181

Cupar: St John's and Dairsie United (F W)
Gavin W.G. Black BD — 2006 2019 — The Manse, 23 Hogarth Drive, Cupar KY15 5YH — GBlack@churchofscotland.org.uk — 01334 650751

East Neuk Trinity (H W) linked with St Monans (H)
Vacant
Session Clerk, East Neuk Trinity: Olive Weir (Mrs) — jamandlor1@gmail.com — 01333 340642

Edenshead (F W)
Vacant
Session Clerk: Rodney McCall — The Manse, Kirk Wynd, Strathmiglo, Cupar KY14 7QS — rodmccall@yahoo.co.uk — 01337 860256 / 01337 827001

Falkland linked with Freuchie (H W)
Guardianship of the Presbytery
Session Clerk, Falkland: Marion Baldie — 1 Newton Road, Falkland, Cupar KY15 7AQ — sessionclerk.falkland@gmail.com — 01337 858557 / 07951 824488

Freuchie See Falkland

Howe of Fife (F W)
William F. Hunter MA BD — 1986 2011 — The Manse, 83 Church Street, Ladybank, Cupar KY15 7ND — WHunter@churchofscotland.org.uk — 01337 832717

Kilrenny (W)
Guardianship of the Presbytery
Session Clerk, Kilrenny: Corinne Peddie (Mrs)   corinne@peddies.com   07939 252012

Kingsbarns (F H)
Guardianship of the Presbytery
Session Clerk: John (Ian) Ramsay   johnvramsay@btinternet.com   01333 451480

Largo (F W)
Gavin R. Boswell BTheol   1993   2018   1 Castaway Lane, Lower Largo KY8 6FA
GBoswell@churchofscotland.org   01333 320850

Largoward (H W)
Guardianship of the Presbytery
Interim Moderator: Catherine Wilson (Mrs)   catherine.wilson15@btinternet.com   01333 310936

Leuchars: St Athernase (F)
John C. Duncan MBE BD MPhil   1987   2016   7 David Wilson Park, Balmullo, St Andrews KY16 0NP
JDuncan@churchofscotland.org.uk   01334 870038

Lindores (F H)
Guardianship of Presbytery
Session Clerk: Rosslynn Scott (Ms)   2 Guthrie Court, Cupar Road, Newburgh, Cupar KY14 6HA
rosslynn6@btinternet.com   01337 842228

Monimail See Cupar: Old and St Michael of Tarvit

Newport-on-Tay (F H W)
Amos B. Chewachong BTh MTh PhD   2005   2017   17 East Station Place, Newport-on-Tay DD6 8EG
AChewachong@churchofscotland.org.uk   01382 542893

Pittenweem See Carnbee

St Andrews: Holy Trinity See Boarhills and Dunino

St Andrews: Hope Park and Martyrs (F H W) linked with Strathkinness (W)   admin@hpmchurch.org.uk   **01334 478144**
Allan McCafferty BSc BD   1993   2011   20 Priory Gardens, St Andrews KY16 8XX   Tel/Fax 01334 478287
AMcCafferty@churchofscotland.org.uk

St Andrews: St Leonard's See Cameron
St Monans See East Neuk Trinity
Strathkinness See St Andrews: Hope Park and Martyrs

Tayport (F W)   27 Bell Street, Tayport DD6 9AP   01382 553879
Vacant

Wormit See Balmerino

In other appointments

Allardice, Michael MA MPhil PGCertTHE FHEA	2014		Ordained Local Minister	2 Station Road, Kingskettle, Cupar KY15 7PR MAllardice@churchofscotland.org.uk	01337 597073
Jeffrey, Kenneth S. BA BD PhD DMin	2002	2014	University of Aberdeen	The North Steading, Dalgairn, Cupar KY15 4PH ksjeffrey@btopenworld.com	07936 203465 01334 653196
MacEwan, Donald G. MA BD PhD	2001	2011	Chaplain: University of St Andrews	Chaplaincy Centre, 3A St Mary's Place, St Andrews KY16 9UY dgm21@st-andrews.ac.uk	01334 462865 07713 322036
Robb, Nigel J. FCP MA BD ThM MTh	1981	2014	Presbytery Clerk St Andrews	Presbytery Office, Hope Park and Martyrs' Church, 1 Howard Place, St Andrews KY16 9UY	07966 286958
Torrance, Alan J. (Prof.) MA BD DrTheol ARCM	1984	1999	University of St Andrews	Kincaple House, Kincaple, St Andrews KY16 9SH	Home 01334 850755 Office 01334 462843

Demitted

Barron, Jane L. (Mrs) BA DipEd BD	1999	2013	(Aberdeen: St Machar's Cathedral)	In USA: contact via the Presbytery Office livialouise888@gmail.com	
Bradley, Ian C. (Prof.) MA BD DPhil	1990	2017	University of St Andrews	4 Donaldson Gardens, St Andrews KY16 9DN icb@st-andrews.ac.uk	01334 475389
Cameron, John U. BA BSc PhD BD ThD	1974	2008	(Dundee: Broughty Ferry St Stephen's and West)	10 Howard Place, St Andrews KY16 9HL jucameron@yahoo.co.uk	01334 474474
Clark, David M. MA BD	1989	2013	(Dundee: The Steeple)	2b Rose Street, St Monans, Anstruther KY10 2BQ dmclark72@gmail.com	01333 738034
Connolly, Daniel BD DipTheol Dip Min	1983	2015	(Army Chaplain)	2 Cairngreen, Cupar KY15 2SY dannyconnolly@hotmail.co.uk	07951 078478
Douglas, Peter C. JP	1966	1993	(Boarhills with Dunino)	12 Greyfriars Gardens, St Andrews KY16 8DR	01334 475868
Fairlie, George BD BVMS MRCVS	1971	2002	(Crail with Kingsbarns)	41 Warrack Street, St Andrews KY16 8DR	01334 475868
Fraser, Ann G. BD CertMin	1990	2007	(Auchtermuchty)	24 Irvine Crescent, St Andrews KY16 8LG anngilfraser@btinternet.com	01334 461329
Gordon, Peter M. MA BD	1958	1995	(Airdrie: West)	3 Cupar Road, Cuparmuir, Cupar KY15 5RH machrie@madasafish.com	01334 652341

Hamilton, Ian W.F. BD LTh ALCM AVCM	1978 2012	(Nairn: Old)	Mossneuk, 5 Windsor Gardens, St Andrews KY16 8XL / reviwfh@btinternet.com	01334 477745
Harrison, Cameron	2006 2011	(Auxiliary Minister)	Woodfield House, Priormuir, St Andrews KY16 8LP / cameron@harrisonleimon.co.uk	01334 478067
Kesting, Sheilagh M. BA BD DD DSG	1980 2016	(Ecumenical Officer, Church of Scotland)	Restalrig, Chance Inn, Cupar KY15 5QJ / smkesting@btinternet.com	01334 829485
McGregor, Duncan J. MIFM	1982 1996	(Channelkirk with Lauder: Old)	14 Mount Melville, St Andrews KY16 8NG	01334 478314
McKimmon, Eric BA BD MTh PhD	1983 2014	(Cargill Burrelton with Collace)	14 Marionfield Place, Cupar KY15 5JN / ericmckimmon@gmail.com	01334 659650
McLean, John P. BSc BPhil BD	1994 2013	(Glenrothes: St Margaret's)	72 Lawmill Gardens, St Andrews KY16 8QS / jpmclean72@gmail.com	01334 470803
Meager, Peter MA BD CertMgmt(Open)	1971 1998	(Elie with Kilconquhar and Colinsburgh)	7 Lorraine Drive, Cupar KY15 5DY / meager52@btinternet.com	01334 656991
Neilson, Peter MA BD MTh	1975 2016	(Mission Consultant)	Linne Bheag, 2 School Green, Anstruther KY10 3HF / neilson.peter@btinternet.com	01333 310477 / 07818 418608
Oxburgh, Brian H. BSc BD	1980 2019	(Tayport)	18 Winram Place, St Andrews KY16 8XH / mjpdht@gmail.com	01334 208743
Paton, Marion J. (Miss) MA BMus BD	1991 2017	(Dundee: St David's High Kirk)		
Robb, Nigel J. FCP MA BD ThM MTh	1981 2014	Presbytery Clerk: St Andrews	Presbytery Office, Hope Park and Martyrs' Church, 1 Howard Place, St Andrews KY16 9UY	07966 286958
Strong, Clifford LTh	1983 1995	(Creich, Flisk and Kilmany with Monimail)	60 Maryknowe, Gauldry, Newport-on-Tay DD6 8SL / cliffstrongman@btinternet.com	01382 330445
Unsworth, Ruth BA BD CertMHS PgDipCBP BABCP	1984 1987	(Glasgow Pollokshaws)	5 Lindsay Gardens, St Andrews KY16 8XB / RUnsworth@churchofscotland.org.uk	07894 802119
Walker, James B. MA BD DPhil	1975 2011	Chaplain: University of St Andrews	5 Priestden Park, St Andrews KY16 8DL	
Wallace, Hugh M. MA BD	1980 2018	(Newhills)	15 West End, St Monans KY10 2BX	01334 472839
Wotherspoon, Ian G. BA LTh	1967 2004	(Coatbridge: St Andrew's)	12 Cherry Lane, Cupar KY15 5DA / wotherspoonrig@aol.com	01334 650710

(27) DUNKELD AND MEIGLE

Meets at Pitlochry on the first Tuesday of February, September and December, on the third Tuesday of April and the fourth Tuesday of October, and at the Moderator's church on the third Tuesday of June.

Clerk:	REV. JOHN RUSSELL MA	Kilblaan, Gladstone Terrace, Birnam, Dunkeld PH8 0DP / dunkeldmeigle@churchofscotland.org.uk	01350 728896
Depute Clerk:	REV. R. FRASER PENNY BA BD	Cathedral Manse, Dunkeld PH8 0AW / RPenny@churchofscotland.org.uk	01350 727249

Aberfeldy (H W) linked with Dull and Weem (H W) linked with Grantully, Logierait and Strathtay (F W)

Neil M. Glover	2005	2017

The Manse, Taybridge Terrace, Aberfeldy PH15 2BS
NGlover@churchofscotland.org.uk

Sheila D. Wallace (Mrs) DCS MA BD	2009	2019

Little Orchard, Blair Atholl, Pitlochry   PH18 5SH
SWallace@churchofscotland.org.uk

01887 820819
07779 280074
01796 481647
07733 243046

Alyth (F H W)

Michael J. Erskine MA BD	1985	2012

The Manse, Cambridge Street, Alyth, Blairgowrie PH11 8AW
erskinemike@gmail.com

01828 632238

Ardler, Kettins and Meigle (F W)

Alison Notman BD		2014

The Manse, Dundee Road, Meigle, Blairgowrie PH12 8SB
ANotman@churchofscotland.org.uk

01828 640074

Bendochy (W) linked with Coupar Angus: Abbey (W)

Andrew F. Graham BTh DPS	2001	2016

Caddam Road, Coupar Angus, Blairgowrie PH13 9EF
Andrew.Graham@churchofscotland.org.uk

01828 627864

Blair Atholl and Struan linked with Braes of Rannoch linked with Foss and Rannoch (H)

Vacant
The Manse, Blair Atholl, Pitlochry PH18 5SX

01796 481213

Session Clerk, Blair Atholl and Struan: H.J. Ingram (Mr)
ingramsparky@btinternet.com

01796 481275

Session Clerk, Braes of Rannoch: A.M. Phillips (Miss)
alisonrannoch@outlook.com

01882 633228

Session Clerk, Foss and Rannoch: R. Anderson (Mr)
lizandrab@live.co.uk

01892 632272

Blairgowrie (F W)

Benjamin J. A. Abelado BTh DipTh PTh	1991	2019

The Manse, Upper David Street, Blairgowrie PH10 6HB
BAbelado@churchofscotland.org.uk

01250 872146

Braes of Rannoch See Blair Atholl and Struan

Caputh and Clunie (H) linked with Kinclaven (H)

Peggy Ewart-Roberts BA BD		2003	2011

Cara Beag, Essendy Road, Blairgowrie PH10 6QU
PEwart-Roberts@churchofscotland.org.uk

01250 876897

Coupar Angus: Abbey See Bendochy
Dull and Weem See Aberfeldy

Dunkeld (H W)

R. Fraser Penny BA BD	1984	2001

Cathedral Manse, Dunkeld PH8 0AW
RPenny@churchofscotland.org.uk

01350 727249

Fortingall, Glenlyon, Kenmore (H) and Lawers (W)

Vacant

The Manse, Balnaskeag, Kenmore, Aberfeldy PH15 2HB   01887 830218
james@remonyestate.co.uk   01887 830209

Session Clerk: J. Duncan Millar   **New charge formed by the union of Fortingall and Glenlyon, and Kenmore and Lawers**

Foss and Rannoch See Blair Atholl and Struan
Grantully, Logierait and Strathtay See Aberfeldy
Kinclaven See Caputh and Clunie

Kirkmichael, Straloch and Glenshee (W) linked with Rattray (H W)

Linda Stewart (Mrs) BD   1996   2012   The Manse, Alyth Road, Rattray, Blairgowrie PH10 7HF   01250 872462
Linda.Stewart@churchofscotland.org.uk

Pitlochry (H W)   **thetryst@btconnect.com**   **01796 474010**

Mary M. Haddow (Mrs) BD   2001   2012   Manse Road, Moulin, Pitlochry PH16 5EP   01796 472774
MHaddow@churchofscotland.org.uk

Rattray See Kirkmichael, Straloch and Glenshee

Tenandry

Guardianship of the Presbytery

Session Clerk: J. Thorpe (Mrs)   johnethorpe@btinternet.com   01796 473252

In other appointments

Nicol, Robert D.   2013   Ordained Local Minister   Rappla Lodge, Camserney, Aberfeldy PH15 2JF   01887 820242
RNicol@churchofscotland.org.uk

Russell, John MA   1959 2000   Presbytery Clerk: Dunkeld and Meigle   Kilblaan, Gladstone Terrace, Birnam, Dunkeld PH8 0DP   01350 728896

Steele, Grace M.F. MA BTh   2014   Ordained Local Minister   12a Farragon Drive, Aberfeldy PH15 2BQ   01887 820025
GSteele@churchofscotland.org.uk

Demitted

Brennan, Anne J. BSc BD MTh   1999 2019   (Fortingall, Glenlyon, Kenmore and Lawers)   Dunmore House, Findo Gask, Auchterarder PH3 1HS   01738 730350
annebrennanyahoo.co.uk

Campbell, Richard S. LTh   1993 2010   (Gargunnock with Kilmadock with Kincardine-in-Menteith)   3 David Farquharson Road, Blairgowrie PH10 6FD   01250 876386
revrichards@yahoo.co.uk

Ewart, William BSc BD   1972 2010   (Caputh and Clunie with Kinclaven)   Cara Beag, Essendy Road, Blairgowrie PH10 6QU   01250 876897
ewe1@btinternet.com

Knox, John W. MTheol	1992 1997	(Lochgelly: Macainsh)	2 Darroch Gate, Blairgowrie PH10 6GT ian.knox5@btinternet.com	01250 872733
MacRae, Malcolm H. MA PhD	1971 2010	(Kirkmichael, Straloch and Glenshee with Rattray)	10B Victoria Place, Stirling FK8 2QU malcolm.macrae1@btopenworld.com	01786 465547
Mowbray, Harry BD CA	2003 2018	(Blairgowrie)	12 Isla Road, Blairgowrie PH10 6RR	
Nelson, Robert C. BA BD	1980 2010	(Isle of Mull, Kilninian and Kilmore with Salen and Ulva with Tobermory with Torosay and Kinlochspelvie)	St Colme's, Perth Road, Birnam, Dunkeld PH8 0BH rcnelson49@btinternet.com	01350 727455
Ormiston, Hugh C. BSc BD MPhil PhD	1969 2004	(Kirkmichael, Straloch and Glenshee with Rattray)	Cedar Lea, Main Road, Woodside, Blairgowrie PH13 9NP	01828 670539
Robertson, Matthew LTh	1968 2002	(Cawdor with Crcy and Dalcross)	Inver, Strathtay, Pitlochry PH9 0PG	01887 840780
Rooney, Malcolm I.G. DPE BEd BD	1993 2017	(The Glens and Kirriemuir: Old)	23 Mart Lane, Northmuir, Kirriemuir DD8 4TL malc.rooney@gmail.com	01575 575334 07909 993233
Sloan, Robert BD	1997 2014	(Fauldhouse St Andrew's)	3 Gean Grove, Blairgowrie PH10 6TL	01250 875286
Tait, Thomas W. BD MBE	1972 1997	(Rattray)	3 Rosemount Park, Blairgowrie PH10 6TZ	01250 874833
Whyte, William B. BD	1973 2004	(Nairn: St Ninian's)	The Old Inn, Park Hill Road, Rattray, Blairgowrie PH10 7DS	01250 874401
Wilson, John M. MA BD	1967 2004	(Altnaharra and Farr)	Berbice, The Terrace, Blair Atholl, Pitlochry PH18 5SZ	01796 481619
Wilson, Mary D. (Mrs) RGN SCM DTM	1990 2004	(Auxiliary Minister)	Berbice, The Terrace, Blair Atholl, Pitlochry PH18 5SZ	01796 481619

(28) PERTH (W)

Meets at 10am on the second Saturday of September, March, and June and at 7pm on the second Tuesday of November in venues throughout the Presbytery.

Clerk:	REV. J. COLIN CASKIE BA BD			
Presbytery Office:		209 High Street, Perth PH1 5PB perth@churchofscotland.org.uk		01738 451177

Aberdalgie and Forteviot (F H W) linked with Aberuthven and Dunning (F H W)

James W. Aitchison BD	1993	2015	The Manse, Aberdalgie, Perth PH2 0QD JAitchison@churchofscotland.org.uk	01738 446771

Abernethy and Dron and Arngask (W)

Stanley Kennon BA BD	1992	2018	3 Manse Road, Abernethy, Perth PH2 9JP SKennon@churchofscotland.org.uk	01738 850194

Aberuthven and Dunning See Aberdalgie and Forteviot

Almondbank Tibbermore linked with Methven and Logiealmond (W) 1987 2019
Robert J. Malloch BD
The Manse, Dalcrue Road, Pitcairngreen, Perth PH1 3EA
RMalloch@churchofscotland.org.uk
01738 850194

Ardoch (H W) linked with Blackford (F H W) 2012 2016
Mairi Perkins BA BTh
info@ardochparishchurch.org
Manse of Ardoch, Feddoch Road, Braco, Dunblane FK15 5RE
MPerkins@churchofscotland.org.uk
01786 880948

Auchterarder (F H T W) 2005 2019
Lynn M. McChlery MA BD PhD
22 Kirkfield Place, Auchterarder PH3 1FP
LMcChlery@churchofscotland.org.uk
01764 662399

Auchtergaven and Moneydie (F W) linked with Redgorton and Stanley (W) 2012
Adrian J. Lough BD
22 King Street, Stanley, Perth PH1 4ND
ALough@churchofscotland.org.uk
01738 **788017**
01738 827952

Blackford See Ardoch

Cargill Burrelton (F) linked with Collace (F) 2001 2016
Steven Thomson BSc BD
The Manse, Manse Road, Woodside, Blairgowrie PH13 9NQ
SThomson@churchofscotland.org.uk
01828 670384

Cleish (H W) linked with Fossoway: St Serf's and Devonside (F W) 2006 2014
Elisabeth M. Stenhouse BD
Station House, Station Road, Crook of Devon, Kinross KY13 0PG
EStenhouse@churchofscotland.org.uk
01577 842128

Collace See Cargill Burrelton

Comrie (F H W) linked with Dundurn (F H)
Vacant
Interim Moderator: John A.H. Murdoch
strathearnkirks@btinternet.com
The Manse, Strowan Road, Comrie, Crieff PH6 2ES
JMurdoch@churchofscotland.org.uk
01764 **679555**
01764 670076
01738 628378
07578 558978

Crieff (F H W) 1996 2013
Andrew J. Philip BSc BD
8 Strathearn Terrace, Crieff PH7 3AQ
APhilip@churchofscotland.org.uk
01764 218976

Dunbarney (H) and Forgandenny (W)
Allan J. Wilson BSc MEd BD   2007

dfpoffice@btconnect.com
Dunbarney Manse, Manse Road, Bridge of Earn, Perth PH2 9DY
AWilson@churchofscotland.org.uk   01738 **812463**
                                               01738 812211

Dundurn See Comrie

Errol (F H) linked with Kilspindie and Rait
John Macgregor BD   2001   2016

South Bank, Errol, Perth PH2 7PZ
John.Macgregor@churchofscotland.org.uk   01821 642279

Fossoway: St Serf's and Devonside See Cleish

Kilspindie and Rait See Errol

Kinross (F H W)
Alan D. Reid MA BD   1989   2009

office@kinrossparishchurch.org
15 Green Wood, Kinross KY13 8FG
AReid@churchofscotland.org.uk   01577 **862570**
                                               01577 862952

Methven and Logiealmond See Almondbank Tibbermore

Mid Strathearn (H W)
Vacant
Session Clerk: Sheena Crawford (Mrs)

Beechview, Abercairney, Crieff PH7 3NF
sheenacrawford@gmail.com   01764 652116
                                               01764 654270

New charge formed by the union of Fowlis Wester, Madderty and Monzie, and Gask

Muthill (F H W) linked with Trinity Gask and Kinkell (F W) 1984   2013
Klaus O.F. Buwert LLB BD DMin

The Manse, Station Road, Muthill, Crieff PH5 2AR
KBuwert@churchofscotland.org.uk   01764 681205

Orwell and Portmoak (F H W)
Angus Morrison MA BD PhD DD   1979   2011

orwellandportmoakchurch@gmail.com
41 Auld Mart Road, Milnathort, Kinross KY13 9FR
AMorrison@churchofscotland.org.uk   01577 **862100**
                                               01577 863461

Perth: Craigie and Moncreiffe (F W)
Vacant
Robert F. Wilkie   2011   2012
(Auxiliary Minister)

The Manse, 46 Abbot Street, Perth PH2 0EE
24 Huntingtower Road, Perth PH1 2JS
RWilkie@churchofscotland.org.uk   01738 623748
                                               01738 628301

Perth: Kinnoull (F H W)
Graham W. Crawford BSc BD STM   1991   2016
1 Mount Tabor Avenue, Perth PH2 7BT
GCrawford@churchofscotland.org.uk
01738 626046
07817 504042

Perth: Letham St Mark's (H W)
James C. Stewart BD DipMin   1997
office@lethamstmarks.org.uk
35 Rose Crescent, Perth PH1 1NT
JStewart@churchofscotland.org.uk
01738 446377
01738 624167

Kenneth D. Mackay DCS   1996   1998
11F Balgowan Road, Perth PH1 2JG
Kenneth.Mackay@churchofscotland.org.uk
01738 621169
07843 883042

Perth: North (F W)
Kenneth D. Stott MA BD   1989   2017
info@perthnorthchurch.org.uk
2 Cragganmore Place, Perth PH1 3GJ
KStott@churchofscotland.org.uk
01738 622298
01738 625728

Perth: Riverside (F W)
David R. Rankin MA BD   2009   2014
perthriverside.bookings@gmail.com
44 Hay Street, Perth PH1 5HS
DRankin@churchofscotland.org.uk
01738 622341
07810 008754

Perth: St John's Kirk of Perth (F H W) linked with Perth: St Leonard's-in-the-Fields (H)   St John's: 01738 633192   St Leonard's: 01738 632238
John A.H. Murdoch BA BD DPSS   1979   2016
Ferntower, Kinfauns Holdings, Perth PH2 7JY
JMurdoch@churchofscotland.org.uk
01738 628378
07578 558978

Alexander T. Stewart MA BD FSAScot   1975   2017
(Associate Minister)
36 Viewlands Terrace, Perth PH1 1BZ
alex.t.stewart@blueyonder.co.uk
01738 566675

Perth: St Leonard's-in-the-Fields See Perth: St John's Kirk of Perth

Perth: St Matthew's (T W)   Office: 01738 636757; Vestry: 01738 630725
Vacant
office@stmatts.org.uk
23 Kincarrathie Crescent, Perth PH2 7HH
01738 626828

Redgorton and Stanley See Auchtergaven and Moneydie

St Madoes and Kinfauns (F W)
Marc F. Bircham BD MTh   2000
Glencarse, Perth PH2 7NF
MBircham@churchofscotland.org.uk
01738 860837

Scone and St Martins
Maudeen I. MacDougall BA BD MTh   1978   2019   The Manse, Burnside, Scone PH2 6LP   01738 551942
Maudeen.MacDougall@churchofscotland.org.uk

Trinity Gask and Kinkell See Muthill

In other appointments

Caskie, J. Colin BA BD   1977 2012   Presbytery Clerk: Perth   13 Anderson Drive, Perth PH1 1JZ   01738 445543
jcolincaskie@gmail.com

McCarthy, David J. BSc BD   1985 2014   Mission and Discipleship Council   121 George Street, Edinburgh EH2 4YN   0131 225 5722
DMcCarthy@churchofscotland.org.uk

MacLaughlan, Grant BA BD   1998 2015   Community Worker, Perth Tulloch Net   Unit 2, Tulloch Square, Perth PH1 2PW   01738 562731 / 07790 518041
grantmac.tullochnet@gmail.com

Michie, Margaret   2013   Ordained Local Minister: Loch Leven Parish Grouping   3 Loch Leven Court, Wester Balgedie, Kinross KY13 9NE   01592 840602
margaretmichie@btinternet.com

Philip, Elizabeth MA BA PGCSE DCS   2007   Deacon   8 Strathearn Terrace, Crieff PH7 3AQ   01764 218976 / 07970 767851
ephilipstich@gmail.com

Stewart, Anne E. BD CertMin   1998 2007   Prison Chaplain: HM Prison Castle Huntly   35 Rose Crescent, Perth PH1 1NT   01738 624167
anne.stewart2@sps.pnn.gov.uk

Thorburn, Susan MTh   2014   Ordained Local Minister   3 Daleally Farm Cottages, St Madoes Road, Errol, Perth PH1 7TJ   01821 642681
SThorburn@churchofscotland.org.uk

Wallace, Catherine PGDipC DCS   1987 2017   Deacon: Honorary Secretary, Diaconate Council   21 Durley Dene Crescent, Bridge of Earn PH2 9RD   01738 621709
secretary@churchofscotland.org.uk

Wylie, Jonathan BSc BD MTh   2000 2015   Chaplain: Strathallan School   Strathallan School, Forgandenny, Perth PH2 9EG   01738 815098
chaplain@strathallan.co.uk

Demitted

Ballentine, Ann M. MA BD   1981 2007   (Kirknewton and East Calder)   17 Nellfield Road, Crieff PH7 3DU   01764 652567
annmballentine@gmail.com

Barr, T. Leslie LTh   1969 1997   (Kinross)   8 Fairfield Road, Kelty KY4 0BY   07727 718076 / 01738 552391
leslie_barr@yahoo.co.uk

Brown, Elizabeth JP RGN   1996 2007   (Auxiliary Minister)   8 Viewlands Place, Perth PH1 1BS
liz.brown@blueyonder.co.uk

Brown, Marina D. MA BD MTh   2000 2012   (Hawick: St Mary's and Old)   Moneydie School Cottage, Luncarty, Perth PH1 3HZ   01738 582163
revmdb1711@btinternet.com

Cairns, Evelyn BD   2004 2012   (Chaplain: Rachel House)   15 Talla Park, Kinross KY13 8AB   01577 863990
revelyn@btinternet.com

Coleman, Sidney H. BA BD MTh   1961 2001   (Glasgow: Merrylea)   'Blaven', 11 Clyde Place, Perth PH2 0EZ   01738 565072
sidney.coleman@blueyonder.co.uk

Craig, Joan H. MTheol	1986	2005	(Orkney: East Mainland)	7 Jedburgh Place, Perth PH1 1SJ joanhcraig@btinternet.com	01738 580180
Donaldson, Robert B. BSocSc	1953	1997	(Kilchoman with Portnahaven)	10 Macrostie Gardens, Crieff PH7 4LP	01764 655178
Dunn, W. Stuart LTh	1970	2006	(Motherwell: Crosshill)	36 Earnmuir Road, Comrie, Crieff PH6 2EY	01764 679178
Fleming, Hamish K. MA	1966	2001	(Banchory Ternan: East)	hamishnan@gmail.com	
Fletcher, Timothy E.G. BA FCMA	1998	2019	(Auxiliary Minister)	3 Ardchoille Park, Perth PH2 7TL fletcherts495@btinternet.com	01738 638189 07747 013985 07747 746418
Gilchrist, Ewen J. BD DipMin DipComm	1982	2017	(Cults)	9 David Douglas Avenue, Scone PH2 6QQ ewengilchrist@btconnect.com	
Graham, Alasdair G. BD DipMin	1981	2019	(Arbroath: West Kirk)	5 Robb Place, Perth PH2 0GB	01738 829350
Graham, Sydney S. DipYL MPhil BD	1987	2009	(Iona with Kilfinichen and Kilvickeon and the Ross of Mull)	'Aspen', Milton Road, Luncarty, Perth PH1 3ES syd@sydgraham.plus.com	
Gregory, J.C. LTh	1968	1992	(Blantyre: St Andrew's)	2 Southlands Road, Auchterarder PH3 1BA	01764 664594
Gunn, Alexander M. MA BD	1967	2006	(Aberfeldy with Amulree and Strathbraan with Dull and Weem)	'Navarone', 12 Cornhill Road, Perth PH1 1LR sandygunn@btinternet.com	01738 443216
Halliday, Archibald R. BD MTh	1964	1999	(Duffus, Spynie and Hopeman)	8 Turretbank Drive, Crieff PH7 4LW roberthalliday343@btinternet.com	01764 656464
Kelly, T. Clifford	1973	1993	(Ferintosh)	20 Whinfield Drive, Kinross KY13 8UB	01577 864946
Lawson, James B. MA BD	1961	2002	(South Uist)	4 Cowden Way, Comrie, Crieff PH6 2NW james.lawson7@btopenworld.com	01764 679180
McCormick, Alastair F.	1962	1998	(Creich with Rosehall)	14 Balmanno Park, Bridge of Earn, Perth PH2 9RJ	01738 813588
McCrum, Robert BSc BD	1982	2014	(Ayr: St James')	28 Rose Crescent, Perth PH1 1NT robert.mccrum@virgin.net	01738 447906
MacDonald, James W. BD	1976	2012	(Crieff)	'Mingulay', 29 Hebridean Gardens, Crieff PH7 3BP rev_up@btinternet.com	01764 654500
McFadzean, Iain MA BD	1989	2019	(Chief Executive: Work Place Chaplaincy Scotland)	2 Lowfield Crescent, Luncarty, Perth PH1 3FG iain.mcfadzean@wpcscotland.co.uk	01738 827338 07969 227696
McGregor, William LTh	1987	2003	(Auchtergaven and Moneydie)	'Ard Choille', 7 Taypark Road, Luncarty, Perth PH1 3FE bill.mcgregor7@btinternet.com	01738 827866
McIntosh, Colin G. MA BD	1976	2013	(Dunblane: Cathedral)	Drumhead Cottage, Drum, Kinross KY13 0PR colinmcintosh4@btinternet.com	01577 840012
MacMillan, Riada M. BD	1991	1998	(Perth: Craigend Moncreiffe with Rhynd)	73 Muirend Gardens, Perth PH1 1JR	01738 628867
McNaughton, David J.H. BA CA	1976	1995	(Killin and Ardeonaig)	14 Rankine Court, Wormit, Newport-on-Tay DD6 8TA	
Main, Douglas M. BD	1986	2014	(Errol with Kilspindie and Rait)	14 Madoch Road, St Madoes, Perth PH2 7TT revdmain@sky.com	01738 860867
Malcolm, Alistair BD DPS	1976	2012	(Inverness: Inshes)	11 Kinclaven Gardens, Murthly, Perth PH1 4EX amalcolm067@btinternet.com	
Milne, Robert B. BTh	1999	2017	(Broughton, Glenholm and Kilbucho with Skirling with Stobo and Drumelzier with Tweedsmuir)	3 Mid Square, Comrie PH6 2EG rbmilne@aol.com	01738 710979

Mitchell, Alexander B. BD	1981	2014	(Dunblane: St Blane's)	24 Hebridean Gardens, Crieff PH7 3BP alex.mitchell6@btopenworld.com	01764 652241
Munro, Gillian BSc BD	1989	2018	(Head of Spiritual Care, NHS Tayside)	The Old Town House, 53 Main Street, Abernethy, Perth PH2 9JH munrooth@aol.com	01738 850066
Munro, Patricia M. BSc DCS	1986	2016	(Deacon)	4 Hewat Place, Perth PH1 2UD patmunrodcs@gmail.com	01738 443088 07814 836314
Paton, Iain F. BD FCIS	1980	2006	(Elie with Kilconquhar and Colinsburgh)	Muldoanich, Stirling Street, Blackford, Auchterarder PH4 1QG iain.f.paton@btinternet.com	01764 682234
Quigley, Barbara D. (Mrs) MTheol ThM DPS	1979	2019	(Glasgow: St Andrew's East)	33 Castle Drive, Auchterarder PH3 1FU	
Redpath, James G. BD DipPTh	1988	2016	(Auchtermuchty with Edenshead and Strathmiglo)	9 Beveridge Place, Kinross KY13 8QY JRedpath@churchofscotland.org.uk	07713 919442
Searle, David C. MA DipTh	1965	2003	(Warden: Rutherford House)	Stonefall Lodge, 30 Abbey Lane, Grange, Errol PH2 7GB dcs@davidsearle.plus.com	01821 641004
Simpson, James A. BSc BD STM DD	1960	1999	(Interim Minister, Brechin Cathedral)	'Dornoch', Perth Road, Bankfoot, Perth PH1 4ED ja@simpsondornoch.co.uk	01738 787710
Sloan, Robert P. MA BD	1968	2007	(Interim Minister, Armadale)	1 Broomhill Avenue, Perth PH1 1EN sloan12@virginmedia.com	01738 443904
Stenhouse, W. Duncan MA BD	1989	2006	(Dunbarney and Forgandenny)	32 Sandport Gait, Kinross KY13 8FB	01577 866992
Stewart, Robin J. MA BD STM	1959	1995	(Orwell with Portmoak)	'Oakbrae', Perth Road, Murthly, Perth PH1 4HF	01738 710220
Thomson, J. Bruce MA BD	1972	2009	(Scone: Old)	47 Elm Street, Errol, Perth PH2 7SQ RevBruceThomson@aol.com	01821 641039 07850 846404
Wallace, James K. MA BD STM	1988	2015	(Perth: St John's Kirk of Perth with St Leonard's-in-the-Fields)	21 Durley Dene Crescent, Bridge of Earn PH2 9RD jkwministry@hotmail.com	01738 621709

PERTH ADDRESSES

Craigie	Abbot Street	Letham St Mark's	Rannoch Road
Kinnoull	Dundee Rd near Queen's Bridge	Moncreiffe	Glenbruar Crescent
		North	Mill Street near Kinnoull Street
		Riverside	Bute Drive

St John's	St John's Street
St Leonard's-in-the-Fields	Marshall Place
St Matthew's	Tay Street

(29) DUNDEE (F W)

Meets at Dundee: The Steeple, Nethergate, on the second Wednesday of February, March, May, September, November and December, and on the fourth Wednesday of June.

Clerk:	REV. JAMES L. WILSON **BD CPS**	dundee@churchofscotland.org.uk	**07885 618659** **01382 774059**
Depute Clerk:	MR COLIN D. WILSON	cd.wilson663@tiscali.co.uk	
Presbytery Office:		Whitfield Parish Church, Haddington Crescent, Dundee DD4 0NA	**01382 503012**

Abernyte (W) linked with Inchture and Kinnaird (F W) linked with Longforgan (F H W)
Marjory A. MacLean LLB BD PhD   1991   2011   The Manse, Longforgan, Dundee DD2 5HB   01382 360238
MMaclean@churchofscotland.org.uk

Auchterhouse (F H W) linked with Monikie and Newbigging and Murroes and Tealing (F H W)   office@sidlawchurches.org.uk   **01382 350182**
Jean de Villiers BATheol BTh HonPsych   2003   2017   29 Oak Lane, Ballumbie Castle Estate, Dundee DD5 3UQ   01382 351680
JdeVilliers@churchofscotland.org.uk

Dundee: Balgay (F H W)
Nardia J. Sandison BAppSc BD MLitt   2019   150 City Road, Dundee DD2 2PW   01382 903446
NSandison@churchofscotland.org.uk

Dundee: Barnhill St Margaret's (H W)   church.office@btconnect.com   **01382 737294**
Alisa L. McDonald BA MDiv   2008   2018   2 St Margaret's Lane, Barnhill, Dundee DD5 2PQ   01382 779278
Alisa.McDonald@churchofscotland.org.uk

Dundee: Broughty Ferry New Kirk (F H T W)   office@broughtyferrynewkirk.org.uk   **01382 738264**
Catherine E.E. Collins (Mrs) MA BD   1993   2006   New Kirk Manse, 25 Ballinard Gardens, Broughty Ferry,   01382 778874
Dundee DD5 1BZ
CCollins@churchofscotland.org.uk

Dundee: Broughty Ferry St James' (F H)
Guardianship of the Presbytery
Session Clerks: Lyn Edwards (Mrs)   lynlocks@hotmail.co.uk   01382 730552
David J.B. Murie   d.j.b.murie@gmail.com   01382 320493

Dundee: Broughty Ferry St Luke's and Queen Street (F W)
C. Graham D. Taylor BSc BD FIAB   2001   22 Albert Road, Broughty Ferry, Dundee DD5 1AZ   **01382 732094**
CTaylor@churchofscotland.org.uk   01382 779212

Dundee: Broughty Ferry St Stephen's and West (H W) linked with Dundee: Dundee (St Mary's) (H W)   office@dundeestmarys.co.uk
Keith F. Hall MA BD   1981   1994   33 Strathern Road, West Ferry, Dundee DD5 1PP   **01382 226271**
KHall@churchofscotland.org.uk   01382 778808

Dundee: Camperdown (H)
Guardianship of the Presbytery
Interim Moderator: Roderick J. Grahame   Camperdown Manse, Myrekirk Road, Dundee DD2 4SF   01382 561872
RGrahame@churchofscotland.org.uk

Dundee: Chalmers-Ardler (F H)
Jonathan W. Humphrey BSc BD PhD   2015   2018   The Manse, Turnberry Avenue, Dundee DD2 3TP   01382 827439
JHumphrey@churchofscotland.org.uk

Dundee: Coldside (F W)
Vacant   9 Abercorn Street, Dundee DD4 7HY   01382 458314

Dundee: Craigiebank (H W) linked with Dundee: Douglas and Mid Craigie (F W)   **01382 731173**
Vacant
Interim Moderator: Kenneth Andrew   kga@scot-int.com   01382 776765

Dundee: Downfield Mains (H W)   **downfieldmainsoffice@gmail.com**   **01382 810624/812166**
Nathan S. McConnell BS MA ThM   2002   2016   9 Elgin Street, Dundee DD3 8NL   01382 690196
NMcConnell@churchofscotland.org.uk

Dundee: Dundee (St Mary's) See Dundee: Broughty Ferry St Stephen's and West

Dundee: Fintry (F W)
Colin M. Brough BSc BD   1998   2002   4 Clive Street, Dundee DD4 7AW   01382 458629
CBrough@churchofscotland.org.uk
Catherine J. Brodie MA BA MPhil PGCE   2017   48h Cleghorn Street, Dundee DD2 2NJ   07432 513375
(Ordained Local Minister)   CBrodie@churchofscotland.org.uk

Dundee: Lochee (F H)
Roderick J. Grahame BD CPS DMin   1991   2018   32 Clayhills Drive, Dundee DD2 1SX   01382 561872
RGrahame@churchofscotland.org.uk

Willie Strachan MBA DipY&C   2013   Ladywell House, Lucky Slap, Monikie, Dundee DD5 3QG   01382 370286
(Ordained Local Minister)   WStrachan@churchofscotland.org.uk

Dundee: Logie and St John's Cross (F H W)
David T. Gray BArch BD   2010   2014   7 Hyndford Street, Dundee DD2 1HQ   **01382 668514** / 01382 668653 / 07789 718622
DGray@churchofscotland.org.uk

Dundee: Meadowside St Paul's (F H T W)
linked with Dundee: St Andrew's (F H T W)
Vacant   mspdundee@outlook.com   **01382 225420**
standrewsdundee@outlook.com   **01382 224860**
Session Clerk, Meadowside St Paul's: Margaret Adamson (Ms)   mspdundee@outlook.com   01382 668624
Session Clerk, St Andrew's: Helen Holden (Mrs)   hholdenuk@yahoo.com   01241 853242

Dundee: Menzieshill (F W)
Robert Mallinson BD   2010   The Manse, Charleston Drive, Dundee DD2 4ED   01382 667446 / 07595 249089
RMallinson@churchofscotland.org.uk

Dundee: St Andrew's See Dundee: Meadowside St Paul's

Dundee: St David's High Kirk (H W)
Emma McDonald BD   2013   2018   St David's High Kirk, 119A Kinghorne Road, Dundee DD3 6PW   01382 322955
EMcDonald@churchofscotland.org.uk

Dundee: The Steeple (F H T W)
Robert A. Calvert BSc BD DMin   1983   2014   128 Arbroath Road, Dundee DD4 7HR   **01382 200031** / 01382 522837 / 07532 029343
office@thesteeplechurch.org.uk
RCalvert@churchofscotland.org.uk

Dundee: Stobswell (F H)
William McLaren MA BD   1990   2007   23 Shamrock Street, Dundee DD4 7AH   **01382 461397** / 01382 459119
WMcLaren@churchofscotland.org.uk

Dundee: Strathmartine (F H W)
Stewart McMillan BD   1983   1990   19 Americanmuir Road, Dundee DD3 9AA   **01382 825817** / 01382 812423
SMcMillan@churchofscotland.org.uk

Dundee: Trinity (H W)
Vacant
Session Clerk: Ian Main
secretary@trinitychurchdundee.org
65 Clepington Road, Dundee DD4 7BQ
ian-main@sky.com
01382 458764
01382 783783

Dundee: West (F W)
Vacant
Interim Moderator: John J. Laidlaw
enquiries@dundeewestchurch.org
jacklaidlaw@blueyonder.co.uk
07341 255354
01382 477458

Dundee: Whitfield (H)
James L. Wilson BD CPS   1986   2001
53 Old Craigie Road, Dundee DD4 7JD
James.Wilson@churchofscotland.org.uk
01382 503012
01382 459249
07885 618659

Fowlis and Liff (F T W) linked with Lundie and Muirhead (F H T W) enquiries@churches-flandlm.co.uk
Donna M. Hays (Mrs) MTheol   2004   149 Coupar Angus Road, Muirhead of Liff, Dundee DD2 5QN
DipEd DipTMHA   DHays@churchofscotland.org.uk
01382 580210

Inchture and Kinnaird See Abernyte

Invergowrie (H W)
Vacant
Interim Moderator: Colin D. Wilson
information@invergowrie.f9.co.uk
2 Boniface Place, Invergowrie, Dundee DD2 5DW
cd.wilson663@tiscali.co.uk
01382 561118
01382 774059

Longforgan See Abernyte
Lundie and Muirhead See Fowlis and Liff

Monifieth (F H W)
Fiona J. Reynolds LLB BD   2018
office@monifiethparishchurch.co.uk
8 Church Street, Monifieth, Dundee DD5 4JP
01382 699183

Monikie and Newbigging and Murroes and Tealing See Auchterhouse

In other appointments

Campbell, Gordon MA BD CDipAF   2001 2004   Auxiliary Minister: an Honorary Chaplain: 2 Falkland Place, Kingoodie, Invergowrie, Dundee DD2 5DY
DipHSM CMgr MCMI MIHM   University of Dundee   g.a.campbell@dundee.ac.uk
AssocCIPD AFRIN ARSGS FRGS
FSAScot
01382 561383

Douglas, Fiona C. MBE MA BD PhD   1989 1997   Chaplain: University of Dundee   10 Springfield, Dundee DD1 4JE
f.c.douglas@dundee.ac.uk
01382 384157

Demitted

Name	Dates	Role	Address / Email	Telephone
Allan, Jean (Mrs) DCS	1989 2011	(Deacon)	12C Hindmarsh Avenue, Dundee DD3 7LW / jeannieallan45@googlemail.com	01382 827299 / 07709 959474
Barrett, Leslie M. BD FRICS	1991 2014	(Chaplain: University of Abertay, Dundee)	Dunelm Cottage, Logie, Cupar KY15 4SJ / lesliembarrett@btinternet.com	01334 870396
Collins, David A. BSc BD	1993 2016	(Auchterhouse with Monikie and Newbigging and Murroes and Tealing)	New Kirk Manse, 25 Ballinard Gardens, Broughty Ferry, Dundee DD5 1BZ / revdacollins@btinternet.com	01382 778874
Dempster, Colin J. BD CertMin	1990 2016	(Mearns Coastal)	35 Margaret Lindsay Place, Monifieth DD6 4RD / Coldcoast@btinternet.com	01382 532368
Fraser, Donald W. MA	1958 2010	(Monifieth)	robandmoiradonald@yahoo.co.uk / 1 Blake Avenue, Broughty Ferry, Dundee DD5 3LH / fraserdonald37@yahoo.co.uk	01382 477491 / 07531 863316
Greaves, Andrew T. BD	1985 2016	(Dundee: West)	Wards of Keithock, Brechin DD9 7PZ	01356 624479
Jamieson, David B. MA BD STM	1974 2011	(Monifieth)	8A Albert Street, Monifieth, Dundee DD5 4JS	01382 532772
Kay, Elizabeth (Miss) DipYCS	1993 2007	(Auxiliary Minister)	1 Kintail Walk, Inchture, Perth PH14 9RY / ekay007@btinternet.com	01828 686029
Laidlaw, John J. MA	1964 1996	(Adviser in Religious Education)	14 Dalhousie Road, Barnhill, Dundee DD5 2SQ / jacklaidlaw@blueyonder.co.uk	01382 477458
Laing, David J.H. BD DPS	1976 2014	(Dundee: Trinity)	18 Kerrington Crescent, Barnhill, Dundee DD5 2TN / david.laing@live.co.uk	01382 739586
Lillie, Fiona L. (Mrs) BA BD MLitt	1995 2017	(Glasgow: St John's Renfield)	4 McVicars Lane, Dundee DD1 4LH / fionalillie@btinternet.com	01382 229082
McLeod, David C. BSc MEng BD	1969 2001	(Dundee: Fairmuir)	6 Carseview Gardens, Dundee DD2 1NE	01382 685811
McMillan, Edith F. (Mrs) MA BD	1981 2018	(Dundee: Craigiebank with Douglas and Mid Craigie)	19 Americanmuir Road, Dundee DD3 9AA / EMcMillan@churchofscotland.org.uk	01382 812423
Mair, Michael V.A. MA BD	1968 2007	(Dundee: Craigiebank with Douglas and Mid Craigie)	48 Panmure Street, Monifieth DD5 4EH / mvamair@gmail.com	01382 530538
Martin, Janie (Miss) DCS	1979 2008	(Deacon)	16 Wentworth Road, Ardler, Dundee DD2 8SD / janimar@aol.com	01382 813786
Mitchell, Jack MA BD CTh	1987 1996	(Dundee: Menzieshill)	29 Carrick Gardens, Ayr KA7 2RT	
Ramsay, Robert J. LLB NP BD	1986 2018	(Invergowrie)	50 Nethergray Road, Dundee DD2 5GT / s3rjr@tiscali.co.uk	01382 562481
Reid, R. Gordon BSc BD MIET	1993 2010	(Carriden)	6 Bayview Place, Monifieth, Dundee DD5 4TN / GordonReid@aol.com	01382 520519
Robertson, James H. BSc BD	1975 2014	(Culloden: The Barn)	'Far End', 35 Mains Terrace, Dundee DD4 7BZ / jimrob838@gmail.com	07952 349884 / 01382 522773
Robson, George K. LTh DPS BA	1983 2011	(Dundee: Balgay)	11 Ceres Crescent, Broughty Ferry, Dundee DD5 3JN / gkrobson@virginmedia.com	07595 465838 / 01382 901212
Rose, Lewis (Mr) DCS	1993 2010	(Deacon)	6 Gauldie Crescent, Dundee DD3 0RR / lewis_rose48@yahoo.co.uk	01382 816580 / 07899 790466

Scott, James MA BD	1973	2010	(Drumoak-Durris)	3 Blake Place, Broughty Ferry, Dundee DD5 3LQ
				jimscott73@yahoo.co.uk 01382 739595
Taylor, Caroline (Mrs)	1995	2014	(Leuchars: St Athernase)	The Old Dairy, 15 Forthill Road, Broughty Ferry, Dundee DD5 3DH 01382 770198
				caro234@btinternet.com
Thornthwaite, Anthony P. MTh	1995	2019	(Dundee: Coldside)	19 Dovecote Way, Haddington EH41 4HY 01620 824385

DUNDEE ADDRESSES

Balgay	200 Lochee Road
Barnhill St Margaret's	10 Invermark Terrace
Broughty Ferry	
New Kirk	370 Queen Street
St James'	5 Fort Street
St Luke's and Queen Street	5 West Queen Street
St Stephen's and West	96 Dundee Road
Camperdown	22 Brownhill Road
Chalmers-Ardler	Turnberry Avenue
Coldside	Isla Street x Main Street
Craigiebank	Craigie Avenue at Greendykes Road
Douglas and Mid Craigie	Balbeggie Place
Downfield Mains	Haldane Street off Strathmartine Road
Dundee (St Mary's)	Nethergate
Fintry	Fintry Road x Fintry Drive
Lochee	191 High Street, Lochee
Logie and St John's Cross	Shaftesbury Rd x Blackness Ave
Meadowside St Paul's	114 Nethergate
Menzieshill	Charleston Drive, Menzieshill
St Andrew's	2 King Street
St David's High Kirk	119A Kinghorne Road
Steeple	Nethergate
Stobswell	170 Albert Street
Strathmartine	507 Strathmartine Road
Trinity	73 Crescent Street
West	130 Perth Road
Whitfield	Haddington Crescent

(30) ANGUS (W)

Meets at Forfar in St Margaret's Church Hall on the first Tuesday of February, March, May, September, November and December, and on the fourth Tuesday of June.

Clerk: **REV IAN A. McLEAN BSc BD DMin**
Acting Depute Clerk: **REV. MARGARET J. HUNT MA BD**
Presbytery Office: angus@churchofscotland.org.uk
St Margaret's Church, West High Street, Forfar DD8 1BJ 01307 464224

Aberlemno (H W) linked with Guthrie and Rescobie (W)
Brian Ramsay BD DPS MLitt 1980 1984 The Manse, Guthrie, Forfar DD8 2TP 01241 828243
BRamsay@churchofscotland.org.uk

Arbirlot linked with Carmyllie
Brian Dingwall BTh CQSW 1999 2016 The Manse, Arbirlot, Arbroath DD11 2NX 01241 874613
brian.d12@btinternet.com 07906 656847

Arbroath: Old and Abbey (F H W)
Dolly Purnell BD 2003 2014 church.office@old-and-abbey-church.org.uk 01241 877068
51 Cliffburn Road, Arbroath DD11 5BA Tel/Fax 01241 872196
DPurnell@churchofscotland.org.uk

Tel/Fax

Arbroath: St Andrew's (F H W)
W. Martin Fair BA BD DMin
1992
office@arbroathstandrews.org.uk   **01241 431135**
92 Grampian Gardens, Arbroath DD11 4AQ   01241 873238
MFair@churchofscotland.org.uk

Arbroath: St Vigeans (F H W)
Guardianship of the Presbytery
Session Clerk: Margaret Pullar (Mrs)
office.stvigeans@gmail.com   **01241 879567**
The Manse, St Vigeans, Arbroath DD11 4RF   01241 873206
margaret.pullar@btinternet.com   01241 876667

Arbroath: West Kirk (H)
Vacant
Session Clerk: William Clark
1 Charles Avenue, Arbroath DD11 2EY   01241 872244
w467clark@btinternet.com
New charge formed by the union of Arbroath: Knox's and Arbroath: West

Barry (W) linked with Carnoustie (F W)
Michael S. Goss BD DPS
1991   2003
44 Terrace Road, Carnoustie DD7 7AR   01241 410194
MGoss@churchofscotland.org.uk   07787 141567

Brechin: Cathedral (H W)
Vacant
office@brechincathedral.org.uk   **01356 629360**
Chanonry Wynd, Brechin DD9 6JS   01356 624980

Brechin: Gardner Memorial (F H T W) linked with Farnell (W)
Vacant
Session Clerk, Gardner Memorial:
Dorothy Black (Miss)
Gardner Memorial: **01356 629191**
office@gardnermemorial.plus.com   01356 622034
15 Caldhame Gardens, Brechin DD9 7JJ   01356 622614
dorothy.black6@btinternet.com

Carmyllie See Arbirlot
Carnoustie See Barry

Carnoustie: Panbride (F H W)
Annette Gordon BD
2017
8 Arbroath Road, Carnoustie DD7 6BL   01241 854478
AGordon@churchofscotland.org.uk

Colliston linked with Friockheim Kinnell linked with Inverkeilor and Lunan (H)
Peter A. Phillips BA
1995   2004
The Manse, Inverkeilor, Arbroath DD11 5SA   01241 830464
PPhillips@churchofscotland.org.uk

Dun and Hillside (F)
Fiona C. Bullock (Mrs) MA LLB BD   2014   4 Manse Road, Hillside, Montrose DD10 9FB   01674 830288
FBullock@churchofscotland.org.uk

Dunnichen, Letham and Kirkden (W)
Guardianship of the Presbytery
Session Clerk: Irene McGugan   7 Braehead Road, Letham, Forfar DD8 2PG   01307 818025
irene.mcgugan@btinternet.com   01307 818436

Eassie, Nevay and Newtyle
Carleen J. Robertson (Miss) BD   1992   2 Kirkton Road, Newtyle, Blairgowrie PH12 8TS   01828 650461
CRobertson@churchofscotland.org.uk

Edzell Lethnot Glenesk (F H W) linked with Fern Careston Menmuir (F W)   **elgparish@btconnect.com**
A.S. Wayne Pearce MA PhD   2002   2017   19 Lethnot Road, Edzell, Brechin DD9 7TG   **01356 647815**
ASWaynePearce@churchofscotland.org.uk   01356 648117

Farnell See Brechin: Gardner Memorial
Fern Careston Menmuir See Edzell Lethnot Glenesk

Forfar: East and Old (F H W)   **eando_office@yahoo.co.uk**
Barbara Ann Sweetin BD   2011   The Manse, Lour Road, Forfar DD8 2BB   01307 248228
BSweetin@churchofscotland.org.uk

Forfar: Lowson Memorial (F H)
Karen Fenwick BSc BD MPhil PhD   2006   1 Jamieson Street, Forfar DD8 2HY   01307 468585
KFenwick@churchofscotland.org.uk

Forfar: St Margaret's (F H W)   **stmargaretsforfar@gmail.com**
Margaret J. Hunt (Mrs) MA BD   2014   St Margaret's Manse, 15 Potters Park Crescent, Forfar DD8 1HH   **01307 464224**
MHunt@churchofscotland.org.uk   01307 462044

Friockheim Kinnell See Colliston

Glamis (H), Inverarity and Kinnettles (W)
Guardianship of the Presbytery
Session Clerk: Mary Reid (Mrs)   mmreid@btinternet.com   01307 840999

Guthrie and Rescobie See Aberlemno
Inverkeilor and Lunan See Colliston

Montrose: Old and St Andrew's (F W)
Ian A. McLean BSc BD DMin   1981   2008   2 Rosehill Road, Montrose DD10 8ST   01674 672447
                                                          IMcLean@churchofscotland.org.uk
Ian Gray   2013   2017   The Mallards, 15 Rossie Island Road, Montrose DD10 9NH   01674 677126
(Ordained Local Minister)   IGray@churchofscotland.org.uk

Montrose: South and Ferryden (W)
Geoffrey Redmayne BSc BD MPhil   2000   2016   Inchbrayock Manse, Usan, Montrose DD10 9SD   01674 675634
                                                          GRedmayne@churchofscotland.org.uk

Oathlaw Tannadice (F W) linked with The Glens and Kirriemuir United (F W)
John K. Orr BD MTh   2012   26 Quarry Park, Kirriemuir DD8 4DR   **01575 572819**
                                                          JOrr@churchofscotland.org.uk   01575 572610
Linda Stevens (Mrs) BSc BD PgDip   2006   17 North Latch Road, Brechin DD9 6LE   01356 623415
(Team Minister)   LStevens@churchofscotland.org.uk   07801 192730

New charge formed by the union of Kirriemuir: St Andrew's and The Glens and Kirriemuir: Old

The Glens and Kirriemuir United See Oathlaw Tannadice

The Isla Parishes (W)
Stephen A. Blakey BSc BD   1977   2018   Balduff House, Kilry, Blairgowrie PH11 8HS   01575 560226
                                                          SBlakey@churchofscotland.org.uk

In other appointments

Milliken, Jamie BD RN   2005 2018   Royal Naval Chaplain   St Christopher's Church, 45 Commando Group, RM Condor,
                                                                    Arbroath DD11 3SP
                                                                    jmilliken@churchofscotland.org.uk

Demitted

Duncan, Robert F. MTheol   1986 2001   (Lochgelly: St Andrew's)   25 Rowan Avenue, Kirriemuir DD8 4TB   01575 573973
Edwards, Dougal BTh   2013 2017   (Ordained Local Minister)   25 Mackenzie Street, Carnoustie DD7 6HD   01241 852666

Gough, Ian G. MA BD MTh DMin	1974 2009	(Arbroath: Knox's with Arbroath: St Vigeans)	23 Keptie Road, Arbroath DD11 3ED ianggough@btinternet.com	07891 838379
Hastie, George I. MA BD	1971 2009	(Mearns Coastal)	23 Borrowfield Crescent, Montrose DD10 9BR	01674 672290
Morrice, Alastair M. MA BD	1968 2000	(Ruberglen: Stonelaw)	5 Brechin Road, Kirriemuir DD8 4BX ambishkek@swissmail.org	01575 574102
Norrie, Graham MA BD	1967 2007	(Forfar: East and Old)	'Novar', 14A Wyllie Street, Forfar DD8 3DN grahamnorrie@hotmail.com	01307 468152
Robertson, George R. LTh	1985 2004	(Udny and Pitmedden)	3 Slateford Gardens, Edzell, Brechin DD9 7SX geomag.robertson@btinternet.com	01356 647322
Smith, Hamish G.	1965 1993	(Auchterless with Rothienorman)	11A Guthrie Street, Letham, Forfar DD8 2PS	01307 818973
Thomas, Martyn R.H. CEng MIStructE	1987 2002	(Fowlis and Liff with Lundie and Muirhead of Liff)	14 Kirkgait, Letham, Forfar DD8 2XQ martyn317thomas@btinternet.com	01307 818084
Thomas, Shirley A. (Mrs) DipSocSci AMIA (Aux)	2000 2006	(Auxiliary Minister)	14 Kirkgait, Letham, Forfar DD8 2XQ martyn317thomas@btinternet.com	01307 818084
Watt, Alan G.N. MTh CQSW DipCommEd	1996 2009	(Edzell Lethnot Glenesk with Fern Careston Menmuir)	6 Pine Way, Friockheim, Arbroath DD11 4WF watt455@btinternet.com	01241 826018
Webster, Allan F. MA BD	1978 2013	(Workplace Chaplain)	42 McCulloch Drive, Forfar DD8 2EB allanfwebster@aol.com	01307 464252 07546 276725

ANGUS ADDRESSES

Arbroath: Old and Abbey		West Abbey Street
St Andrew's		Hamilton Green
St Vigeans		St Vigeans Brae
West Kirk		Keptie Street
Brechin: Cathedral		Bishops Close
	Gardner Memorial	South Esk Street
Carnoustie		Dundee Street
	Panbride	Arbroath Road
Forfar: East and Old		East High Street
	Lowson Memorial	Jamieson Street
	St Margaret's	West High Street
Kirriemuir: United		High Street
Montrose: South and Ferryden		Church Road, Ferryden
	Old and St Andrew's	High Street

(31) ABERDEEN (F W)

Meets on the first Tuesday of February, March, May, September, October, November and December, and on the fourth Tuesday of June. The venue varies.

Clerk:	REV. JOHN A. FERGUSON BD DipMin DMin	
Depute Clerk:	MRS CHERYL BRANKIN BA	
Treasurer:	MR ALAN MORRISON	
Presbytery Office:	Mastrick Church, Greenfern Road, Aberdeen AB16 6TR aberdeen@churchofscotland.org.uk	01224 698119

Aberdeen: Bridge of Don Oldmachar (F H W) secretary@oldmacharchurch.org
Vacant   60 Newburgh Circle, Aberdeen AB22 8QZ   **01224 709299**
Joseph K. Somevi BSc MSc PhD MRICS   2015   2018   97 Ashwood Road, Aberdeen AB22 8QX   01224 823283
MRTPI MIEMA CertCRS   (Ordained Local   JSomevi@churchofscotland.org.uk   01224 826362
Minister)   07886 533259

Aberdeen: Craigiebuckler (F H W)   **office@craigiebuckler.org.uk**   **01224 315649**
Kenneth L. Petrie MA BD   1984   1999   185 Springfield Road, Aberdeen AB15 8AA   01224 315125
                                                                      KPetrie@churchofscotland.org.uk

Aberdeen: Ferryhill (F H W)   **office@ferryhillparishchurch.org**   **01224 213093**
J. Peter N. Johnston BSc BD   2001   2013   54 Polmuir Road, Aberdeen AB11 7RT   01224 949192
                                                                      PJohnston@churchofscotland.org.uk

Aberdeen: Garthdee (F H W)   **admin@garthdeechurch.co.uk**
Vacant
Session Clerk: Hilda Smith (Mrs)   smithh09@hotmail.com   01224 311309

Aberdeen: High Hilton (F H W)   **01224 494717**
G. Hutton B. Steel MA BD   1982   2013   24 Rosehill Drive, Aberdeen AB24 4JJ   01224 493552
                                                                      Hutton.Steel@churchofscotland.org.uk

Aberdeen: Holburn West (F H W)   **churchoffice@holburnwestchurch.org.uk**   **01224 571120**
Duncan C. Eddie MA BD   1992   1999   31 Cranford Road, Aberdeen AB10 7NJ   01224 325873
                                                                      DEddie@churchofscotland.org.uk

Aberdeen: Mannofield (F H T W)   **office@mannofieldchurch.org.uk**   **01224 310087**
Keith T. Blackwood BD DipMin   1997   2007   21 Forest Avenue, Aberdeen AB15 4TU   01224 315748
                                                                      KBlackwood@churchofscotland.org.uk

Aberdeen: Mastrick (F H W)   **01224 694121**
Susan J. Sutherland (Mrs) BD   2009   2017   8 Corse Wynd, Kingswells, Aberdeen AB15 8TP   01224 279562
                                                                      SSutherland@churchofscotland.org.uk

Aberdeen: Middlefield (F H)   **01224 682310**
Guardianship of the Presbytery
Session Clerk: Linda A. Forbes (Mrs)   linda56forbes@yahoo.co.uk   01224 691165

Aberdeen: Midstocket (H W)
Vacant
Session Clerk: Alison McLeod (Mrs)
secretary@midstocketchurch.org.uk — **01224 319519**
alisonmcleod99@sky.com — 01224 732227

Aberdeen: Northfield (F H)
Scott C. Guy BD — 1989 1998
28 Byron Crescent, Aberdeen AB16 7EX — **01224 692332**
SGuy@churchofscotland.org.uk — 01224 692332

Aberdeen: Queen's Cross (F H W)
Scott M. Rennie MA BD STM — 1999 2009
office@queenscrosschurch.org.uk — **01224 644742**
1 St Swithin Street, Aberdeen AB10 6XH — 01224 322549
SRennie@churchofscotland.org.uk

Aberdeen: Rubislaw (F H W)
Robert L. Smith BS MTh PhD — 2000 2013
rubislawchurch@btconnect.com — **01224 645477**
13 Oakhill Road, Aberdeen AB15 5ERR — 01224 314773
RSmith@churchofscotland.org.uk

Aberdeen: Ruthrieston West (F W)
Benjamin D.W. Byun BS MDiv MTh PhD — 1992 2008
53 Springfield Avenue, Aberdeen AB15 8JJ — 01224 312706
BByun@churchofscotland.org.uk

Aberdeen: St Columba's Bridge of Don (F H W)
Louis Kinsey BD DipMin TD — 1991
administrator@stcolumbaschurch.org.uk — **01224 825653**
151 Jesmond Avenue, Aberdeen AB22 8UG — 01224 705337
LKinsey@churchofscotland.org.uk

Aberdeen: St George's Tillydrone (F H W)
Vacant
Session Clerk: Kenneth Williamson
admin@tillydrone.church — **01224 482204**
kdwllmsn@yahoo.co.uk — 01224 487302

Aberdeen: St John's Church for Deaf People
Mary Whittaker BSc BD — 2011 2018
11 Templand Road, Lhanbryde, Elgin IV30 8BR — Text only 07501 454766
MWhittaker@churchofscotland.org.uk — or contact Aberdeen: St Mark's

Aberdeen: St Machar's Cathedral (F H T W)
Vacant
Session Clerk: Alan Grant
office@stmachar.com — **01224 485988**
bryce.grant@outlook.com — 07801 078000

Aberdeen: St Mark's (F H W)
Vacant
Session Clerks: Helen Burr (Mrs)
                Dianne Morrison (Miss)

office@stmarksaberdeen.org.uk
helen.burr@hotmail.co.uk
diannemorrison@talktalk.net

01224 640672
07751 851610
07767 140582

Aberdeen: St Mary's (F H)
Elsie J. Fortune (Mrs) BSc BD   2003

stmaryschurch924@btinternet.com
456 King Street, Aberdeen AB24 3DE
EFortune@churchofscotland.org.uk

01224 487227
01224 633778

Aberdeen: St Nicholas Kincorth, South of (W)
Edward C. McKenna BD DPS   1989   2002

The Manse, Kincorth Circle, Aberdeen AB12 5NX
EMcKenna@churchofscotland.org.uk

01224 872820

Aberdeen: St Nicholas Uniting, Kirk of (F H W)
B. Stephen C. Taylor BA BBS MA MDiv   1984   2005

mither.kirk@btconnect.com
12 Louisville Avenue, Aberdeen AB15 4TX
BSCTaylor@churchofscotland.org.uk

01224 643494 (ext 21)
01224 314318
01224 649242 (Fax)

St Nicholas Uniting is a Local Ecumenical Partnership with the United Reformed Church

Aberdeen: St Stephen's (F H W)
Maggie Whyte BD   2010

6 Belvidere Street, Aberdeen AB25 2QS
Maggie.Whyte@churchofscotland.org.uk

01224 624443
01224 635694

Aberdeen: South Holburn (H W)
David J. Stewart BD MTh DipMin   2000   2018

54 Woodstock Road, Aberdeen AB15 5JF
DStewart@churchofscotland.org.uk

07498 781457
01224 317975

Aberdeen: Stockethill (W)
Ian M. Aitken MA BD   1999

52 Ashgrove Road West, Aberdeen AB16 5EE
IAitken@churchofscotland.org.uk

01224 686929

Aberdeen: Summerhill (F H W)
Michael R.R. Shewan MA BD CPS   1985   2010

36 Stronsay Drive, Aberdeen AB15 6JL
MShewan@churchofscotland.org.uk

01224 324669

Aberdeen: Torry St Fittick's (F H W)
Edmond Gatima BEng BD MSc MPhil PhD   2013

11 Devanha Gardens East, Aberdeen AB11 7UN
EGatima@churchofscotland.org.uk

01224 899183
01224 588245

Aberdeen: Woodside (F H W)
Markus Auffermann DipTheol — 1999 2006
322 Clifton Road, Aberdeen AB24 4HQ
officewpc@talktalk.net
MAuffermann@churchofscotland.org.uk
01224 277249
01224 484562

Bucksburn Stoneywood (H W)
Nigel Parker BD MTh DMin — 1994
23 Polo Park, Stoneywood, Aberdeen AB21 9JW
NParker@churchofscotland.org.uk
01224 712411
01224 712635

Cults (F H T W)
Shuna M. Dicks BSc BD — 2010 2018
1 Cairnlee Terrace, Bieldside, Aberdeen AB15 9AE
cultsparishchurch@btinternet.com
SDicks@churchofscotland.org.uk
01224 869028
01224 861692

Dyce (F H T W)
Manson C. Merchant BD CPS — 1992 2008
100 Burnside Road, Dyce, Aberdeen AB21 7HA
dyceparishchurch@outlook.com
MMerchant@churchofscotland.org.uk
01224 771295
01224 722380

Kingswells (F H W)
Laurene M. Lafontaine BA MDiv — 1987 2019
Kingswells Manse, Lang Stracht, Aberdeen AB15 8PN
LLafontaine@churchofscotland.org.uk
01224 749986

Newhills (F H W)
Vacant
Session Clerk: Myra Kinnaird (Mrs)
office@newhillschurch.org.uk
myra@no24.co.uk
01224 716161
07833 197202

Peterculter (F H W)
John A. Ferguson BD DipMin DMin — 1988 1999
7 Howie Lane, Peterculter AB14 0LJ
secretary@culterkirk.co.uk
JFerguson@churchofscotland.org.uk
01224 735845
01224 735041

In other appointments

Craig, Gordon T. BD DipMin — 1988 2012
Chaplain to UK Oil and Gas Industry
Shell Exploration and Production, Tullos Complex, 1 Altens Farm Road, Aberdeen AB12 3FY
gordon.craig@ukoilandgaschaplaincy.com
01224 882600

Hutchison, David S. BSc BD ThM — 1991 2015
Chaplain: University of Aberdeen
The Den of Keithfield, Tarves, Ellon AB41 7NU
d.hutchison@abdn.ac.uk
01651 851501

Rodgers, D. Mark BA BD MTh — 1987 2003
Head of Spiritual Care, NHS Grampian
63 Cordiner Place, Hilton, Aberdeen AB24 4SB
mrodgers@nhs.net
01224 379135

Swinton, John (Prof.) BD PhD — 1999
University of Aberdeen
51 Newburgh Circle, Bridge of Don, Aberdeen AB22 8XA
j.swinton@abdn.ac.uk
01224 825637

Demitted

Gardner, Bruce K. MA BD PhD	1988 2011	(Aberdeen: Bridge of Don Oldmachar)	21 Hopetoun Crescent, Bucksburn, Aberdeen AB21 9QY drbrucekgardner@aol.com	07891 186724
Groves, Ian B. BD CPS	1989 2016	(Inverurie West)	28 Parkhill Circle, Dyce, Aberdeen AB21 7FN ian@thegroves.me.uk	01224 774380
Lundie, Ann V. (Miss) DCS	1972 2007	(Deacon)	20 Langdykes Drive, Cove, Aberdeen AB12 3HW ann.lundie@btopenworld.com	01224 898416
Maciver, Norman MA BD DMin	1976 2006	(Newhills)	4 Mundi Crescent, Newmachar, Aberdeen AB21 0LY norirene@aol.com	01651 869434
Main, Alan (Prof.) TD MA BD STM PhD DD	1963 2001	(University of Aberdeen)	Kirkfield, Barthol Chapel, Inverurie AB51 8TD amain@alktalk.net	01651 806773
Montgomerie, Jean B. (Miss) MA BD	1973 2006	(Forfar: St Margaret's)	12 St Ronan's Place, Peterculter, Aberdeen AB14 0QX revjeanb@tiscali.co.uk	01224 732350
Phillippo, Michael MTh BSc BVetMed MRCVS	2003 2011	(Auxiliary Minister)	126 St Michael's Road, Newtonhill AB39 3XW	01569 739475
Richardson, Thomas C. LTh ThB	1971 2004	(Cults: West)	19 Kinkell Road, Aberdeen AB15 8HR tomandpatrich@gmail.com	01224 315328
Sheret, Brian S. MA BD DPhil	1982 2009	(Glasgow: Drumchapel Drumry St Mary's)	59 Airyhall Crescent, Aberdeen AB15 7QS	01224 323032
Stewart, James C. MA BD STM FSAScot	1960 2000	(Aberdeen: Kirk of St Nicholas)	54 Murray Terrace, Aberdeen AB11 7SB study@jascstewart.co.uk	01224 587071
Weir, James J.C.M. BD	1991 2018	(Aberdeen: St George's Tillydrone)	114 Hilton Heights, Woodside, Aberdeen AB24 4QF	01224 901430
Youngson, Elizabeth J.B. BD	1996 2015	(Aberdeen: Mastrick)	47 Corse Drive, The Links, Dubford, Aberdeen AB23 8LN elizabeth.youngson@btinternet.com	07788 294745

ABERDEEN ADDRESSES

Bridge of Don Oldmachar	Ashwood Park
Craigiebuckler	Springfield Road
Cults	Quarry Road, Cults
Dyce	Victoria Street, Dyce
Ferryhill	Fonthill Road x Polmuir Road
Garthdee	Ramsay Gardens
High Hilton	Hilton Drive
Holburn West	Great Western Road
Kingswells	Old Skene Road, Kingswells
Mannofield	Great Western Road x Craigton Road
Mastrick	Greenfern Road
Middlefield	Manor Avenue
Midstocket	Mid Stocket Road
Northfield	Byron Crescent
Peterculter	Craigton Crescent
Queen's Cross	Albyn Place
Rubislaw	Queen's Gardens
Ruthrieston West	Broomhill Road
St Columba's Bridge of Don	Braehead Way, Bridge of Don
St George's Tillydrone	Hayton Road, Tillydrone
St John's for the Deaf	at St Mark's
St Machar's Cathedral	The Chanonry
St Mark's	Rosemount Viaduct
St Mary's	King Street
St Nicholas Kincorth, South of	Kincorth Circle
St Nicholas Uniting, Kirk of	Union Street
St Stephen's	Powis Place
South Holburn	Holburn Street
Stockethill	Cairncy Community Centre
Summerhill	Stronsay Drive
Torry St Fittick's	Walker Road
Woodside	Church Street, Woodside

(32) KINCARDINE AND DEESIDE (W)

Meets in various locations as arranged on the first Tuesday of September, October, November, December, March and May, and on the last Tuesday of June at 7pm.

Clerk:	REV. HUGH CONKEY BSc BD	39 St Ternans Road, Newtonhill, Stonehaven AB39 3PF kincardinedeeside@churchofscotland.org.uk	01569 739297

Aberluthnott (F W) linked with Laurencekirk (F H W)
Vacant
Interim Moderator: Brian D. Smith
contact@parishchurchofaberluthnottandlaurencekirk.co.uk
Aberdeen Road, Laurencekirk AB30 1AJ
BSmith@churchofscotland.org.uk
01561 378838
01561 340203

Aboyne-Dinnet (F H W) linked with Cromar (F W)
Frank Ribbons MA BD DipEd 1985
49 Charlton Crescent, Aboyne AB34 5GN
FRibbons@churchofscotland.org.uk   2011
01339 887267

Arbuthnott, Bervie and Kinneff (F T W)
Andrew Morrison MA BD   2019
5 West Park Place, Inverbervie, Montrose DD10 0XA
Andrew.Morrison@churchofscotland.org.uk
01561 362530

Banchory-Ternan: East (F H W)
Alan J.S. Murray BSc BD PhD   2003   2013
info@banchoryeastchurch.com
East Manse, Station Road, Banchory AB31 5YP
AJSMurray@churchofscotland.org.uk
01330 820380
01330 822481

Banchory-Ternan: West (F H T W)
Antony A. Stephen MA BD   2001   2011
office@banchorywestchurch.com
The Manse, 2 Wilson Road, Banchory AB31 5UY
TStephen@churchofscotland.org.uk
01330 822006
01330 822811

Birse and Feughside (W)
Amy C. Pierce BA BDiv   2017   2019
The Manse, Finzean, Banchory AB31 6PB
ACPierce@churchofscotland.org.uk
01330 850776
07814 194997

Braemar and Crathie (F W)
Kenneth I. Mackenzie DL BD CPS   1990   2005
The Manse, Crathie, Ballater AB35 5UL
KMacKenzie@churchofscotland.org.uk
01339 742208

Cromar See Aboyne-Dinnet

Charge / Minister			Address / Contact	Telephone
Drumoak-Durris (F H W) Jean A. Boyd MSc BSc BA	2016		26 Sunnyside Drive, Drumoak, Banchory AB31 3EW JBoyd@churchofscotland.org.uk	01330 811031
Glenmuick (Ballater) (H W) David L.C. Barr	2014		The Manse, Craigendarroch Walk, Ballater AB35 5ZB DBarr@churchofscotland.org.uk	01339 756111
Laurencekirk See Aberluthnott				
Maryculter Trinity (W) Melvyn J. Griffiths BTh DipTheol DMin	1978	2014	**thechurchoffice@tiscali.co.uk** The Manse, Kirkton of Maryculter, Aberdeen AB12 5FS MGriffiths@churchofscotland.org.uk	**01224 735983** 01224 730150
Mearns Coastal (F W) Guardianship of the Presbytery Norman D. Lennox-Trewren (Ordained Local Minister)	2018		32 Haulkerton Crescent, Laurencekirk AB30 1FB NLennoxTrewren@churchofscotland.org.uk	01561 377359
Mid Deeside (W) Holly Smith BSIS MDiv MEd	2009	2019	Lochnagar, Torphins, Banchory AB31 4JU Holly.smith@churchofscotland.org.uk	**01339 889160** 01339 882915
Newtonhill (W) Hugh Conkey BSc BD	1987	2001	39 St Ternans Road, Newtonhill, Stonehaven AB39 3PF HConkey@churchofscotland.org.uk	01569 730143
Portlethen (F H W) Rodolphe Blanchard-Kowal (Exchange Minister)	2013	2017	**portlethenpc@btconnect.com** 18 Rowanbank Road, Portlethen, Aberdeen AB12 4NX RKowal@churchofscotland.org.uk	**01224 782883** 01224 780211
Stonehaven: Carronside (H W) Vacant Interim Moderator: David Galbraith			**secretary.dunnottarchurch@outlook.com** Dunnottar Manse, Stonehaven AB39 3XL David.Galbraith@churchofscotland.org.uk	**01569 760930** 01569 762166 01561 320779

New charge formed by the union of Stonehaven: Dunnottar and Stonehaven; South

Stonehaven: Fetteresso (H W) office@fetteresso.org **01569 767689**
Vacant
Interim Moderator: William F. Wallace williamwallace39@talktalk.net 01330 822259

West Mearns (F W)

Brian D. Smith BD	1990	2016	The Manse, Fettercairn, Laurencekirk AB30 1UE BSmith@churchofscotland.org.uk		01561 340203

Demitted

Blair, Fyfe BA BD DMin	1989	2019	(Stonehaven: Fetteresso)	19 Crichie Place, Fettercairn, Laurencekirk AB30 1EZ Fyfe.Blair@churchofscotland.org.uk	01561 340579
Broadley, Linda J. (Mrs) LTh DipEd	1996	2013	(Dun and Hillside)	Snaefell, Lochside Road, St Cyrus, Montrose DD10 0DB lindabroadley@btinternet.com	01674 850141
Brown, J.W.S. BTh	1960	1995	(Cromar)	10 Forestside Road, Banchory AB31 5ZH iainisobel@aol.com	01330 824353
Duncan, Rosslyn P. BD MTh	2007	2018	(Stonehaven: Dunnottar with Stonehaven: South)	Four Oaks, Broomdykes, Duns TD1 3LZ rosslynpduncan@gmail.com	07899 878427
Lamb, A. Douglas MA	1964	2002	(Dalry: St Margaret's)	9 Luther Drive, Laurencekirk AB30 1FE lamb.edzell@talk21.com	01561 376816
Purves, John P. S. MBE BSc BD	1978	2013	(Colombo, Sri Lanka: St Andrew's Scots Kirk)	Lonville Cottage, 20 Viewfield Road, Ballater AB35 5RD john@thepurves.com	01339 754081
Wallace, William F. BDS BD	1968	2008	(Wick: Pulteneytown and Thrumster)	Lachan Cottage, 29 Station Road, Banchory AB31 5XX williamwallace39@talktalk.net	01330 822259
Watson, John M. LTh	1989	2009	(Aberdeen: St Mark's)	20 Greystone Place, Newtonhill, Stonehaven AB39 3UL johnmutchwatson2065@btinternet.com	01569 730604 07733 334380

(33) GORDON (F W)

Meets at various locations on the first Tuesday of February, March, April, May, September, October, November and December; and on the last Tuesday of June.

Clerk: REV. G. EUAN D. GLEN BSc BD The Manse, 26 St Ninians, Monymusk, Inverurie AB51 7HF **01467 651470**
gordon@churchofscotland.org.uk

Barthol Chapel (F) linked with Tarves (F W)

Alison I. Swindells (Mrs) LLB BD DMin	1998	2017	8 Murray Avenue, Tarves, Ellon AB41 7LZ ASwindells@churchofscotland.org.uk		01651 851295

Belhelvie (F H W)
Paul McKeown BSc PhD BD   2000   2005
belhelviecofs@btconnect.com
Belhelvie Manse, Balmedie, Aberdeen   AB23 8YR
PMcKeown@churchofscotland.org.uk
01358 742227

Blairdaff and Chapel of Garioch (F W)
Martyn S. Sanders BA CertEd   2013   2015
The Manse, Chapel of Garioch, Inverurie   AB51 5HE
MSanders@churchofscotland.org.uk
01467 681619
07814 164373

Cluny (F H W) linked with Monymusk (F H W)
G. Euan D. Glen BSc BD   1992
The Manse, 26 St Ninians, Monymusk, Inverurie   AB51 7HF
GGlen@churchofscotland.org.uk
01467 651470

Culsalmond and Rayne (F W) linked with Daviot (H W)
Mary M. Cranfield MA BD DMin   1989
The Manse, Daviot, Inverurie   AB51 0HY
MCranfield@churchofscotland.org.uk
01467 671241

Cushnie and Tough (H)
Vacant
Session Clerk: Ronald Ferguson
The Manse, Muir of Fowlis, Alford   AB33 8JU
ronald_ferguson@btinternet.com
01975 581239
01975 563404

Daviot See Culsalmond and Rayne

Echt and Midmar (F H W)
Sheila M. Mitchell BD MTh   1995   2018
The Manse, Echt, Westhill   AB32 7AB
SMitchell@churchofscotland.org.uk
01330 860004

Ellon (F T W)
Alastair J. Bruce   BD MTh PGCE   2015
info@ellonparishchurch.co.uk
The Manse, 12 Union Street, Ellon   AB41 9BA
ABruce@churchofscotland.org.uk
01358 725690
01358 723787

Fintray Kinellar Keithhall (F W)
Vacant
01224 790439

Foveran (W)
Richard M.C. Reid BSc BD MTh   1991   2013
The Manse, Foveran, Ellon   AB41 6AP
RReid@churchofscotland.org.uk
01358 789288

Howe Trinity (F W)
John A. Cook MA BD DMin — 1986 2000
enquiries@howetrinity.org.uk
The Manse, 110 Main Street, Alford   AB33 8AD
John.Cook@churchofscotland.org.uk
01975 562829
01975 562282

Huntly Cairnie Glass
Thomas R. Calder LLB BD WS — 1994
The Manse, Queen Street, Huntly   AB54 8EB
TCalder@churchofscotland.org.uk
01466 792630

Insch-Leslie-Premnay-Oyne (F H W)
Kay F. Gauld BD STM PhD — 1999 2015
66 Denwell Road, Insch   AB52 6LH
KGauld@churchofscotland.org.uk
01464 820404

Inverurie: St Andrew's (F)
Vacant
standrews@btinternet.com
27 Buchan Drive, Newmachar, Aberdeen   AB21 0NR
01467 628740
01651 862281

Inverurie: West (F T W)
Rhona P. Cathcart BA BSc BD — 2017
admin@inveruriewestchurch.org
West Manse, 1 Westburn Place, Inverurie   AB51 5QS
RCathcart@churchofscotland.org.uk
01647 620285
01467 620285

Kemnay (F T W)
Joshua M. Mikelson BA MDiv — 2008 2015
office@kemnayparish.church
15 Kirkland, Kemnay, Inverurie   AB51 5QD
JMikelson@churchofscotland.org.uk
Tel/Fax
01467 643883
01467 642219

Kintore (F H W)
Neil W. Meyer BD MTh — 2000 2014
28 Oakhill Road, Kintore, Inverurie   AB51 0FH
NMeyer@churchofscotland.org.uk
01467 632219

Meldrum and Bourtie (F W)
Vacant
info@meldrumandbourtiechurch.com
The Manse, Urquhart Road, Oldmeldrum, Inverurie   AB51 0EX
01651 872250

Methlick (F W)
William A. Stalder BA MDiv MLitt PhD — 2014
The Manse, Manse Road, Methlick, Ellon   AB41 7DG
WStalder@churchofscotland.org.uk
01651 806264

Monymusk See Cluny

New Machar (F W)
Douglas G. McNab BA BD   1999   2010   The New Manse, Newmachar, Aberdeen AB21 0RD   01651 862278
DMcNab@churchofscotland.org.uk

Noth
Regine U. Cheyne (Mrs) MA BSc BD   1988   2010   Manse of Noth, Kennethmont, Huntly AB54 4NP   01464 831690
RCheyne@churchofscotland.org.uk

Skene (F H W)   **info.skeneparish@gmail.com**   **01224 742512**
Stella Campbell MA (Oxon) BD   2012   The Manse, Manse Road, Kirkton of Skene, Westhill AB32 6LX   01224 745955
SCampbell@churchofscotland.org.uk
Marion G. Stewart (Miss) DCS   1991   1994   Kirk Cottage, Kirkton of Skene, Westhill AB32 6XE   01224 743407
MStewart@churchofscotland.org.uk

Strathbogie Drumblade
Vacant   49 Deveron Park, Huntly AB54 8UZ   01466 792702

Tarves See Barthol Chapel

Udny and Pitmedden (F W)
Vacant   The Manse, Manse Road, Udny Green, Ellon AB41 7RS   01651 843794

Upper Donside (F H)
Vacant   **upperdonsideparishchurch@btinternet.com**   01464 861745
Session Clerk: Margaret Thomson (Mrs)   margaret.thomson9@btpenworld.com

In other appointments
Irvine, Carl J. BA   2017   Ordained Local Minister, Presbytery   Northside of Glack, Meikle Wartle, Inverurie AB51 5AR   01467 671135
CIrvine@churchofscotland.org.uk

Demitted
Christie, Andrew C. LTh   1975 2000   (Banchory-Devenick and Maryculter/Cookney)   17 Broadstraik Close, Elrick, Aberdeen AB32 6JP   01224 746888
Craggs, Sheila (Mrs)   2001 2016   (Auxiliary Minister)   7 Morar Court, Ellon AB41 9GG   01358 723055

Craig, Anthony J.D. BD	1987	2009	(Glasgow: Maryhill)	4 Hightown, Collieston, Ellon AB41 8RS / aacraig@btinternet.com	01358 751247
Dryden, Ian MA DipEd	1988	2001	(New Machar)	16 Glenhome Gardens, Dyce, Aberdeen AB21 7FG / ian@idryden.freeserve.co.uk	01224 722820
Falconer, James B. BD	1982	2018	(Hospital Chaplain)	3 Brimmond Walk, Westhill AB32 6XH	01224 744621
Ford, Carolyn (Carol) H.M. DSD RSAMD BD	2003	2018	(Edinburgh: St Margaret's)	4 Mitchell Avenue, Huntly AB54 8DW	
Greig, Alan BSc BD	1977	2017	(Interim Minister)	1 Dunnydeer Place, Insch AB52 6HP / greig@kincarr.free-online.co.uk	01464 820332
Hawthorn, Daniel MA BD DMin	1965	2004	(Belhelvie)	7 Crimond Drive, Ellon AB41 8BT / danhawthorn@compuserve.com	01358 723981
Jones, Robert A. LTh CA	1966	1997	(Marnoch)	13 Gordon Terrace, Inverurie AB51 4GT	01467 622691
Macalister, Eleanor	1994	2006	(Ellon)	Quarryview, Ythan Bank, Ellon AB41 7TH / macall ster@aol.com	01358 761402
MacGregor, Neil I.M. BD	1995	2019	(Strathbogie Drumblade)	1 Abban Place, Inverness IV3 8GZ	01464 820387
Mack, John C. JP	1985	2008	(Auxiliary Minister)	The Willows, Auchleven, Insch AB52 6QB	01464 820749
McLeish, Robert S.	1970	2000	(Insch-Leslie-Premnay-Oyne)	19 Western Road, Insch AB52 6JR	01224 743184
Rodger, Matthew A. BD	1978	1999	(Ellon)	15 Meadowlands Drive, Westhill AB32 6EJ	01464 821124
Stoddart, A. Grainger	1975	2001	(Meldrum and Bourtie)	6 Mayfield Gardens, Insch AB52 6XL	07749 993070
Telfer, Iain J.M. BD DPS	1978	2018	(Chaplain: Royal Infirmary of Edinburgh)	66 High Street, Inverurie AB51 3XS / iain_telfer@yahoo.co.uk	
Thomson, Iain U. MA BD	1970	2011	(Skene)	4 Keirhill Gardens, Westhill AB32 6AZ / iainuthomson@googlemail.com	01224 746743

(34) BUCHAN (W)

Meets at St Kane's Centre, New Deer, Turriff on the first Tuesday of February, March, May, September, October, November and December, and on the third Tuesday of June.

Clerk:	REV. SHEILA M. KIRK BA LLB BD	The Manse, Old Deer, Peterhead AB42 5JB / **buchan@churchofscotland.org.uk**	01771 623582

Aberdour linked (W) with Pitsligo (F W)
Vacant
Interim Moderator: Ruth Mackenzie (Miss) — 31 Blairmore Park, Rosehearty, Fraserburgh AB43 7NZ / ursular@tiscali.co.uk — 01346 571823 / 01779 480680

Auchaber United (W) linked with Auchterless (W)
Stephen J. Potts BA — 2012 — The Manse, Auchterless, Turriff AB53 8BA / SPotts@churchofscotland.org.uk — 01888 511058

Auchterless See Auchaber United

Banff (F W) linked with King Edward (F W)
David I.W. Locke MA MSc BD 2000 2012 info@banffparishchurchofscotland.org.uk **01262 818211**
7 Colleonard Road, Banff AB45 1DZ 01261 812107
DLocke@churchofscotland.org.uk 07776 448301

Crimond (F W) linked with Lonmay (W)
Vacant The Manse, Crimond, Fraserburgh AB43 8QJ 01346 532431
Session Clerk, Crimond: Irene Fowlie (Mrs) fowlie@hotmail.com
Session Clerk, Lonmay: Roy Kinghorn strathelliefarm@btinternet.com 01346 532436

Cruden (F H W)
Sean Swindells BD DipMin MTh 1996 2019 8 Murray Avenue, Tarves, Ellon AB41 7LZ 01651 851295
SSwindells@churchofscotland.org.uk 07791 755976

Deer (F H)
Sheila M. Kirk BA LLB BD 2007 2010 The Manse, Old Deer, Peterhead AB42 5JB 01771 623582
SKirk@churchofscotland.org.uk

Fraserburgh: Old (W)
Vacant fraserburghopc@btconnect.com **01346 510139**
Interim Moderator: James Givan 4 Robbie's Road, Fraserburgh AB43 7AF 01346 515332
jim.givan@btinternet.com 01261 833318

Fraserburgh: South (H) linked with Inverallochy and Rathen: East
Vacant 15 Victoria Street, Fraserburgh AB43 9PJ 01346 518244
Session Clerk, Fraserburgh: South: William J. Smith bill.moira.smith@gmail.com 01346 513991

Fraserburgh: West (F H T W) linked with Rathen: West (T W)
Vacant 4 Kirkton Gardens, Fraserburgh AB43 8TU 01346 513303
Session Clerk, Fraserburgh: West: Jill Smith (Mrs) jill@fraserburgh-harbour.co.uk 01346 517972
Session Clerk, Rathen: West: Ian J. Campbell cicfarmers@hotmail.co.uk 01346 532062

Fyvie linked with Rothienorman (F)
Alison Jaffrey (Mrs) MA BD FSAScot 1990 2019 The Manse, Fyvie, Turriff AB53 8RD 01651 891961
AJaffrey@churchofscotland.org.uk

Inverallochy and Rathen: East See Fraserburgh: South
King Edward See Banff

Longside (W)
Robert A. Fowlie BD 2007
The Manse, Old Deer, Peterhead AB42 5JB
RFowlie@churchofscotland.org.uk
01771 622228

Lonmay See Crimond

Macduff (F T W)
Hugh O'Brien CSS MTheol 2001 2016
contactus@macduffparishchurch.org
10 Ross Street, Macduff AB44 1NS
HOBrien@churchofscotland.org.uk
01261 832316

Marnoch (F W)
Alan Macgregor BA BD PhD 1992 2013
Marnoch Manse, 53 South Street, Aberchirder, Huntly AB54 7TS
AMacgregor@churchofscotland.org.uk
01466 781143

Maud and Savoch (F W) linked with New Deer: St Kane's (F W)
Aileen M. McFie (Mrs) BD 2003 2018
The Manse, Fordyce Terrace, New Deer, Turriff AB53 6TD
ARobson@churchofscotland.org.uk
01771 644097
01771 644631

Monquhitter and New Byth linked with Turriff: St Andrew's
James M. Cook MA MDiv 1999 2002
info@standrewsturriff.co.uk
St Andrew's Manse, Balmellie Road, Turriff AB53 4SP
JCook@churchofscotland.org.uk
01888 560304

New Deer: St Kane's See Maud and Savoch

New Pitsligo linked with Strichen and Tyrie (F W)
Vacant
Interim Moderator: Hugh O'Brien
Kingsville, Strichen, Fraserburgh AB43 6SQ
HOBrien@churchofscotland.org.uk
01771 637365
01261 832316

Ordiquhill and Cornhill (H) linked with Whitehills
W. Myburgh Verster BA BTh LTh MTh 1981 2011
6 Craigneen Place, Whitehills, Banff AB45 2NE
WVerster@churchofscotland.org.uk
01261 861317

Peterhead: New (F)
Vacant
Session Clerk: Ruth Mackenzie (Miss)
1 Hawthorn Road, Peterhead AB42 2DW
ursular@tiscali.co.uk
01779 480680

Peterhead: St Andrew's (H W)
Guardianship of the Presbytery
Session Clerk: John Leslie   eil.ian@btinternet.com   01779 470571

Pitsligo See Aberdour

Portsoy (W)
Vacant   The Manse, 4 Seafield Terrace, Portsoy, Banff AB45 2QB   01261 842272
Interim Moderator: Kevin R. Gruer   KGruer@churchofscotland.org.uk   01888 563850

Rathen: West See Fraserburgh: West
Rothienorman See Fyvie

St Fergus (F)
Jeffrey Tippner BA MDiv MCS PhD   1991   2012   26 Newton Road, St Fergus, Peterhead AB42 3DD   01779 838287
JTippner@churchofscotland.org.uk

Sandhaven
Guardianship of the Presbytery
Interim Moderator: David I.W. Locke   DLocke@churchofscotland.org.uk   01261 812107
07776 448301

Strichen and Tyrie See New Pitsligo
Turriff: St Andrew's See Monquhitter and New Byth

Turriff: St Ninian's and Forglen (H L W)   info@stniniansandforglen.org.uk   **01888 560282**
Kevin R. Gruer BSc BA   2011   4 Deveronside Drive, Turriff AB53 4SP   01888 563850
KGruer@churchofscotland

Whitehills See Ordiquhill and Cornhill

In other appointments

Stewart, William   2015 2016   Ordained Local Minister, Presbytery-wide   Denend, Strichen, Fraserburgh AB43 6RN   01771 637256
billandjunes@live.co.uk

| van Sittert, Paul BA BD | 1997 | 2011 | Chaplain: Army | 4Bn The Royal Regiment of Scotland, Bourlon Barracks, Plumer Road, Catterick Garrison DL9 3AD
padre.pvs@gmail.com | |

Demitted

Coutts, Fred MA BD	1973	1989	(Hospital Chaplain)	Ladebank, 1 Manse Place, Hatton, Peterhead AB42 0UQ fred.coutts@btinternet.com	01779 841320
Fawkes, G.M. Allan BA BSc JP	1979	2000	(Lonmay with Rathen: West)	3 Northfield Gardens, Hatton, Peterhead AB42 0SW afawkes@aol.com	01779 841814
Macnee, Iain LTh BD MA PhD	1975	2011	(New Pitsligo with Strichen and Tyrie)	Wardend Cottage, Alvah, Banff AB45 3TR macneeiain4@googlemail.com	01261 815647
Noble, George S. DipTh	1972	2000	(Carfin with Newarthill)	Craigowan, 3 Main Street, Inverallochy, Fraserburgh AB43 8XX	01346 582749
Ross, David S. MSc PhD BD	1978	2013	(Chaplain: Scottish Prison Service)	3–5 Abbey Street, Old Deer, Peterhead AB42 5LN padsross@btinternet.com	01771 623994
Thorburn, Robert J. BD	1978	2017	(Fyvie with Rothienorman)	12 Slackadale Gardens, Turriff AB53 4UA rjthorburn@aol.com	

(35) MORAY (F W)

Meets at St Andrew's-Lhanbryd and Urquhart on the first Tuesday of February, March, May, September, October, November and December, and at the Moderator's church on the fourth Tuesday of June.

| Clerk: | **REV. ALASTAIR H. GRAY MA BD** | **North Manse, Church Road, Keith AB55 5FX**
moray@churchofscotland.org.uk | **01542 886840**
07944 287777 |

Aberlour (F H W)

| Vacant | | |
| Session Clerk: Linda Cordiner | The Manse, Mary Avenue, Aberlour AB38 9QU
lwcordiner@outlook.com | 01340 871687 |

Alves and Burghead (F W) linked with Kinloss and Findhorn (W)

Vacant		
Session Clerk, Alves and Burghead: Barrie Wallace	The Manse, 4 Manse Road, Kinloss, Forres IV36 3GH abcsessionclerk@aim.com	01309 690474
		01343 850372
Session Clerk, Kinloss and Findhorn: Corinne Davies	cozzerdavies@gmail.com	01309 690359

Bellie and Speymouth (F W)

| Seóras I. Orr MSc MTh | 2018 | **bellieandspeymouth@gmail.com**
11 The Square, Fochabers IV32 7DG
SOrr@churchofscotland.org.uk | **01343 823802**
01343 820256 |

Birnie and Pluscarden (W) linked with Elgin: High (W)
Stuart M. Duff BA   1997   2014   The Manse, Daisy Bank, 5 Forteath Avenue, Elgin IV30 1TQ   01343 545703
                                                              SDuff@churchofscotland.org.uk

Buckie: North (H) linked with Rathven
Vacant   The Manse, 14 St Peter's Road, Buckie AB56 1DL   01542 832118

Buckie: South and West (F H W) linked with Enzie (F W)
Wesley C. Brandon BA MDiv   2003   2019   WBrandon@churchofscotland.org.uk

Cullen and Deskford (F T W)
Douglas F. Stevenson BD DipMin DipHE   1991   2010   14 Seafield Road, Cullen, Buckie AB56 4AF   01542 841963
MCOSCA MBACP   DStevenson@churchofscotland.org.uk

Dallas linked with Forres: St Leonard's (F H W) linked with Rafford (F)   stleonardsforres@gmail.com
Donald K. Prentice BSc BD   1989   2010   St Leonard's Manse, Nelson Road, Forres IV36 1DR   01309 672380
                                                              DPrentice@churchofscotland.org.uk
John A. Morrison BSc BA PGCE   2013   35 Kirkton Place, Elgin IV30 6JR   01343 550199
(Ordained Local Minister)   JMorrison@churchofscotland.org.uk

Duffus, Spynie and Hopeman (H W)
Jennifer M. Adams BEng BD   2013   The Manse, Duffus, Elgin IV30 5QP   01343 830276
                                                              JAdams@churchofscotland.org.uk

Dyke and Edinkillie (F W)
Richard G. Moffat BD   1994   2019   Dyke and Edinkillie Manse, Westview, Mundole, Forres IV36 2TA   01309 271321
                                                              RMoffat@churchofscotland.org.uk

Elgin: High See Birnie and Pluscarden

Elgin: St Giles' (H) and St Columba's South (F W)   stgileselgin@gmail.com   **01343 551501**
Deon Oelofse BA MDiv LTh MTh   2002   2017   18 Reidhaven Street, Elgin IV30 1QH   01343 208786
                                                              DOelofse@churchofscotland.org.uk
Sonia Palmer RGN   2017   94 Ashgrove Park, Elgin IV30 1UT   07748 700929
(Ordained Local Minister)   Sonia.Palmer@churchofscotland.org.uk

Enzie See Buckie: South and West

Findochty (F T W) linked with Portknockie (F T W)
Vacant
Session Clerk, Findochty: David Pirie
Session Clerk, Portknockie: Morag Ritchie (Mrs)

20 Netherton Terrace, Findochty, Buckie AB56 4QD
hdpirie@aol.com
moragritchie8@btinternet.com

01542 833180
01542 834123
01542 840951

Forres: St Laurence (H W)
Barry J. Boyd LTh DPS   1993

12 Mackenzie Drive, Forres IV36 2JP
BBoyd@churchofscotland.org.uk

01309 672260
07778 731018 (Mbl)

Forres: St Leonard's See Dallas

Keith: North, Newmill, Boharm and Rothiemay (F H W)
Alastair H. Gray MA BD   1978   2015

knnbrchurch@btconnect.com
North Manse, Church Road, Keith AB55 5BR
AGray@churchofscotland.org.uk

01542 886390
01542 886840

Keith: St Rufus, Botriphnie and Grange (F H W)
Vacant
Session Clerk: Nicola Smith (Ms)

St Rufus' Manse, Church Road, Keith AB55 5BR
nicolasmith1099@gmail.com

01542 882799
01542 488673

Kinloss and Findhorn See Alves and Burghead

Knockando, Elchies and Archiestown (H W) linked with Rothes (W)   info@moraykirk.co.uk
Robert J.M. Anderson BD FInstLM   1993   2000

The Manse, Rothes, Aberlour AB38 7AF
RJMAnderson@churchofscotland.org.uk

01340 831497
01340 831381

Lossiemouth: St Gerardine's High (H W) linked with Lossiemouth: St James (F T W)
Geoffrey D. McKee BA   1997   2014

The Manse, St Gerardine's Road, Lossiemouth IV31 6RA
GMcKee@churchofscotland.org.uk

01343 208852

Lossiemouth: St James' See Lossiemouth: St Gerardine's High

Mortlach and Cabrach (F H)
Vacant
Session Clerk: Elizabeth Cameron

Mortlach Manse, Dufftown, Keith AB55 4AR
stevie.liz@btinternet.com

01340 820380
01340 820846

Portknockie See Findochty
Rafford See Dallas
Rathven See Buckie: North
Rothes See Knockando, Elchies and Archiestown

St Andrew's-Lhanbryd (H) and Urquhart (F W)
Vacant
Session Clerk: Alastair Rossetter — 39 St Andrews Road, Lhanbryde, Elgin IV30 8PU — alastair@rossetter.plus.com — 01343 843765 / 07751 323975

In other appointments

Munro, Sheila BD	1995	2003	RAF Station Chaplain	Chaplaincy Centre, RAF Wyton, Huntingdon PE28 2EA sheila.munro781@mod.gov.uk	

Demitted

Attenburrow, Anne BSc MB ChB	2006	2018	(Auxiliary Minister)	4 Jock Inksons Brae, Elgin IV30 1QE AAttenburrow@churchofscotland.org.uk	01343 552330
Bain, Brian LTh	1980	2007	(Gask with Methven and Logiealmond)	Bayview, 13 Stewart Street, Portgordon, Buckie AB56 5QT bricoreen@gmail.com	01542 831215
Buchan, Alexander MA BD PGCE	1975	1992	(North Ronaldsay with Sanday)	The Manse, 14 St Peter's Road, Buckie AB56 1DL revabuchan@bluebucket.org	01542 832118
Buchan, Isabel C. (Mrs) BSc BD RE(PgCE)	1975	2019	(Buckie: North with Rathven)	59 Cliffburn Road, Arbroath DD11 5BA	
King, Margaret MA DCS	2002	2012	(Deacon)	56 Murrayfield, Fochabers IV32 7EZ margaretking889@gmail.com	01343 820937
Legge, Rosemary (Mrs) BSc BD MTh	1992	2017	(Cushnie and Tough)	57 High Street, Archiestown, Aberlour AB38 7QZ revrl192@aol.com	01340 810304
Morton, Alasdair J. MA BD DipEd FEIS	1960	2000	(Bowden with Newtown)	16 St Leonard's Road, Forres IV36 1DW alasgilmor@hotmail.co.uk	01309 671719
Morton, Gillian M. (Mrs) MA BD PGCE	1983	1996	(Hospital Chaplain)	16 St Leonard's Road, Forres IV36 1DW gillianmorton@hotmail.co.uk	01309 671719
Robertson, Peter BSc BD	1988	1998	(Dallas with Forres: St Leonard's with Rafford)	17 Ferryhill Road, Forres IV36 2GY peterrobertsonforres@talktalk.net	01309 676769
Rollo, George B. BD	1974	2010	(Elgin: St Giles' and St Columba's South)	'Struan', 13 Meadow View, Hopeman, Elgin IV30 5PL rollos@gmail.com	01343 835226
Ross, William B. LTh CPS	1988	2016	(Aberdour with Pitsligo)	5 Strathlene Court, Rathven AB55 3DD williamross278@btinternet.com	01542 834418
Smith, Morris BD	1988	2013	(Cromdale and Advie with Dulnain Bridge with Grantown-on-Spey)	1 Urquhart Grove, New Elgin IV30 8TB mosmith.themanse@btinternet.com	01343 545019
Watts, Anthony BD	1999	2013	(Glenmuick (Ballater))	tonyewatts@yahoo.co.uk	01309 672418

Whyte, David LTh	1993	2011	(Boat of Garten, Duthil and Kincardine)	1 Lemanfield Crescent, Garmouth, Fochabers IV32 7LS whytedj@btinternet.com	01343 870667
Wright, David L. MA BD	1957	1998	(Stornoway: St Columba)	84 Wyvis Drive, Nairn IV12 4TP	01667 451613

(36) ABERNETHY

Meets at Boat of Garten on the first Tuesday of February, March, May, September, October, November and December, and on the last Tuesday of June.

Clerk: **REV JAMES A.I. MacEWAN MA BD**   **Rapness, Station Road, Nethy Bridge PH25 3DN**   **01479 821116**
abernethy@churchofscotland.org.uk

Abernethy (F H W) linked with Boat of Garten (H), Carrbridge (H) and Kincardine (F W)
Vacant   The Manse, Deshar Road, Boat of Garten PH24 3BN   01479 831252
DWalker@churchofscotland.org.uk

Session Clerk, Abernethy: Lorimer Gray   lorimer.gray@gmail.com   01479 821110
Session Clerk, Boat of Garten, Carrbridge and Kincardine: Tim Walker tim@drumullie.co.uk   01479 831316

Alvie and Insh (H W) linked with Rothiemurchus and Aviemore (H W)
Charles J. Finnie LTh DPS   1991   2019   The Manse, 8 Dalfaber Park, Aviemore PH22 1QF   01479 810280
CFinnie@churchofscotland.org.uk

Boat of Garten, Carrbridge and Kincardine See Abernethy

Cromdale (H) and Advie (F W) linked with Dulnain Bridge (H W) linked with Grantown-on-Spey (F H W)
Gordon I. Strang BSc BD   2014   The Manse, Golf Course Road, Grantown-on-Spey PH26 3HY   01479 872084
GStrang@churchofscotland.org.uk

Dulnain Bridge See Cromdale and Advie
Grantown-on-Spey See Cromdale and Advie

Kingussie (F H W) linked with Laggan (H) and Newtonmore (H W)
Catherine A. Buchan (Mrs) MA MDiv   2002   2009   The Manse, Fort William Road, Newtonmore PH20 1DG   01540 673238
CBuchan@churchofscotland.org.uk
New charge formed by the union of Laggan and Newtonmore: St Bride's and linkage with Kingussie

Laggan and Newtonmore See Kingussie

Rothiemurchus and Aviemore See Alvie and Insh

Tomintoul (H), Glenlivet and Inveraven
Guardianship of the Presbytery
Session Clerk: Margo Stewart (Mrs)

The Manse, Tomintoul, Ballindalloch AB37 9HA
margoandedward@hotmail.co.uk

01807 580239

In other appointments

Duncanson, Mary (Ms) BTh	2013	(Ordained Local Minister: Presbytery Pastoral Support)	3 Balmenach Road, Cromdale, Grantown-on-Spey PH26 3LJ MDuncanson@churchofscotland.org.uk	01479 872165
Thomson, Mary Ellen (Mrs)	2013	Ordained Local Minister: Presbytery Chaplain to Care Homes	Kerrowside, 3 Hillside Avenue, Kingussie PH21 1PA Mary.Thomson@churchofscotland.org.uk	01540 661772

Demitted

Atkinson, Graham T. MA BD MTh	2006	2017	(Glasgow: Sandyhills) gtatkinson75@yahoo.co.uk	15 Lockhart Place, Aviemore PH22 1SW	07715 108837
MacEwan, James A.I. MA BD	1973	2012	(Abernethy with Cromdale and Advie) wurrus@hotmail.co.uk	Rapness, Station Road, Nethy Bridge PH25 3DN	01479 821116
Ritchie, Christine A.Y. (Mrs) BD DipMin	2002	2012	(Braes of Rannoch with Foss and Rannoch) gandcritchie70@gmail.com	25 Beachen Court, Grantown-on-Spey PH26 3JD	01479 873419
Walker, Donald K. BD	1979	2018	(Abernethy with Boat of Garten, Carrbridge and Kincardine) dwalkerjabulani@gmail.com	Jabulani, Seafield Avenue, Grantown-on-Spey PH26 3JQ	01479 870104

(37) INVERNESS (W)

Meets at Inverness, in Inverness: Inshes (2019) on the third Saturday of September, the third Tuesday of November, (2020) the first Saturday in March and the fourth Tuesday in June; Saturday meetings preceded by a presbytery conference.

Clerk: REV. TREVOR G. HUNT BA BD

7 Woodville Court, Culduthel Avenue, Inverness IV2 6BX
inverness@churchofscotland.org.uk

01463 250355
07753 423333

Ardersier (H) linked with Petty
Robert Cleland

1997   2014

The Manse, Ardersier, Inverness IV2 7SX
RCleland@churchofscotland.org.uk

01667 462224

Auldearn and Dalmore linked (F W) with Nairn: St Ninian's (F H W)
Thomas M. Bryson BD   1997   2015   The Manse, Auldearn, Nairn IV12 5SX
TBryson@churchofscotland.org.uk   01667 451675

Cawdor (F H) linked with Croy and Dalcross (F H)
Robert E. Brookes BD   2009   2016   Hillswick, Regoul, Geddes, Nairn IV12 5SB
RBrookes@churchofscotland.org.uk   01667 404686

Croy and Dalcross See Cawdor

Culloden: The Barn (F H W)
Michael Robertson BA   2014   **admin@barnchurch.org.uk**   **01463 798946**
45 Oakdene Court, Culloden IV2 7XL   01463 795430
Mike.Robertson@churchofscotland.org.uk   07740 984395

Daviot and Dunlichity (W) linked with Moy, Dalarossie and Tomatin (W)
Vacant
Session Clerk, Daviot and Dunlichity: Kathleen Matheson (Mrs)   k.matheson@btconnect.com   01808 521767
Session Clerk, Moy, Dalarossie and Tomatin: Vivian Roden (Mrs)   vroden@btinternet.com   01808 511355

Dores and Boleskine
Vacant
Session Clerk: Iain King   kingdores@btinternet.com   01463 751293

Inverness: Crown (F H W)
Vacant   **office@crown-church.co.uk**   **01463 231140**
39 Southside Road, Inverness IV2 4XA
Morven Archer (Mrs)   2013   2018   42 Firthview Drive, Inverness IV3 8QE   01463 230537
(Ordained Local Minister)   MArcher@churchofscotland.org.uk   01463 237840

Inverness: Dalneigh and Bona (GD H W)
Stewart A. MacKay   2009   2018   9 St Mungo Road, Inverness IV3 5AS   01463 232339
S.A.Mackay@churchofscotland.org.uk

Inverness: East (F GD H W)
Vacant   **invernesseastoffice@gmail.com**   **01463 236695**
Interim Moderator: Hugh F. Watt   39 Appin Drive, Inverness IV2 7AL   01456 450231
HWatt@churchofscotland.org.uk

Inverness: Hilton (F W)
Duncan A.C. MacPherson LLB BD
1994
office@hiltonchurch.org.uk
66 Culduthel Mains Crescent, Inverness IV2 6RG
DMacPherson@churchofscotland.org.uk
01463 233310
01463 231417

Inverness: Inshes (H W)
David S. Scott MA BD
1987   2013
48 Redwood Crescent, Milton of Leys, Inverness IV2 6HB
David.Scott@churchofscotland.org.uk
01463 226727
01463 772402

Farquhar A.M. Forbes MA BD
(Associate Minister)
2016
The Heights, Inverarnie, Inverness IV2 6XA
FForbes@churchofscotland.org.uk
01808 521450

Inverness: Kinmylies (F H W)
Scott Polworth LLB BD
2009   2018
2 Balnafettack Place, Inverness IV3 8TQ
SPolworth@churchofscotland.org.uk
01463 714035
01463 559137

Inverness: Ness Bank (F H T W)
Fiona E. Smith (Mrs) LLB BD
2010
15 Ballifeary Road, Inverness IV3 5PJ
FSmith@churchofscotland.org.uk
01463 234653

Inverness: Old High St Stephen's (T W)
Peter W. Nimmo BD ThM
1996   2004
invernesschurch@gmail.com
24 Damfield Road, Inverness IV2 3HU
PNimmo@churchofscotland.org.uk
07934 285924
01463 250802

Inverness: St Columba (New Charge Development) (F H T W)
Scott A. McRoberts BD MTh
2012
info@stcolumbainverness.org
20 Bramble Close, Inverness IV2 6BS
SMcRoberts@churchofscotland.org.uk
01463 230308
07535 290092

Inverness: Trinity (F H W)
Vacant
Session Clerk: Iain Macdonald
invernesstrinitychurch@yahoo.co.uk
60 Kenneth Street, Inverness IV3 5PZ
iain2567@gmail.com
01463 221490
01463 234756
01463 223238

Kilmorack and Erchless (F W)
Ian A. Manson BA BD
1989   2016
'Roselynn', Croyard Road, Beauly IV4 7DJ
IManson@churchofscotland.org.uk
01463 783824

Kiltarlity (F W) linked with Kirkhill (F W)
Vacant
Wardlaw Manse, Wardlaw Road, Kirkhill IV5 7NZ
01463 831247

Kirkhill See Kiltarlity
Moy, Dalarossie and Tomatin See Daviot and Dunlichity

Nairn: Old (H W)
Alison C. Mehigan BD DPS
2003 2015
secretary.nairnold@btconnect.com
15 Chattan Gardens, Nairn IV12 4QP
AMehigan@churchofscotland.org.uk
01667 **452382**
01667 453777

Nairn: St Ninian's See Auldearn and Dalmore
Petty See Ardersier

Urquhart and Glenmoriston (H)
Hugh F. Watt BD DPS DMin
1986 1996
Blairbeg, Drumnadrochit, Inverness IV3 6UG
HWatt@churchofscotland.org.uk
01456 450231

In other appointments

Name	Years	Appointment	Address / Email	Phone
Brown, Derek G. BD DipMin DMin	1989 1994	Lead Chaplain: NHS Highland	1 Allan Gardens, Dornoch IV25 3PD / derek.brown1@nhs.net	01862 810296
Getliffe, Dot L.J. (Mrs) BA BD DipEd DCS	2006	Deacon	136 Ardness Place, Lochardil, Inverness IV2 4QY / DGetliffe@churchofscotland.org.uk	01463 716051
Mackenzie, Seóras L. BD	1996 1998	Chaplain: Army	39 Engr Regt (Air Support), Kinloss Barracks, Kinloss, Forres IV36 3XL	
Morrison, Hector BSc BD MTh	1981 2009	Principal: Highland Theological College	24 Oak Avenue, Inverness IV2 4NX	01463 238561

Demitted

Name	Years	Charge	Address / Email	Phone
Black, Archibald T. BSc	1964 1997	(Inverness: Ness Bank)	16 Elm Park, Inverness IV2 4WN	01463 230588
Buell, F. Bart BA MDiv	1980 1995	(Urquhart and Glenmoriston)	6 Towerhill Place, Cradlehall, Inverness IV2 5FN / bartbuell@talktalk.net	01463 794634
Chisholm, Archibald F. MA	1957 1997	(Braes of Rannoch with Foss and Rannoch)	32 Seabank Road, Nairn IV12 4EU / arch32@btinternet.com	01667 452001
Craw, John DCS	1998 2009	(Deacon)	5 Larchfield Court, Nairn IV12 4SS / johncraw607@btinternet.com	07544 761653
Fraser, Jonathan MA(Div) MTh ThM	2012 2019	(Associate, Inverness: Inshes)	9 Broom Drive, Inverness IV2 4EG / Jonathan.Fraser@uhi.ac.uk	07749 539981
Hunt, Trevor G. BA BD	1986 2011	(Evie with Firth with Rendall)	7 Woodville Court, Culduthel Avenue, Inverness IV2 6BX / trevorhunt@gmail.com	01463 250355 / 07753 423333
Jeffrey, Stewart D. BSc BD	1962 1997	(Banff with King Edward)	10 Grigor Drive, Inverness IV2 4LP / stewart.jeffrey@talktalk.net	01463 230085
Lyon, B. Andrew LTh	1971 2007	(Fraserburgh Wes: with Rathen West)	20 Barnview, Culloden, Inverness IV2 7EX / balyon2018@hotmail.com	01463 559609
MacQuarrie, Donald A. BSc BD	1979 2012	(Fort William: Duncansburgh MacIntosh with Kilmonivaig)	Birch Cottage, 4 Craigrorie, North Kessock, Inverness IV1 3XH / pdmacq@ukgateway.net	01463 731050

McRoberts, T. Douglas BD CPS FRSA	1975 2014	(Malta)	24 Redwood Avenue, Inverness IV2 6HA doug.mcroberts@btinternet.com	01463 772594
Mitchell, Joyce (Mrs) DCS	1994 2010	(Deacon)	Sunnybank, Farr, Inverness IV2 6XG joyce@mitchell71.freeserve.co.uk	01808 521285
Rettie, James A. BTh	1981 1999	(Melness and Eriboll with Tongue)	2 Trantham Drive, Westhill, Inverness IV2 5QT	01463 798896
Ritchie, Bruce BSc BD PhD	1977 2013	(Dingwall: Castle Street)	16 Brinckman Terrace, Westhill, Inverness IV2 5BL brucezomba@hotmail.com	01463 791389
Robertson, Fergus A. MA BD	1972 2010	(Inverness: Dalneigh and Bona)	16 Druid Temple Way, Inverness IV2 6UQ faavrobertson@yahoo.co.uk	01463 718462
Stirling, G. Alan S. MA	1960 1999	(Leochel Cushnie and Lynturk with Tough)	97 Lochlann Road, Culloden, Inverness IV2 7HJ	01463 798313
Turner, Fraser K. LTh	1994 2007	(Kiltarlity with Kirkhill)	20 Caulfield Avenue, Inverness IV2 5GA fraseratq@yahoo.co.uk	01463 794004
Waugh, John L. LTh	1973 2002	(Ardclach with Auldearn and Dalmore)	58 Wyvis Drive, Nairn IV12 4TP jswaugh@gmail.com	Tel/Fax 01667 456397
Younger, Alastair S. BScEcon ASCC	1969 2008	(Inverness: St Columba High)	33 Duke's View, Slackbuie, Inverness IV2 6BB younger873@btinternet.com	01463 242873

INVERNESS ADDRESSES

Inverness

Crown	Kingsmills Road x Midmills Road
Dalneigh and Bona	St Mary's Avenue
East	Academy Street x Margaret Street
Hilton	Druid Road x Tomatin Road
Inshes	Inshes Retail Park
Kinmylies	Kinmylies Way
Ness Bank	Ness Bank x Castle Road
Old High	Church Street x Church Lane
St Columba	Drummond School
St Stephen's	Old Edinburgh Road x Southside Road
Trinity	Huntly Place x Upper Kessock Street

Nairn

Old	Academy Street x Seabank Road
St Ninian's	High Street x Queen Street

(38) LOCHABER (F W)

Meets at Caol, Fort William, in Kilmallie Church Hall at 6pm, on the first Tuesday of September and December, on the last Tuesday of October and on the fourth Tuesday of March. The June meeting is held at 6pm on the second Tuesday in the church of the incoming Moderator. The Presbytery Annual Conference is held in February.

Clerk: REV DONALD G. B. McCORKINDALE   The Manse, 2 The Meadows, Strontian, Acharacle PH36 4HZ   01967 402234
              BD DipMin   lochaber@churchofscotland.org.uk
Treasurer: MRS CONNIE ANDERSON   faoconnie@gmail.com   07554 176580

Acharacle (F H W) linked with Ardnamurchan (F W)
M. Fiona Ogg (Mrs) BA BD   2012
The Church of Scotland Manse, Acharacle PH36 4JU
Fiona.Ogg@churchofscotland.org.uk
01967 431654

Ardgour and Kingairloch (F H T W) linked with Morvern (F H T W)
Donald G.B. McCorkindale BD DipMin   1992   2011
The Manse, 2 The Meadows, Strontian, Acharacle PH36 4HZ
DMcCorkindale@churchofscotland.org.uk
01967 402234
07554 176580

Ardnamurchan See Acharacle

Duror (F H W) linked with Glencoe: St Munda's (F H W)
Alexander C. Stoddart BD   2001   2016
9 Cameron Brae, Kentallen, Duror PA38 4BF
AStoddart@churchofscotland.org.uk
01631 740285

Fort Augustus (W) linked with Glengarry (W)
Anthony M. Jones   1994   2018
BD DPS DipTheol CertMin FRSA
The Manse, Fort Augustus PH32 4BH
AJones@churchofscotland.org.uk
01320 366210

Fort William: Duncansburgh MacIntosh (F H W) linked with Kilmonivaig (F W)
Richard Baxter MA BD   1997   2016
The Manse, The Parade, Fort William PH33 6BA
RBaxter@churchofscotland.org.uk
01397 702297
07958 541418

Morag Muirhead (Mrs)   2013
(Ordained Local Minister)
6 Dumbarton Road, Fort William PH33 6UU
MMuirhead@churchofscotland.org.uk
01397 703643

Glencoe: St Munda's See Duror
Glengarry See Fort Augustus

Kilmallie (W)
Vacant
Session Clerk: Margaret Antonios
m.antonios@btinternet.com
01397 703559

Kilmonivaig See Fort William: Duncansburgh MacIntosh

Kinlochleven (H W) linked with Nether Lochaber (H W)
Malcolm A. Kinnear MA BD PhD   2010
The Manse, Lochaber Road, Kinlochleven PH50 4QW
MKinnear@churchofscotland.org.uk
01855 831227

Morvern See Ardgour

Nether Lochaber See Kinlochleven

North West Lochaber (F H W)
Stewart Goudie BSc BD   2010   2018   Church of Scotland Manse, Annie's Brae, Mallaig PH41 4RG   01687 462514
SGoudie@churchofscotland.org.uk

Strontian See Ardgour

In other appointments

Kinnear, Marion (Mrs)   2009   Auxiliary Minister   The Manse, Lochaber Road, Kinlochleven PH50 4QW   01855 831227
Marion.Kinnear@churchofscotland.org.uk   07563 180662

Demitted

Anderson, David M. MSc FCOptom   1984 2018   (Ordained Local Minister)   'Mirlos', 1 Dumfries Place, Fort William PH33 6UQ   01397 702091
david@mirlos.co.uk

Corbett, Richard T. BSc MSc PhD BD   1992 2019   (Kilmallie)   Flat 309, Knight's Court, North William Street, Perth PH1 5NB   01687 450227

Lamb, Alan H.W. BA MTh   1959 2001   (Associate, Fort Augustus with Glengarry)   Smiddy House, Arisaig PH39 4NH
h.a.lamb@handalamb.plus.com

Millar, John L. MA BD   1981 1990   (Fort William: Duncansburgh with Kilmonivaig)   Flat 0/1, 12 Chesterfield Gardens, Glasgow G12 0BF   0141 339 4090
johnmillar123@btinternet.com

Varwell, Adrian P.J. BA BD PhD   1983 2011   (Fort Augustus with Glengarry)   19 Enrick Crescent, Kilmore, Drumnadrochit, Inverness IV63 6TP   01456 459352
adrian.varwell@btinternet.com

Winning, A. Ann MA DipEd BD   1984 2006   (Morvern)   'Westering', 13C Carnoch, Glencoe, Ballachulish PH49 4HQ   01855 811929
awinning009@btinternet.com

(39) ROSS (W)

Meets on the first Tuesday of September in the church of the incoming Moderator, and in Dingwall: Castle Street Church on the first Tuesday of October, November, December, February, March and May, and on the last Tuesday of June.

Clerk: **MRS CATH CHAMBERS**   **184 Kirkside, Alness IV17 0RH**   **01349 882026**
ross@churchofscotland.org.uk

Alness
Vacant
Michael J. Macdonald   2004   2014   27 Darroch Brae, Alness IV17 0SD
(Auxiliary Minister)   73 Firhill, Alness IV17 0RT   01349 882238
                                                Michael.Macdonald@churchofscotland.org.uk   01349 884268

Avoch (W) linked with Fortrose and Rosemarkie (W)
Warren R. Beattie BSc BD MSc PhD   1990   2019   5 Ness Way, Fortrose IV10 8SS   01381 620111
                                                        WBeattie@churchofscotland.org.uk

Contin (H W) linked with Fodderty and Strathpeffer (H W)
Vacant   The Manse, Contin, Strathpeffer IV14 9ES   01997 421028
James Bissett   2016   JBissett@churchofscotland.org.uk
(Ordained Local Minister)

Cromarty (W) linked with Resolis and Urquhart (W)
Terrance Burns BA MA   2004   2017   The Manse, Culbokie, Dingwall IV7 8JN   01349 877452
                                        TBurns@churchofscotland.org.uk

Dingwall: Castle Street (F H W)
Drausio P. Goncalves   1993   2019   16 Achany Road, Dingwall IV15 9JB   01349 866792
                                        DGoncalves@churchofscotland.org.uk

Dingwall: St Clement's (H W)
Bruce Dempsey BD   1997   2014   8 Castlehill Road, Dingwall IV15 9PB   01349 292055
                                    BDempsey@churchofscotland.org.uk

Fearn Abbey and Nigg (W) linked with Tarbat (W)
Vacant   Church of Scotland Manse, Fearn, Tain IV20 1WN   01862 832282
Session Clerk, Fearn Abbey and Nigg: Alex Gordon   alex@balmuchy.co.uk
Session Clerk, Tarbat: Douglas Gordon   d.gordon123@btinternet.com

Ferintosh (F W)
Stephen Macdonald BD MTh   2008   2018   Ferintosh Manse, Leanaig Road, Conon Bridge,   01349 861275
                                            Dingwall IV7 8BE   07570 804193
                                            SMacdonald@churchofscotland.org.uk

Fodderty and Strathpeffer See Contin
Fortrose and Rosemarkie See Avoch

Invergordon (W)
Kenneth Donald MacLeod BD CPS   1989   2000

invergordonparishchurch@live.co.uk
The Manse, Cromlet Drive, Invergordon IV18 0BA   01349 852273
KMacLeod@churchofscotland.org.uk

Killearnan (F H W) linked with Knockbain (F H W)
Susan Cord   2016

14 First Field Avenue, North Kessock, Inverness IV1 3JB   01463 731930
SCord@churchofscotland.org.uk

Kilmuir and Logie Easter (F)
Vacant
Session Clerk: George Morrison

The Manse, Delny, Invergordon IV18 0NW   01862 842280
ga.morrison@virgin.net

Kiltearn (H)
Donald A. MacSween BD   1991   1998

The Manse, Swordale Road, Evanton, Dingwall IV16 9UZ   01349 830472
DMacSween@churchofscotland.org.uk

Knockbain See Killearnan

Lochbroom and Ullapool (F GD)
Heidi J. Hercus BA   2018

The Manse, 11 Royal Park, Mill Street, Ullapool IV26 2XT   01854 613146
HHercus@churchofscotland.org.uk

Resolis and Urquhart See Cromarty

Rosskeen (F W)
Vacant
Carol Rattenbury   2017
(Ordained Local Minister)

Rosskeen Manse, Perrins Road, Alness IV17 0XG   01349 882265
Balloan Farm House, Alcaig, Conon Bridge, Dingwall IV7 8HU   01349 877323
CRattenbury@churchofscotland.org.uk

Tain (F W)
Andrew P. Fothergill BA   2012   2017

14 Kingsway Avenue, Tain IV19 1NJ   01862 89296
AFothergill@churchofscotland.org.uk

Tarbat See Fearn Abbey and Nigg

Urray and Kilchrist (F)
The Manse, Corry Road, Muir of Ord IV6 7TL   01463 870259
duncell153@btinternet.com   01463 870860
Vacant
Session Clerk: Duncan Cromb

Demitted

Name			(Former Charge)	Address / Email	Phone
Archer, Nicholas D.C. BA BD	1971	1992	(Dores and Boleskine)	2 Aldie Cottages, Tain IV19 1LZ na.2ac777@btinternet.com	01862 821494
Bell, Graeme K. BA BD	1983	2017	(Glasgow: Carnwadric)	4 Munro Terrace, Rosemarkie, Fortrose IV10 8UR graemekbell@googlemail.com	07591 180101
Dupar, Kenneth W. BA BD PhD	1965	1993	(Christ's College., Aberdeen)	The Old Manse, The Causeway, Cromarty IV11 8XJ	01381 600428
Forsyth, James LTh	1970	2000	(Fearn Abbey with Nigg Chapelhill)	Rhives Lodge, Golspie, Sutherland KW10 6DD	
Horne, Douglas A. BD	1977	2009	(Tain)	151 Holm Farm Road, Culduthel, Inverness IV2 6BF douglas.horne@talktalk.net	01463 712677
Lincoln, John BA BD MPhil	1986	2014	(Balquhidder with Killin and Ardeonaig)	59 Obsdale Park, Alness IV17 0TR johnlincoln@minister.com	01349 882791
McDonald, Alan D. LLB BD MTh DLitt DD	1979	2016	(Cameron with St Andrews: St Leonard's)	7 Duke Street, Cromarty IV11 8YH alan.d.mcdonald@talk21.com	01381 600954
McGowan, Andrew T. B. (Prof) BD STM PhD	1979	2019	(Inverness: East)	18 Davis Drive, Alness IV17 0ZD AMcGowan@churchofscotland.org.uk	01340 880762
MacLennan, Alasdair J. BD DCE	1979	2001	(Resolis and Urquhart)	Airdale, Seaforth Road, Muir of Ord IV6 7TA	01463 870704
McLeod, John MA	1958	1993	(Resolis and Urquhart)	'Benview', 19 Balvaird, Muir of Ord IV6 7RQ sheilaandjohn@yahoo.co.uk	01463 871286
Munro, James A. BA BD DMS	1979	2013	(Port Glasgow: Hamilton Bardrainney)	1 Wyvis Crescent, Conon Bridge, Dingwall IV7 8BZ james781munro@btinternet.com	01349 865752
Scott, David V. BTh	1994	2014	(Fearn Abbey and Nigg with Tarbat)	29 Sunnyside, Culloden Moor, Inverness IV2 5ES	01463 795802
Smith, Russel BD	1994	2013	(Dingwall: St Clement's)	1 School Road, Conon Bridge, Dingwall IV7 8AE russamtwo@btinternet.com	01349 861011
Warwick, Ivan C. MA BD TD	1980	2014	(Paisley: St James')	Ardcruidh Croft, Heights of Dochcarty, Dingwall IV15 9UF L70rev@btinternet.com	01349 861464 07787 535083

(40) SUTHERLAND (F)

Meets at Lairg on the first Tuesday of March, May, September, November and December, and on the first Tuesday of June at the Moderator's church.

Clerk:	REV. IAN W. McCREE BD	Tigh Ardachu, Mosshill, Brora KW9 6NG sutherland@churchofscotland.org.uk	01408 621185

Altnaharra and Farr (W) linked with Melness and Tongue (F H)
Beverly W. Cushman MA MDiv BA PhD   1977   2017
The Manse, Bettyhill, Thurso KW14 7SS
BCushman@churchofscotland.org.uk
01641 521208

Assynt and Stoer
Vacant
Interim Moderator: John MacPherson
Canisp Road, Lochinver, Lairg IV27 4LH
JMacPherson@churchofscotland.org.uk
01571 844342
01971 502431

Clyne (H W) linked with Kildonan and Loth Helmsdale (H W)
Vacant
Session Clerk, Clyne: Sydney L. Barnett
info@brorachurchofscotland.org
Golf Road, Brora KW9 6QS
sydneylb43@gmail.com
01408 621239
01408 621569

Creich (W) linked with Kincardine Croick and Edderton (W) linked with Rosehall (W)   info@kyleofsutherlandchurches.org
Vacant
Session Clerk, Creich: Jeani Hunter (Mrs)
Session Clerk, Kincardine Croick and Edderton: Rev. Mary J. Stobo
Session Clerk, Rosehall: Lt. Col. Colin Gilmour MBE DL
The Manse, Ardgay IV24 3BG
nielsonhunter@btinternet.com
MStobo@churchofscotland.org.uk
shenaval@btinternet.com
01863 766285
01862 810544
01863 766868
01549 441374

Dornoch Cathedral (F H W)
Susan M. Brown (Mrs) BD DipMin DUniv   1985   1998
1 Allan Gardens, Dornoch IV25 3PD
Susan.Brown@churchofscotland.org.uk
01862 810296

Durness and Kinlochbervie (F W)
Andrea M. Boyes (Mrs) RMN BA(Theol)   2013   2017
Manse Road, Kinlochbervie, Lairg IV27 4RG
ABoyes@churchofscotland.org.uk
01971 521287

Eddrachillis
John MacPherson BSc BD   1993
Church of Scotland Manse, Scourie, Lairg IV27 4TQ
JMacPherson@churchofscotland.org.uk
01971 502431

Golspie
John B. Sterrett BA BD PhD   2007
pray@standrewgolspie.org
The Manse, Fountain Road, Golspie KW10 6TH
JSterret@churchofscotland.org.uk
Tel/Fax 01408 633295

Kildonan and Loth Helmsdale See Clyne
Kincardine Croick and Edderton See Creich

Lairg (F H W) linked with Rogart (H W)
Vacant
Hilary M. Gardner (Miss)   2010   2018   The Manse, Lairg IV27 4EH
(Auxiliary Minister)   Cayman Lodge, Kincardine Hill, Ardgay IV24 3DJ   01863 766107
HGardner@churchofscotland.org.uk

Melness and Tongue See Altnaharra and Farr
Rogart See Lairg
Rosehall See Creich

In other appointments

Stobo, Mary J. (Mrs)   2013   Ordained Local Minister; Community Healthcare Chaplain   Druim-an-Sgairnich, Ardgay IV24 3BG   01863 766868
MStobo@churchofscotland.org.uk

Demitted

Chambers, S. John OBE BSc   1972 2009   (Inverness: Ness Bank)   Bannlagan Lodge, 4 Earls Cross Gardens, Dornoch IV25 3NR   01862 811520
chambersdornoch@btinternet.com
Goskirk, J.L. LTh   1968 2010   (Lairg with Rogart)   Rathvilly, Lairgmuir, Lairg IV27 4ED   01549 402569
leslie_goskirk@sky.com
McCree, Ian W. BD   1971 2011   (Clyne with Kildonan and Loth Helmsdale)   Tigh Ardachu, Mosshill, Brora KW9 6NG   01408 621185
ianmccree@live.co.uk
McKay, Margaret (Mrs) MA BD MTh   1991 2003   (Auchaber United with Auchterless)   2 Mackenzie Gardens, Dornoch IV25 3RU   01862 811859
megsie38@gmail.com

(41) CAITHNESS (W)

Meets alternately at Wick and Thurso on the first Tuesday of February, March, May, September, November and December, and the third Tuesday of June.

Clerk: REV. HEATHER STEWART   Burnthill, Thrumster, Wick KW1 5TR   01955 651717
caithness@churchofscotland.org.uk

Halkirk Westerdale linked with Watten
Vacant
Session Clerk, Halkirk: Janet Mowat (Mrs)   The Manse, Station Road, Watten, Wick KW1 5YN   01955 621220
jsmowat25@btinternet.com   01847 831638
Session Clerk, Watten: vacant

Latheron (W)
Vacant

Heather Stewart (Mrs)   2013   2017
(Ordained Local Minister)
Central Manse, Main Street, Lybster KW3 6BN
parish-of-latheron@btconnect.com
Burnthill, Thrumster, Wick KW1 5TR   Work
Heather.Stewart@churchofscotland.org.uk

01593 721706

01955 651717
01955 603333

North Coast (F)
David J.B. Macartney BA   2017
Church of Scotland Manse, Reay, Thurso KW14 7RE
DMacartney@churchofscotland.org.uk

01847 811734

Pentland
Vacant
Session Clerk: Christine Shearer (Mrs)
The Manse, Canisbay, Wick KW1 4YH

01955 611271

Thurso: St Peter's and St Andrew's (F H W)
David S.M. Malcolm BD   2011   2014
The Manse, 46 Rose Street, Thurso KW14 8RF
David.Malcolm@churchofscotland.org.uk

01847 895186

Thurso: West (H W)
Vacant
Interim Moderator: David J.B. Macartney
Thorkel Road, Thurso KW14 7LW
DMacartney@churchofscotland.org.uk

01847 893898
01847 811734

Watten See Halkirk Westerdale

Wick: Pulteneytown (H) and Thrumster (W)
Andrew A. Barrie BD   2013   2017
The Manse, Coronation Street, Wick KW1 5LS
Andrew.Barrie@churchofscotland.org.uk

01955 606192
07791 663439

Wick: St Fergus (F W)
John Nugent BD   1999   2011
Mansefield, Miller Avenue, Wick KW1 4DF
JNugent@churchofscotland.org.uk

01955 602167
07511 503946

Demitted

Duncan, Esme (Miss)   2013 2017   (Ordained Local Minister)
Avalon, Upper Warse, Canisbay, Wick KW1 4YD
EDuncan@churchofscotland.org.uk

01955 611455

Rennie, Lyall	2014	2019	(Ordained Local Minister)	Ruachmarra, Lower Warse, Canisbay, Wick KW1 4YB	01955 611756
				LRennie@churchofscotland.org.uk	
Warner, Kenneth BD	1981	2008	(Halkirk and Westerdale)	Kilearnan, Clayock, Halkirk KW12 6UZ	01847 831825
				wrnkenn@btinternet.com	

CAITHNESS Communion Sundays

Halkirk Westerdale	Apr, Jul, Oct	
Latheron	Apr, Jul, Sep, Nov	
North Coast	Mar, Easter, Jun, Sep, Dec	
Pentland:		
Canisbay	1st Jun, Nov	
Dunnet	last May, Nov	
Keiss	1st May, 3rd Nov	
Thurso: Clrig	last May, Nov	
S Peter's and S Andrew's	Mar, Jun, Sep, Dec	
West	4th Mar, Jun, Nov	
Watten	1st Jul, Dec	
Wick: Pulteneytown and Thrumster		1st Mar, Jun, Sep, Dec
St Fergus		Apr, Oct

(42) LOCHCARRON – SKYE

Meets in Kyle on Tuesdays (normally the first Tuesday) in August, September, November, December, February, March and June.

Clerk: REV. RODERICK A.R. MacLEOD MA MBA BD DMin The Manse, 6 Upper Breakish, Isle of Skye IV42 8PY **01471 822416**
lochcarronskye@churchofscotland.org.uk

Applecross, Lochcarron and Torridon (GD)
Anita Stutter Drs (MA) 2008 2017 The Manse, Colonel's Road, Lochcarron, Strathcarron IV54 8YG 01520 722783
AStutter@churchofscotland.org.uk

Bracadale and Duirinish (GD)
Janet Easton-Berry BA (SocSc) BA (Theol) 2016 Duirinish Manse, Dunvegan, Isle of Skye IV55 8WQ 01470 521668
JEaston-Berry@churchofscotland.ork.uk

Gairloch and Dundonnell (F W)
Stuart J. Smith BEng BD MTh 1994 2016 Church of Scotland Manse, The Glebe, Gairloch IV21 2BT 01445 712645
Stuart.Smith@churchofscotland.org.uk

Glenelg Kintail and Lochalsh (W)
Vacant The Manse, Main Street, Kyle of Lochalsh IV40 8DA 01599 534294 / 01599 534393
Session Clerk: John Adamson (Dr) sandvika2428@gmail.com

Kilmuir and Stenscholl (GD W) John W. Murray LLB BA	2003	2015	1 Totescore, Kilmuir, Isle of Skye IV51 9YN JMurray@churchofscotland.org.uk	01470 542297
Portree (GD W) Sandor Fazakas BD MTh	1976	2007	Viewfield Road, Portree, Isle of Skye IV51 9ES SFazakas@churchofscotland.org.uk	01478 611868
Snizort (GD H) Alisdair T. MacLeod-Mair MEd DipTheol	2001	2019	The Manse, Kensaleyre, Snizort, Portree, Isle of Skye IV51 9XE AMacLeod-Mair@churchofscotland.org.uk	01470 532453
Strath and Sleat (F GD W) Roderick A.R. MacLeod MA MBA BD DMin	1994	2015	The Manse, 6 Upper Breakish, Isle of Skye IV42 8PY RMacLeod@churchofscotland.org.uk	01471 822416

In other appointments

MacKenzie, Hector M.	2008		Chaplain: Army	HQ Military Corrective Training Centre, Berechurch Hall Camp, Berechurch Hall Road, Colchester CO2 9NU mackenziehector@hotmail.com	

Demitted

Martin, George M. MA BD	1987	2005	(Applecross, Lochcarron and Torridon)	8(1) Buckingham Terrace, Edinburgh EH4 3AA	0131 343 3937
Morrison, Derek	1995	2013	(Gairloch and Dundonnell)	2 Cliffton Place, Poolewe, Achnasheen IV22 2IU derekmorrison1@aol.com	01445 781333

LOCHCARRON – SKYE Communion Sundays – see websites and local notices for current arrangements

(43) UIST

Meets on the first Tuesday of February, March, September and November in Lochmaddy, and on the third Tuesday of June in Leverburgh.

| Clerk: | REV. GAVIN J. ELLIOTT MA BD | 5a Aird, Isle of Benbecula HS7 5LT
uist@churchofscotland.org.uk | 01870 602726 |

Benbecula (F GD H) linked with Carinish (GD H W)   info@carinish-church.org.uk

Andrew (Drew) P. Kuzma BA	2007	2016	Church of Scotland Manse, Griminish, Isle of Benbecula HS7 5QA AKuzma@churchofscotland.org.uk	01870 602180
Ishabel Macdonald, (Ordained Local Minister)	2011		'Cleat Afe Ora', 18 Carinish, Isle of North Uist HS6 5HN Ishie.Macdonald@churchofscotland.org.uk	01876 580367

Berneray and Lochmaddy (GD H) linked with Kilmuir and Paible (GD)

Alen J.R. McCulloch MA BD	1990	2017	Church of Scotland Manse, Paible, Isle of North Uist HS6 5HD AMcCulloch@churchofscotland.org.uk	01876 510310

Carinish See Benbecula
Kilmuir and Paible See Berneray and Lochmaddy

Manish-Scarista (GD H)

Vacant		Church of Scotland Manse, Scarista, Isle of Harris HS3 3HX	01859 550200
Session Clerk: Paul Alldred		paul.alldred@outlook.com	01859 520494

Tarbert (GD H T W)

Ian Murdo M. MacDonald DPA BD	2001	2015	The Manse, Manse Road, Tarbert, Isle of Harris HS3 3DF Ian.MacDonald@churchofscotland.org.uk	01859 502231

Demitted

Elliott, Gavin J. MA BD	1976	2015	(Ministries Council)	5a Aird, Isle of Benbecula HS7 5LT gavkondwani@gmail.com	01870 602726
MacIver, Norman BD	1976	2011	(Tarbert)	57 Boswell Road, Wester Inshes, Inverness IV2 3EW norman@n-cmaciver.freeserve.co.uk	
Morrison, Donald John	2001	2019	(Auxiliary Minister)	22 Kyles, Tarbert, Isle of Harris HS3 3BS DMorrison@churchofscotland.org.uk	01859 502341

Petrie, Jackie G.	1989	2011	(South Uist)	7B Malaclete, Isle of North Uist HS6 5BX	01876 560804
				jackiegpetrie@yahoo.com	
Smith, John M.	1956	1992	(Lochmaddy)	Hamersay, Clachan, Locheport, Lochmaddy,	
				Isle of North Uist HS6 5HD	
Smith, Murdo MA BD	1988	2011	(Manish-Scarista)	Aisgeir, 15A Upper Shader, Isle of Lewis HS3 3MX	01876 580332

UIST Communion Sundays

Benbecula	2nd Mar, Sep	Carinish	4th Mar, Aug
Berneray and Lochmaddy	4th Jun, last Oct	Kilmuir and Paible	1st Jun, 3rd Nov
		Manish-Scarista	3rd Apr, 1st Oct
		Tarbert	2nd Mar, 3rd Sep

(44) LEWIS

Meets at Stornoway, in St Columba's Church Hall, on the second Tuesday of February, March, June, September and November and at other times as required.

| Clerk: | MR JOHN CUNNINGHAM | 1 Raven's Lane, Stornoway, Isle of Lewis HS2 0EG | 01851 709977 |
| | | lewis@churchofscotland.org.uk | 07789 878840 |

Barvas (F GD H W)
| Dougie Wolf BA(Theol) | 2017 | Church of Scotland Manse, Lower Barvas, Isle of Lewis HS2 0QY | 01851 840218 |
| | | mrdougiewolf@gmail.com | |

Carloway (F GD H)
| Donald Macaskill BD MPhil DMin | 1989 | 2019 | Church of Scotland Manse, Knock, Carloway, Isle of Lewis HS2 9AU | 01851 **643211** |
| | | | DMacaskill@churchofscotland.org.uk | 01851 643255 |

Cross Ness (GD H T W)
Vacant
| Interim Moderator: to be appointed | crossnesschurch@gmail.com | |
| | Cross Manse, Swainbost, Ness, Isle of Lewis HS2 0TB | 01851 810375 |

Kinloch (GD H)
| Iain M. Campbell BD | 2004 | 2008 | Laxay, Lochs, Isle of Lewis HS2 9LA | 01851 830218 |
| | | | i455@btinternet.com | |

Knock (GD H)
Guardianship of the Presbytery
Interim Moderator: Iain M. Campbell
i455@btinternet.com
01851 830218

Lochs-Crossbost (GD H)
Guardianship of the Presbytery
Interim Moderator: Donald Macleod
donaldmacleod25@btinternet.com
01851 704516

Lochs-in-Bernera (F GD H) linked with Uig (F GD H)
Hugh Maurice Stewart DPA BD   2008
Church of Scotland Manse, Uigen, Miavaig, Isle of Lewis   HS2 9HX
berneralwuig@btinternet.com
01851 672388

Stornoway: High (GD H)
Gordon M. Macleod BA   2017   2019
High Manse, 1 Goathill Road, Stornoway, Isle of Lewis   HS1 2NJ
GMacleod@churchofscotland.org.uk
07717 065739

Stornoway: Martin's Memorial (F H W)
Thomas MacNeil MA BD   2002   2006
enquiries@martinsmemorial.org.uk
Matheson Road, Stornoway, Isle of Lewis   HS1 2LR
tommymacneil@hotmail.com
01851 700820
01851 704238

John M. Nicolson BD DipMin   1997   2017
(Assistant Minister)
33 Westview Terrace, Stornoway, Isle of Lewis   HS1 2HP
johnmurdonicolson@gmail.com
07899 235355

Stornoway: St Columba (F GD H)
William J. Heenan BA MTh   2012
St Columba's Manse, Lewis Street, Stornoway, Isle of Lewis   HS1 2JF
wmheenan@hotmail.com
01851 701546
01851 705933
07837 770589

Uig See Lochs-in-Bernera

In other appointments

Shadakshari, T.K. BTh BD MTh   1998   2006   Head of Spiritual Care, Western Isles
Health Board
23D Benside, Newmarket, Stornoway, Isle of Lewis HS2 0DZ
tk.shadakshari@nhs.net
Home 01851 701727
01851 704704
07403 697138
Office

Demitted

Amed, Paul LTh DPS   1992   2015   (Barvas)
6 Scotland Street, Stornoway, Isle of Lewis HS1 2JQ
paul.amed@outlook.com
01851 706450

Jamieson, Esther M.M. (Mrs) BD   1984   2002   (Glasgow: Penilee St Andrew's)
1 Redburn, Bayview, Stornoway, Isle of Lewis HS1 2UU
iandejamieson@btinternet.com
01851 704789

Johnstone, Ben MA BD DMin	1973 2013	(Strath and Sleat)	Loch Alainn, 5 Breaclete, Great Bernera, Isle of Lewis HS2 9LT	01851 612445
			benonbernera@gmail.com	
Maclean, Donald A. DCS	1988 1990	(Deacon)	8 Upper Barvas, Isle of Lewis HS2 0QX	01851 840454
MacLennan, Donald Angus	1975 2006	(Kinloch)	4 Kestrel Place, Inverness IV2 3YH	01463 243750
				07799 668270
			maclennankinloch@btinternet.com	
Macleod, William	1957 2006	(Uig)	54 Lower Barvas, Isle of Lewis HS2 0QY	01851 840217

LEWIS Communion Sundays

Barvas	3rd Mar, Sep	Knock	3rd Apr, 1st Nov
Carloway	1st Mar, last Sep	Lochs-Crossbost	4th Mar, Sep
Cross Ness	2nd Mar, Oct	Lochs-in-Bernera	1st Apr, 2nd Sep
Kinloch	3rd Mar, 2nd Jun, 2nd Sep	Stornoway: High	3rd Feb, last Aug

Stornoway: Martin's Memorial	3rd Feb, last Aug, 1st Dec, Easter
Stornoway: St Columba	3rd Feb, last Aug
Uig	3rd Jun, 4th Oct

(45) ORKNEY (W)

Normally meets at Kirkwall on the first Wednesday of September, November, February, April, and the third Wednesday of June.

Clerk: KAREN McKNIGHT CIMA CertBA		8 Fletts Corner, Finstown, Orkney KW17 2EE	**01856 761554**
		orkney@churchofscotland.org.uk	
Depute Clerk: MS MARGARET A.B. SUTHERLAND LLB BA		13 Cursiter Crescent, Kirkwall, Orkney KW15 1XN	**01856 873747**
		mabs2@tiscali.co.uk	

Birsay, Harray and Sandwick (F W)

David G. McNeish MB ChB BSc BD	2015	The Manse, North Biggings Road, Dounby, Orkney KW17 2HZ	01856 771599
		DMcNeish@churchofscotland.org.uk	

East Mainland (W)

		eastmainlandchurch@gmail.com	
Wilma A. Johnston MTheol MTh	2006 2014	The Manse, Holm, Orkney KW17 2SB	01856 781797
		Wilma.Johnston@churchofscotland.org.uk	

Eday
Vacant
Session Clerk: Johan Robertson

essonquoy@btinternet.com	01857 622251

Evie (H) linked with Firth (H) linked with Rendall linked with Rousay　　　　**Firth: 01856 761117**
Vacant　　The Manse, Finstown, Orkney KW17 2EG　　01856 761328
Session Clerk, Firth: Janis Dickey　　rbdickey@hotmail.com　　01856 761396
Session Clerk, Rendall: Eileen Fraser　　eileenocot@hotmail.co.uk　　01856 761409
Session Clerk, Rousay: Elizabeth Firth　　liznedyar@gmail.com　　01856 821477

Firth　See Evie

Flotta (W) linked with Hoy and Walls (F) linked with Orphir and Stenness (H W)
Vacant　　Stenness Manse, Stenness, Stromness, Orkney KW16 3HH
Session Clerk, Flotta: Isobel Smith　　01856 701219
Session Clerk, Hoy and Walls:　　01856 701363
　Anderson Sutherland

Hoy and Walls　See Flotta

Kirkwall: East (F H W) linked with Shapinsay (F W)
Julia M. Meason MTh　2013　East Church Manse, Thoms Street, Kirkwall, Orkney KW15 1PF　01856 874789
　　JMeason@churchofscotland.org.uk

Kirkwall: St Magnus Cathedral (F H T W)
G. Fraser H. Macnaughton MA BD　1982　2002　Berstane Road, Kirkwall, Orkney KW15 1NA　01856 873312
　　FMacnaughton@churchofscotland.org.uk

North Ronaldsay
Guardianship of the Presbytery
Presbytery Clerk: Karen McKnight　orkney@churchofscotland.org.uk　01856 761554

Orphir and Stenness　See Flotta

Papa Westray (W) linked with Westray (W)
Iain D. MacDonald BD　1993　The Manse, Hilldavale, Westray, Orkney KW17 2DW　Tel/Fax　01857 677357
　　IMacDonald@churchofscotland.org.uk　07710 443780

Rendall　See Evie
Rousay　See Evie

Sanday
Vacant
Interim Moderator: John A. Butterfield
JButterfield@churchofscotland.org.uk
01856 850203

Shapinsay See Kirkwall: East

South Ronaldsay and Burray
Vacant
St Margaret's Manse, Church Road, St Margaret's Hope, Orkney KW17 2SR
01856 831670
Interim Moderator: Wilma A. Johnston
Wilma.Johnston@churchofscotland.org.uk
01856 781797

Stromness (F H)
John A. Butterfield BA BD MPhil   1990   2016
5 Manse Lane, Stromness, Orkney KW16 3AP
JButterfield@churchofscotland.org.uk
01856 850203

Stronsay: Moncur Memorial (W)
Vacant
Session Clerk: Elsie Dennison
elsie.dennison@live.co.uk
01857 616238

Westray See Papa Westray

In other appointments

Freeth, June BA MA		2015	Ordained Local Minister	Cumlaquoy, Birsay, Orkney KW17 2ND JFreeth@churchofscotland.org.uk	01856 721449
Prentice, Martin W.M.		2013	Ordained Local Minister	Cott of Howe, Cairston, Stromness, Orkney KW16 3JU MPrentice@churchofscotland.org.uk	01856 851139 07795 817213

Demitted

Clark, Thomas L. BD	1985	2008	(Orphir with Stenness)	7 Headland Rise, Burghead, Elgin IV30 5HA toml.clark@btinternet.com	01343 830144
Graham, Jennifer D. (Mrs) BA MDiv PhD	2000	2011	(Eday with Stronsay: Moncur Memorial)	Lodge, Stronsay, Orkney KW17 2AN jdgraham67@gmail.com	01857 616487
Tait, Alexander	1967	1995	(Glasgow: St Enoch's Hogganfield)	Ingermas, Evie, Orkney KW17 2PH	01856 751477

Wishart, James BD   1986 2009   (Deer)   Upper Westshore, Burray, Orkney KW17 2TE   01856 731672
jwishart06@btinternet.com

(46) SHETLAND (F)

Meets at Tingwall on the second Tuesday of February, April, June, September, November and December.

Acting Clerk: REV. B. IAN MURRAY BD   **Kilmorie House, 6 Institution Road, Elgin IV30 1RP**
Depute Clerk: MRS CHERYL BRANKIN BA   **Mastrick Church, Greenfern Road, Aberdeen AB16 6TR   01224 698119**
shetland@churchofscotland.org.uk

Burra Isle (F) linked with Tingwall (F)
Vacant   25 Hogalee, East Voe, Scalloway, Shetland ZE1 0UU   01595 881184
Session Clerk, Tingwall: John Jarmson   john.jarmson@btinternet.com   01595 840502

Delting linked with Northmavine
Vacant
Session Clerk, Delting: Isobel Morrice (Ms)   isobelmorrice@btinternet.com

Dunrossness and St Ninian's inc. Fair Isle linked with Sandwick, Cunningsburgh and Quarff
Vacant   dbuddleunst@btinternet.com   01595 431575
Session Clerk, Sandwick, Cunningsburgh and
Quarff: Dennis Buddle

Lerwick and Bressay (F)
Vacant   The Manse, 82 St Olaf Street, Lerwick, Shetland ZE1 0ES   01595 692125
Interim Moderator: B. Ian Murray   BMurray@churchofscotland.org.uk   01343 546265

Nesting and Lunnasting linked with Whalsay and Skerries
Irene A. Charlton (Mrs) BTh   1994   1997   The Manse, Marrister, Symbister, Whalsay, Shetland ZE2 9AE   01806 566767
ICharlton@churchofscotland.org.uk

Northmavine See Delting

Sandsting and Aithsting linked with Walls and Sandness
Vacant
Session Clerk, Sandsting and Aithsting: Creighton Williamson   creightonwilliamson@tiscali.co.uk
Session Clerk, Walls and Sandness: Barbara Taylor (Mrs)   barbarataylor534@btinternet.com   01595 809344

Sandwick, Cunningsburgh and Quarff See Dunrossness and St Ninian's
Tingwall See Burra Isle

Unst and Fetlar (F) linked with Yell
Vacant   North Isles Manse, Gutcher, Yell, Shetland ZE2 9DF   01957 744258
Session Clerk, Yell: Barbara Priest (Mrs)   barbara@aistgatesgirt.plus.com   01957 711512

Walls and Sandness See Sandsting and Aithsting
Whalsay and Skerries See Nesting and Lunnasting
Yell See Unst and Fetlar

In other appointments

Henderson, Frances M. BA BD PhD	2006	2018	Transition Minister, Shetland	Brae Church of Scotland Manse, Brae ZE2 9QJ 01806 522469 FHenderson@churchofscotland.org.uk
Murray, B. Ian BD	2002	2018	Interim Minister and Acting Clerk, Shetland	Kilmorie House, 6 Institution Road, Elgin IV30 1RP 01343 546265 BMurray@churchofscotland.org.uk

Demitted

Greig, Charles H.M. MA BD	1976	2016	(Dunrossness and St Ninian's inc. Fair Isle with Sandwick, Cunningsburgh and Quarff)	6 Hayhoull Place, Bigton, Shetland ZE2 9GA 01950 422468 chm.greig@btinternet.com
Kirkpatrick, Alice H. (Miss) MA BD FSAScot	1987	2000	(Northmavine)	1 Daisy Park, Baltasound, Unst, Shetland ZE2 9EA
Macintyre, Thomas MA BD	1972	2011	(Sandsting and Aithsting with Walls and Sandness)	Lappideks, South Voxter, Cunningsburgh, Shetland ZE2 9HF 01950 477549 the2macs.macintyre@btinternet.com
Smith, Catherine (Mrs) DCS	1964	2003	(Deacon)	21 Lingaro, Bixter, Shetland ZE2 9NN 01595 810207
Williamson, Magnus J.C.	1982	1999	(Fetlar with Yell)	Creekhaven, Houl Road, Scalloway, Shetland ZE1 0XA 01595 880023

(47) ENGLAND (F)

Meets at London, in Crown Court Church, on the second Tuesday of February, and at St Columba's, Pont Street, on the second Tuesday of June and the second Saturday of October.

| Clerk: | REV. ALISTAIR CUMMING MSc CCS FInstLM FLPI | 64 Prince George's Avenue, London SW20 8BH england@churchofscotland.org.uk | 07534 943986 |

Corby: St Andrew's (F H W)
A. Norman Nicoll BD 2003 2016
43 Hempland Close, Corby, Northants NN18 8LR
NNicoll@churchofscotland.org.uk
07930 988863

Corby: St Ninian's (H W)
Kleber Machado BTh MA MTh PhD 1998 2012
The Manse, 46 Glyndebourne Gardens, Corby, Northants NN18 0PZ
KMachado@churchofscotland.org.uk
01536 265245
01536 669478

Guernsey: St Andrew's in the Grange (F H W)
David G. Coulter CB OStJ QHC
BA BD MDA PhD 1989 2019
The Manse, Le Villocq, Castel, Guernsey GY5 7SB
DCoulter@churchofscotland.org.uk
01481 257345

Jersey: St Columba's (F H T W)
Graeme M. Glover BD 2017
18 Claremont Avenue, St Saviour, Jersey JE2 7SF
GGlover@churchofscotland.org.uk
01534 730659

London: Crown Court (F H T W)
Philip L. Majcher BD 1982 2007
53 Sidmouth Street, London WC1H 8JX
PMajcher@churchofscotland.org.uk
020 7836 5643
020 7278 5022

London: St Columba's (F H T W) linked with Newcastle: St Andrew's (H T W)   office@stcolumbas.org.uk
C. Angus MacLeod MA BD 1996 2012
29 Hollywood Road, Chelsea, London SW10 9HT
Angus.MacLeod@churchofscotland.org.uk
St Columba's: 020 7584 2321
Office   020 7584 2321

In other appointments

Name	Years	Appointment	Address / Email	Telephone
Anderson, David P. BSc BD	2002 2007	Senior Army Chaplain	Infantry Training Centre, Vimy Barracks, Catterick Garrison DL9 3PS / padre.anderson180@mod.gov.uk	07590 507917
Binks, Mike	2007 2015	Auxiliary Minister – Churches Together in Corby	Hollybank, 10 Kingsbrook, Corby NN18 9HY / MBinks@churchofscotland.org.uk	
Cumming, Alistair MSc CCS FInstLM FLPI	2010 2013	Presbytery Clerk: Auxiliary Minister	64 Prince George's Avenue, London SW20 8BH / ACumming@churchofscotland.org.uk	020 8540 7365 / 07534 943986
Francis, James MBE BD PhD	2002 2009	Army Chaplain	37 Millburn Road, Coleraine BT52 1QT	02870 353869
Lancaster, Craig MA BD	2004 2011	RAF Chaplain	52 Suffolk Avenue, RAF Honington, Bury St Edmunds IP31 1LW / craig.lancaster102@mod.gov.uk	
Langlands, Cameron H. BD MTh ThM PhD MInstLM	1995 2012	Head of Chaplaincy, South London and Maudsley NHS Foundation Trust	Maudsley Hospital, Denmark Road, London SE5 8EZ	07989 642544
Lovett, Mairi F. BSc BA DipPS MTh	2005 2013	Hospital Chaplain	Royal Brompton Hospital, Sydney Street, London SW3 6NP / m.lovett@rbht.nhs.uk	020 7352 8121 ext. 4736
McLay, Neil BA BD	2006 2012	Army Chaplain	1 R Welsh, Lucknow Barracks, Lowa Road, Tidworth SP9 7BU	01344 754098
McMahon, John K.S. MA BD	1998 2012	Head of Spiritual and Pastoral Care, West London NHS Trust	Broadmoor Hospital, Crowthorne, Berkshire RG45 7EG / john.mcmahonrev@westlondon.nhs.uk	
Mather, James BA DipArch MA MBA	2010	Auxiliary Minister: University Chaplain	24 Ellison Road, Barnes, London SW13 0AD / JMather@churchofscotland.org.uk	Home 020 8876 6540 / Work 020 7361 1670 / Mbl 07836 715655
Middleton, Paul (Prof) BMus BD ThM PhD	2000 2017	Biblical Studies, University of Chester	97B Whipcord Lane, Chester CH1 4DG / revdj@gmail.com	
Thom, David J. BD DipMin	1999 2015	Army Chaplain	Flat 5, 18 Northside Wandsworth Common, London SW18 2SL / revrfw@gmail.com	020 8870 0953
Walker, R. Forbes BSc BD ThM	1987 2013	School Chaplain, Emmanuel School, London		
Ward, Michael J. BSc BD PhD MA PGCE	1983 2009	Training and Development Officer: Presbyterian Church of Wales	Apt 6, Bryn Hedd, Conwy Road, Penmaen-mawr, Gwynedd LL34 6BS / revmw@btopenworld.com	07765 598816

Demitted

Name	Years	Charge	Address / Email	Telephone
Anderson, Andrew F. MA BD	1981 2011	(Edinburgh: Greenside)	58 Reliance Way, Oxford OX4 2FG / andrew.relianceway@gmail.com	01865 778397
Cairns, W. Alexander BD	1978 2006	(Corby: St Andrew's)	Kirkton House, Kirkton of Craig, Montrose DD10 9TB / sandy.cairns@btinternet.com	07808 588045
Cameron, R. Neil	1976 2005	(Chaplain: Army)	neilandminacameron@yahoo.co.uk	
Lunn, Dorothy I.M.	2002 2017	(Auxiliary Minister)	14 Bellerby Drive, Ouston, Co.Durham DH2 1TW / dorothylunn@hotmail.com	0191 492 0647
Macfarlane, Peter T. BA LTh	1970 1994	(Chaplain: Army)	4 rue de Rives, 37160 Abilly, France	
McIndoe, John H. MA BD STM DD	1960 2000	(London: St Columba's with Newcastle: St Andrew's)	5 Dunlin, Westerlands Park, Glasgow G12 0FE / johnandeve@mcindoe555.fsnet.co.uk	0141 579 1366

MacLeod, Rory N. BA BD	1986 2017	154 Regt RLC, Bothwell House, Elgin Street, Dunfermline KY12 7SB	
Mills, Peter W. CB BD DD CPD	1984 2017	16 Pearce Drive, Lawley, Telford TF3 5JQ	
Wallace, Donald S.	1950 1990	7 Dellfield Close, Watford, Herts WD1 3BL	01923 223289

Chaplain: Army
(Largoward with St Monans)
(Chaplain: Royal Caledonian Schools)

ENGLAND – Church Addresses

Corby: St Andrew's	Occupation Road	Jersey:	Midvale Road, St Helier	Newcastle:	Sandyford Road
Corby: St Ninian's	Beanfield Avenue	London: Crown Court	Crown Court WC2		
Guernsey:	The Grange, St Peter Port	London: St Columba's	Pont Street SW1		

(48) PRESBYTERY OF INTERNATIONAL CHARGES (W)

Meets over the weekend of the second Sunday of March and October, hosted by congregations in mainland Europe.

Clerk: REV. JAMES SHARP   102 Rue des Eaux-Vives, CH-1207 Geneva, Switzerland   **0041 22 786 4847**
clerk@internationalpresbytery.net
www.internationalpresbytery.net

Depute Clerk: REV. DEREK G. LAWSON LLB BD   Schiedamse Vest 121, 3012BH, Rotterdam, The Netherlands   **0031 10 412 5709**
deputeclerk@internationalpresbytery.net

Amsterdam: English Reformed Church (F T W)
Lance Stone BD MTh PhD   1980   Jan Willem Brouwersstraat 9, NL-1071 LH Amsterdam,   0031 20 672 2288
The Netherlands
minister@ercadam.nl
Church address: Begijnhof 48, 1012WV Amsterdam

Bermuda: Christ Church, Warwick (F H W)
Alistair G. Bennett BSc BD   1978 2016   christchurch@logic.bm   **001 441 236 1882**
The Manse, 6 Manse Road, Paget PG 01, Bermuda   001 441 236 0400
Church address: Christ Church, Middle Road, Warwick, Bermuda
Mailing address: PO Box WK 130, Warwick WK BX, Bermuda

Bochum (Associated congregation) (W)
James M. Brown MA BD   1982 1983   Neustrasse 15, D-44787 Bochum, Germany   0049 234 133 65
JBrown@churchofscotland.org.uk
Church address: Pauluskircke, Grabenstrasse 9, 44787 Bochum

Brussels St Andrew's (F H W)
Vacant

Interim Moderator: Lance Stone, Amsterdam

secretary@churchofscotland.be
23 Square des Nations, B-1000 Brussels, Belgium
minister@churchofscotland.be
Church address: Chaussée de Vieurgat 181, 1050 Brussels

0032 2 649 02 19
0032 2 672 40 56

Budapest St Columba's (F W)
Aaron C. Stevens BA MDiv MACE

2004   2006

Stefánia út 32, H-1143, Budapest, Hungary
AStevens@churchofscotland.org.uk
Church address: Vörösmarty utca 51, 1064 Budapest

0036 30 567 6356
0036 70 615 5394

Colombo, Sri Lanka: St Andrew's Scots Kirk (F W)
Vacant

Session Clerk: Chandan de Silva

churchofficer@scotskirk.lk
73 Galle Road, Colpetty, Colombo 3, Sri Lanka
minister@standrewsscotskirk.org
chandan59@yahoo.com

0094 112 323 765
0094 112 386 774

0094 112 588 687

Costa del Sol (W)
Guardianship of the Presbytery

Interim Moderator: Derek Lawson, Rotterdam

Avenida Jesus Santos Rein, 24 Edf. Lindamar 4 – 3Q,
Fuengirola, 29640 Malaga, Spain
Church address: Lux Mundi Ecumenical Centre, Calle Nueva 3,
29460 Fuengirola

0034 951 260 982

Geneva (F W)
Laurence H. Twaddle MA BD MTh

1977   2017

6 chemin Taverney, 1218 Geneva, Switzerland
cofsg@pingnet.ch
Church address: Auditoire de Calvin, 1 Place de la Taconnerie, Geneva

0041 22 788 08 31
0041 22 788 08 31

Gibraltar St Andrew's (W)
Ewen MacLean BA BD

1995   2009

St Andrew's Manse, 29 Scud Hill, Gibraltar
scotskirk@gibraltar.gi
Church address: Governor's Parade, Gibraltar

00350 200 77040

Lausanne: The Scots Kirk (F H W)
Gillean P. MacLean (Ms) BA BD

1994   2019

26 Avenue de Rumine, CH-1005 Lausanne, Switzerland
GMacLean@churchofscotland.org.uk

0041 21 323 98 28

Lisbon St Andrew's (F W)
Guardianship of the Presbytery
lisbonstandrewschurch@gmail.com
Rua Coelho da Rocha, N°75 - 1°
Campa de Ourique, 1350-073 Lisbon, Portugal
cofslx@netcabo.pt
Church address: Rua da Arriaga, Lisbon
00351 213 951 165

Session Clerk: Nina O'Donnell
sessionclerklisbon@gmail.com
00351 21 483 8750

Malta St Andrew's Scots Church (H W)
Vacant
La Romagnola, 15 Triq is-Seiqia, Misrah Kola, Attard ATD 1713, Malta
minister@saintandrewsmalta.com
Church address: 210 Old Bakery Street, Valletta, Malta
Tel/Fax 00356 214 15465

Interim Moderator: James Brown, Bochum

Paris: The Scots Kirk (F W)
Jan J. Steyn   1988   2017
10 Rue Thimmonier, F-75009 Paris, France
Church address: 17 Rue Bayard, 75009 Paris
JSteyn@churchofscotland.org.uk
0033 1 48 78 47 94

Rome: St Andrew's (F W)
Vacant
scotskirkrome@gmail.com
Via XX Settembre 7, 00187 Rome, Italy
scotskirkrome@gmail.com
Tel 0039 06 482 7627
Fax 0039 06 487 4370

Session Clerk: Inge Weustink

Rotterdam: Scots International Church (F W)   1998   2016
Derek G. Lawson LLB BD
info@scotsintchurch.com
Schiedamse Vest 121, 3012BH Rotterdam, The Netherlands
DLawson@churchofscotland.org.uk
Church address: Schiedamsesingel 2, Rotterdam, The Netherlands
0031 10 412 4779
0031 10 412 5709

Trinidad: Greyfriars St Ann's, Port of Spain (W) linked with Arouca and Sangre Grande
Vacant
50 Frederick Street, Port of Spain, Trinidad
Interim Moderator: Rev Aaron Stevens, Budapest
001 868 623 6684

In other appointments

Bom, Irene   2008   Ordained Local Minister-Worship and Prayer Promoter
Bergpolderstraat 53A, NL-3038 KB Rotterdam, The Netherlands
ibsalem@xs4all.nl
0031 10 265 1703

Evans-Boiten, Joanne H.G. BD	2004 2018	Retreat Centre Director	Colomba le Roc, 510 Chemin du Faurat, Belmontet, 46800 Montecuq, France Joanne.evansboiten@gmail.com	0033 5 65 22 13 11
McGeoch, Graham G. MA BD MTh	2009 2017	Lecturer	Faculdade Unida de Vitoria. R.Eng. Fabio Ruschi 161 Bento Ferreira, Vitoria ES 29050-670, Brazil	
Ross, Matthew Z. LLB BD MTh FSAScot	1998 2018	Programme Executive for Diakonia and Capacity Building, World Council of Churches	World Council of Churches, Route de Ferney 150. Case Postale 2100, CH-1211 Geneva 2, Switzerland Matthew.Ross@wcc-coe.org	work 0041 22 791 6322 mob 0041 79 155 8638
Sharp, James	2005 2013	Ordained Local Minister, Presbytery Clerk	102 Rue des Eaux-Vives, 1207 Geneva, Switzerland jim.sharp@churchofscotland.org.uk	0041 22 786 4847

Demitted

Foggitt, Eric W. MA BSc BD	1991 2009	(Dunbar)	Christiaan de Wetstraat 19/2, 1091 NG Amsterdam, Netherlands ericfoggitt@gmail.com	0031 639 541 203
Herbold Ross, Kristina M.	2008 2018	(Work Place Chaplain)	c/o Rev Matthew Z. Ross (see above)	
Pitkeathly, Thomas C. MA CA BD	1984 2004	(Brussels)	77 St Thomas Road, Lytham St. Anne's FY8 1JP tpitkeathly@yahoo.co.uk	01253 789634
Reamonn, Paraic BA BD	1982 2018	(Jerusalem: St Andrew's)	395B Route de Mandement, 1281 Ruissin, Switzerland PReamonn@churchofscotland.org.uk	0041 22 776 4834

(49) JERUSALEM

Clerk:	JOANNA OAKLEY-LEVSTEIN		St Andrew's, Galilee, PO Box 104, Tiberias 14100, Israel j.oakley@gmail.com	00972 50 5842517

Jerusalem and Tiberias: St Andrew's (F W)

John McCulloch BA BA (Theol) PhD	2018		jerusalem@churchofscotland.org.uk St Andrew's Scots Memorial Church, 1 David Remez Street, PO Box 8619, Jerusalem 91086, Israel JMcCulloch@churchofscotland.org.uk	00972 2 673 2401
			tiberias@churchofscotland.org.uk	
Katharine S. McDonald BA MSc BD MLitt (Associate Minister) (Scottish Episcopal Church)	2012	2015	St Andrew's, Galilee, 1 Gdud Barak Street, PO Box 104, Tiberias 14100, Israel kmcdonald@churchofscotland.org.uk	00972 54 244 6736

SECTION 6

Additional Lists of Personnel

LIST A – ORDAINED LOCAL MINISTERS

Those engaged in active service. Where only one date is given it is the year of ordination and appointment. Contact details may be found under the Presbytery in Section 5 to which an OLM belongs.

NAME	ORD	APP	APPOINTMENT	PRESBYTERY
Allardice, Michael MA MPhil PGCertTHE FHEA	2014	—		25 Kirkcaldy
Archer, Morven (Mrs)	2013	2018	Inverness: Crown	37 Inverness
Bellis, Pamela A. BA	2014	2014	Inch linked with Portpatrick linked with Stranraer: Trinity	9 Wigtown and Stranraer
Bissett, James	2016		Contin linked with Fodderty and Strathpeffer	39 Ross
Born, Irene	2008		Worship Resourcing	48 International Charges
Breingan, Mhairi	2011	2019	Paisley: Stow Brae	14 Greenock and Paisley
Brodie, Catherine J. MA BA MPhil PGCE	2017		Dundee: Fintry	29 Dundee
Crossan, Morag BA	2016		Dalmellington linked with Patna Waterside	10 Ayr
Crossan, William	2014	2018	Campbeltown: Lorne and Lowland	19 Argyll
Dee, Oonagh	2014	2016	Castle Douglas linked with The Bengairn Parishes	8 Dumfries and Kirkcudbright
Dempster, Eric T. MBA	2016	2018	Lockerbie: Dryfesdale, Hutton and Corrie Newton	7 Annandale and Eskdale
Don, Andrew MBA	2006	2013		3 Lothian
Duncanson, Mary (Ms) BTh	2013		Presbytery Pastoral Support	36 Abernethy
Finnie, Bill H. BA PgDipSW CertCRS	2015		Kirkintilloch: Hillhead	16 Glasgow
Forsythe, Ruth (Mrs) MCS	2017	2018	Glasgow: Temple Anniesland	16 Glasgow
Freeth, June BA MA	2015			45 Orkney
Fulcher, Christine P. BEd	2012	2018	Presbytery Ministries Co-ordinator – South Argyll	19 Argyll
Geddes, Elizabeth (Mrs)	2013			14 Greenock and Paisley
Gray, Ian	2013	2017	Montrose: Old and St Andrew's	30 Angus
Grieve, Leslie E.T. BSc BA	2014		Glasgow: Colston Wellpark	16 Glasgow
Hardman Moore, Susan (Prof.) MA MAR PhD	2013		New College, University of Edinburgh	1 Edinburgh
Harrison, Frederick	2013			3 Lothian
Henderson, Derek R.	2017		Abercorn linked with Pardovan, Kingscavil and Winchburgh	2 West Lothian
Hogg, James	2018		Troon: St Meddan's	10 Ayr
Hunt, Roland BSc PhD CertEd	2016		Glasgow: Carmyle linked with Glasgow: Mount Vernon	16 Glasgow
Irvine, Carl J. BA	2017		Presbytery-wide	33 Gordon
Johnston, June E. BSc MEd BD	2013	2018	Bonnyrigg	3 Lothian
Lennox-Trewren, Norman D.	2018		Mearns Coastal	32 Kincardine and Deeside
McCutcheon, John	2014			18 Dumbarton
Macdonald, Ishabel	2011		Benbecula linked with Carinish	43 Uist
MacDonald, Monica (Mrs)	2014		Slamannan	22 Falkirk

Name			Charge		Presbytery
Mack, Lynne (Mrs)	2013	2014	Gargunnock linked with Kilmadock linked with Kincardine-in-Menteith	23	Stirling
McKenzie, Janet R. (Mrs)	2016		Edinburgh: Tron Kirk (Gilmerton and Moredun)	1	Edinburgh
MacLeod, Iain A.	2012	—		16	Glasgow
McLeod, Tom	2014	2015	Craigie Symington linked with Prestwick: South	10	Ayr
Mateos, Margaret	2018	—	Dunfermline: St Leonard's	24	Dunfermline
Maxwell, David	2014	—		16	Glasgow
Michie, Margaret (Mrs)	2013		Loch Leven Parish Grouping	28	Perth
Morrison, John A. BSc BA PGCE	2013		Dallas linked with Forres: St Leonard's linked with Rafford	35	Moray
Muirhead, Morag Y. (Mrs)	2014	2017	Fort William: Duncansburgh MacIntosh linked with Kilmonivaig	38	Lochaber
Murphy, Jim	2013		East Kilbride: Mossneuk	17	Hamilton
Nicol, Robert D.	2014	—		27	Dunkeld and Meigle
Nutter, Margaret A.E.	2017	2019	Presbytery-wide	18	Dumbarton
Palmer, Sonia RGN	2018		Elgin: St Giles' and St Columba's South	35	Moray
Porteous, Brian BSc DipCS	2013	—	Kirkcaldy: Torbain	25	Kirkcaldy
Prentice, Martin W.M.	2018	—		45	Orkney
Quilter, Alison	2013		Polbeth Harwood linked with West Kirk of Calder	2	West Lothian
Ralph, Mandy R. RGN	2017			12	Ardrossan
Rattenbury, Carol	2013		Rosskeen	39	Ross
Sarle, Andrew BSc BD	2005	2013	Falkirk: Bainsford	22	Falkirk
Sharp, James	2015	2018	Presbytery Clerk, International Charges	48	International Charges
Somevi, Joseph K. BSc MSc PhD MRICS MRTPI MIEMA CertCRS	2014		Aberdeen: Bridge of Don Oldmachar	31	Aberdeen
Steele, Grace M.F. MA BTh	2011	2017		27	Dunkeld and Meigle
Stevenson, Stuart	2013	2017	Paisley: St Ninian's Ferguslie	14	Greenock and Paisley
Stewart, Heather (Mrs)	2015	2016	Latheron	41	Caithness
Stewart, William	2013		Presbytery-wide	34	Buchan
Stobo, Mary J. (Mrs)	2014		Community Healthcare Chaplain	40	Sutherland
Strachan, Pamela D. (Lady) MA (Cantab)	2013		Eddleston linked with Peebles: Old	4	Melrose and Peebles
Strachan, Willie MBA DipY&C	2014		Dundee: Lochee	29	Dundee
Sturrock, Roger D. (Prof.) BD MD FCRP	2011	2014	Glasgow: Kelvinside Hillhead linked with Glasgow: Wellington	16	Glasgow
Thomson, Mary Ellen (Mrs)	2013	2017	Presbytery Chaplain to Care Homes	36	Abernethy
Thorburn, Susan (Mrs) MTh	2013	2019		28	Perth
Tweedie, Fiona J. BSc PhD	2015		Mission Statistics Co-ordinator, Church Offices	1	Edinburgh
Wallace, Mhairi (Mrs)	2017		Kirkmichael, Tinwald and Torthorwald	8	Dumfries and Galloway
Watson, Michael D.	2018		Athelstaneford linked with Whitekirk and Tyninghame	3	Lothian
Watt, Kim			Presbytery-wide	11	Irvine and Kilmarnock
Welsh, Rita M. BA PhD	2017		Edinburgh: Holy Trinity	1	Edinburgh
White, Ann BA DipTh	2018		Falkirk: Grahamston United	22	Falkirk

ORDAINED LOCAL MINISTERS (Retired)

Those who are retired and registered under the Registration of Ministries Act (Act 2, 2017, as amended) as 'O' or 'R' (Retaining). There are presently no OLMs registered as 'I'(Inactive). Contact details may be found under the Presbytery in Section 5 to which an OLM belongs.

NAME	ORD	RET	PRESBYTERY
Anderson, David M. MSc FCOptom	1984	2018	38 Lochaber
Brown, Kathryn I. (Mrs)	2014	2019	22 Falkirk
Duncan, Esme (Miss)	2013	2017	41 Caithness
Edwards, Dougal BTh	2013	2017	30 Angus
Harvey, Joyce (Mrs)	2013	2019	47 England (not a member of Presbytery) 2 Beaufort Court, West Bridford, Nottingham NG2 7TB JHarvey@churchofscotland.org.uk 07510 136575
Kiehlmann, Peter BA (Dr)	2016	2018	47 England (not a member of Presbytery) PKiehlmann@churchofscotland.org.uk
Mathers, Alexena (Sandra)	2015	2018	22 Falkirk
McAllister, Anne C. (Mrs) BSc DipEd CCS	2013	2016	11 Irvine and Kilmarnock
McLaughlin, Cathie H. (Mrs)	2014	2018	16 Glasgow
Rennie, Lyall	2014	2019	41 Caithness
Robertson, Ishbel A.R. MA BD	2013	2018	18 Dumbarton

LIST B – AUXILIARY MINISTERS

Those engaged in active service. Contact details may be found under the Presbytery in Section 5 to which an Auxiliary Minister belongs.

NAME	ORD	APP	APPOINTMENT	PRESBYTERY
Binks, Mike	2007	2015	Churches Together in Corby	47 England
Buck, Maxine	2007	2015	Presbytery-wide	17 Hamilton
Cameron, Ann J. (Mrs) CertCS DCE TEFL	2005	2017	Craigrownie linked with Garelochhead linked with Rosneath St. Modan's	18 Dumbarton
Campbell, Gordon A. MA BD CDipAF DipHSM CMgr MCMI MIHM AssocCIPD AFRIN ARSGS FRGS FSAScot	2001	2004	An Honorary Chaplain, University of Dundee	29 Dundee
Cumming, Alistair MSc CCS FInstLM FLPI	2010	2013	Presbytery Clerk, England	47 England
Gardner, Hilary M. (Miss)	2010	2018	Lairg linked with Rogart	40 Sutherland
Griffiths, Ruth I. (Mrs)	2004		Dunoon: The High Kirk linked with Innellan linked with Toward	19 Argyll
Howie, Marion L.K. (Mrs) MA ARCS	1992	2016	Dalry: St Margaret's	12 Ardrossan

NAME	ORD	RET		PRESBYTERY
Jackson, Nancy	2009	—	—	10 Ayr
Kemp, Tina MA	2005	2017	Helensburgh linked with Rhu and Shandon	18 Dumbarton
Kinnear, Marion (Mrs)	2009	—	—	38 Lochaber
Macdonald, Michael J.	2004	2014	Alness	39 Ross
Mack, Elizabeth A. (Miss) DipPEd	1994	2018	Lochend and New Abbey	8 Dumfries and Kirkcudbright
Manson, Eileen (Mrs) DipCE	1994	—	—	14 Greenock and Paisley
Mather, James BA DipArch MA MBA	2010	—	University Chaplain	47 England
Paterson, Andrew E. JP	1994	2016	Presbytery-wide	24 Dunfermline
Riddell, Thomas S. BSc CEng FIChemE	1993	1994	Linlithgow: St Michael's	2 West Lothian
Robson, Brenda PhD	2005	2014	Kirknewton and East Calder	2 West Lothian
Shearer, Anne F. BA DipEd	2010	2018	Alva	23 Stirling
Walker, Linda	2008	2014	Presbytery-wide	16 Glasgow
Wandrum, David C.	1993	2017	Carriden	22 Falkirk
Wilkie, Robert F.	2011	2012	Perth: Craigie and Moncrieffe	28 Perth

AUXILIARY MINISTERS (Retired)

Those who are retired and registered under the Registration of Ministries Act (Act 2, 2017, as amended) as 'O', 'R' (Retaining) or 'I' (Inactive). Only those 'Inactive' Auxiliary Ministers who have given consent under the GDPR to publication of their details are included. Contact details may be found under the Presbytery in Section 5 to which an Auxiliary Minister belongs.

NAME	ORD	RET	PRESBYTERY
Attenburrow, Anne BSc MB ChB	2006	2018	35 Moray
Birch, James PgDip FRSA FIOC	2001	2007	16 Glasgow
Brown, Elizabeth (Mrs) JP RGN	1996	2007	28 Perth
Cloggie, June (Mrs)	1997	2006	23 Stirling
Craggs, Sheila (Mrs)	2001	2016	33 Gordon
Fletcher, Timothy E. G. BA FCMA	1998	2019	28 Perth
Harrison, Cameron	2006	2011	26 St Andrews
Kay, Elizabeth (Miss) DipYCS	1993	2007	29 Dundee
Landale, William S.	2005	2016	5 Duns
Lunn, Dorothy I. M.	2002	2017	47 England
McAlpine, John BSc	1988	2004	17 Hamilton (not member of Presbytery) Braeside, 201 Bonkle Road, Newmains, Wishaw ML2 9AA 01698 384610
MacDonald, Kenneth BA MA	2001	2006	16 Glasgow
MacFadyen, Anne M. (Mrs) BSc BD FSAScot	1995	2003	16 Glasgow
Mack, John C. JP	1985	2008	33 Gordon

Mailer, Colin M. 1996 2005 22 Falkirk (not member of Presbytery) 25 Saltcoats Drive, Grangemouth FK3 9JP 01324 712401

Morrison, Donald John 2001 2019 43 Uist

Paterson, Maureen (Mrs) BSc 1992 2010 25 Kirkcaldy

Phillippo, Michael MTh BSc BVetMed MRCVS 2003 2011 31 Aberdeen

Pot, Joost BSc 1992 2004 48 International Charges (not member of Presbytery) joostpot@gmail.com

Ramage, Alastair E. MA BA ADB CertEd 1996 2016 18 Dumbarton

Shaw, Catherine A.M. MA 1998 2006 11 Irvine and Kilmarnock

Thomas, Shirley A. (Mrs) DipSocSci AMIA 2000 2006 30 Angus

Wilson, Mary D. (Mrs) RGN SCM DTM 1990 2004 27 Dunkeld and Meigle

Zambonini, James LIADip 1997 2015 17 Hamilton

LIST C – THE DIACONATE

Those engaged in active service. Contact details may be found under the Presbytery in Section 5 to which a Deacon belongs.

Prior to the General Assembly of 2002, Deacons were commissioned. In 2002 existing Deacons were ordained, as have been those subsequently.

NAME	ORD	APP	APPOINTMENT	PRESBYTERY
Beck, Isobel BD DCS	2014	2016	Kilwinning: Old	12 Ardrossan
Blair, Fiona (Miss) DCS	1994	2015	Ardrossan and Saltcoats: Kirkgate	12 Ardrossan
Brydson, Angela (Mrs) DCS	2015	2014	Lochmaben, Moffat and Lockerbie Grouping	7 Annandale and Eskdale
Cathcart, John Paul (Mr) DCS	2000	2017	Glasgow: Castlemilk	16 Glasgow
Corrie, Margaret (Miss) DCS	1989	2013	Armadale	2 West Lothian
Crawford, Morag (Miss) MSc DCS	1977	1998	Rosyth	24 Dunfermline
Crocker, Liz (Mrs) DipComEd DCS	1985	2015	Edinburgh: Tron Kirk (Gilmerton and Moredun)	1 Edinburgh
Cuthbertson, Valerie (Mrs) DipTMus DCS	2003		Cumbernauld: Old	22 Falkirk
Evans, Mark (Mr) BSc MSc DCS	1988	2006	Head of Spiritual Care and Bereavement Lead, NHS Fife	1 Edinburgh
Gargrave, Mary S. (Mrs) DCS	1989	2002	Glasgow: Carnwadric	16 Glasgow
Getliffe, Dot L.J. (Mrs) BA BD DipEd DCS	2006	—	—	37 Inverness
Gilroy, Lorraine (Mrs) DCS	1988	—	—	17 Hamilton
Hamilton, James (Mr) DCS	1997	2000	Glasgow: Maryhill	16 Glasgow
Hamilton, Karen M. (Mrs) DCS	1995	2014	Glasgow: Cambuslang	16 Glasgow
Love, Joanna (Ms) BSc DCS	1992	2009	Iona Community: Wild Goose Resource Group	16 Glasgow
Lyall, Ann (Miss) DCS	1980	2017	Interim Deacon, Avonbridge linked with Torphichen	2 West Lothian
MacDonald, Anne (Miss) BA DCS	1980	2002	Healthcare Chaplain, Glasgow Royal Infirmary	16 Glasgow
McIntosh, Kay (Mrs) DCS	1990	2018	Edinburgh: Mayfield Salisbury	2 West Lothian
Mackay, Kenneth D. (Mr) DCS	1996	1998	Perth: Letham St Mark's	28 Perth

NAME				PRESBYTERY
McLaren, Glenda M. (Mrs) DCS	1990	2006	Dunoon: St John's linked with Kirn and Sandbank	19 Argyll
McPheat, Elspeth (Miss) DCS	1985	2001	CrossReach: Manager, St Margaret's House, Polmont	1 Edinburgh
Nicholson, David (Mr) DCS	1994	1993	Cumbernauld: Kildrum	22 Falkirk
Pennykid, Gordon J. BD DCS	2015	2018	Chaplain, HM Prison Edinburgh	1 Edinburgh
Philip, Elizabeth (Mrs) MA BA BA PGCSE DCS	2007	—	—	28 Perth
Porter, Jean T. (Mrs) BD DCS	2006	2008	Stirling: St Mark's	23 Stirling
Robertson, Pauline (Mrs) BA CertTheol DCS	2003	2016	Port Chaplain, Sailors' Society	1 Edinburgh
Scott, Pamela (Mrs) DCS	2017	2017	Lochgelly and Benarty: St Serf's	24 Dunfermline
Stewart, Marion G. (Miss) DCS	1991	1994	Skene	33 Gordon
Thomson, Jacqueline (Mrs) MTh DCS	2004	2008	Buckhaven and Wemyss	25 Kirkcaldy
Wallace, Catherine (Mrs) PGDipC DCS	1987	2017	Honorary Secretary, Diaconate Council	28 Perth
Wallace, Sheila D. BA BD DCS	2009	2019	Grantully, Logierait and Strathtay	27 Dunkeld and Meigle
Wright, Lynda (Miss) BEd DCS	1979	2016	Community Chaplaincy Listening Co-ordinator, NHS Fife	25 Kirkcaldy

THE DIACONATE (Registered as Retaining or Inactive)

Those who are retired and registered under the Registration of Ministries Act (Act 2, 2017, as amended) as 'Retaining' or 'Inactive.' Only those 'Inactive' Deacons who have given consent under the GDPR to publication of their details are included. Contact details may be found under the Presbytery in Section 5 to which a Deacon belongs. Where a retired Deacon does not have a seat on Presbytery, contact details are given here. The list is shorter than in previous years, as some have not registered under the new arrangements.

NAME	COM/ORD	RET	PRESBYTERY
Allan, Jean (Mrs) DCS	1989	2011	29 Dundee
Beaton, Margaret S. (Miss) DCS	1989	2015	16 Glasgow
Bell, Sandra L.N. (Mrs) DCS	2001		39 Ross (not a member of Presbytery) 4 Munro Terrace, Rosemarkie, Fortrose IV10 8UR
Buchanan, John (Mr) DCS	1988		3 Lothian
Buchanan, Marion (Mrs) MA DCS	1983	2019	3 Lothian
Craw, John (Mr) DCS	1998	2009	37 Inverness
Dunnett, Linda (Mrs) BA DCS	1976	2016	23 Stirling
Gordon, Margaret (Mrs) DCS	1998	2012	1 Edinburgh
Gray, Christine M. (Mrs) DCS	1969	2003	16 Glasgow (not a member of Presbytery) 11 Woodside Avenue, Thornliebank, Glasgow G46 7HR 0141 571 1008
Gray, Greta (Miss) DCS	1992	2014	14 Greenock and Paisley
Hughes, Helen (Miss) DCS	1977	2008	16 Glasgow
Johnston, Mary (Miss) DCS	1988	2003	14 Greenock and Paisley (not a member of Presbytery) 19 Lounsdale Drive, Paisley PA2 9ED 0141 849 1615
King, Margaret MA DCS	2002	2012	35 Moray

NAME	ORD	PRES	ADDRESS
Lundie, Ann V. (Miss) DCS	1972	2007	31 Aberdeen
McCully, M. Isobel (Miss) DCS	1974	1999	14 Greenock and Paisley (not a member of Presbytery) 10 Broadstone Avenue, Port Glasgow PA14 5BB 01475 742240 mi.mccully@btinternet.com
MacKinnon, Ronald M. (Mr) DCS	1996	2012	12 Ardrossan
Maclean, Donald A. (Mr) DCS	1988	1990	44 Lewis
McLellan, Margaret DCS	1986	2018	16 Glasgow
McNaughton, Janette (Miss) DCS	1982	2007	22 Falkirk (not a member of Presbytery) 4 Dunellan Avenue, Moodiesburn, Glasgow G69 0GB 01236 870180
Martin, Janie (Miss) DCS	1979	2008	29 Dundee
Merrilees, Ann (Miss) DCS	1994	2006	2 West Lothian
Miller, Elsie M. (Miss) DCS	1974	2001	16 Glasgow
Mitchell, Joyce (Mrs) DCS	1994	2010	37 Inverness
Mulligan, Anne MA DCS	1974	2013	1 Edinburgh
Munro, Patricia BSc DCS	1986	2016	28 Perth
Nicol, Joyce (Mrs) BA DCS	1974	2006	14 Greenock and Paisley
Ogilvie, Colin (Mr) BA DCS	1998	2015	17 Hamilton
Rennie, Agnes M. (Miss) DCS	1974	2012	1 Edinburgh
Rose, Lewis (Mr) DCS	1993	2010	29 Dundee
Ross, Duncan (Mr) DCS	1996	2015	14 Greenock and Paisley
Smith, Catherine (Mrs) DCS	1964	2003	46 Shetland
Steele, Marilynn J. (Mrs) BD DCS	1999	2012	3 Lothian
Steven, Gordon R. BD DCS	1997	2012	3 Lothian
Tait, Agnes (Mrs) DCS	1995	2014	17 Hamilton
Teague, Yvonne (Mrs) DCS	1965	2002	1 Edinburgh
Thomson, Phyllis (Miss) DCS	2003	2010	2 West Lothian
Trimble, Robert DCS	1988	1998	2 West Lothian
Urquhart, Barbara (Mrs) DCS	1986	2017	11 Irvine and Kilmarnock
Wilson, Muriel (Miss) MA BD DCS	1997	2011	10 Ayr (not a member of Presbytery) 28 Bellevue Crescent, Ayr KA7 2DR 01292 264039 me.wilson28@btinternet.com

LIST D – MINISTERS NOT IN PRESBYTERIES REGISTERED AS RETAINING OR EMPLOYED

Those who are not members of a Presbytery but, under the Registration of Ministries Act (Act 2, 2017, as amended), are registered as 'Retaining' and authorised to perform the functions of ministry outwith an appointment covered by Category O or Category E. This list also includes a few ministers registered as 'Employed' (or 'O' for up to 3 years) who are not members of a Presbytery. The list is shorter than in previous years, as some have not registered under the new arrangements.

NAME	ORD	ADDRESS	TEL	PRES
Aitken, Ewan R. BA BD	1992	159 Restalrig Avenue, Edinburgh EH7 6PJ	0131 467 1660	1

Name	Year	Address	Phone	No.
Anderson, David MA BD	1975	Rowan Cottage, Aberlour Gardens, Aberlour AB38 9LD / maurvid@hotmail.com	01340 871906	35
Anderson, Susan M. (Mrs) BD	1997	32 Murrayfield, Bishopbriggs, Glasgow G64 3DS / susanbriggs32@gmail.com	0141 772 6338	16
Auld, A. Graeme (Prof.) MA BD PhD DLit FSAScot FRSE	1973	Nether Swanshiel, Hobkirk, Bonchester Bridge, Hawick TD9 8JU / a.g.auld@ed.ac.uk	01450 860636	6
Barclay, Neil W. BSc BEd BD	1986	4 Gibsongray Street, Falkirk FK2 7LN / neil.barclay@virginmedia.com	01324 874681	22
Bardgett, Frank D. MA BD PhD	1987	Tigh an Iasgair, Street of Kincardine, Boat of Garten PH24 3BY / iasgair1@icloud.com	01479 831751	36
Black, James S.	1976	7 Breck Terrace, Penicuik EH26 0RJ / jsb.black@btopenworld.com	01968 677559	3
Blackley, Jane M. MA BD	2009	38 Garvel Road, Milngavie, Glasgow G62 7JE	0141 931 5344	18
Bradley, Andrew W. BD	1975	Flat 1/1, 38 Cairnhill View, Bearsden, Glasgow G61 1RP / andrewwbradley@hotmail.com		16
Brown, Robert F. MA BD ThM	1971	55 Hilton Drive, Aberdeen AB24 4NJ / Bjacob546@aol.com	01224 491451	31
Cowie, James M. BD	1977	24 Cowdrait, Burnmouth, Eyemouth TD14 5SW / jimcowie@europe.com	01890 781394	3
Cowieson, Roy J. BD	1979	22 The Paddock, Hamilton ML3 0RB / arjay1232@gmail.com	001 250 650 7568	13
Currie, David E.P. BSc BD	1983	42 Onslow Gardens, Muswell Hill, London N10 3JX / davidepcurrie@gmail.com	01355 248510	17
Davidson, Mark R. MA BD STM PhD RN	2005	The Manse, Main Street, Kippen FK8 3DN / mark.davidson122@mod.gov.uk	01786 871249	33
Dick, John H.A. (Ian) MA MSc BD	1982	18 Fairfield Road, Kelty KY4 0BY	01383 271147	24
Dilbey, Mary D. (Miss) BD	1997	41 Bonaly Rise, Edinburgh EH13 0QU	0131 441 9092	1
Donaghy, Leslie G. BD DipMin PGCE FSAScot	1990	53 Oak Avenue, East Kilbride G75 9ED / leslie@donaghy.org.uk	07809 484812	18
Douglas, Colin R. MA BD STM	1969	34 West Pilton Gardens, Edinburgh EH4 4EQ / colin.r.douglas@gmail.com	0131 551 3808	1
Drake, Wendy F. (Mrs) BD	1978	21 William Black Place, South Queensferry EH30 9QR / revwdrake@hotmail.co.uk	0131 331 1520	1
Drummond, Norman W. (Prof.) CBE MA BD DUniv FRSE	1976	c/o Columba 1400 Ltd., Staffin, Isle of Skye IV51 9JY	01478 611400	42
Espie, Howard	2011	1 Sprucebank Avenue, Langbank, Port Glasgow PA14 6YX / howardespie.me.com	01475 540391	1
Finlay, Quintin BA BD	1975	Ivy Cottage, Greenlees Farm, Kelso TD5 8BT	07901 981171	6
Forbes, John W.A. BD	1973	Little Ennochie Steading, Finzean, Banchory AB31 6LX / jrbbbb@icloud.com	01330 850785	32
Gauld, Beverly G.D.D. MA BD	1972	7 Rowan View, Lanark ML11 9FQ	01555 665765	13
Gillies, Janet E. BD	1998	33 Castle Road, Stirling FK9 5JD / jan.gillies@yahoo.com	01786 446222	3
Gordon, Elinor J. (Miss) BD	1988	6 Balgibbon Drive, Callander FK17 8EU / elinorgordon@btinternet.com	01877 331049	23

Name	Ord.	Address / Email	Tel.	No.
Grainger, Alison J. BD	1995	2 Hareburn Avenue, Avonbridge, Falkirk FK1 2NR, revajgrainger@btinternet.com	01324 861632	2
Green, Alex H. MA BD	1986	44 Laburnum Drive, Milton of Campsie, Glasgow G66 8HY, lesvert@btinternet.com	01360 313001	16
Hamilton, Helen (Miss) BD	1991	The Cottage, West Tilbouries, Maryculter, Aberdeen AB12 5GD, helenhamilton125@gmail.com	01224 739632	32
Harper, Anne J.M. (Miss) BD STM MTh CertSocPsych	1979	122 Greenock Road, Bishopton PA7 5AS	01505 862466	16
Haslett, Howard J. BA BD	1972	26 The Maltings, Haddington EH41 4EF, howard.haslett@btinternet.com	01620 481208	3
Hobson, Diane L. (Mrs) BA BD	2002	Flat 3, Marldon Cross Hill, Marldon, Paignton TQ3 1NE, diane.hobson@me.com	07850 962007	31
Hudson, Eric V. LTh	1971	2 Murrayfield Drive, Bearsden, Glasgow G61 1JE, norman.hutcheson@gmail.com	0141 942 6110	18
Hutcheson, Norman M. MA BD	1973	66 Maxwell Park, Dalbeattie DG5 4LS	01556 610102	8
Hutchison, Alison M. (Mrs) BD DipMin	1988	Ashfield, Drumoak, Banchory AB31 5AG, ahutch@hotmail.co.uk	01330 811309	32
Kerr, Hugh F. MA BD	1968	134C Great Western Road, Aberdeen AB10 6QE	01224 580091	16
Knox, R. Alan MA LTh AInstAM	1965	27 Killyvalley Road, Garvagh, Co. Londonderry, Northern Ireland BT51 5LX	02829 558925	46
Lawrie, Robert M. BD MSc DipMin LLCM(TD) MCMI FCMI	1994	West Benview, Main Road, Langbank PA14 6XP, revrmlawrie@gmail.com	01475 540240 07789 824479	14
Lockerbie, Caroline R. BA MDiv DMin	1978	102 3300 Centennial Drive, Vernon, BC, Canada V1T 9Md5, lockerbie21@gmail.com	001 519 429 5563	46
Logan, Thomas M. LTh	1971	3 Duncan Court, Kilmarnock KA3 7TF	01563 524398	11
Lusk, Alastair S. BD	1974	9 MacFie Place, Stewartfield, East Kilbride, Glasgow G74 4TY		17
McHaffie, Robin D. BD	1979	Shepherd's Cottage, Castle Heaton, Cornhill-on-Tweed TD12 4XQ, robinmchaffie@btinternet.com	01890 885946	5
MacKay, Alan H. BD	1974	Flat 1/1, 18 Newburgh Street, Glasgow G43 2XR, alanhmackay@aol.com	0141 632 0527	16
McKay, Johnston R. MA BA PhD	1969	15 Montgomerie Avenue, Fairlie, Largs KA29 0EE, johnston.mckay@btopenworld.com	01475 568802	16
McKean, Alan T. BD CertMin	1982	15 Park Road, Kirn, Dunoon PA23 8JL	01369 700016	39
MacLaine, Marilyn (Mrs) LTh	1995	37 Bankton Brae, Livingston EH54 9LA, marilynmaclaine@btinternet.com	01506 400619	2
McLean, Gordon LTh	1972	Beinn Dhorain, Kinnettas Square, Strathpeffer IV14 9BD, gmaclean@hotmail.co.uk	01997 421380	39
McWilliam, Thomas M. MA BD	1964	Flat 3, 13 Culduthel Road, Inverness IV2 4AG, tommcw@tommcwl.plus.com	01463 718981	39
Melville, David D. BD	1989	28 Porterfield, Comrie, Dunfermline KY12 9HJ, revddm@gmail.com	01383 850075	24
Messeder, Lee BD PgDipMin	1988	59 Miles End, Cavalry Park, Kilsyth G65 0BH, lee.messeder@gmail.com	07469 965934	23

Name	Year	Address / Email	Phone	No.
Millar, Peter W. MA BD PhD	1971	6/5 Etrickdale Place, Edinburgh EH3 5JN / ionacottage@hotmail.com	0131 557 0517	1
Monteith, W. Graham MA BD BPhil PhD	1974	20/3 Grandfield, Edinburgh EH6 4TL	0131 552 2564	1
Muckart, Graeme W.M. MTh MSc FSAScot	1983	Kildale, Clashmore, Dornoch IV25 3RG / gw2m.kildale@gmail.com	01862 881715	40
Muir, Margaret A. (Miss) MA LLB BD	1989	59/4 South Beechwood, Edinburgh EH12 5YS	0131 313 3240	1
Munro, Flora J. BD DMin	1993	87 Gairn Terrace, Aberdeen AB10 6AY / floramunro@aol.com	07762 966393	31
Murray, George M. MTh	1995	6 Mayfield, Lesmahagow ML11 0FH / george.murray7@gmail.com	01555 895216	16
Newell, Alison M. (Mrs) BD	1986	1A Inverleith Terrace, Edinburgh EH3 5NS / alinewell@aol.com	0131 556 3505	1
Newell, J. Philip MA BD PhD	1982	1A Inverleith Terrace, Edinburgh EH3 5NS	0131 556 3505	1
Niven, William W. LTh	1982	4 Obsdale Park, Alness IV17 0TP	01349 884053	39
Parker, Carol Anne (Mrs) BEd BD	2009	The Cottages, Dornoch Firth Caravan Park, Meikle Ferry South, Tain IV19 1JX / CParker@churchofscotland.org.uk	01862 892292	39
Patterson, Philip W. BMus BD	1999	Carver Barracks, Wimbish, Saffron Walden CB10 2YA	0131 664 0673	28
Penman, Iain D. BD	1977	33/5 Carnbee Avenue, Edinburgh EH16 6GA / iainpenmanklm@aol.com	07931 993427	1
Pieterse, Ben BA BTh LTh	1974	15 Bakeoven Close, Seaforth Sound, Simon's Town 7975, South Africa / benhp1@gmail.com		25
Provan, Iain W. (Prof.) MA BA PhD	1991	Regent College, 5800 University Boulevard, Vancouver BC V6T 2E4, Canada	001 604 224 3245	1
Robertson, Blair MA BD ThM	1990	West Erd Guest House, 282 High Street, Elgin IV30 1AG / info@westendguesthouse.co.uk	01343 549629	35
Roderick, Maggie R. BA BD FRSA FTSI	2010	34 Craiglea, Stirling FK9 5EE / MRoderick@churchofscotland.org.uk		23
Saunders, Keith BD	1983	1/2, 10 Rutherford Drive, Lenzie G66 3US / revchap53@hotmail.com	0141 558 4338	16
Scotland, Ronald J. BD	1993	7A Rose Avenue, Elgin IV30 1NX / ronnieandjill@thescotlands.co.uk	01343 543086	35
Scouler, Michael D. MBE BSc BD	1988	Head of Spiritual Care, NHS Borders, Chaplaincy Centre, Borders General Hospital, Melrose TD6 9BS / michael.scouler@borders.scot.nhs.uk	01896 826565	6
Shackleton, Scott J.S. (Prof.) QCVS BA BD PhD RN	1993	Deputy Chaplain of the Fleet, Naval Command HQ, MP1.2 Leach Building, Whale Island, Portsmouth PO2 8BY / scott.shackleton674@mod.gov.uk		47
Shanks, Norman J. MA BD DD	1983	1 Marchmont Terrace, Glasgow G12 9LT / rufuski@btinternet.com	0141 339 4421	16
Smith, Albert E. BD	1983	25 Alloway Drive, Paisley PA2 7DS / aesmith42@googlemail.com	0141 533 5879	32
Smith, Elizabeth (Mrs) BD	1996	smithrevb44@gmail.com		1
Smith, Hilary W. BD DipMin MTh PhD	1999	hilaryoxfordsmith1@gmail.com	0131 441 5858	35

Name	Year	Address / Email	Telephone	No.
Smith, Ronald W. BA BEd BD	1979	1F1, 2 Middlefield, Edinburgh EH7 4PF	0131 553 1174 / 07900 896954	1
Smith, William A. LTh	1972	82 Ashgrove Road West, Aberdeen AB16 5EE / bill2us@aol.com	01224 681866	31
Spence, Sheila M. (Mrs) MA BD	1979	12 Machan Avenue, Larkhall ML9 2HE	01698 310370	17
Stewart, Charles E. BSc BD MTh PhD	1976	105 Sinclair Street, Helensburgh G84 9HY / c.e.stewart@btinternet.com	01436 678113	18
Stewart, Fraser M.C. BSc BD	1980	12a Crowlista, Uig, Isle of Lewis HS2 9JF / fraserstewart1955@hotmail.com	01851 672413	39
Stewart, Margaret L. (Mrs) BSc MB ChB BD	1985	28 Inch Crescent, Bathgate EH48 1EU / famstewart@ormail.co.uk	01506 653428	2
Storrar, William F. (Prof.) MA BD PhD	1984	Director, Center of Theological Inquiry, 50 Stockton Street, Princeton, NJ 08540, USA		1
Strachan, Alexander E. MA BD	1974	2 Leafield Road, Dumfries DG1 2DS / aestrachan@aol.com	01387 279460	8
Strachan, David G. BD DPS	1978	24 Kemnay Place, Aberdeen AB15 8SG	01224 324032	31
Strachan, Ian M. MA BD	1959	'Cardenwell', Glen Drive, Dyce, Aberdeen AB21 7EN	01224 772028	31
Tallach, John MA MLitt	1970	29 Firthview Drive, Inverness IV3 8NS / johntallach@talktalk.net	01463 418721	39
Thomas, W. Colville ChLJ BTh BPhil DPS DSc	1964	11 Muirfield Crescent, Gullane EH31 2HN	01620 842415	3
Thomson, Alexander BSc BD MPhil PhD	1973	4 Munro Street, Dornoch IV25 3RA / alexander.thomson6@btinternet.com	01862 811650	40
Thrower, Charles D. BSc	1965	Grange House, Wester Grangemuir, Pittenweem, Anstruther KY10 2RB / charlesandsteph@btinternet.com	01333 312631	26
Turnbull, John LTh	1994	4 Rathmor Road, Biggar ML12 6QG / john.moiraturnbull62@btinternet.com	01899 221502	13
Turnbull, Julian S. BSc BD MSc CEng MBCS	1980	39 Suthren Yett, Prestonpans EH32 9GL / jules@turnbull25.plus.com	01875 818305	3
Webster, John G. BSc	1964	Plane Tree, King's Cross, Brodick, Isle of Arran KA27 8RG	01770 700747	12
Whyte, Ron C. BD CPS	1990	13 Hillside Avenue, Kingussie PH21 1PA / ron4xst@btinternet.com	01540 661101 / 07979 026973	36
Wood, James L.K.	1967	1 Glen Drive, Dyce, Aberdeen AB21 7EN	01224 722543	31

LIST E – MINISTERS NOT IN PRESBYTERIES (REGISTERED AS INACTIVE)

Those who are not members of a Presbytery but, under the Registration of Ministries Act (Act 2, 2017, as amended), are registered as 'Inactive'. Only those who have given consent under the GDPR to publication of their details are included. The list is shorter than in previous years, as some have not registered under the new arrangements.

NAME	ORD	ADDRESS	TEL	PRES
Abernethy, William LTh	1979	120/1 Willowbrae Road, Edinburgh EH8 7HW	0131 661 0390	1
Alexander, Douglas N. MA BD	1961	West Morningside, Main Road, Langbank, Port Glasgow PA4 6XP	01475 540249	14
Beckett, David M. BA BD	1964	31/1 Sciennes Road, Edinburgh EH9 1NT	0131 667 2672	1
		davidbeckett3@aol.com		
Campbell, J. Ewen R. MA BD	1967	20 St Margaret's Road, North Berwick EH39 4PJ	01620 890835	25
			07840 353887	
Cook, John MA BD	1967	26 Silverknowes Court, Edinburgh EH4 5NR	0131 312 8447	1
Craig, Ronald A.S. BAcc BD	1983	29 Third Avenue, Auchinloch, Kirkintilloch, Glasgow G66 5EB	0141 573 9220	16
		rascraig@ntlworld.com		
Davidson, Ian M.P. MBE MA BD	1954	13/8 Craigend Park, Edinburgh EH16 5XX	0131 664 0074	1
		ian.m.p.davidson@btinternet.com		
Dickson, Graham T. MA BD	1985	43 Hope Park Gardens, Bathgate EH48 2QT	01506 237597	2
		gtd194@googlemail.com		
Donaldson, Colin V.	1982	3A Playfair Terrace, St Andrews KY16 9HX	01334 472889	3
		colinmarion80@gmail.com		
Forbes, John W.A. BD	1973	Little Ennochie Steading, Finzean, Banchory AB31 4LX	01330 850785	32
		jrf6666@icloud.com		
Gale, Ronald A.A. LTh	1982	Dorset		5
Galloway, Kathy (Mrs) BD MA MLitt	1977	20 Hamilton Park Avenue, Glasgow G12 8UU	0141 357 4079	16
		kathygalloway200@btinternet.com		
Gillon, D. Ritchie M. BD DipMin	1994	12 Fellhill Street, Ayr KA7 3JF	01292 270018	10
		revgillon@hotmail.com		
Gordon, Laurie Y.	1960	1 Alder Drive, Portlethen, Aberdeen AB12 4WA	01224 782703	31
Grainger, Harvey L. LTh	1975	13 St Ronan's Crescent, Peterculter, Aberdeen AB14 0RL	01224 739824	31
		harveygrainger@btinternet.com		
Hamilton, David S.M. MA BD STM	1958	Linfield, Milton of Lawton, Arbroath DD11 4RU	01241 238369	30
		dandmhamilton@gmail.com		
Harvey, W. John BA BD DD	1965	501 Shields Road, Glasgow G41 2RF	0141 429 3774	16
		jonmol@phonecoop.coop	07709 651335	
Huie, David F. MA BD	1962	17 St Mary's Mead, Witney OX28 4EZ	01993 778310	47
Liddiard, F.G.B. MA	1957	34 Trinity Fields Crescent, Brechin DD9 6YF	01356 622966	30
		bernardliddiard@btinternet.com		
Lithgow, Anne R. (Mrs) MA BD	1992	13 Cameron Park, Edinburgh EH16 5JY		3
		anne.lithgow@btinternet.com		
McAlister, D.J.B. MA BD PhD	1951	2 Duff Avenue, Moulin, Pitlochry PH16 5EN	01796 473591	27

Name	Year	Address	Phone	No.
McGillivray, A. Gordon MA BD STM	1951	36 Larchfield Neuk, Balerno EH14 7NL	0131 449 3901	1
McIntyre, Allan G. BD	1985	9a Templehill, Troon KA10 6BQ agmcintyre@lineone.com	07876 445626	10
McLachlan, Fergus C. BD	1982	46 Queen Square, Glasgow G41 2AZ	0141 423 3830	16
McPhee, Duncan C. MA BD	1953	8 Belvedere Park, Edinburgh EH6 4LR	0131 552 6784	1
Macpherson, Colin C.R. MA BD	1958	7 Eva Place, Edinburgh EH9 3ET	0131 667 1456	1
Minto, Joan E. (Mrs) MA BD	1993	1 Lochaber Cottages, Forres IV36 2RL joanminto.123@gmail.com	07800 669074	3
Murray, Douglas R. MA BD	1965	32 Forth Park, Bridge of Allan, Stirling FK9 5NT d-smurray@supanet.com	01786 831081	23
Newlands, George M. (Prof.) MA BD PhD DLitt FRSA FRSE	1970	49 Highsett, Cambridge CB2 1NZ gnewlsnds@icloud.com	01223 569984 07786 930941	47
Plate, Maria A.G. (Miss) CQSW DSW BA LTh DSW	1983	Flat 29, 77 Barnton Park View, Edinburgh EH4 6EL riaplate@gmail.com	0131 339 8539	1
Poole, Ann McColl (Mrs) DipEd ACE LTh	1983	Kirkside Cottage, Dyke, Forres IV36 2TF		35
Prentice, George BA BTh	1964	46 Victoria Gardens, Corsebar Road, Paisley PA2 9AQ g-prentice04@talktalk.net	0141 842 1585	14
Ramsay, Alan MA	1967	12 Riverside Grove, Lochyside, Fort William PH33 7RD	01397 702054	38
Seath, Thomas J.G. BD	1980	Orchard House Care Home, Crossford, Carluke ML8 5PY		13
Sefton, Henry R. MA BD STM PhD	1957	25 Albury Place, Aberdeen AB11 6TQ	01224 572305	31
Shannon, W.G. MA BD	1955	19 Knockard Road, Pitlochry PH16 5HJ	01796 473533	27
Webster, Brian G. BD BSc CEng MIET	1988	3/1 Cloch Court, 57 Albert Road, Gourock PA19 1NJ revwebby@aol.com		14
Wilkie, William E. LTh	1978	32 Broomfield Park, Portlethen, Aberdeen AB12 4XT william.wilkie5@btinternet.com	01224 782052	31
Wilson, Andrew G.N. MA BD DMin	1977	Auchintarph, Coull, Tarland, Aboyne AB34 4TT agn.wilson@gmail.com	01339 880918	32
Wilson, John M. (Ian) MA	1964	27 Bellfield Street, Edinburgh EH15 2BR tom54wilson@aol.com	0131 669 5257	1

LIST F – HEALTH AND SOCIAL CARE CHAPLAINS

LOTHIAN

Head of Spiritual Care and Bereavement
Rev. Dr Duncan MacLaren; duncan.maclaren@nhs.net; 0131 242 1991

Spiritual Care Office: The Royal Infirmary of Edinburgh, 51 Little France Crescent, Edinburgh EH16 4SA
Full details of chaplains and contacts in all hospitals: www.nhslothian.scot.nhs.uk > Services > Spiritual Care > The Team

Chaplaincy team includes from the Church of Scotland:
Rev. Lynne MacMurchie, Royal Edinburgh Hospital, Community Mental Health, Astley Ainslie Hospital; lynne.macmurchie@nhslothian.scot.nhs.uk; 0131 537 6775
Rev. Georgina Nelson, St John's Hospital, Tippethill House Hospital; georgina.nelson@nhslothian.scot.nhs.uk; 01506 522188
Rev. Alistair Ridland, Western General, Ferryfield House; alistair.ridland@nhslothian.scot.nhs.uk; 0131 537 1400

Outwith NHS
Rev. Suzie Stark, St Columba's Hospice, 15 Boswall Road, Edinburgh EH5 3RW; SStark@churchofscotland.org.uk; 0131 551 1381

BORDERS

Head of Spiritual Care
Rev. Michael Scouler; michael.scouler@borders.scot.nhs.uk; 01896 826565
Spiritual Care Department: Chaplaincy Centre, Borders General Hospital, Melrose TD6 9BS; 01896 826564
Further information: www.nhsborders.scot.nhs.uk > Patients and Visitors > Our services > Chaplaincy Centre

DUMFRIES AND GALLOWAY

Head of Spiritual Care
Vacant, Dumfries and Galloway Royal Infirmary; 01387 246246 Ext 31544; 07795 120965
DGRI Sanctuary Office, Cargenbridge, Dumfries DG2 8RX
Further information: www.nhsdg.scot.nhs.uk > Focus on > Search > Chaplaincy

AYRSHIRE AND ARRAN

Service Lead for Chaplaincy and Staff Care
Rev. Judith A. Huggett, Crosshouse Hospital, Kilmarnock KA2 0BE; judith.huggett@aapct.scot.nhs.uk; 01563 577301
Chaplaincy Office: Ailsa Hospital, Dalmellington Road, Ayr KA6 6AB; 01292 610556
Further information: www.nhsaaa.net > Services A-Z > Chaplaincy service

LANARKSHIRE

Head of Spiritual Care and Wellbeing
Paul Graham, paul.graham@lanarkshire.scot.nhs.uk

Spiritual Care and Wellbeing Office: Law House, Airdrie Road, Carluke ML8 5EP; spiritualcare@lanarkshire.scot.nhs.uk; 01698 377637
Further information: www.nhslanarkshire.org.uk > Our services A–Z > Spiritual care

Chaplaincy team includes from Church of Scotland:
Rev. Ali Pandian, University Hospital Wishaw; 01698 366779

GREATER GLASGOW AND CLYDE

Lead Healthcare Chaplain: Dawn Allan; chaplains@ggc.scot.nhs.uk
Spiritual Care: The Sanctuary, Queen Elizabeth University Hospital, Govan Road, Glasgow G51 4TF; 0141 211 3026
Further information: www.nhsggc.org.uk > Services Directory > Spiritual Care

Chaplaincy team includes from Church of Scotland:
Anne MacDonald DCS, Glasgow Royal Infirmary; 0141 211 4661

Outwith NHS
Rev. David Hood, Marie Curie Hospice, Balornock Road, Glasgow G21 3US; 0141 557 7400

FORTH VALLEY

Head of Spiritual Care: Tim Bennison
Spiritual Care Centre: Forth Valley Royal Hospital, Larbert FK5 4WR; 01324 566071
Further information: www.nhsforthvalley.com > Services A–Z > Spiritual Care Centre

FIFE

Head of Spiritual Care and Bereavement Lead
Mr Mark Evans DCS, Department of Spiritual Care, Queen Margaret Hospital, Whitefield Road, Dunfermline KY12 0SU; mark.evans59@nhs.net; 01383 623623 ext 24136
Victoria Hospital, Kirkcaldy: Chaplain's Office: 01592 648158 or 01592 729675
Queen Margaret Hospital, Dunfermline: Department of Spiritual Care: 01383 674136
Mental Health and Community Chaplain, Adamson and Stratheden Hospitals: 07976 918909
Glenrothes Community Hospital: Chaplain's Office: 01592 648158

Cameron Community Hospital: Chaplain's Office: 01592 729675

St Andrews Community Hospital: Rev Dr James Connolly: jamesconnolly@nhs.net; 07711 177655

Community Chaplaincy Listening Co-ordinator (NHS Fife): Miss Lynda Wright DCS; lynda.wright1@nhs.net; 07835 303395

Further information: www.nhsfife.org > Spiritual Care

TAYSIDE

Head of Spiritual Care: Rev. Alan Gibbon

The Wellbeing Centre, Royal Victoria Hospital, Dundee DD2 1SP; lynne.downie@nhs.net; 01382 423110

Further information: www.nhstayside.scot.nhs.uk > Our Services A-Z > Spiritual Care

GRAMPIAN

Lead Chaplain

Rev. Mark Rodgers, Chaplains' Office, Aberdeen Royal Infirmary, Foresterhill, Aberdeen AB25 2ZN; nhsg.chaplaincy@nhs.net; 01224 553166

Further information: www.nhsgrampian.co.uk > Home > Our services > A-Z > Spiritual Care

HIGHLAND

Lead Chaplain

Rev. Dr Derek Brown, Raigmore Hospital, Old Perth Road, Inverness IV2 3UJ; derek.brown1@nhs.net; 01463 704463

Further information: www.nhshighland.scot.nhs.uk/Services/Pages/Chaplaincy-Raigmore.aspx

WESTERN ISLES HEALTH BOARD

Lead Chaplain

Rev. T. K. Shadakshari, 23D Benside, Newmarket, Stornoway, Isle of Lewis HS2 0DZ; tk.shadakshari@nhs.net;
(Office) 01851 704704; (Home) 01851 701727; (Mbl) 07403 697138

NHS SCOTLAND

Head of Programme, Health & Social Care Chaplaincy & Spiritual Care, NHS Education for Scotland

Rev. Canon Dr Iain Macritchie BSc BD STM PhD; iain.macritchie@nes.scot.nhs.uk; 01463 255705

NHS Education for Scotland, Centre for Health Sciences, Old Perth Road, Inverness IV2 3JH

Spiritual Care Specialist Research Lead
Rev. Iain J.M.Telfer, iain.telfer@nes.scot.nhs.uk; 01224 805120; 07554 222232
NHS Education for Scotland, Forest Grove House, Foresterhill Road, Aberdeen AB25 2ZP

LIST G – CHAPLAINS TO HM FORCES

The three columns give dates of ordination and commissioning, and branch where the chaplain is serving: Royal Navy, Army, Royal Air Force, Royal Naval Reserve, Army Reserve, or where the person is an Officiating Chaplain to the Military.

NAME	ORD	COM	BCH	ADDRESS
Anderson, David P. BSc BD	2002	2007	A	Senior Chaplain, Infantry Training Centre, Vimy Barracks, Catterick Garrison DL9 3PS
Ashley-Emery, Stephen BD DPS	2006		RNR	HMS Scotia, MoD Caledonia, Hilton Road, Rosyth, Dunfermline KY11 2XH
Begg, Richard MA BD	2008	2016	A	3 Signal Regiment, Kiwi Barracks, Bulford Barracks, Salisbury SP4 9NY
Berry, Geoff T. BD BSc	2009	2012	A	4 Regiment Royal Artillery, Alanbrooke Barracks, Topcliffe, Thirsk YO7 3EY
Blakey, Stephen A. BSc BD	1977	1977	OCM	Staff Chaplain, HQ Scotland, Forthside, Stirling FK7 7RR
Cobain, Alan R. BD	2000	2017	A	1 Yorks, Battlesbury Barracks, Woodcock Lane, Warminster BH12 9DT 1yorks-ai-bhq-padre@mod.gov.uk
Dalton, Mark F. BD DipMin RN	2002	2003	RN	The Chaplaincy, HMS Seahawk, Royal Naval Air Station Culdrose, Helston, Cornwall TR12 7RH mark.dalton242@mod.gov.uk
Davidson, Mark R. MA BD STM PhD RN	2005	2011	RN	The Chaplaincy, HMS Neptune, HM Naval Base Clyde, Faslane, Helensburgh G84 8HL mark.davidson122@mod.gov.uk
Duncan, John C. MBE BD MPhil	1987	2001	OCM	Waterloo Lines, Leuchars Station, St Andrews KY1 0JX
Frail, Nicola BLE MBA MDiv	2000	2012	A	Royal Memorial Chapel, Royal Military Academy, Haig Road, Camberley GU15 4PQ
Francis, James MBE BD PhD	2002	2009	A	Deputy Assistant Chaplain General, 38 (Irish) Brigade, Thiepval Barracks, Lisburn B28 3NP
Gardner, Neil N. MA BD RNR	1991	1991	OCM	Edinburgh Universities Officers' Training Corps, 301 Colinton Road, Edinburgh EH13 0LA
Gardner, Neil N. MA BD RNR	1991	1991	RNR	Honorary Chaplain, Royal Navy
Goodison, Michael J. BSc BD	2013	2013	A	5 Regiment Royal Artillery, Marne Barracks, Catterick Garrison DL10 7NP
Kellock, Chris N. MA BD	1998	2012	A	HQ 12 Armoured Infantry Brigade, Ward Barracks, Bulford, Wiltshire SP4 9NA
Kinsey, Louis BD DipMin TD	1991	1992	AR	205 (Scottish) Field Hospital (V), Graham House, Whitefield Road, Glasgow G51 6JU
Lancaster, Craig MA BD	2004	2011	RAF	Chaplaincy Centre, RAF Honington, Bury St Edmunds, Suffolk IP31 1EE craig.lancaster102@mod.gov.uk
MacKay, Stewart A.	2009	2009	AR	7 Scots, Queens Barracks, 131 Dunkeld Road, Perth PH1 5BT
MacKenzie, Hector M.	2008	2008	A	HQ Military Corrective Training Centre, Berechurch Hall Camp, Berechurch Hall Road, Colchester CO2 9NU
Mackenzie, Seoras L. BD	1996	1998	A	39 Engineer Regiment (Air Support), Kinloss Barracks, Kinloss, Forres IV36 3XL
McLaren, William MA BD	1990		OCM	225 GS Medical Regiment (V), Oliver Barracks, Dalkeith Road, Dundee DD4 7DL
McLay, Neil BA BD	2006	2012	A	1 R Welsh, Lucknow Barracks, Lowa Road, Tidworth SP9 7BU

MacLeod, Rory N. BA BD	AR	1986	154 Regiment RLC, Bothwell House, Elgin Street, Dunfermline KY12 7SB
Macpherson, Duncan J. BSc BD	A	1993	Army Personnel Centre, MP413, Kentigern House, 65 Brown Street, Glasgow G2 8EX
Mair, Michael J. BD	AR	2014	32 (Scottish) Signal Regiment, 21 Jardine Street, Glasgow G20 6JU
Milliken, Jamie BD	RN	2005	45 Commando, RM Condor, Forfar Road, Arbroath DD11 3SP
Munro, Sheila BD	RAF	1995	Chaplaincy Centre, RAF Cosford, Albrighton, Wolverhampton WV7 3EX; sheila.munro781@mod.gov.uk
Patterson, Philip W. BMus BD	A	1999	32 Engineer Regiment, Marne Barracks, Catterick Garrison DL10 7NP
Rankin, Lisa-Jane BD CPS	OCM	2003	2 Bn Royal Regiment of Scotland, Glencorse Barracks, Penicuik EH26 0QH
Rowe, Christopher J. BA BD	AR	2008	5 Military Intelligence Battalion, Redford Barracks, Colinton Road, Edinburgh EH13 0LA
Selemani, Ecilo LTh MTh	OCM	1993	51 Infantry Brigade and HQ Scotland, Forthside, Stirling FK7 7RR
Shackleton, Scott J.S. (Prof.) QCVS BA BD PhD RN	RN		Deputy Chaplain of the Fleet, Naval Command HQ, MP1.2 Leach Building, Whale Island, Portsmouth PO2 8BY; scott.shackleton674@mod.gov.uk
Taylor, Gayle J.A. MA BD	OCM	1999	3 Bn The Rifles, Redford Barracks, Colinton Road, Edinburgh EH13 0PP
Thom, David J. BD DipMin	A	1999	3 Royal Horse Artillery, Albemarle Barracks, Harlaw Hill, Newcastle upon Tyne NE15 0RF
van Sittert, Paul BA BD	A	1997	4 Bn The Royal Regiment of Scotland, Bourlon Barracks, Plumer Road, Catterick Garrison DL9 3AD
Young, David T. BA BD MTh	RNR	2007	HMS Dalriada, Govan, Glasgow G51 3JH

ACF: Army Cadet Force

Blackwood, Keith T. BD DipMin	2 Bn The Highlanders, ACF, Cadet Training Centre, Rocksley Drive, Boddam, Peterhead AB42 3BA
Dicks, Shuna M. BSc BD	2 Bn The Highlanders, ACF, Cadet Training Centre, Rocksley Drive, Boddam, Peterhead AB42 3BA
McCulloch, Alen J.R. MA BD	1 Highlanders Bn, ACF, Gordonville Road, Inverness IV2 4SU
Mackenzie, Cameron BD	Lothian and Borders Bn, ACF, Drumshoreland House, Broxburn EH52 5PF
McLaren, William MA BD	Angus and Dundee Bn, ACF, Barry Buddon, Carnoustie DD7 7RY
Selemani, Ecilo LTh MTh	Glasgow and Lanark Bn, ACF, Gilbertfield Road, Cambuslang, Glasgow G72 8YP
Warwick, Ivan C. MA BD TD	1 Highlanders Battalion, ACF, Gordonville Road, Inverness IV2 4SU
Wilson, Fiona A. BD	West Lowland Battalion, ACF, Fusilier House, Seaforth Road, Ayr KA8 9HX

ATC: Air Training Corps

Highland Wing

Role	Name	Email / Contact
Regional Chaplain, Scotland & N. Ireland	Alistair K. Ridland RAFAC	chaplain.sni@aircadets.org
Wing Chaplain & 2405 Sqn	Russel Smith	russanntwo@yahoo.co.uk
Assistant Wing Chaplain	Alan H.W. Lamb	01687 450227
52 (Aviemore) & 832 (Wester Ross) Sqn	Ron C. Whyte	ron4xst@btinternet.com
379 (County of Ross) Sqn	Michael J. Macdonald	Michael.Macdonald@churchofscotland.org.uk
432DF (Speyside) Sqn	Robert J.M. Anderson	revrjmanderson-moray@outlook.com
446 (Forres) Sqn	Donald K. Prentice	DPrentice@churchofscotland.org.uk
1796 (Thurso) Sqn	David J.B. Macartney	DMacartney@churchofscotland.org.uk

North East Scotland Wing

Role	Name	Email / Contact
Wing Chaplain & 107 (Aberdeen) Sqn	James L.K. Wood	nescot@aircadets.org
102 (Aberdeen Airport) Sqn	Nigel Parker	NParker@churchofscotland.org.uk
1296 (Turriff) Sqn	James M. Cook	JCook@churchofscotland.org.uk
1298 (Huntly) Sqn	Kay F. Gauld	KGauld@churchofscotland.org.uk
2288 (Montrose) Sqn	Ian A. McLean	IMcLean@churchofscotland.org.uk
2367 (Banchory) Sqn	Frank Ribbons	FRibbons@churchofscotland.org.uk

South East Scotland Wing

Wing Chaplain & 2450 (Dudhope) Sqn	C. Graham D. Taylor	CTaylor@churchofscotland.org.uk
132 (North Berwick) Sqn	Neil J. Dougall	NDougall@churchofscotland.org.uk
775 (Burntisland) Sqn	Alan Sharp	Unity Hall, Links Place, Burntisland KY3 9DY
859 (Dalgety) Sqn	Christine M. Sime	CSime@churchofscotland.org.uk
1370 (Leven) Sqn	Jacqueline Thomson DCS	Jacqueline.Thomson@churchofscotland.org.uk
1716 (Roxburgh) Sqn	Sheila W. Moir	SMoir@churchofscotland.org.uk
1756 (Broxburn) Sqn	Jacobus Boonzaaier	JBoonzaaier@churchofscotland.org.uk
2345 (Leuchars) Sqn	John C. Duncan	JDuncan@churchofscotland.org.uk
2519 (Strathmore) Sqn	Thomas W. Tait	TA Centre, Union Street, Blairgowrie PH10 6BG
2535 (Livingston) Sqn	Nelu I. Balaj	NBalaj@churchofscotland.org.uk

West Scotland Wing

Wing & 1333 (Grangemouth Spitfire) Sqn	Aftab Gohar	AGohar@churchofscotland.org.uk
49F (Greenock) Sqn	Alan K. Sorensen	ASorensen@churchofscotland.org.uk
327 (Kilmarnock) Sqn	Kristina I. Hine	KHine@churchofscotland.org.uk
396 (Paisley) Sqn	Peter G. Gill	PGill@churchofscotland.org.uk
498 (Wishaw) Sqn	Ian Douglas (Mr)	ian@paphosab.demon.co.uk
1138 (Ardrossan) Sqn	Jonathan C. Fleming	JFleming@churchofscotland.org.uk
2166 (Hamilton) Sqn	I. Ross Blackman	RBlackman@churchofscotland.org.uk

SC: Sea Cadets

Campbell, Gordon MA BD	Sea Cadets Dundee, East Camperdown Street, Dundee DD1 3LG
Fletcher, Suzanne G. BA MDiv MA	Sea Cadets Dunbar, ACF Building, Castle Park Barracks, 33 North Road, Dunbar EH42 1EU
MacKay, Colin (Mr)	Sea Cadets Wick, The Scout Hall, Kirkhill, Wick KW1 4PN
May, John S. (Iain) BSc MBA BD	Sea Cadets Leith, Prince of Wales Dock, Leith, Edinburgh EH6 7DX
Robertson, Pauline DCS BA CertTheol	Sea Cadets Musselburgh, 9-11 South Street, Musselburgh EH21 6AT
Templeton, James L. BSc BD	Sea Cadets Methil, Harbour View, Methil KY8 3RF
Wallace, Douglas W. MA BD	Sea Cadets East Kilbride, Army Reserve Centre, Whitemoss, East Kilbride G74 2HP

LIST H – READERS

This list comprises active Readers only.

1. EDINBURGH

Devoy, Fiona (Mrs)	196 The Murrays Brae, Edinburgh EH17 8UH	fiona.devoy@yahoo.co.uk	0131 558 8210
Farrow, Edmund	14 Brunswick Terrace, Edinburgh EH7 5PG	edmundfarrow@blueyonder.co.uk	0131 664 2366
Jackson, Kate (Ms)	3 Kedslie Road, Edinburgh EH16 6NT	katejackson1252@gmail.com	0131 554 1326
Johnston, Alan	36 Foster Road, Penicuik EH26 0FL	alanacj2@gmail.com	07901 501819
Kerrigan, Herbert A. (Prof.) MA LLB QC	Airdene, 20 Edinburgh Road, Dalkeith EH22 1JY	kerrigan@kerriganqc.com	0131 660 3007 07725 953772

Name	Address	Email	Phone
Pearce, Martin J.	4 Corbiehill Avenue, Edinburgh EH4 5DR	martin.j.pearce@blueyonder.co.uk	0131 336 4864 07801 717222
Sherriffs, Irene (Mrs)	22/2 West Mill Bank, Edinburgh EH13 0QT	reenie.sherriffs@blueyonder.co.uk	0131 466 9530
Tew, Helen (Mrs)	5/5 Moat Drive, Edinburgh EH14 1NU	helentew.9@gmail.com	07986 170802

2. WEST LOTHIAN

Elliott, Sarah (Miss)	105 Seafield Rows, Seafield, Bathgate EH47 7AW	sarah.elliott6@btopenworld.com	01506 654950
Galloway, Brenda (Dr)	16 Baron's Hill Court, Linlithgow EH49 7SP	dr.b.galloway82@gmail.com	01506 842069
Holden, Louise (Mrs)	Am Batnach, Easter Breich, West Calder EH55 8PP	louise.holden@btinternet.com	01506 873030
McFadzean, John	121 South Street, Armadale, Bathgate EH48 3JT	jmcfadzean2@gmail.com	01501 730260
Middleton, Alex	19 Cramond Place, Dalgety Bay KY11 9LS	alex.middleton@btinternet.com	01383 820800
Orr, Elizabeth (Mrs)	64a Marjoribanks Street, Bathgate EH48 1AL	liz-orr@hotmail.co.uk	01596 653116
Paxton, James	5 Main Street, Longridge, Bathgate EH47 8AE	jim_paxton@btinternet.com	01501 772192
Wilkie, David	55 Goschen Place, Broxburn EH52 5JH	david-fmu_09@tiscali.co.uk	01506 238644

3. LOTHIAN

Name	Address	Email	Phone
Evans, W. John IEng MIIE(Elec)	Waterlily Cottage, 10 Fenton Steading, North Berwick EH39 5AF	jevans7is@hotmail.com	01620 842990
Hogg, David MA	82 Eskhill, Penicuik EH26 8DQ	hogg-d2@sky.com	01968 676350 07821 693946
Millan, Mary (Mrs)	33 Polton Vale, Loanhead EH20 9DF	marymillan@gmail.com	0131 440 1624 07814 466104
Trevor, A. Hugh MA MTh	29A Fidra Road, North Berwick EH39 4NE	htrevor@talktalk.net	01620 894924
Waugh, Jacqueline (Mrs)	15 Garleton Drive, Haddington EH41 3BL	jacqueline.waugh@yahoo.com	01620 825007
Yeoman, Edward T.N. FSAScot	75 Newhailes Crescent, Musselburgh EH21 6EF	edwardyeoman6@aol.com	0131 653 2291 07896 517666

4. MELROSE AND PEEBLES

Selkirk, Frances (Mrs)	21 Park Crescent, Newtown St Boswells, Melrose TD6 0QR	f.selkirk@hillview2selkirk.plus.com	01835 823669

5. DUNS

Landale, Alison (Mrs)	Green Hope Guest House, Ellemford, Duns TD11 3SG	alison@greenhope.co.uk	01361 890242

6. JEDBURGH

Findlay, Elizabeth (Mrs)	7e Rose Lane, Kelso TD5 7AP	findlay290@gmail.com	01573 226641
Knox, Dagmar (Mrs)	3 Stichill Road, Ednam, Kelso TD5 7QQ	dagmar.knox.riding@btinternet.com	01573 224883

7. ANNANDALE AND ESKDALE

Boncey, David	Redbrae, Beattock, Moffat DG10 9RF	david.boncey613@btinternet.com	01683 300613
Brown, Martin J.	Lochhouse Farm, Beattock, Moffat DG10 9SG	martin.j.brown1967@gmail.com	01683 300451
Brown, S. Jeffrey BA	Skara Brae, Holm Park, 8 Ballplay Road,	sjbrown@btinternet.com	01683 220475

Name	Address	Email	Phone
Dodds, Alan	Moffat DG10 9JU	alanandjen46@talktalk.net	01461 201235
Jackson, Susan (Mrs)	Trinco, Battlehill, Annan DG12 6SN 48 Springbells Road, Annan DG12 6LQ	peter-jackson24@sky.com	07498 714675
Morton, Andrew A. BSc	19 Sherwood Park, Lockerbie DG11 2DX	andrew_morton@mac.com	01576 203164

8. DUMFRIES AND KIRKCUDBRIGHT

Name	Address	Email	Phone
Corson, Gwen (Mrs)	7 Sunnybrae, Borgue, Kirkcudbright DG46 4SJ	gwendolyn@hotmail.com	01557 870328
Matheson, David	44 Auchenkeld Avenue, Heathhall, Dumfries DG1 3QY	davidb.matheson44@btinternet.com	01387 252042
Monk, Geoffrey	Hilbre Cottage, Laurieston, Castle Douglas DG7 2PW		01644 450679
Smith, Nicola (Mrs)	Brightwater Lodge, Kelton, Castle Douglas DG7 1SZ	nickysasmith@btinternet.com	01556 680453

9. WIGTOWN AND STRANRAER

Name	Address	Email	Phone
Cash, Marlane (Mrs)	5 Maxwell Drive, Newton Stewart DG8 6EL	marlaneg690@btinternet.com	01671 401375
McQuistan, Robert	Old Schoolhouse, Carsluith, Newton Stewart DG8 7DT	mcquistan@mcquistan.plus.com	01671 820327

10. AYR

Name	Address	Email	Phone
Anderson, James (Dr) BVMS PhD DVM FRCPath FIBiol MRCVS	67 Henrietta Street, Girvan KA26 9AN	jc.anderson2@talktalk.net	01465 710059 07952 512720
Jamieson, Ian A.	2 Whinfield Avenue, Prestwick KA9 2BH	ian4189.jamieson@gmail.com	01242 476898 01292 479313
Morrison, James	27 Monkton Road, Prestwick KA9 1AP	jim.morrison@talktalk.net	07773 287852
Murphy, Ian	56 Lamont Crescent, Netherthird, Cumnock KA18 3DU	ianm_cummock@yahoo.co.uk	01290 423675
Ogston, Jean (Mrs)	14 North Park Avenue, Girvan KA26 9DH	jeanogston@gmail.com	01465 713081
Riome, Elizabeth (Mrs)	Monkwood Mains, Minishant, Maybole KA19 8EY	aj.riome@btinternet.com	01292 443440
Ronald, Glenn	188 Prestwick Road, Ayr KA8 8NP	glenronald@btinternet.com	01292 286861
Stewart, Christine (Mrs)	52 Kilnford Drive, Dundonald KA2 9ET	christistewart@btinternet.com	01563 850486

11. IRVINE AND KILMARNOCK

Name	Address	Email	Phone
Bircham, James F.	8 Holmlea Place, Kilmarnock KA1 1UU	james.bircham@sky.com	01563 532287
Cooper, Fraser	5 Balgray Way, Irvine KA11 1RP	frasercooper1560@gmail.com	01294 211235
Crosbie, Shona (Mrs)	4 Campbell Street, Darvel KA17 0DA	fawltytowersdarvel@yahoo.co.uk	01560 322229
Dempster, Ann (Mrs)	20 Graham Place, Kilmarnock KA3 7JN	ademp99320@aol.com	01563 529361 07729 152945
Gillespie, Janice (Miss)	12 Jeffrey Street, Kilmarnock KA1 4EB	janice.gillespie@tiscali.co.uk	01563 540009
Graham, Barbara (Miss) MA MLitt MPhil CertChSt	42 Annanhill Avenue, Kilmarnock KA1 2LQ	barbara.graham74@btinternet.com	01563 522108
Hamilton, Margaret A. (Mrs)	59 South Hamilton Street, Kilmarnock KA1 2DT	mahamilton1@outlook.com	01563 534431

Name	Address	Email	Phone
Jamieson, John H. (Dr) BSc DEP DEdPsy AFBPsS CPsychol	22 Moorfield Avenue, Kilmarnock KA1 1TS	johnhjamieson@tiscali.co.uk	01563 534065
McGeever, Gerard	23 Kinloch Avenue, Stewarton, Kilmarnock KA3 3HQ	mcgeege1@gmail.com	01560 484331
MacLean, Donald	1 Four Acres Drive, Kilmaurs, Kilmarnock KA3 2ND	donanmac@yahoo.co.uk	01563 538475
Mills, Catherine (Mrs)	59 Crossdene Road, Crosshouse, Kilmarnock KA2 0JU	cfmills5lib@hotmail.com	01563 535305
Raleigh, Gavin	21 Landsborough Drive, Kilmarnock KA3 1RY	gavin.raleigh@lineone.net	01563 539377
Whitelaw, David	9 Kirkhill, Kilwinning KA13 6NB	whitelawfam@talktalk.net	01294 551695

12. ARDROSSAN

Name	Address	Email	Phone
Barclay, Elizabeth (Mrs)	2 Jacks Road, Saltcoats KA21 5NT	mfiz98@dsl.pipex.com	01294 471855
Brookens, Aileen J. (Mrs)	Willow Cottage, Glenashdale, Whiting Bay, Isle of Arran KA27 8QW	aileenbrokens@gmail.com	01770 700535
Bruce, Andrew	57 Dockers Gardens, Ardrossan KA22 8GB	andrew_bruce2@sky.com	01294 605113
Clarke, Elizabeth (Mrs)	Swallowbrae, Torbeg, Isle of Arran KA27 8HE	lizahclarke@gmail.com	01770 860219 / 07780 574367
Currie, Archie BD	55 Central Avenue, Kilbirnie KA25 6JP	Archie.Currie@churchofscotland.org.uk	01505 681474 / 07881 452115
McCool, Robert	17 McGregor Avenue, Stevenston KA20 4BA		01294 466548
MacLeod, Sharon (Mrs)	Creag Dhubh, Golf Course Road, Whiting Bay, Isle of Arran KA27 8QT	macleodsharon@hotmail.com	01770 700353
Murray, Brian	19 Snowdon Terrace, Seamill KA23 9HN	brian.murray100@btinternet.com	01294 822272
Robertson, William	1 Archers Avenue, Irvine KA11 2GB	willie.robert@yahoo.co.uk	01294 203577
Ross, Magnus M.B. BA MEd	39 Beachway, Largs KA30 8QH	m.b.ross@btinternet.com	01475 689572

13. LANARK

Name	Address	Email	Phone
Grant, Alan	25 Moss-side Avenue, Carluke ML8 5UG	amgrant25@aol.com	01555 771419
Love, William	30 Barmore Avenue, Carluke ML8 4PE	janbill30@tiscali.co.uk	01555 751243

14. GREENOCK AND PAISLEY

Name	Address	Email	Phone
Banks, Russell	18 Aboyne Drive, Paisley PA2 7SJ	margaret.banks2@ntlworld.com	0141 884 6925
Bird, Mary Jane (Miss)	Greenhill Farm, Barochan Road, Houston PA6 7HS	mjbird55@gmail.com	
Boag, Jennifer (Miss)	11 Madeira Street, Greenock PA16 7UJ	jenniferboag@hotmail.com	01475 720125
Davey, Charles L.	16 Divert Road, Gourock PA19 1DT	charlesdavey16@hotmail.co.uk	01475 631544
Glenny, John C.	49 Cloch Road, Gourock PA19 1AT	jacklizg@aol.com	01475 636415
Hood, Eleanor (Mrs)	12 Clochoderick Avenue, Kilbarchan, Johnstone PA10 2AY	eleanor.hood.kilbarchan@ntlworld.com	01505 704208
MacDonald, Christine (Ms)	33 Collier Street, Johnstone PA5 8AG	christine.macdonald10@ntlworld.com	01505 355779
McFarlan, Elizabeth (Miss)	20 Fauldswood Crescent, Paisley PA2 9PA	elizabeth.mcfarlan@ntlworld.com	01505 358411
McHugh, Jack	Earlshaugh, Earl Place, Bridge of Weir PA11 3HA	jackmchugh1@btinternet.com	01505 612789
Marshall, Leon M.	Glenisla, Gryffe Road, Kilmacolm PA13 4BA	lm@stevenson-kyles.co.uk	01505 872417

Name	Address	Email	Phone
Maxwell, Margaret A. (Sandra) (Mrs) BD	2 Grants Avenue, Paisley PA2 6AZ	sandra@maxwellmail.co.uk	0141 884 3710
Rankin, Kenneth	20 Bruntsfield Gardens, Glasgow G53 7QJ	krankin@hotmail.co.uk	0141 880 7474
Spooner, John R. BSc PGC(Mgt)	Onslow, Uplawmoor Road, Neilston, Glasgow G78 3LB	jrspooner@btopenworld.com	0141 881 5182 / 07481 008033

16. GLASGOW

Name	Address	Email	Phone
Allan, Phillip	34 Muirhead Way, Bishopbriggs, Glasgow G64 1YG	hampdenhorror@gmail.com	07954 497930
Dickson, Hector M.K.	61 Whitton Drive, Giffnock, Glasgow G46 6EF	hectordickson@hotmail.com	0141 637 0080 / 0141 883 9518
Fullarton, Andrew	2/2, 2263 Paisley Road West, Glasgow G52 3QA		01786 609594
Grant, George	8 Erskine Street, Stirling FK7 0QN	georgegrant@gmail.com	07921 168057
Horner, David J.	20 Ledi Road, Glasgow G43 2AJ	djhorner@btinternet.com	0141 637 7369
Joansson, Tordur (Todd)	1/2, 18 Eglinton Court, Glasgow G5 9NE	to41jp@yahoo.co.uk	0141 429 6733
Kelly, George	25 Westerton, Lennoxtown G66 7LR	geojkelly@btinternet.com	01360 311739
Kilpatrick, Joan (Mrs)	39 Brent Road, Regent's Park, Glasgow G46 8JG	je-kilpatrick@sky.com	0141 621 1809
McColl, John		solfolly11@gmail.com	07757 303195
McFarlane, Robert	25 Avenel Road, Glasgow G13 2PB	robertmcfrln@yahoo.co.uk	0141 954 5540
McInally, Gordon	10 Melville Gardens, Bishopbriggs, Glasgow G64 3DF	gmcinally@sky.com	0141 563 2685
Mackenzie, Norman	55 Culzean Crescent, Newton Mearns, Glasgow G77 5SW		07935 861530
Millar, Kathleen (Mrs)	18 Greenwood Grove West, Stewarton Road Glasgow G77 6ZF		07793 203045
Morrison, Graham	1/1, 40 Gardner Street, Glasgow G11 5DF		0141 579 4772 / 0141 942 3024
Morrison, Katie (Miss)	3b Lennox Court, 16 Stockiemuir Avenue, Bearsden G61 3JL	katiemorrison2003@hotmail.co.uk	07852 373840
Nicolson, John C.	2 Lindsaybeg Court, Chryston, Glasgow G69 9DD	john.c.nicolson@btinternet.com	0141 779 2447
Phillips, John B.	2/3, 30 Handel Place, Glasgow G5 0TP	johnphillips@fish.co.uk	0141 429 7716
Robertson, Lynne M. (Mrs) MA MEd	2 Greenhill, Bishopbriggs, Glasgow G64 1LE	emrobertsonmed@btinternet.com	0141 772 1323 / 07720 053981
Roy, Shona (Mrs)	81 Busby Road, Clarkston, Glasgow G76 8BD	theroyfamily@yahoo.co.uk	0141 644 3713
Smith, Ann	52 Robslee Road, Thornliebank, Glasgow G46 7BX		0141 621 0638
Stead, May (Mrs)	9A Carrick Drive, Mount Vernon, Glasgow G32 0RW	maystead@hotmail.co.uk	07917 785109
Stewart, James	45 Airthrey Avenue, Glasgow G14 9LY	jmstewart325@btinternet.com	0141 959 5814
Tindall, Mararget (Mrs)	23 Ashcroft Avenue, Lennoxtown, Glasgow G65 7EN	margarettindall@aol.com	01360 310911

17. HAMILTON

Allan, Angus J.	Blackburn Mill, Chapelton, Strathaven ML10 6RR	angus.allan@hotmail.com	01357 300916
Beattie, Richard	4 Bent Road, Hamilton ML3 6QB	richardbeattie1958@hotmail.com	01698 420806

Name	Address	Email	Phone
Chirnside, Peter	141 Kyle Park Drive, Uddingston, Glasgow G71 7DB	petefiona@btinternet.com	01698 813769
Codona, Joy (Mrs)	Dykehead Farm, 300 Dykehead Road, Airdrie ML6 7SR	jcodona772@btinternet.com	01236 767063, 07810 770609
Douglas, Ian	24 Abbotsford Crescent, Strathaven ML10 6EQ	lDouglas@churchofscotland.org.uk	01742 022423
Fyfe, Lorna K.	8b Glenavon Court, Larkhall ML9 2WA	lorna.fyfe@yahoo.com	07929 031068
Haggarty, Francis	46 Glen Road, Caldercuix ML6 7PZ	frank_h@fsmail.com	01236 842182
Hastings, William Paul	186 Glen More, East Kilbride, Glasgow G74 2AN	wphastings@hotmail.co.uk	01355 521228, 07954 167158
Hislop, Eric	1 Castlegait, Strathaven ML10 6FF	eric.hislop@tiscali.co.uk	01357 520003
Jardine, Lynette	1 Hume Drive, Uddingston, Glasgow G71 4DW	lpjardine@blueyonder.co.uk	01698 812404
Leckie, Elizabeth	8 Montgomery Place, Larkhall ML9 2EZ	elizleckie@blueyonder.co.uk	01698 325625
McCleary, Isaac	719 Coatbridge Road, Bargeddie, Glasgow G69 7PH	isaacmccleary@gmail.com	07908 547040
Preston, Steven J.	24 Glen Prosen, East Kilbride, Glasgow G74 3TA	steven.preston1@btinternet.com	01355 237359, 07752 120536
Stevenson, Thomas	34 Castle Wynd, Quarter, Hamilton ML3 7XD	weetamgtr@gmail.com	01698 282263, 07860 477344
White, Ian T.	4 Gilchrist Walk, Lesmahagow ML11 0FQ	iantwhite@aol.com	01555 890704

18. DUMBARTON

Name	Address	Email	Phone
Galbraith, Iain B. MA MPhil MTh ThD FTCL	Beechwood, Overton Road, Alexandria G83 0LJ	iainbg@icloud.com	01389 753563
McEwan, Alex	1/1 The Riggs, Milngavie G62 8LX	aleximcewan@gmail.com	0141 384 0274
Morgan, Richard	Annandale, School Road, Rhu, Helensburgh G84 8RS	themorgans@hotmail.co.uk	01436 821269

19. ARGYLL

Name	Address	Email	Phone
Alexander, John	11 Cullipool Village, Isle of Luing, Oban PA34 4UB	jandjalex@gmail.com	01852 314242
Allan, Douglas	1 Camplen Court, Rothesay, Isle of Bute PA20 0NL	douglasallan984@btinternet.com	
Binner, Aileen (Mrs)	Ailand, North Connel, Oban PA37 1QX England	binners@ailand.plus.com	01631 710264
Garrett, William	3 Braeface, Tayvallich, Lochgilphead PA31 89N	we.garrett@btinternet.com	
Logue, David	Laurel Bank, 23 George Street, Dunoon PA23 8JT	david@loguenet.co.uk	01546 870647
MacKellar, Janet BSc	West Drimvore, Lochgilphead PA31 8SU	jkmackellar@aol.com	01369 705549
McLellan, James A.	Northton, Gianavan, Oban PA34 5TU	james.mclellan8@btinternet.com	01546 606403
Mills, Peter A.	Tigh na Barnashaig, Tayvallich, Lochgilphead PA31 8PN	peter@peteramills.com	
Morrison, John L.		jolomo@thejolomostudio.com	01546 870637
Ramsay, Matthew M.	Portnastorm, Carradale, Campbeltown PA28 6SB	kintyre@fishermensmission.org.uk	01583 431381
Scouller, Alastair	15 Allanwater Apartments, Bridge of Allan, Stirling FK9 4DZ	scouller@globalnet.co.uk	01786 832496
Sinclair, Margaret (Ms)	2 Quarry Place, Furnace, Inveraray PA32 8XW	margaret_sinclair@btinternet.com	01499 500633
Stather, Angela (Ms)	1 Dunlossit Cottages, Port Askaig, Isle of Islay PA46 7RB	angstat@btinternet.com	01496 840726

Thornhill, Christopher R. — 4 Ardfern Cottages, Ardfern, Lochgilphead PA31 8QN — c.thornhill@btinternet.com — 01852 300011

Waddell, Martin — Fasgadh, Clachan Seil, Oban PA34 4TJ — waddell715@btinternet.com — 01852 300395
Zielinski, Jeneffer C. (Mrs) — 7 Wallace Court, Ferguslie Street, Sandbank Dunoon P A23 8QA — jeneffierzielinski@gmail.com — 01369 706136

22. FALKIRK
Duncan, Lorna M. (Mrs) BA — 28 Solway Drive, Head of Muir, Denny FK6 5NS — ell.dee@blueyonder.co.uk — 01324 813020
Jalland, Darren — 62 Rosebank Avenue, Falkirk FK1 5JP — larbertred@googlemail.com — 01324 558436
McMillan, Isabelle (Mrs) — 17 Castle Avenue, Airth, Falkirk FK2 8GA — 07896 433314
Stewart, Arthur MA — 51 Bonnymuir Crescent, Bonnybridge FK4 1GD — arthur.stewart1@btinternet.com — 01324 812667
Struthers, Ivar B. — 7 McVean Place, Bonnybridge FK4 1QZ — ivar.struthers@btinternet.com — 01324 841145 / 07921 778208

23. STIRLING
Grier, Hunter — 17 Station Road, Bannockburn, Stirling FK7 8LG — anneandhunter@gmail.com — 01786 815192
McPherson, Alistair M. — Springpark, Doune Road, Dunblane FK15 9AR — 01786 826850

24. DUNFERMLINE
Brown, Gordon — Nowell, Fossoway, Kinross KY13 0UW — brown.nowell@hotmail.com.uk — 01577 840248
Conway, Bernard — 4 Centre Street, Kelty KY4 0EQ — 01383 830442
Grant, Allan — 6 Normandy Place, Rosyth KY11 2HJ — allan75@talktalk.net — 01383 428760 / 07449 278378
McCaffery, Joyce (Mrs) — 53 Foulford Street, Cowdenbeath KY4 9AS — mccafferyjo@tiscali.co.uk — 01383 515775
Meiklejohn, Barry — 40 Lilac Grove, Dunfermline KY11 8AP — meiklejohn.ib@gmail.com — 01383 731550
Mitchell, Ian G. QC — 17 Carlingnose Point, North Queensferry, Inverkeithing KY11 1ER — igmitchell@easynet.co.uk — 01383 416240

Monk, Alan — 36 North Road, Saline KY12 9UQ — alanmonk@talktalk.net — 01383 851283
Muirhead, Sandy — sandy_muirhead@hotmail.com

25. KIRKCALDY
Biernat, Ian — 2 Formonthills Road, Glenrothes KY6 3EF — ian.biernat@btinternet.com — 01592 741487

26. ST ANDREWS
Elder, Morag Anne (Ms) — 5 Provost Road, Tayport DD6 9JE — benuardin@tiscali.co.uk — 01382 552218
Peacock, Graham — 6 Balgove Avenue, Gauldry, Newport-on-Tay DD6 8SQ — grahampeacock6@btinternet.com — 01382 330124
Smith, Elspeth (Mrs) — Glentarkie Cottage, Glentarkie, Strathmiglo, Cupar KY14 7RU — elspeth.smith@btinternet.com — 01337 860824

27. DUNKELD AND MEIGLE

Howat, David P.	Lilybank Cottage, Newton Street, Blairgowrie PH10 6HZ	david@thehowats.net	01250 874715
Patterson, Rosemary (Mrs)	Rowantree, Golf Course Road, Blairgowrie PH10 6LJ	pattersonrose.c@gmail.com	01250 876607
Theaker, Phillip D. (Dr)	5 Altamount Road, Blairgowrie PH10 6QL	ptheaker@talktalk.net	01250 871162

28. PERTH

Archibald, Michael	Wychwood, Culdeesland Road, Methven, Perth, PH1 3QE	michael.archibald@gmail.com	01783 840995
Begg, James	8 Park Village, Turretbank Road, Crieff PH7 4JN	bjimmy37@aol.com	01764 655907
Benneworth, Michael	7 Hamilton Place, Perth PH1 1BB	mbenneworth@hotmail.com	01738 628093
Davidson, Andrew	95 Needless Road, Perth PH2 0LD	a.r.davidson.91@cantab.net	01738 620839
Laing, John	10 Graybank Road, Perth PH2 0GZ	johnandmarylaing@hotmail.co.uk	01738 623888
McChlery, Stuart	22 Kirkfield Place, Auchterarder PH3 1FP	s.mcchlery@gcu.ac.uk	01764 662399
Ogilvie, Brian	67 Whitecraigs, Kinnesswood, Kinross KY13 9JN	brianj.ogilvie1@btopenworld.com	01592 840823 / 07815 759864
Stewart, Anne	Ballcraine, Murthly Road, Stanley, Perth PH1 4PN	anne.stewart13@btinternet.com	01738 828637
Yellowlees, Deirdre (Mrs)	Ringmill House, Gannochy Farm, Perth PH2 7JH	d.yellowlees@btinternet.com	01738 633773 / 07920 805399

29. DUNDEE

Sharp, Gordon	6 Kelso Street, Dundee DD2 1SJ	gordonsharp264@gmail.com	01382 643002
Xenphontos-Hellen, Tim	23 Ancrum Drive, Dundee DD2 2JG	tim.xsf@btinternet.com	01382 630355 / 01382 567756 (Work)

30. ANGUS

Beedie, Alexander W. (William)	6B Carnegie Street, Arbroath DD11 1TX	a.w.beedie38@gmail.com	01241 875001
Gray, Linda (Mrs)	8 Inchgarth Street, Forfar DD8 3LY	lindamgray@sky.com	01307 464039
Walker, Eric	12 Orchard Brae, Kirriemuir DD8 4JY	eric.line15@btinternet.com	01575 572082
Walker, Pat (Mrs)	12 Orchard Brae, Kirriemuir DD8 4JY	pat.line15@btinternet.com	01575 572082

31. ABERDEEN

Cooper, Gordon	1 Kirkbrae View, Cults, Aberdeen AB15 9RU	ga_cooper@hotmail.co.uk	01224 964165
Gray, Peter (Prof.)	165 Countesswells Road, Aberdeen AB15 7RA	pmdgray@bcs.org.uk	01224 318172
Greig, Martin	85 Macaulay Drive, Aberdeen AB15 8FL	mgreig@aberdeencity.gov.uk	07920 806332

32. KINCARDINE AND DEESIDE

Bell, Robert	27 Mearns Drive, Stonehaven AB39 2DZ	r.bell282@btinternet.com	01569 767173 / 07733 014826
Broere, Teresa (Mrs)	3 Balnastraid Cotages, Dinnet, Aboyne AB34 5NE	broere@btinternet.com	01339 880058
Coles, Stephen	43 Mearns Walk, Laurencekirk AB30 1FA	steve@sbcco.com	01561 378400

Name	Address	Email	Phone
McCafferty, W. John	Lynwood, Cammachmore, Stonehaven AB39 3NR	wjmccafferty@yahoo.co.uk	01569 730281
Middleton, Robin B. (Capt.)	7 St Terran's Road, Newtonhill, Stonehaven AB39 3PF	robbiemiddleton7@hotmail.com	07768 925122 01569 730852
Platt, David	2 St Michael's Road, Newtonhill, Stonehaven AB39 3RW	daveplatt01@btinternet.com	01569 730465
Simpson, Elizabeth (Mrs)	Connemara, 33 Golf Road, Ballater AB35 5RS	connemara33@yahoo.com	01339 755597
33. GORDON			
Bichard, Susanna (Mrs)	Beechlee, Haddo Lane, Tarves, Ellon AB41 7JZ	smbichard@aol.com	01651 851345
Crouch, Simon	Greenbank, Corgarff, Strathdon AB36 8YL	scassents@aol.com	01975 651779
			07713 101358
Doak, Alan B.	17 Chieves Place, Ellon AB41 9WH	alanbdoak@aol.com	01358 721819
Findlay, Patricia (Mrs)	Douglas View, Tullynessle, Alford AB33 8QR	p.a.findlay@btopenworld.com	01975 562379
Lord, Noel (Dr)	15 Milton Way, Kemnay AB51 5EW	drnolly@gmail.com	01467 643937
Mitchell, Jean (Mrs)	6 Cowgate, Oldmeldrum, Inverurie AB51 0EN	j.g.mitchell@btinternet.com	01651 872745
Robb, Margaret (Mrs)	Chrislouan, Keithhall, Inverurie AB51 0LN	mdmrobb@btinternet.com	01651 822310
34. BUCHAN			
Barker, Tim	South Silverford Croft, Longmanhill, Banff AB45 3SB	tbarker05@aol.com	01261 851839
Brown, Lillian (Mrs)	45 Main Street, Aberchirder, Huntly AB54 7ST	mabroon64@gmail.com	01466 780330
Forsyth, Alicia (Mrs)	Rothie Inn Farm, Forgue Road, Rothienorman, Inverurie AB51 8YH	aliciaforsyth56@gmail.com	01651 821359
Givan, James	Zimra, Longmanhill, Banff AB45 3RP	jim.givan@btinternet.com	01261 833318
			07753 458664
Grant, Margaret (Mrs)	22 Elphin Street, New Aberlour, Fraserburgh AB43 6LH	mgrant3120@gmail.com	01346 561341
Hine, Kath (Ms)	2 Burnside Cottage, Rothiemay, Huntly AB54 7JX	kath.hine@gmail.com	01542 870680
Lumsden, Vera (Mrs)	8 Queen's Crescent, Portsoy, Banff AB45 2PX	veralumsden53@gmail.com	01261 842712
McColl, John	East Cairnchina, Lonmay, Fraserburgh AB43 8RH	solfolly11@gmail.com	07757 303195
McDonald, Rhoda (Miss)	16 St Andrew's Drive, Fraserburgh AB43 2PX	techmc@callnetuk.com	01346 514052
McFie, David	The Manse, Fordyce Terrace, New Deer, Turriff AB53 6TD	waverley7100@gmx.co.uk	01771 644631
MacLeod, Ali (Ms)	11 Pitfour Crescent, Fetterangus, Peterhead AB42 4EL	aliowl@hotmail.com	01771 622992
			07821 670705
Macnee, Anthea (Mrs)	Wardend Cottage, Alvah, Banff AB45 3TR	macneeiain4@googlemail.com	01261 815647
Mair, Dorothy L.T. (Miss)	Flat F, 15 The Quay, Newburgh, Ellon AB41 6DA	dorothymair2@aol.com	01358 788832
			07505 051305
Noble, John M.	44 Henderson Park, Peterhead AB42 2WR	john_m_noble@hotmail.co.uk	01779 472522
Ogston, Norman	Rowandale, 6 Rectory Road, Turriff AB53 4SU	norman.ogston@gmail.com	01888 560342
Simpson, Andrew C.	10 Wood Street, Banff AB45 1JX	andy.louise1@btinternet.com	01261 812538

Name	Address	Email	Telephone
Sneddon, Richard	100 West Road, Peterhead AB42 2AQ	richard.sneddon@btinternet.com	
35. MORAY			
Forbes, Jean (Mrs)	Greenmoss, Drybridge, Buckie AB56 5JB	dancingfeet@tinyworld.co.uk	01542 831646 / 07974 760337
36. ABERNETHY			
Bardgett, Alison (Mrs)	Tigh an Iasgair, Street of Kincardine, Boat of Garten PH24 3BY	iasgair10@icloud.com	01479 831751
Black, Barbara J. (Mrs)	Carn Eilrig, Nethy Bridge PH25 3EE	bjcarneilrig54@gmail.com	01479 821641
37. INVERNESS			
Appleby, Jonathan	91 Cradlehall Park, Inverness IV2 5DB	jon.wyvis@gmail.com	01463 791470
Cazaly, Leonard	9 Moray Park Gardens, Culloden, Inverness IV2 7FY	len_cazaly@lineone.net	01463 794469
Cook, Arnett D.	66 Millerton Avenue, Inverness IV3 8RY	arnett.cook@btinternet.com	01463 224795
Dennis, Barry	5 Loch Ness View, Dores, Inverness IV2 6TW	barrydennis@live.co.uk	01463 751393
MacInnes, Ailsa (Mrs)	Kilmartin, 17 Southside Road, Inverness IV2 3BG	ailsa.macinnes@btopenworld.com	01463 230321 / 07704 485055
Robertson, Hendry	Park House, 51 Glenurquhart Road, Inverness IV3 5PB	hendryrobertson046@btinternet.com	01463 231858 / 07929 766102
Roberston, Stewart J.H.	6 Raasay Road, Inverness IV2 3LR	sjhro@tiscali.co.uk	01463 417937
Roden, Vivian (Mrs)	15 Old Mill Road, Tomatin, Inverness IV13 7YW	vroden@btinternet.com	01808 511355 / 07887 704915
38. LOCHABER			
Gill, Ella (Mrs)	5 Camus Inas, Acharacle PH36 4JQ	ellagill768@gmail.com	01967 431834
Skene, William	Tiree, Gairlochy, Spean Bridge PH34 4RQ	bill.skene@lochaber.presbytery.org.uk	01397 712594
39. ROSS			
Finlayson, Michael R.	Amberlea, Glenskiach, Evanton, Dingwall IV16 9UU	finlayson935@btinternet.com	01349 830598
Greer, Kathleen (Mrs) MEd	17 Duthac Wynd, Tain IV19 1LP	greer2@talktalk.net	01862 892065
Jamieson, Patricia A. (Mrs)	9 Craig Avenue, Tain IV19 1JP	hapjiam179@yahoo.co.uk	01862 893154
McAlpine, James	5 Cromlet Park, Invergordon IV18 0RN	jmca2@tiscali.co.uk	01349 852801
Munro, Irene (Mrs)	1 Wyvis Crescent, Conan Bridge, Dingwall IV7 8BZ	irenemunro@rocketmail.com	01349 865752
40. SUTHERLAND			
Baxter, A. Rosie (Dr)	Daylesford, Invershin, Lairg IV27 4ET	drrosiereid@yahoo.co.uk	01549 421326 / 07748 761694
Roberts, Irene (Miss)	Flat 4, Harbour Buildings, Main Street, Portmahomack, Tain IV20 1YG	ireneroberts43@hotmail.com	01862 871166 / 07854 436854
Weidner, Karl	6 St Vincent Road, Tain IV19 1JR	kweidner@btinternet.com	01862 894202

41. CAITHNESS

Name	Address	Email	Phone
MacDonald, Morag (Dr)	Orkney View, Portskerra, Melvich KW14 7YL	liliasmacdonald@btinternet.com	01641 531281
O'Neill, Leslie	Holytree Cottage, Parkside, Lybster KW3 6AS	leslie_oneill@hotmail.co.uk	01593 721738
O'Neill, Maureen (Mrs)	Holytree Cottage, Parkside, Lybster KW3 6AS	oneill.maureen@yahoo.com	01593 721738

42. LOCHCARRON-SKYE

Lamont, John H. BD	6 Tigh na Filine, Aultbea, Achnasheen IV22 2JE	jhlamont@btinternet.com	07714 720753
MacRae, Donald E.	Nethania, 52 Strath, Gairloch IV21 2DB	dmgair@aol.com	01445 712235

43. UIST

MacNab, Ann (Mrs)	Druim Skilivat, Scolpaig, Lochmaddy, Isle of North Uist HS6 5DH	annabhan@hotmail.com	01876 510701

44. LEWIS

Macleod, Donald	14 Balmerino Drive, Stornoway, Isle of Lewis HS1 2TD	donaldmacleod25@btinternet.com	01851 704516
Macmillan, Iain	34 Scotland Street, Stornoway, Isle of Lewis HS1 2JR	macmillan@brocair.fsnet.co.uk	01851 704826 / 07775 027987

45. ORKNEY

Dicken, Marion (Mrs)	12 MacDonald Park, St Margaret's Hope, Orkney KW17 2AL	mj44@hotmail.co.uk	01856 831687
Gillespie, Jean (Mrs)	16 St Colm's Quadrant, Eday, Orkney KW16 3PH	jrw2810@btinterent.com	01856 701406
Jones, Josephine (Mrs) BA CertEd LRAM	Moorside, Firth, Orkney KW17 2JZ	yetminstermusic@googlemail.com	01856 761899
Pomfret, Valerie (Mrs)	3 Clumly Avenue, Kirkwall, Orkney KW15 1YU	vpomfret@btinternet.com	01857 622251
Robertson, Johan (Mrs)	Essonquoy, Eday, Orkney KW17 2AB	essonquoy@btinternet.com	

46. SHETLAND

Name	Address	Email	Phone
Harrison, Christine (Mrs) BA	Gerdavatn, Baltasound, Unst, Shetland ZE2 9DY	chris4242@btinternet.com	01957 711578

47. ENGLAND

Menzies, Rena (Mrs)	40 Elizabeth Avenue, St Brelade's, Jersey JE3 8GR	menzfamily@jerseymail.co.uk	01534 741095
Milligan, Elaine (Mrs)	16 Surrey Close, Corby, Northants NN17 2TG	elainemilligan@ntlworld.com	01536 205259

48. INTERNATIONAL CHARGES

Campbell, Cindy (Mrs)	9 Cavello Heights, Sandys MA 05, Bermuda	Ccampbell@argus.bm	001 441 234 3797
Goodman, Alice (Mrs)	Route de Sallaz 23, Rivaz 1071, Switzerland	alice.goodman@epfl.ch	0041 21 946 1727

49. JERUSALEM
Oakley-Levstein, Joanna (Mrs) BA   Mevo Hamma, 12934, Israel   j.oak.lev@gmail.com   00972 50584 2517

LIST I – MINISTRIES DEVELOPMENT STAFF

Ministries Development Staff support local congregations, parish groupings and presbyteries in a wide variety of ways, bringing expertise or experience to pastoral work, development, and outreach in congregation and community. Some may be ministers and deacons undertaking specialist roles: they are listed also in Section 5 (Presbyteries), with deacons further in List C of the present section.

1. EDINBURGH

Crocker, Liz DipComEd DCS	Edinburgh: Tron Kirk (Gilmerton and Moredun) – Parish Assistant	ECrocker@churchofscotland.org.uk
Fejszes, Violetta (Dr)	Edinburgh: Old Kirk and Muirhouse – Parish Development Worker	VFejszes@churchofscotland.org.uk
de Jager, Lourens (Rev) PgDip MDiv BTh	Edinburgh: Portobello and Joppa – Associate Minister	LDeJager@churchofscotland.org.uk
Hirani, Hina	Edinburgh: Old Kirk and Muirhouse – Project Development Worker	HHirani@churchofscotland.org.uk
Lewis, Christein	Edinburgh: Old Kirk and Muirhouse – Young Person Development Worker	CLewis@churchofscotland.org.uk
Luscombe, Kenneth L. (Rev)	Edinburgh: Greyfriars Kirk – Associate Minister	KLuscombe@churchofscotland.org.uk
McMullin, Michael BA	Edinburgh: Craigmillar Park; Priestfield; Reid Memorial – Ministries Development Worker	MMcMullin@churchofscotland.org.uk
MacPherson, Gigha K.	Edinburgh: St David's Broomhouse – Children and Family Worker	GMacPherson@churchofscotland.org.uk
Marshall, Zoe	Edinburgh: Willowbrae – Community Development Worker	ZMarshall@churchofscotland.org.uk
Midwinter, Alan	Edinburgh: St David's Broomhouse – Pastoral Assistant	AMidwinter@churchofscotland.org.uk
Moodie, David	Edinburgh: Granton – Parish Assistant	DMoodie@churchofscotland.org.uk
Richardson, Ian (Dr)	Edinburgh: Holy Trinity – Discipleship Team Leader	IRichardson@churchofscotland.org.uk
Robertson, Douglas S. BEng BA MTh	Edinburgh: Gracemount – Church Leader	Douglas.Robertson@churchofscotland.org.uk
Stark, Jennifer MA MATheol	Edinburgh: Richmond Craigmillar – Community Development Worker	JStark@churchofscotland.org.uk
Wilson-Tagoe, Jacqueline	Edinburgh: Meadowbank - Programme and Outreach Worker	Wilson-Tagoe@churchofscotland.org.uk

2. WEST LOTHIAN

Brown, Kenneth (Rev)	Livingston United – Church and Community Development Worker	Kenneth.Brown@churchofscotland.org.uk
Corrie, Margaret (Miss) DCS	Armadale – Mission Development Worker	MCorrie@churchofscotland.org.uk
Philip, Darren BSc	Livingston United – Youth and Children's Worker	DPhilip@churchofscotland.org.uk

3. LOTHIAN

Glen, Ewen A.	Tranent Cluster and Presbytery – Family and Youth Development Worker	EGlen@churchofscotland.org.uk
Middlemass, Deborah	Tranent Cluster – Family and Youth Development Worker	DMiddlemass@churchofscotland.org.uk
Morley, Anthea	Newbattle – Project Development Worker	AMorley@churchofscotland.org.uk
Muir, Malcolm T. (Rev)	Newbattle – Associate Minister	MMuir@churchofscotland.org.uk
Pryde, Erika	Newbattle – Mission and Outreach Co-ordinator	EPryde@churchofscotland.org.uk

4. MELROSE AND PEEBLES

5. DUNS

6. JEDBURGH

7. ANNANDALE AND ESKDALE

Brydson, Angela (Mrs) DCS	Lochmaben, Moffat and Lockerbie grouping – Deacon	ABrydson@churchofscotland.org.uk
Campbell, Alasdair D. BA	Annan and Gretna grouping – Parish Assistant	Alasdair.Campbell@churchofscotland.org.uk
Hislop, Donna	Canonbie, Langholm & Border grouping - Youth Worker	DHislop@churchofscotland.org.uk

8. DUMFRIES AND KIRKCUDBRIGHTSHIRE

9. WIGTOWN AND STRANRAER

10. AYR

Algeo, Paul	North Ayr Parish Grouping – Family/Development Worker	PAlgeo@churchofscotland.org.uk
Crossan, Morag (Rev) BA	Dalmellington linked with Patna Waterside – Youth and Children's Worker	MCrossan@churchofscotland.org.uk

11. IRVINE AND KILMARNOCK

Wardrop, Elaine	Kilmarnock: St Andrew's and St Marnock's: Mission Development Worker	EWardrop@churchofscotland.org.uk

12. ARDROSSAN

Beck, Isobel BD DCS	Kilwinning Old – Deacon	IBeck@churchofscotland.org.uk
Blair, Fiona DCS	Beith – Parish Assistant	FBlair@churchofscotland.org.uk
Boyd, Carol	Kilwinning Mansefield Trinity – Young Adults Community Development W.	CBoyd@churchofscotland.org.uk
Devlin, Brian	Stevenston: Ardeer linked with Livingstone – Community Mission Worker	BDevlin@churchofscotland.org.uk
Hunter, Jean C.Q. BD	Brodick linked with Corrie linked with Lochranza and Pirnmill linked with Shiskine – Parish Assistant	JHunter@churchofscotland.org.uk
Isbister, Gordon (Dr)	Ardrossan: Park – Family and Outreach Worker	GIsbister@churchofscotland.org.uk
McKay, Angus	Cumbrae linked with Largs St John's – Parish Assistant	AMcKay@churchofscotland.org.uk

13. LANARK

14. GREENOCK AND PAISLEY

McCallum, Graham	Paisley St Ninian's Ferguslie – Outreach Worker	GMcCallum@churchofscotland.org.uk
Murphy, Natasha C.	Greenock Parish Grouping – Youth and Children's Worker	NMurphy@churchofscotland.org.uk

16. GLASGOW

Baird, Janette Y.	Glasgow: Castlemilk – Community Development Worker	JBaird@churchofscotland.org.uk
Barrett, Geoffrey	Presbytery – Local Congregational Review Officer	GBarrett@churchofscotland.org.uk
Cameron, Lisa	Glasgow: St James' (Pollok) – Youth and Children's Ministry Leader	LCameron@churchofscotland.org.uk
Cathcart, John Paul DCS	Glasgow: Castlemilk – Deacon	Paul.Cathcart@churchofscotland.org.uk
Christie, Jacqueline F. (Dr)	Glasgow: Ruchazie – Project Support Worker	Jacqueline.Christie@churchofscotland.org.uk
Dinsmore, Yvonne	Glasgow: Colston Wellpark – Parish Project Development Worker	YDinsmore@churchofscotland.org.uk
Durning, Ashley	Glasgow: Possilpark – Youth Development Worker	ADurning@churchofscotland.org.uk
Evans, Andrew	Glasgow: Gorbals – Community Development Worker	AEvans@churchofscotland.org.uk
Gargrave, Mary S. (Mrs) DCS	Glasgow: Carnwadric – Deacon	Mary.Gargrave@churchofscotland.org.uk
Hamilton, James DCS	Glasgow: Maryhill – Parish Assistant	James.Hamilton@churchofscotland.org.uk
Hamilton, Karen (Mrs) DCS	Cambuslang – Deacon	KHamilton@churchofscotland.org.uk
Herbert, Claire BD	Lodging House Mission, Glasgow - Chaplain	CHerbert@churchofscotland.org.uk
Hyndman, Graham	Church House, Bridgeton – Youth Worker	GHyndman@churchofscotland.org.uk
Macdonald-Haak, Aileen D.	Glasgow: Carntyne – Development Worker, Older People	AMacdonald-Haak@churchofscotland.org.uk
McDougall, Hilary N. (Rev) MA PGCE BD	Presbytery Congregational Facilitator (Glasgow)	HMcDougall@churchofscotland.org.uk
McElhinney, Amy	Glasgow: Garthamlock and Craigend East – Research and Development Facilitator	AMcElhinny@churchofscotland.org.uk
McGreechin, Anne	Glasgow: Cranhill, Ruchazie and Garthamlock and Craigend East Parish Grouping – Congregational Support Worker	AMcGreechin@churchofscotland.org.uk
McIlreavy, Gillian M.	Glasgow: Govan and Linthouse – Communication Co-ordinator	GMcIlreavy@churchofscotland.org.uk
McKeown, Mark W.J. (Rev) MEng MDiv	Glasgow: Chryston – Associate Minister	MMcKeown@churchofscotland.org.uk
Macphie, Caroline	Glasgow: Drumchapel St Andrew's – Parish Assistant	CMacphie@churchofscotland.org.uk
McMahon, Deborah	Glasgow: Easterhouse – Children's Development Worker	DKeenan@churchofscotland.org.uk
Marshall, Kirsteen	Glasgow: St Christopher's Priesthill and Nitshill – Parish Assistant	KMarshall@churchofscotland.org.uk
Miller, Susan	Glasgow: Shettleston New – Youth and Children's Worker	SMiller@churchofscotland.org.uk
Morrin, Jonathan	Glasgow: Barlanark Greyfriars – Youth and Children's Worker	JMorrin@churchofscotland.org.uk
Morrison, Iain J.	Glasgow: Colston Milton – Community Arts Worker	IMorrison@churchofscotland.org.uk
Mubengo, Eddison	Rutherglen: West and Wardlawhill – Mission and Discipleship Worker	EMubengo@churchofscotland.org.uk
Pettigrove, Kaila	Glasgow: Wallacewell – Children and Youth Development Worker	KPettigrove@churchofscotland.org.uk
Quinteros Virreira, Marcos	Glasgow: Ruchazie – Congregational Leader	MQuinterosVirreira@churchofscotland.org.uk
Robertson, Douglas J.	Glasgow: Shettleston New – Discipleship Facilitator	DJRobertson@churchofscotland.org.uk
Sutton, Naomi	Glasgow: St Christopher's Priesthill and Nitshill – Children and Family Worker	NSutton@churchofscotland.org.uk
Taylor, Rachel E.	Glasgow: Sherbrooke Mosspark – Project Development Worker	RTaylor@churchofscotland.org.uk
Usher, Eileen	Glasgow: Cranhill, Ruchazie, Garthamlock and Craigend East Parish Grouping – Family Worker	EUsher@churchofscotland.org.uk
Willis, Mags	Glasgow: Easterhouse – Youth Development Worker	MWillis@churchofscotland.org.uk
Wilson, Marie	Netherlee linked with Stamperland – Pastoral Assistant	Marie.Wilson@churchofscotland.org.uk
Young, Neil J.	Glasgow: St Paul's – Youth Worker	NYoung@churchofscotland.org.uk
Ziegler, Melanie	Fernhill and Cathkin – Family Worker	MZiegler@churchofscotland.org.uk

17. HAMILTON

Binnie, Michelle	Hamilton: Gilmour and Whitehill linked with Hamilton: West -	MBinnie@churchofscotland.org.uk

Douglas, Ian — Motherwell: Crosshill linked with St Margaret's – Parish Assistant — IDouglas@churchofscotland.org.uk
Pope, Helen — Motherwell: North linked with Wishaw: Craigneuk and Belhaven – Church and Community Development Worker — HPope@churchofscotland.org.uk
Quammie, Shannon E.M. — Strathaven: Trinity – Children's and Young People Development Worker — SQuammie@churchofscotland.org.uk
Wood, Elaine — Airdrie: Cairnlea linked with Calderbank – Family/Youth Ministry Co-ordinator — EWood@churchofscotland.org.uk

18. DUMBARTON

Burke, Maureen — Dumbarton churches - Pastoral Assistant — MBurke@churchofscotland.org.uk
Dungavel, Marie Claire — Dumbarton: Riverside linked with West, Development Worker — MCDungavell@churchofscotland.org.uk
Graham, Gillian — Clydebank Waterfront linked with Dalmuir Barclay – Children, Young People and Family Worker — GGraham@churchofscotland.org.uk
Kemp, Tina (Rev) MA — Helensburgh linked with Rhu and Shandon – Ministries Assistant — TKemp@churchofscotland.org.uk
White, David M. (Rev) BA BD DMin — Baldernock linked with Milgavie St Paul's – Associate Minister — drdavidmwhite@btinternet.com
Wilson, Lorraine — Clydebank: Waterfront linked with Dalmuir Barclay – Pastoral Assistant — LWilson@churchofscotland.org.uk

19. ARGYLL

Burton, Rebecca A. — Presbytery - Youth and Children's Worker — RBurton@churchofscotland.org.uk
Fulcher, Christine P. (Rev) BEd — Presbytery Ministries Co-ordinator – South Argyll — CFulcher@churchofscotland.org.uk
Hay, Alison — Presbytery Ministries Co-ordinator – North and East Argyll — AHay@churchofscotland.org.uk
McLaren, Glenda M. (Ms) DCS — Dunoon: St John's linked with Kirn and Sandbank – Deacon — Glenda.McLaren@churchofscotland.org.uk
Wilson, John K. (Kenny) — Presbytery - Youth and Children's Worker — KWilson@churchofscotland.org.uk

22. FALKIRK

Bogle, Albert O. (Very Rev) BD MTh — Sanctuary First (Presbytery Mission Initiative) – Pioneer Minister — AlbertBogle@churchofscotland.org.uk
Boland, Susan (Mrs) DipHE(Theol) — Cumbernauld: Abronhill – Family Development Worker — SBoland@churchofscotland.org.uk
Cuthbertson, Valerie S. (Miss) DCS — Cumbernauld: Old – Deacon — VCuthbertson@churchofscotland.org.uk
du Toit, George (Erick) (Rev) — Falkirk: Camelon – Associate Minister — EduToit@churchofscotland.org.uk
Nicholson, David DCS — Cumbernauld: Kildrum – Deacon — DNicholson@churchofscotland.org.uk

23. STIRLING

Allen, Valerie L (Rev) BMus MDiv DMin — Presbytery – Chaplain — VL2allen@btinternet.com
Anderson, Dorothy U. (Rev) LLB DipPL BD — Dunblane: Cathedral – Associate Minister — DAnderson@churchofscotland.org.uk
McDowell, Bonnie J. — Presbytery - Dementia Project Co-ordinator — BMcDowell@churchofscotland.org.uk
Porter, Jean T. (Mrs) BD DCS — Stirling: St Mark's – Deacon — JPorter@churchofscotland.org.uk

24. DUNFERMLINE

Christie, Aileen — Lochgelly and Benarty: St Serf's – Outreach Worker — Aileen.Christie@churchofscotland.org.uk
Crawford, Morag (Miss) MSc DCS — Rosyth – Deacon — MCrawford@churchofscotland.org.uk
Scott, Pamela (Mrs) DCS — Lochgelly and Benarty: St Serf's – Parish Assistant — PScott@churchofscotland.org.uk

25. KIRKCALDY

Hutchison, John BA	Rothes Trinity Parish Grouping – Families Worker and Parish Assistant	JHutchison@churchofscotland.org.uk
Kerr, Fiona	Methil: Wellesley – Parish Assistant	FKerr@churchofscotland.org.uk
Livingstone, Ruth M.	Glenrothes: St Margaret's – Congregational Support Worker	RLivingstone@churchofscotland.org.uk
Pringle, Iona M. BD	Kennoway, Windygates and Balgonie: St Kenneth's – Parish Assistant	IPringle@churchofscotland.org.uk
Thomson, Jacqueline (Mrs) MTh DCS	Buckhaven and Wemyss – Deacon	Jacqueline.Thomson@churchofscotland.org.uk

26. ST ANDREWS

Thorburn, Susan (Rev) MTh	Eden Tay Cluster – Mission Development Worker	SThorburn@churchofscotland.org.uk

27. DUNKELD AND MEIGLE

Name	Role	Email
Wallace, Sheila D. (Mrs) BA BD DCS	Grantully, Logierait and Strathtay - Parish Deacon	SWallace@churchofscotland.org.uk

28. PERTH

Mackay, Kenneth D. DCS	Perth: Letham St Mark's – Pastoral Worker	Kenneth.Mackay@churchofscotland.org.uk
Stewart, Alexander T. (Rev) MA BD FSAScot	Perth: St John's Kirk of Perth linked with Perth: St Leonard's-in-the-Fields – Associate Minister	alex.t.stewart@blueyonder.co.uk
Stott, Anne M.	Presbytery Pioneer Worker – Bertha Park	AStott@churchofscotland.org.uk
Wellstood, Keith A. PGDipCG MICG	Perth: Riverside – Community Worker	KWellstood@churchofscotland.org.uk

29. DUNDEE

Berry, Gavin R.	Dundee: Camperdown/Lochee - Parish Assistant	GBerry@churchofscotland.org.uk
Campbell, Neil MA	Dundee: Craigiebank linked with Douglas and Mid Craigie – Youth and Young Adult Development Worker	Neil.Campbell@churchofscotland.org.uk
Clark, Ross	Dundee: Fintry – Discipleship, Mission and Development Worker	Ross.Clark@churchofscotland.org.uk
McKenzie, Matthew	Dundee: Lochee / Dundee: Camperdown – Youth and Families Worker	MMcKenzie@churchofscotland.org.uk
Stirling, Diane BSc DipCPC BTh	Dundee: Craigiebank linked with Douglas and Mid Craigie – Parish Assistant	DStirling@churchofscotland.org.uk

30. ANGUS

Name	Role	Email
Read, Rebecca	Montrose area churches – Youth and Children's Worker	RRead@churchofscotland.org.uk
Stevens, Linda (Rev) BSc BD PgDip	The Glens and Kirriemuir: Old – West Angus Area Team Minister	LStevens@churchofscotland.org.uk

31. ABERDEEN

Amalanand, John C.	Aberdeen: Garthdee – Parish Assistant	JAmalanand@churchofscotland.org.uk
Angus, Natalie	Dyce – Youth and Family Worker	NAngus@churchofscotland.org.uk
Broere, Teresa	Aberdeen: Mastrick – Parish Assistant	PBroere@churchofscotland.org.uk
Griesse, Dorte	Aberdeen: Mannofield – Children's and Family Worker	DGriesse@churchofscotland.org.uk
Lightbody, Philip (Rev)	Presbytery - Mission Development Leader and Presbytery Planning Officer	PLightbody@churchofscotland.org.uk
Mitchell, William	Aberdeen: St George's Tillydrone / Middlefield – Community Development Worker	WMitchell@churchofscotland.org.uk
Sangbarini, Curtis	Aberdeen: St Nicholas Kincorth, South of / Torry St Fittick's – Parish Assistant, Mission Development	CSangbarini@churchofscotland.org.uk
Taylor, Valerie AssocCIPD PGDip	Aberdeen: Torry St Fittick's – Ministry Assistant	VTaylor@churchofscotland.org.uk

Thomas, Jay MA BA	Aberdeen: 'West End' churches – Youth Ministry Leader	JThomas@churchofscotland.org.uk

32. KINCARDINE AND DEESIDE

Benton, Margaret MA BD	Stonehaven churches - Pastoral Assistant	MBenton@churchofscotland.org.uk

33. GORDON

Adam, Pamela BD	Ellon – Parish Assistant	PAdam@churchofscotland.org.uk
Bruce, Nicola P.S. BA MTh	Ellon – Parish Assistant, Mission Development	NBruce@churchofscotland.org.uk
Cross, Peter	Ellon – Parish Assistant	PCross@churchofscotland.org.uk
Mikelson, Heather (Rev)	Presbytery - Mission Development Worker	HMikelson@churchofscotland.org.uk
Stewart, Marion G. (Miss) DCS	Skene – Deacon	MStewart@churchofscotland.org.uk
Stigant, Victoria J.	Presbytery - Youth Work Facilitator	VStigant@churchofscotland.org.uk

34. BUCHAN

Dick, Janet	Presbytery – Mission and Discipleship Development Worker	Janet.Dick@churchofscotland.org.uk

35. MORAY

Baker, Paula (Mrs)	Birnie and Pluscarden linked with Elgin: High – Parish Assistant	PBaker@churchofscotland.org.uk
Bosch, Eckhardt	Keith churches – Parish Assistant	EBosch@churchofscotland.org.uk

36. ABERNETHY

Orr, Gillian BA	Presbytery - Youth Worker	GOrr@churchofscotland.org.uk

37. INVERNESS

Haringman, Paul MSc	Culloden: The Barn – Community Worker	Paul.Haringman@churchofscotland.org.uk

38. LOCHABER

39. ROSS

40. SUTHERLAND

41. **CAITHNESS**

42. **LOCHCARRON-SKYE**

43. **UIST**

44. **LEWIS**

45. **ORKNEY**

46. **SHETLAND**
Weir, K. Ellen   Presbytery – Youth and Children's Worker   EWeir@churchofscotland.org.uk

47. **ENGLAND**

48. **INTERNATIONAL CHARGES**

LIST J – OVERSEAS LOCATIONS

AFRICA
MALAWI   **Church of Central Africa Presbyterian Synod of Livingstonia**
Dr Linus Malu (2018)   Legal Officer, Church and Society Department, Church and Society   office +265 265 1 311 133
                                    Department, PO Box 112, Mzuzu, Malawi   mobile +265 994 652 345
                                    nnabuikemalu@yahoo.com   www.ccapsolinia.org
Mr Gary Brough (2019)   Resource, Mobilisation & Communications Manager, Church and   office +265 265 1 311 133
                                    Society Department, PO Box 112, Mzuzu, Malawi   mobile +265 883 626 500
                                    churchsociety@sdnp.org.mw   www.ccapsolinia.org

MALAWI: CCAP Livingstonia, Nkhoma and Blantyre; MOZAMBIQUE: **Evangelical Church of Christ**; SOUTH SUDAN: **Presbyterian Church of South Sudan and Sudan**
Rev Dr Kenneth R Ross (2019)   Theological Educator: Africa, based at Zomba Theological College,   +265 1 524 419
                                    PO Box 130, Zomba
                                    KRoss@churchofscotland.org.uk

ZAMBIA   **United Church of Zambia**
Mr Keith and Mrs Ida Waddell (2016) UCZ Synod, Nationalist Road at Burma Road, PO Box 50122,   office 00260 964 761 039
                                     15101 Ridgeway, Lusaka, Zambia   mobile +260 977 143 692
                                     keithida2014@gmail.com   http://uczsynod.org

ASIA

NEPAL — Ms Jenny Featherstone (2007) (Ecumenical appointment: Methodist Church UK) — Adviser, Chodort Training Centre, PO Box 630451, Choma, Zambia; jenny.featherstone@googlemail.com — 00260 979 703 130

NEPAL — Mr Joel Hafvenstein (2015) — c/o United Mission to Nepal, PO Box 126, Kathmandu, Nepal; ed@umn.org.np — 00 977 1 4228 118; www.umn.org.np

LAOS — Mr Tony and Mrs Catherine Paton (2009) (Mission Associates, staff of CMS) — Church Mission Society, Church of the Holy Spirit, Vientiane Lao People's Democratic Republic — www.the-chs.org.

EUROPE

PRAGUE — Rev Dr David I. Sinclair (2017) — Evangelical Church of the Czech Brethren, Jungmannova 9, CZ111 21, Prague 1; DSinclair@churchofscotland.org.uk — 00 420 224 999 230

ROME — Ms Fiona Kendall (2018) (Ecumenical appointment: Methodist Church UK; Global Ministries USA) — Mediterranean Hope, Federation of Protestant Churches in Italy, Via Firenze 38, 00138 Roma, Italy; FKendall@churchofscotland.org.uk — 00 39 (0)6 4825 120; www.mediterraneanhope.com

MIDDLE EAST

ISRAEL & PALESTINE

JERUSALEM — Rev Dr John McCulloch (2018) — St Andrew's Jerusalem, PO Box 8619, Jerusalem 91086, Israel; JMcCulloch@churchofscotland.org.uk — +972 2 673 2401; www.standrewsjerusalem.org/

TIBERIAS — Rev Kate McDonald (2015) — St Andrew's Galilee, PO Box 104, Tiberias 14100, Israel; KMcDonald@churchofscotland.org.uk — +972 4 244 6736; https://standrewsgalilee.com/

JAFFA — Vacant — Tabeetha School, PO Box 8170, 21 Jeffet Street, Jaffa, 61081 Israel; office@tabeethaschool.org — +972 3 682 1581; www.tabeethaschool.org

See also the Presbyteries of International Charges and Jerusalem (Section 5: 48 and 49)

LIST K – PRISON CHAPLAINS

SCOTTISH PRISON SERVICE CHAPLAINCY ADVISER (Church of Scotland)

Rev Sheena Orr
SPS HQ, Calton House, 5 Redheughs Rigg, Edinburgh EH12 9HW
sheena.orr@sps.pnn.gov.uk
0131 330 3575

ADDIEWELL
Rev. Jim Murphy
HM Prison Addiewell, Station Road, Addiewell, West Calder EH55 8QA
jim.murphy@sodexojusticeservices.com
01506 874500
ext. 3606

CASTLE HUNTLY
Rev. Anne E. Stewart
HM Prison Castle Huntly, Longforgan, Dundee DD2 5HL
anne.stewart2@sps.pnn.gov.uk
01382 319388

CORNTON VALE
Rev. Sheena Orr
Mrs Deirdre Yellowlees
HM Prison and Young Offender Institution, Cornton Vale, Cornton Road, Stirling   FK9 5NU
sheena.orr@sps.pnn.gov.uk
deirdre.yellowlees@sps.pnn.gov.uk
01786 835365

DUMFRIES
Rev. Neil Campbell
HM Prison Dumfries, Terregles Street, Dumfries DG2 9AX
neil.campbell2@sps.pnn.gov.uk
01387 294214

EDINBURGH
Mr Gordon Pennykid DCS
Rev. Keith Graham
Rev. David Swan
HM Prison Edinburgh, 33 Stenhouse Road, Edinburgh EH11 3LN
gordon.pennykid@sps.pnn.gov.uk
keith.graham@sps.pnn.gov.uk
david.swan@sps.pnn.gov.uk
0131 444 3115

GLASGOW: BARLINNIE
Rev. Jill Clancy
Rev. Jonathan Keefe
Rev. Ian McInnes
HM Prison Barlinnie, 81 Lee Avenue, Riddrie, Glasgow G33 2QX
jill.clancy@sps.pnn.gov.uk
jonathan.keefe@sps.pnn.gov.uk
ian.mcinnes@sps.pnn.gov.uk
0141 770 2059

GLENOCHIL
Rev. Graham Bell (Baptist)
Rev. Elizabeth Kenny
HMPrison Glenochil, King o' Muir Road, Tullibody FK10 3AD
graham.bell@sps.pnn.gov.uk
elizabeth.kenny@sps.pnn.gov.uk
01259 767211

GRAMPIAN
Rev. Alison Harvey (Episcopal)
HM Prison and Young Offender Institution, South Road, Peterhead AB42 2YY
alison.harvey@sps.pnn.gov.uk
01779 485744

GREENOCK
Rev. Neil Campbell
HM Prison Greenock, Old Inverkip Road, Greenock PA16 9AH
neil.campbell2@sps.pnn.gov.uk
01475 787801
ext. 393287

INVERNESS
Rev. Hugh Watt
HM Prison Inverness, Duffy Drive, Inverness IV2 3HN
hugh.watt@sps.pnn.gov.uk
01463 229020

KILMARNOCK
Rev. Jill Clancy
HM Prison Kilmarnock, Mauchline Road, Kilmarnock KA1 5AA
pamela.clancy@serco.com
01563 548928

LOW MOSS
Rev. Martin Forrest
HM Prison Low Moss, 190 Crosshill Road, Bishopbriggs, Glasgow G64 2PZ
martin.forrest@sps.pnn.gov.uk
0141 762 9727

PERTH
Rev. Kenneth G. Russell
Mrs Deirdre Yellowlees
Chaplaincy Centre, HM Prison Perth, 3 Edinburgh Road, Perth PH2 7JH
kenneth.russell@sps.pnn.gov.uk
deirdre.yellowlees@sps.pnn.gov.uk
01738 458216

POLMONT
Craig Bryan (Baptist)
Chaplaincy Centre, HM Young Offender Institution Polmont, Brightons, Falkirk FK2 0AB
craig.bryan@sps.pnn.gov.uk
01324 722241

SHOTTS
Ms Dorothy Russell
Rev. Murdo MacLean
HM Prison Shotts, Canthill Road, Shotts ML7 4LE
dorothy.russell@sps.pnn.gov.uk
murdo.maclean@sps.pnn.gov.uk
01501 824071

LIST L – UNIVERSITY CHAPLAINS

ABERDEEN
Rev. Marylee Anderson MA BD
Rev. David S. Hutchison BSC BD ThM
m.anderson@abdn.ac.uk
d.hutchison@abdn.ac.uk
01224 272137
01224 272137

ABERTAY, DUNDEE
Rev. Robert A. Calvert BSc BD DMin
RCalvert@churchofscotland.org.uk
07532 029343

CAMBRIDGE
Rev. Nigel Uden (U.R.C. and C. of S.)
minister@stcolumbaschurch.org
01223 314586

DUNDEE
Rev. Fiona C. Douglas MBE MA BD PhD
f.c.douglas@dundee.ac.uk
01382 384157

EDINBURGH
Rev. Harriet A. Harris MBE BA DPhil
Rev. Alison M. Newell BD (Associate Chaplain)
Rev. Geoffrey Baines (Associate Chaplain)
chaplain@ed.ac.uk
ali.newell@ed.ac.uk
g.baines@ed.ac.uk
0131 650 2595
0131 650 2597
0131 650 9502

GLASGOW
Rev. Stuart D. MacQuarrie JP BD BSc MBA
chaplain@glasgow.ac.uk
0141 330 5419

GLASGOW CALEDONIAN
Rev. Alastair S. Duncan MA BD
ADuncan@churchofscotland.org.uk
07968 852083

HERIOT-WATT, EDINBURGH
Rev. Alistair P. Donald MA PhD BD
chaplaincy@hw.ac.uk
0131 451 4508

OXFORD
Rev. Helen Garton (U.R.C. and C. of S.) minister@saintcolumbas.org 01865 606910
07399 027532

ROBERT GORDON, ABERDEEN
Rev. Canon Isaac. M. Poobalan BD MTh DMin chaplaincy@rgu.ac.uk 01224 640119

ST ANDREWS
Rev. Donald G. MacEwan MA BD PhD dgm21@st-andrews.ac.uk 01334 462866
07713 322036
Rev. Samantha J. Ferguson MTheol sjf6@st-and-ews.ac.uk 01334 461766
(Assistant Chaplain) 07546 526280

STIRLING
Rev. Janet P. Foggie MA BD PhD janet.foggie@stir.ac.uk 07899 349246

STRATHCLYDE, GLASGOW
Vacant (Honorary Chaplain) chaplaincy@strath.ac.uk 0141 548 4144

LIST M – WORK PLACE CHAPLAINS

CHIEF EXECUTIVE, WORK PLACE CHAPLAINCY SCOTLAND
Vacant info@wpcscotland.co.uk 0131 441 2271

For a full list of Regional Organisers, Team Leaders and Chaplaincy Locations see: www.wpcscotland.co.uk > Contact Us

Chaplain to the UK Oil and Gas Industry Rev. Gordon T. Craig gordon.craig@ukoilandgaschaplaincy.com 01224 882600

LIST N – REPRESENTATIVES ON COUNCIL EDUCATION COMMITTEES

For a full list see: www.churchofscotland.org.uk > Resources > Yearbook > Section 6-N

LIST O – MINISTERS ORDAINED FOR SIXTY YEARS AND UPWARDS

For a full list see: www.churchofscotland.org.uk > Resources > Yearbook > Section 6-O

LIST P – DECEASED MINISTERS AND DEACONS

The Editor has been made aware of the following ministers and deacons who have died since the compilation of the previous volume of the Year Book.

Anderson, Janet DCS	(Deacon)
Barrington, Charles William Harcourt	(Associate, Edinburgh: Balerno)
Bertram, Thomas Alexander	(Patna Waterside)
Brown, William Dixon	(Wishaw: Thornlie)
Butters, David	(Turriff: St Ninian's and Forglen)
Byers, Mairi Catriona	(Jura)
Campbell, John Anthony	(Irvine: St Andrew's)
Cassells, Alexander Ketchen	(Leuchars: St Athernase and Guardbridge)
Chestnut, Alexander	(Greenock: St Mark's Greenbank)
Douglas, Andrew Morrison	(Aberdeen: High Hilton)
Doyle, Ian Bruce	(Secretary, Department of National Mission)
Drummond, Rhoda Elizabeth DCS	(Chaplain's Assistant, RAF)
Duncan, Charles Alexander	(Heriot with Stow: St Mary of Wedale)
Forrest, Alan Bell	(Uphall: South)
Galbraith, William James Lethem	(Kilchrenan and Dalavich with Muckairn)
Gisbey, John Edward	(Thornhill)
Goldie, George Dymock	(Aberdeen: Greyfriars)
Goss, Alister John	(Industrial Chaplain)
Grant, James Gordon	(Edinburgh: Dean)
Greer, Arthur David Courtenay	(Barra)
Hare, Malcolm McNeill Walker	(Kilmarnock: St Kentigern's)
Hibbert, Frederick William	(Tiberias: St Andrew's)
Hood, Catriona Anne	Auxiliary Minister, South Argyll
Houghton, Christine	(Whitburn: South)
Ingram, Joseph Ross	(Chaplain, Royal Air Force)
Johnston, William Roger	(Ochiltree with Stair)
Johnstone, Ronald	(Thurso: West)
Lawson, Ronald George	(Greenock: Wellpark Mid Kirk)
McDonald, William Gordon	(Falkirk: Grahamston United)
McGill, Thomas Wilkinson	(Portpatrick with Stranraer: St Ninian's)
Mackinnon, Roderick Maclean	(Kilmuir and Logie Easter)
MacLeod, Norman	(Hamilton: St Andrew's)
McMillan, William Johnstone	(Sandsting and Aithsting with Walls and Sandness)
Macnaughton, John Anderson	(Glasgow: Hyndland)
MacRae, Norman Iain	(Inverness: Trinity)
Martin, James	(Glasgow: High Carntyne)
Mathers, Daniel Lamb	(Grangemouth: Charing Cross and West)
Maxton, Ronald McNish	(Associate, Dollar with Glendevon with Muckhart)
Melrose, James Henderson Loudon	(Associate, Gourock: Old Gourock and Ashton)

Morton, Andrew Queen	(Culross and Torryburn)
Munro, David Peacock	(Bearsden: North)
Munro, George Alexander Morrison	(Edinburgh: Cluny)
Nicol, Robert Morrison	(Jersey: St Columba's)
Orr, James McMichael	(Aberfoyle with Port of Menteith)
Paton, John Harris	Kilninian and Kilmore with Salen and Ulva with Tobermory with Torosay and Kinlochspelvie
Philip, George Mackenzie	(Glasgow: Sandyford Henderson Memorial)
Sawers, Hugh	(Motherwell: St Andrew's)
Schofield, Melville Frederick	(Chaplain, Western General Hospital, Edinburgh)
Scoular, Stanley	(Rosyth)
Smith, Hugh MacCommach Croll	(Mortlach and Cabrach)
Stitt, Ronald John Maxwell	(Hamilton: Gilmour and Whitehill)
Thomson, Peter David	(Comrie with Dundurn)
Walker, Wikje DCS	(Deacon, Glenrothes: St Columba's)
Webster, Elspeth DCS	(Deacon, Rosyth)
Wedderburn, Alexander John Maclagan	(University of Munich)
Whitley, Laurence Arthur Brown	(Glasgow: Cathedral (High or St Mungo's))
Williams, Trevor Charles	(Hoddom with Kirtle-Eaglesfield with Middlebie with Waterbeck)

SECTION 7

Legal Names and Scottish Charity Numbers for Congregations

All congregations in Scotland, and congregations furth of Scotland which are registered with OSCR, the Office of the Scottish Charity Regulator

For a complete list of legal names see:

www.churchofscotland.org.uk > Resources > Yearbook > Section 7

Further information

All documents, as defined in the Charities References in Documents (Scotland) Regulations 2007, must specify the Charity Number, Legal Name of the congregation, any other name by which the congregation is commonly known and the fact that it is a Charity. For more information, please refer to the Law Department circular on the Regulations on the Church of Scotland website.

www.churchofscotland.org.uk > Resources > Law Department Circulars > Charity Law

SECTION 8

Church Buildings: Ordnance Survey National Grid References

Please go to: www.churchofscotland.org.uk > Resources > Yearbook > Section 8

SECTION 9

Parish and Congregational Changes

The parish structure of the Church of Scotland is constantly being reshaped as the result of unions, linkages and the occasional dissolution.

Section 9A, 'Parishes and Congregations: names no longer in use', records one of the inevitable consequences of these changes, the disappearance of the names of many former parishes and congregations. There are, however, occasions when for legal and other reasons it is important to be able to identify the present-day successors of those parishes and congregations whose names are no longer in use and which can therefore no longer be easily traced. A list of all such parishes and congregations, with full explanatory notes, may be found at:

www.churchofscotland.org.uk/Resources/Yearbook > Section 9A

Section 9B, 'Recent Readjustment and other Congregational Changes', printed below, incorporates all instances of union, linkage and dissolution, together with certain other congregational changes, which have taken place since the publication of the 2018–19 Year Book.

3: Lothian	**Howgate** and **Pencuik: South** united as **Penicuik: South and Howgate**
8: Dumfries and Kirkcudbright	**Balmaclellan and Kells** and **Dalry** united as **Balmaclellan, Kells and Dalry**
10: Ayr	**Girvan: North (Old and St Andrew's)** renamed **Girvan: North**
16: Glasgow	**Glasgow: Anderston Kelvingrove** and **Glasgow: Renfield St Stephen's** united as **Glasgow: St Andrew's West**
19: Argyll	**Ardchattan** linked with **Coll** linked with **Connel**
22: Falkirk	**Cumbernauld: Kildrum** linked with **Cumbernauld: St Mungo's**

	Falkirk: Grahamston United and **Falkirk: St James'** united as **Falkirk: Grahamston United**
26: St Andrews	**Anstruther and Cellardyke: St Ayle** linked with **Kilrenny**: linkage severed
	Crail linked with **Kingsbarns**: linkage severed
	Anstruther and Cellardyke: St Ayle linked with **Crail**
27: Dunkeld and Meigle	**Fortingall and Glenlyon** and **Kenmore and Lawers** united as **Fortingall, Glenlyon, Kenmore and Lawers**
28: Perth	**Fowlis Wester, Madderty and Monzie** and **Gask** united as **Mid Strathearn**
30: Angus	**Arbroath: Knox's** linked with **Arbroath: St Vigeans**: linkage severed
	Arbroath: Knox's and **Arbroath: West Kirk** united as **Arbroath: West Kirk**
	Kirriemuir: St Andrew's linked with **Oathlaw Tannadice**: linkage severed
	Kirriemuir: St Andrew's and **The Glens and Kirriemuir: Old** united as **The Glens and Kirriemuir United**
	Oathlaw Tannadice linked with **The Glens and Kirriemuir United**
32: Kincardine and Deeside	**Stonehaven: Dunnottar** and **Stonehaven: South** united as **Stonehaven: Carronside**
36: Abernethy	**Laggan** and **Newtonmore** united as **Laggan and Newtonmore**
	Kingussie linked with **Laggan and Newtonmore**
41: Caithness	**Bower** dissolved

SECTION 10

Congregational
Statistics
2018

Comparative Statistics: 1978–2018

	2018	2008	1998	1988	1978
Communicants	325,695	471,894	641,340	822,985	987,196
Elders	26,607	36,360	44,388	47,061	48,309

NOTES ON CONGREGATIONAL STATISTICS

Com   Number of communicants at 31 December 2018.

Eld   Number of elders at 31 December 2018.

G   Membership of the Guild including Young Woman's Groups and others as recorded on the 2018 annual return submitted to the Guild Office.

In 18   Ordinary General Income for 2018. Ordinary General Income consists of members' offerings, contributions from congregational organisations, regular fund-raising events, income from investments, deposits and so on. This figure does not include extraordinary or special income, or income from special collections and fund-raising for other charities.

M&M   Final amount allocated to congregations to contribute for Ministries and Mission after allowing for Presbytery-approved amendments up to 31 December 2018, but before deducting stipend endowments and normal allowances given for locum purposes in a vacancy or guardianship.

–18   This figure shows 'the number of children and young people aged 17 years and under who are involved in the life of the congregation'.

NB: Figures may not be available for new charges created or for congregations which have entered into readjustment late in 2018 or during 2019. Figures may also not be available for congregations which failed to submit the appropriate schedule. Where the figure for the number of elders is missing, then in nearly every case the number of communicants relates to the previous year.

Congregation	Com	Eld	G	In18	M&M	–18
1. Edinburgh						
Balerno	526	68	23	133,774	79,828	20
Barclay Viewforth	302	28	-	151,743	126,567	62
Blackhall St Columba's	654	65	-	199,844	113,394	20
Bristo Memorial Craigmillar	56	5	-	45,208	29,339	80
Broughton St Mary's	172	23	-	59,946	51,143	45
Canongate	330	35	-	150,209	73,734	12
Carrick Knowe	336	45	58	62,425	40,985	261
Colinton	813	53	-	191,416	119,049	75
Corstorphine: Craigsbank	399	29	-	96,463	65,159	73
Corstorphine: Old	382	28	40	164,392	70,640	41
Corstorphine: St Anne's	356	55	55	110,498	67,372	40
Corstorphine: St Ninian's	611	78	51	165,366	99,837	-
Craiglockhart	362	46	25	149,625	88,337	20
Craigmillar Park	174	12	20	61,110	49,799	4
Reid Memorial	275	14	-	110,799	58,021	5
Cramond	954	89	-	245,444	182,006	58
Currie	459	29	48	142,814	89,452	65
Dalmeny	98	9	-	30,782	14,378	8
Queensferry	553	53	42	117,446	66,541	-
Davidson's Mains	425	58	-	-	117,962	55
Drylaw	65	12	-	-	6,346	9
Duddingston	400	44	-	165,206	72,472	170
Fairmilehead	503	58	34	105,155	82,250	65
Gorgie Dalry Stenhouse	214	24	-	105,491	78,476	96
Gracemount	14	4	-	18,516	1,991	21
Liberton	690	56	39	216,389	125,956	75
Granton	170	21	-	-	27,606	6
Greenbank	679	78	36	262,288	141,254	195
Greenside	103	21	-	-	32,784	7
Greyfriars Kirk	298	32	-	-	94,723	21
High (St Giles')	463	32	-	313,411	183,430	17
Holy Trinity	221	28	-	137,537	104,899	149
Inverleith St Serf's	311	35	21	116,342	73,439	80
Juniper Green	291	26	-	104,043	64,336	30
Kirkliston	236	31	43	98,849	59,595	27
Leith: North	159	24	-	-	51,201	15
Leith: St Andrew's	176	21	-	77,236	54,649	40
Leith: South	290	71	-	112,298	75,242	130
Liberton Northfield	166	8	-	48,689	27,345	288
Marchmont St Giles'	207	26	16	120,009	72,753	58
Mayfield Salisbury	503	59	-	294,086	148,031	60
Meadowbank	60	4	-	40,848	68,027	2
Morningside	415	69	-	180,945	127,611	207
Morningside United	95	11	-	61,465	7,123	14
Murrayfield	464	38	-	139,358	94,676	115
Newhaven	143	16	-	132,545	49,512	165
Old Kirk and Muirhouse	96	18	-	-	18,126	96
Palmerston Place	375	37	-	166,500	109,612	95

Congregation	Com	Eld	G	In18	M&M	–18
Pilrig St Paul's	207	16	19	51,235	31,345	4
Polwarth	182	17	13	90,567	58,954	1
Portobello and Joppa	813	75	70	225,870	132,319	201
Priestfield	106	16	18	85,172	54,407	60
Ratho	176	13	-	-	35,495	11
Richmond Craigmillar	84	8	-	-	6,147	20
St Andrew's and St George's West	321	42	-	255,623	165,986	48
St Andrew's Clermiston	173	10	-	58,615	31,044	9
St Catherine's Argyle	109	7	-	59,663	34,364	32
St Cuthbert's	275	28	-	117,458	92,986	8
St David's Broomhouse	119	15	-	37,757	11,783	39
St John's Colinton Mains	214	19	-	63,164	36,154	50
St Margaret's	212	-	19	-	41,903	-
St Martin's	85	11	-	21,954	683	6
St Michael's	314	26	28	62,489	50,106	10
St Nicholas' Sighthill	326	18	-	-	27,901	15
St Stephen's Comely Bank	133	9	-	145,630	57,198	17
Slateford Longstone	188	11	32	-	23,637	21
Stockbridge	174	15	-	80,360	59,287	19
Tron Kirk (Gilmerton and Moredun)	85	8	-	-	12,308	93
Wardie	505	51	45	153,990	87,416	185
Willowbrae	111	13	-	55,561	45,683	2

2. West Lothian

Congregation	Com	Eld	G	In18	M&M	–18
Abercorn	63	7	-	15,363	9,996	-
Pardovan, Kingscavil and Winchburgh	253	28	-	68,513	40,947	216
Armadale	478	39	25	83,846	50,426	157
Avonbridge	61	6	-	13,553	7,178	4
Torphichen	199	16	-	31,712	23,535	3
Bathgate: Boghall	220	28	24	-	56,106	166
Bathgate: High	449	33	30	98,810	54,500	65
Bathgate: St John's	329	15	30	-	37,750	94
Blackburn and Seafield	249	29	-	-	47,119	81
Blackridge	63	8	-	27,463	10,500	2
Harthill: St Andrew's	179	10	23	60,421	34,675	44
Breich Valley	104	11	18	36,987	23,649	5
Broxburn	340	22	25	82,481	46,831	25
Fauldhouse: St Andrew's	180	10	-	48,062	36,337	10
Kirknewton and East Calder	294	33	31	101,523	65,776	55
Kirk of Calder	494	37	21	86,966	52,649	-
Linlithgow: St Michael's	1,278	98	46	-	170,765	235
Linlithgow: St Ninian's Craigmailen	378	39	38	69,292	43,699	125
Livingston: Old	310	34	19	95,948	57,491	57
Livingston: United	278	32	-	-	43,287	173
Polbeth Harwood	163	17	-	31,256	14,946	9
West Kirk of Calder	237	18	12	62,457	44,438	29
Strathbrock	272	25	16	89,990	68,427	80
Uphall South	181	24	-	59,832	42,757	20
Whitburn: Brucefield	203	18	26	92,963	55,020	8
Whitburn: South	338	31	-	75,597	52,292	85

Congregation	Com	Eld	G	In18	M&M	–18
3. Lothian						
Aberlady	191	18	-	51,404	22,458	3
Gullane	347	25	25	-	36,852	58
Athelstaneford	195	13	-	23,560	17,794	14
Whitekirk and Tyninghame	132	12	-	-	21,255	10
Belhaven	526	37	65	93,440	54,584	39
Spott	99	7	-	-	10,293	4
Bilston	83	4	15	14,711	5,741	-
Glencorse	286	12	19	27,029	16,268	-
Roslin	219	9	-	23,570	16,519	-
Bonnyrigg	576	57	48	-	67,879	10
Cockenzie and Port Seton: Chalmers Memorial	168	26	24	92,987	52,768	97
Cockenzie and Port Seton: Old	208	19	25	59,871	34,396	14
Cockpen and Carrington	143	25	42	30,161	24,536	10
Lasswade and Rosewell	263	20	-	28,151	24,925	25
Dalkeith: St John's and King's Park	459	36	33	165,964	62,300	70
Dalkeith: St Nicholas Buccleuch	320	17	-	58,980	32,891	-
Dirleton	208	16	-	-	38,145	9
North Berwick: Abbey	255	31	32	100,382	54,727	40
Dunbar	328	19	29	106,448	72,841	59
Dunglass	268	10	-	26,038	21,032	20
Garvald and Morham	36	9	-	-	7,383	6
Haddington: West	210	18	24	53,163	35,091	6
Gladsmuir	164	15	-	-	16,477	4
Longniddry	304	42	27	74,263	47,676	9
Gorebridge	130	11	-	97,849	64,715	100
Haddington: St Mary's	481	37	-	-	69,968	33
Howgate	26	5	-	22,378	11,986	8
Penicuik: South	70	7	-	-	40,152	2
Humbie	71	9	-	27,540	17,059	18
Yester, Bolton and Saltoun	266	32	-	54,454	37,738	36
Loanhead	280	21	29	-	35,809	40
Musselburgh: Northesk	285	25	22	59,435	39,373	146
Musselburgh: St Andrew's High	264	26	18	61,876	42,474	-
Musselburgh: St Clement's & St Ninian's	71	10	-	-	16,367	-
Musselburgh: St Michael's Inveresk	359	36	-	84,855	51,412	5
Newbattle	319	23	14	77,293	37,586	130
Newton	92	1	-	17,383	13,845	10
North Berwick: St Andrew Blackadder	561	35	30	170,449	98,759	70
Ormiston	137	9	20	49,112	26,466	13
Pencaitland	152	3	-	-	20,714	8
Penicuik: North	385	30	-	75,893	45,795	42
Penicuik: St Mungo's	290	22	18	69,567	42,978	20
Prestonpans: Prestongrange	242	18	14	60,010	36,702	11
Tranent	223	16	31	68,371	34,435	73
Traprain	407	31	30	69,429	54,423	50
Tyne Valley	287	20	-	72,548	56,008	83
4. Melrose and Peebles						
Ashkirk	37	4	-	-	5,559	1

Congregation	Com	Eld	G	In18	M&M	–18
Selkirk	348	20	-	71,670	42,836	37
Bowden and Melrose	670	54	25	117,183	77,428	45
Broughton, Glenholm and Kilbucho	137	9	18	17,327	12,253	1
Skirling	57	3	-	8,684	5,126	-
Stobo and Drumelzier	81	-	-	18,775	14,735	3
Tweedsmuir	37	-	-	-	4,057	-
Caddonfoot	156	13	-	17,529	10,348	6
Galashiels: Trinity	353	39	25	56,660	37,866	1
Carlops	50	12	-	-	11,883	15
Kirkurd and Newlands	86	12	12	13,472	16,232	10
West Linton: St Andrew's	165	15	-	41,142	23,346	-
Channelkirk and Lauder	382	20	16	-	40,812	12
Earlston	344	21	8	46,086	33,527	32
Eddleston	99	4	-	-	10,018	10
Peebles: Old	387	27	-	105,591	64,396	8
Ettrick and Yarrow	168	17	-	38,345	31,811	-
Galashiels: Old and St Paul's	222	16	27	65,658	41,956	1
Galashiels: St John's	177	10	-	41,773	20,429	5
Innerleithen, Traquair and Walkerburn	306	24	40	-	36,810	2
Lyne and Manor	87	7	-	-	21,064	2
Peebles: St Andrew's Leckie	479	37	-	116,237	67,362	65
Maxton and Mertoun	78	11	-	11,284	6,022	-
Newtown	106	8	-	18,022	9,912	20
St Boswells	168	18	16	32,796	22,708	3
Stow: St Mary of Wedale and Heriot	173	12	-	28,245	23,886	9

5. Duns

Congregation	Com	Eld	G	In18	M&M	–18
Ayton and District Churches	293	-	11	28,506	29,786	-
Berwick-upon-Tweed: St Andrew's Wallace Green & Lowick	289	-	-	123,483	38,038	-
Chirnside	88	-	12	19,441	11,063	-
Hutton and Fishwick and Paxton	59	-	10	15,035	10,692	-
Coldingham and St Abbs	66	-	-	40,856	26,202	-
Eyemouth	104	-	21	-	24,369	-
Coldstream and District Parishes	422	-	-	47,374	39,302	-
Eccles and Leitholm	147	-	11	27,480	17,539	-
Duns and District Parishes	629	-	40	92,758	74,458	-
Fogo	44	-	-	-	4,492	-
Gordon: St Michael's	59	-	-	-	6,837	-
Greenlaw	85	-	14	20,910	12,245	-
Legerwood	61	-	-	7,710	5,827	-
Westruther	38	-	-	5,327	4,166	-

6. Jedburgh

Congregation	Com	Eld	G	In18	M&M	–18
Ale and Teviot United	379	23	19	35,374	42,833	17
Cavers and Kirkton	97	7	-	11,152	9,491	-
Hawick: Trinity	484	35	34	45,391	28,408	55
Cheviot Churches	291	25	32	-	47,288	-
Hawick: Burnfoot	70	11	-	25,644	14,485	79
Hawick: St Mary's and Old	350	19	22	43,423	29,022	107

Congregation	Com	Eld	G	In18	M&M	–18
Hawick: Teviot and Roberton	251	8	9	49,776	31,016	9
Hawick: Wilton	268	24	-	-	30,132	55
Teviothead	51	4	-	5,726	3,433	5
Hobkirk and Southdean	123	16	12	15,890	16,776	5
Ruberslaw	234	17	10	31,402	23,970	-
Jedburgh: Old and Trinity	554	13	33	64,229	46,609	-
Kelso Country Churches	176	16	13	23,693	31,775	11
Kelso: North and Ednam	927	40	27	140,905	73,118	-
Kelso: Old and Sprouston	436	22	-	45,455	33,317	8
Oxnam	123	9	-	-	7,462	12

7. Annandale and Eskdale

Congregation	Com	Eld	G	In18	M&M	–18
Annan: Old	340	40	43	64,328	43,755	20
Dornock	105	10	-	9,902	6,266	-
Annan: St Andrew's	579	-	43	64,457	40,055	-
Brydekirk	45	4	-	8,400	6,562	1
Applegarth, Sibbaldbie and Johnstone	115	7	10	-	9,408	-
Lochmaben	244	18	34	69,453	40,552	20
Canonbie United	85	16	-	-	19,708	14
Liddesdale	94	6	10	28,685	21,313	-
Dalton and Hightae	173	-	-	19,778	15,565	-
St Mungo	73	-	-	10,877	9,763	-
Gretna: Old, Gretna: St Andrew's Half Morton & Kirkpatrick Fleming	302	-	17	-	37,386	-
Hoddom, Kirtle-Eaglesfield and Middlebie	192	20	14	30,774	17,751	49
Kirkpatrick Juxta	99	-	-	12,815	6,482	-
Moffat: St Andrew's	335	27	20	70,339	43,375	47
Wamphray	53	5	-	8,066	4,870	8
Langholm Eskdalemuir Ewes and Westerkirk	416	26	10	58,444	53,271	45
Lockerbie: Dryfesdale, Hutton and Corrie	670	40	33	62,529	46,835	15
The Border Kirk	292	-	-	67,929	39,502	-
Tundergarth	28	6	-	6,697	6,270	-

8. Dumfries and Kirkcudbright

Congregation	Com	Eld	G	In18	M&M	–18
Balmaclellan and Kells	52	5	16	9,487	13,097	4
Carsphairn	84	7	-	7,769	6,620	3
Dalry	67	11	-	-	15,002	-
Caerlaverock	105	7	-	13,282	7,452	-
Dumfries: St Mary's-Greyfriars	335	28	26	-	45,000	10
Castle Douglas	339	20	22	64,282	39,834	10
The Bengairn Parishes	180	-	-	29,145	27,279	-
Closeburn	177	12	-	29,915	20,078	20
Kirkmahoe	229	13	6	-	18,372	-
Colvend, Southwick and Kirkbean	178	10	20	84,724	58,739	-
Corsock and Kirkpatrick Durham	49	10	-	24,809	13,636	8
Crossmichael, Parton and Balmaghie	203	10	15	23,757	24,211	5
Cummertrees, Mouswald and Ruthwell	177	-	-	29,747	21,150	-
Dalbeattie and Kirkgunzeon	491	-	36	-	34,477	-
Urr	168	9	-	-	16,375	-
Dumfries: Maxwelltown West	333	36	26	-	57,000	56

Congregation	Com	Eld	G	In18	M&M	–18
Dumfries: Northwest	270	9	-	25,438	28,471	3
Dumfries: St George's	465	48	25	109,199	70,870	75
Dumfries: St Michael's and South	631	42	19	99,960	63,727	50
Dumfries: Troqueer	238	18	23	-	59,327	36
Dunscore	173	18	-	-	20,352	2
Glencairn and Moniaive	145	10	-	40,384	25,831	-
Durisdeer	135	6	-	21,975	15,562	10
Penpont, Keir and Tynron	151	10	-	24,433	19,973	8
Thornhill	143	8	-	-	24,909	-
Gatehouse and Borgue	265	18	-	54,289	33,896	17
Tarff and Twynholm	135	12	27	22,631	17,824	11
Irongray, Lochrutton and Terregles	159	20	-	25,876	22,683	-
Kirkconnel	215	12	-	21,678	22,462	-
Sanquhar: St Bride's	366	20	11	44,269	29,423	-
Kirkcudbright	471	28	-	86,447	55,222	65
Kirkmichael, Tinwald and Torthorwald	373	37	18	-	38,966	2
Lochend and New Abbey	195	19	11	37,800	21,160	-

9. Wigtown and Stranraer

Ervie Kirkcolm	167	13	-	21,921	13,057	8
Leswalt	260	-	-	25,877	18,244	-
Glasserton and Isle of Whithorn	88	7	-	-	11,740	-
Whithorn: St Ninian's Priory	293	6	13	33,766	26,804	30
Inch	175	-	10	-	14,267	45
Portpatrick	211	-	21	25,358	17,059	-
Stranraer: Trinity	465	40	29	85,370	62,067	20
Kirkcowan	106	8	-	33,623	20,777	8
Wigtown	143	11	12	33,232	22,381	4
Kirkinner	126	-	6	15,792	10,255	-
Mochrum	228	-	20	18,200	15,548	-
Sorbie	99	8	-	21,799	15,916	-
Kirkmabreck	116	11	23	19,378	12,653	-
Monigaff	186	9	-	20,669	19,288	7
Kirkmaiden	206	16	-	-	21,428	-
Stoneykirk	284	-	17	-	25,321	-
Luce Valley	210	18	23	-	33,652	10
Penninghame	397	-	17	94,532	58,518	-
Stranraer: High Kirk	511	-	-	67,723	54,490	-

10. Ayr

Alloway	962	94	-	244,308	123,224	425
Annbank	240	21	15	26,289	19,569	-
Tarbolton	288	24	18	48,851	38,730	12
Auchinleck	312	16	24	-	24,178	6
Catrine	102	9	-	21,164	17,088	-
Ayr: Auld Kirk of Ayr	478	53	29	72,574	49,244	-
Ayr: Castlehill	524	34	49	76,511	60,745	187
Ayr: Newton Wallacetown	346	38	42	109,567	67,041	70
Ayr: St Andrew's	278	21	15	-	50,212	108
Ayr: St Columba	1,204	114	74	317,237	155,789	40

Congregation	Com	Eld	G	In18	M&M	–18
Ayr: St James'	330	32	-	68,098	50,094	133
Ayr: St Leonard's	364	47	20	107,315	48,802	-
Dalrymple	121	13	-	-	16,161	1
Ayr: St Quivox	208	19	-	36,932	32,531	45
Ballantrae	228	15	13	35,992	27,444	3
St Colmon (Arnsheen Barrhill and Colmonell)	203	8	-	29,029	18,230	4
Barr	64	2	-	2,433	3,113	-
Dailly	108	8	-	12,769	10,654	-
Girvan: South	241	23	27	33,603	21,432	10
Coylton	306	18	-	37,776	25,183	15
Drongan: The Schaw Kirk	165	15	16	39,266	23,347	56
Craigie and Symington	264	22	19	50,418	34,788	12
Prestwick: South	244	31	28	84,925	56,446	95
Crosshill	168	9	28	15,131	5,507	-
Maybole	297	23	21	67,860	43,667	1
Dalmellington	204	12	-	20,146	20,179	-
Patna: Waterside	131	7	-	-	15,734	-
Dundonald	451	35	40	-	52,201	3
Fisherton	112	11	-	14,950	8,310	5
Kirkoswald	187	14	22	35,301	20,670	12
Girvan: North	580	40	-	75,899	46,542	-
Kirkmichael	190	15	21	24,444	14,660	2
Straiton: St Cuthbert's	156	11	18	22,019	12,838	6
Lugar	153	10	15	20,595	8,380	4
Old Cumnock: Old	323	17	26	62,972	37,166	18
Mauchline	364	24	34	81,292	46,561	40
Sorn	138	11	14	21,328	11,277	5
Monkton and Prestwick: North	275	25	21	89,327	56,364	80
Muirkirk	152	13	-	19,864	12,079	7
Old Cumnock: Trinity	298	22	24	46,107	34,629	11
New Cumnock	449	28	22	85,958	45,189	45
Ochiltree	212	21	11	31,610	20,339	10
Stair	206	17	21	45,195	22,831	27
Prestwick: Kingcase	575	77	45	101,897	77,933	200
Prestwick: St Nicholas'	555	67	40	124,599	77,595	74
Troon: Old	890	63	-	151,384	82,454	120
Troon: Portland	463	46	-	-	80,993	12
Troon: St Meddan's	618	71	31	-	93,141	135

11. Irvine and Kilmarnock

Congregation	Com	Eld	G	In18	M&M	–18
Caldwell	209	20	-	61,161	40,191	2
Dunlop	365	35	18	-	53,914	60
Crosshouse	241	27	20	59,351	37,221	45
Darvel	289	25	24	44,887	35,176	38
Dreghorn and Springside	365	-	23	84,308	57,649	38
Fenwick	283	-	28	-	34,046	-
Kilmarnock: Riccarton	221	23	17	64,651	41,683	71
Galston	507	61	52	90,120	67,790	9
Hurlford	283	21	23	58,389	40,470	70
Irvine: Fullarton	351	33	52	-	61,186	254

Congregation	Com	Eld	G	In18	M&M	–18
Irvine: Girdle Toll	153	13	21	-	21,380	60
Irvine: St Andrew's	223	-	23	57,733	30,629	-
Irvine: Mure	277	27	18	59,278	43,643	46
Irvine: Old	314	20	-	152,578	48,492	4
Irvine: Relief Bourtreehill	196	21	20	36,431	26,488	8
Kilmarnock: Kay Park	447	71	18	141,978	81,807	173
Kilmarnock: New Laigh Kirk	784	73	44	229,584	125,391	160
Kilmarnock: St Andrew's & St Marnock's	739	91	35	180,000	104,333	395
Kilmarnock: St John's Onthank	176	19	16	-	30,330	4
Kilmarnock: St Kentigern's	269	23	-	56,029	32,018	108
Kilmarnock: South	210	14	14	36,389	24,411	15
Kilmaurs: St Maur's Glencairn	280	-	24	64,666	32,605	-
Newmilns: Loudoun	173	-	-	-	23,619	-
Stewarton: John Knox	242	19	27	102,031	58,349	50
Stewarton: St Columba's	400	-	40	79,330	57,857	-

12. Ardrossan

Ardrossan: Park	375	30	37	75,783	46,303	157
Ardrossan and Saltcoats Kirkgate	202	32	25	89,133	53,178	2
Beith	662	58	20	96,945	69,148	66
Brodick	119	-	-	52,738	34,668	-
Corrie	30	5	-	20,324	11,280	-
Lochranza and Pirnmill	56	11	-	23,175	14,209	-
Shiskine	62	10	17	32,573	23,470	8
Cumbrae	232	-	28	51,078	38,634	-
Largs: St John's	630	43	39	-	79,071	19
Dalry: St Margaret's	492	56	26	-	94,201	26
Dalry: Trinity	177	19	-	87,540	50,634	190
Fairlie	189	21	21	70,204	49,391	39
Largs: St Columba's	339	-	46	69,140	59,395	-
Kilbirnie: Auld Kirk	286	-	-	53,174	39,612	-
Kilbirnie: St Columba's	483	32	-	69,408	39,581	22
Kilmory	30	5	-	-	8,044	1
Lamlash	83	13	24	40,271	23,248	4
Kilwinning: Mansefield Trinity	181	-	23	53,907	36,507	-
Kilwinning: Old	548	-	28	108,466	68,772	-
Largs: Clark Memorial	629	79	36	150,678	84,634	134
Saltcoats: North	267	-	18	62,594	31,560	-
Saltcoats: St Cuthbert's	228	33	12	80,457	50,984	78
Stevenston: Ardeer	187	28	25	42,242	23,728	27
Stevenston: Livingstone	222	28	19	51,243	34,215	5
Stevenston: High	215	20	15	81,017	57,335	38
West Kilbride	405	43	16	115,482	74,590	119
Whiting Bay and Kildonan	75	9	-	41,693	27,162	6

13. Lanark

Biggar	291	20	27	88,384	59,131	30
Black Mount	69	10	14	15,464	11,832	5
Cairngryffe	137	14	12	-	21,032	4
Libberton and Quothquan	77	12	-	16,141	11,249	12

Congregation	Com	Eld	G	In18	M&M	–18
Symington	136	15	19	32,212	22,946	3
Carluke: Kirkton	657	55	27	132,796	80,638	370
Carluke: St Andrew's	180	11	16	-	32,588	32
Carluke: St John's	543	50	29	-	56,631	72
Carnwath	120	11	18	-	11,528	-
Carstairs	172	13	19	45,298	33,112	190
Coalburn and Lesmahagow Old	450	29	28	-	55,129	4
Crossford	137	5	-	34,326	21,462	44
Kirkfieldbank	72	6	-	-	10,398	-
Douglas Valley	271	20	30	48,310	35,708	1
Forth: St Paul's	316	26	35	-	37,222	120
Kirkmuirhill	144	9	45	86,791	46,926	20
Lanark: Greyfriars	493	47	30	104,101	54,234	156
Lanark: St Nicholas'	470	42	18	105,372	68,188	58
Law	170	8	29	46,911	28,009	94
Lesmahagow: Abbeygreen	109	14	-	53,844	39,810	155
Upper Clyde	181	7	17	24,319	22,926	8

14. Greenock and Paisley

Congregation	Com	Eld	G	In18	M&M	–18
Barrhead: Bourock	421	37	29	87,001	59,132	200
Barrhead: St Andrew's	354	40	32	-	91,276	278
Bishopton	607	53	-	115,118	65,670	102
Bridge of Weir: Freeland	384	49	-	142,327	77,637	121
Bridge of Weir: St Machar's Ranfurly	302	25	26	95,003	57,900	16
Elderslie Kirk	417	34	34	102,398	63,003	-
Erskine	321	30	56	-	64,565	150
Gourock: Old Gourock and Ashton	590	59	12	123,627	73,208	210
Gourock: St John's	403	51	9	136,437	73,852	258
Greenock: East End	52	6	-	-	6,057	12
Greenock: Mount Kirk	301	32	-	57,456	43,320	90
Greenock: Lyle Kirk	721	45	20	-	84,834	110
Greenock: St Margaret's	163	29	-	44,623	19,719	20
Greenock: St Ninian's	212	16	-	-	13,788	34
Greenock: Wellpark Mid Kirk	451	46	12	-	59,652	80
Greenock: Westburn	539	65	21	113,756	79,201	38
Houston and Killellan	658	63	60	150,875	87,264	160
Howwood	131	15	20	44,868	26,979	10
Inchinnan	248	33	27	62,718	39,679	33
Inverkip	292	29	19	70,940	48,758	19
Skelmorlie and Wemyss Bay	227	35	-	-	52,578	7
Johnstone: High	190	30	21	-	58,468	85
Johnstone: St Andrew's Trinity	191	27	-	38,767	24,726	59
Johnstone: St Paul's	350	62	-	80,190	48,517	135
Kilbarchan	415	49	42	114,202	76,521	120
Kilmacolm: Old	367	44	-	123,726	81,414	30
Kilmacolm: St Columba	137	16	-	95,620	63,682	8
Langbank	118	14	-	43,055	26,625	2
Port Glasgow: St Andrew's	397	57	21	74,017	52,843	309
Linwood	169	21	30	56,310	34,814	11
Lochwinnoch	87	13	-	-	27,403	152

Congregation	Com	Eld	G	In18	M&M	–18
Neilston	412	29	19	107,228	69,157	150
Paisley: Abbey	681	44	-	145,510	106,808	73
Paisley: Glenburn	146	-	-	39,959	29,322	-
Paisley: Lylesland	266	37	26	-	59,924	51
Paisley: Martyrs' Sandyford	353	55	23	98,446	72,590	110
Paisley: Oakshaw Trinity	434	64	-	156,363	64,146	25
Paisley: St Columba Foxbar	154	21	-	25,719	20,162	30
Paisley: St Luke's	177	22	-	-	33,798	10
Paisley: St Mark's Oldhall	413	54	48	108,741	69,167	77
Paisley: St Ninian's Ferguslie	44	6	-	-	5,000	4
Paisley: Sherwood Greenlaw	518	61	24	120,833	74,672	136
Paisley: Stow Brae Kirk	329	-	45	93,133	66,568	-
Paisley: Wallneuk North	312	30	-	59,230	39,570	11
Port Glasgow: Hamilton Bardrainney	214	18	13	38,386	29,332	41
Port Glasgow: St Martin's	137	10	-	-	13,152	12
Renfrew: North	604	69	29	108,916	77,487	161
Renfrew: Trinity	302	24	34	90,919	63,515	50

16. Glasgow

Banton	60	-	-	12,293	5,585	-
Twechar	69	-	-	19,653	8,979	-
Bishopbriggs: Kenmure	241	18	32	94,037	68,453	93
Bishopbriggs: Springfield Cambridge	566	39	80	123,132	75,940	132
Broom	432	49	17	114,872	76,940	461
Burnside Blairbeth	444	35	77	-	141,645	203
Busby	214	29	20	76,353	47,198	15
Cadder	599	74	48	-	90,629	126
Cambuslang	560	45	33	114,914	87,721	194
Cambuslang: Flemington Hallside	307	-	37	60,400	35,566	-
Campsie	143	-	19	52,610	36,939	-
Chryston	570	-	13	204,095	112,798	-
Eaglesham	490	-	40	139,742	86,367	-
Fernhill and Cathkin	232	-	9	-	33,446	-
Gartcosh	137	-	-	23,422	18,737	-
Glenboig	104	9	-	13,487	8,248	7
Giffnock: Orchardhill	322	44	10	157,713	93,521	219
Giffnock: South	572	63	31	185,095	99,193	25
Giffnock: The Park	243	-	-	72,844	44,640	-
Greenbank	747	74	66	235,372	135,981	350
Kilsyth: Anderson	243	17	47	-	42,499	89
Kilsyth: Burns and Old	358	27	30	69,103	57,682	108
Kirkintilloch: Hillhead	65	8	8	19,499	9,804	-
Kirkintilloch: St Columba's	199	36	34	-	54,921	10
Kirkintilloch: St David's Memorial Park	497	46	28	-	53,955	97
Kirkintilloch: St Mary's	636	40	-	122,069	67,516	24
Lenzie: Old	406	43	-	122,320	63,328	82
Lenzie: Union	550	57	61	185,027	108,534	225
Maxwell Mearns Castle	244	24	-	165,028	95,416	180
Mearns	584	41	-	196,000	123,730	45
Milton of Campsie	288	31	40	74,679	48,595	110

Congregation	Com	Eld	G	In18	M&M	–18
Netherlee	588	62	33	205,057	116,293	-
Stamperland	276	25	16	70,299	51,643	15
Newton Mearns	366	36	31	105,185	71,335	74
Rutherglen: Old	210	25	-	80,892	40,102	5
Rutherglen: Stonelaw	285	-	-	138,953	85,729	-
Rutherglen: West and Wardlawhill	428	43	38	71,663	48,262	115
Stepps	203	19	-	57,162	35,946	64
Thornliebank	131	12	23	-	28,364	11
Torrance	192	19	-	-	60,446	109
Williamwood	401	-	26	-	68,055	-
Glasgow: Anderston Kelvingrove	41	6	-	-	24,265	6
Glasgow: Baillieston Mure Memorial	326	36	59	-	53,093	255
Glasgow: Baillieston St Andrew's	248	22	23	60,781	43,952	128
Glasgow: Balshagray Victoria Park	125	25	12	92,139	62,735	18
Glasgow: Barlanark Greyfriars	73	16	10	34,578	17,237	175
Glasgow: Blawarthill	166	-	20	-	13,686	-
Glasgow: Bridgeton St Francis in the East	74	-	13	37,760	22,602	-
Glasgow: Broomhill Hyndland	494	-	33	182,243	112,201	-
Glasgow: Calton Parkhead	78	12	-	16,683	5,062	2
Glasgow: Cardonald	300	46	-	-	68,741	85
Glasgow: Carmunnock	275	23	14	45,975	32,430	48
Glasgow: Carmyle	77	5	-	22,098	13,054	27
Glasgow: Kenmuir Mount Vernon	114	10	22	63,711	38,197	38
Glasgow: Carntyne	255	22	32	-	51,601	60
Glasgow: Carnwadric	81	-	-	29,802	21,375	-
Glasgow: Castlemilk	137	-	22	-	16,265	-
Glasgow: Cathcart Old	252	-	23	69,483	53,604	-
Glasgow: Cathcart Trinity	321	45	31	202,000	111,635	45
Glasgow: Cathedral (High or St Mungo's)	394	-	-	88,813	75,034	-
Glasgow: Causeway (Tollcross)	158	23	20	-	39,835	89
Glasgow: Clincarthill	215	-	34	-	58,268	-
Glasgow: Colston Milton	56	7	-	16,207	6,746	9
Glasgow: Colston Wellpark	89	11	-	21,426	19,347	24
Glasgow: Cranhill	35	6	-	-	4,702	264
Glasgow: Croftfoot	262	39	33	-	47,728	80
Glasgow: Dennistoun New	158	28	-	82,180	60,972	81
Glasgow: Drumchapel St Andrew's	138	29	-	-	28,993	50
Glasgow: Drumchapel St Mark's	76	-	-	15,688	1,121	-
Glasgow: Easterhouse	52	7	-	-	13,028	111
Glasgow: Eastwood	174	42	18	81,934	61,834	112
Glasgow: Gairbraid	119	-	-	27,198	19,195	-
Glasgow: Gallowgate	34	7	-	25,720	16,849	-
Glasgow: Garthamlock and Craigend East	55	-	-	-	2,294	-
Glasgow: Gorbals	93	-	-	51,271	17,522	-
Glasgow: Govan and Linthouse	162	44	41	-	60,853	312
Glasgow: Hillington Park	261	-	26	67,932	39,860	-
Glasgow: Ibrox	113	29	12	-	28,089	60
Glasgow: John Ross Memorial (for Deaf People)	52	-	-	-	-	-
Glasgow: Jordanhill	347	52	24	163,508	98,823	40

Congregation	Com	Eld	G	In18	M&M	–18
Glasgow: Kelvinbridge	50	16	-	32,890	33,606	33
Glasgow: Kelvinside Hillhead	151	-	-	-	46,263	-
Glasgow: King's Park	518	50	-	126,532	85,068	125
Glasgow: Kinning Park	122	12	-	32,704	22,947	-
Glasgow: Knightswood St Margaret's	154	18	-	45,885	27,409	11
Glasgow: Langside	199	33	-	88,385	56,710	22
Glasgow: Maryhill	144	14	9	-	21,697	90
Glasgow: Merrylea	253	47	23	65,051	47,025	34
Glasgow: Newlands South	402	56	-	148,495	83,872	22
Glasgow: Partick South	104	14	-	59,994	43,341	30
Glasgow: Partick Trinity	120	23	-	-	59,848	25
Glasgow: Pollokshaws	97	22	-	36,228	26,909	14
Glasgow: Pollokshields	145	28	20	-	48,853	60
Glasgow: Possilpark	101	-	-	-	15,727	-
Glasgow: Queen's Park Govanhill	223	29	26	88,596	70,543	13
Glasgow: Renfield St Stephen's	131	15	15	-	47,851	-
Glasgow: Robroyston	47	4	-	44,289	3,920	22
Glasgow: Ruchazie	26	-	-	1,221	2,648	-
Glasgow: Ruchill Kelvinside	73	-	-	-	32,332	-
Glasgow: St Andrew and St Nicholas	304	32	11	73,045	55,899	381
Glasgow: St Andrew's East	57	15	19	-	18,109	60
Glasgow: St Christopher's Priesthill and Nitshill	193	16	-	29,664	24,266	29
Glasgow: St Columba	125	-	-	-	13,188	-
Glasgow: St David's Knightswood	187	17	25	89,004	48,072	24
Glasgow: St Enoch's Hogganfield	103	14	16	32,214	21,669	5
Glasgow: St George's Tron	-	-	-	-	1,470	-
Glasgow: St James' (Pollok)	152	-	33	43,843	30,352	-
Glasgow: St John's Renfield	290	43	-	144,277	83,216	141
Glasgow: St Paul's	33	5	-	10,908	2,968	350
Glasgow: St Rollox	74	-	-	43,037	21,823	-
Glasgow: Sandyford Henderson Memorial	113	-	-	157,491	108,241	-
Glasgow: Sandyhills	221	26	43	72,890	47,939	23·
Glasgow: Scotstoun	98	-	-	58,869	36,340	-
Glasgow: Shawlands Trinity	300	-	-	81,951	83,020	-
Glasgow: Sherbrooke Mosspark	327	-	18	-	113,414	-
Glasgow: Shettleston New	205	-	25	-	49,620	-
Glasgow: Springburn	187	-	23	-	41,108	-
Glasgow: Temple Anniesland	248	20	-	84,459	58,727	114
Glasgow: Toryglen	53	9	-	11,076	9,689	6
Glasgow: Trinity Possil and Henry Drummond	56	6	-	101,336	34,102	4
Glasgow: Tron St Mary's	88	-	-	36,781	26,758	-
Glasgow: Wallacewell	126	-	-	16,840	1,457	-
Glasgow: Wellington	169	-	-	98,841	72,745	-
Glasgow: Whiteinch	69	5	-	54,497	35,708	38
Glasgow: Yoker	94	-	-	-	15,069	-

17. Hamilton

Airdrie: Cairnlea	507	49	24	-	84,556	115
Calderbank	115	9	16	25,356	12,647	-
Airdrie: Clarkston	328	35	16	78,308	50,948	129

Congregation	Com	Eld	G	In18	M&M	−18
Airdrie: High	279	35	-	69,026	39,661	129
Caldercruix and Longriggend	151	9	-	66,966	36,828	92
Airdrie: Jackson	329	49	21	88,263	53,991	190
Airdrie: New Monkland	279	30	23	72,812	40,666	71
Greengairs	117	9	-	22,367	14,363	-
Airdrie: St Columba's	206	14	-	46,148	12,876	2
Airdrie: The New Wellwynd	704	88	-	185,806	92,905	165
Bargeddie	85	-	-	-	43,599	-
Bellshill: Central	152	30	16	57,041	33,861	12
Bellshill: West	430	32	-	77,914	39,815	18
Blantyre: Livingstone Memorial	180	21	-	52,795	28,993	225
Blantyre: St Andrew's	170	20	-	50,684	31,304	12
Blantyre: Old	246	16	22	74,801	48,455	30
Bothwell	486	51	47	200,949	67,799	93
Chapelhall	192	24	28	43,968	27,322	35
Kirk o' Shotts	161	9	-	26,532	17,446	9
Cleland	141	9	-	25,694	15,356	-
Wishaw: St Mark's	262	28	38	69,921	46,349	119
Coatbridge: Blairhill Dundyvan	231	19	21	52,162	34,808	76
Coatbridge: Middle	257	28	31	36,095	31,620	119
Coatbridge: Calder	255	15	11	50,205	36,527	-
Coatbridge: Old Monkland	95	18	-	37,879	35,624	36
Coatbridge: New St Andrew's	553	69	32	111,453	76,224	199
Coatbridge: Townhead	124	17	-	33,595	24,847	30
Dalserf	183	21	24	57,284	51,657	4
East Kilbride: Claremont	393	36	-	135,584	79,422	20
East Kilbride: Greenhills	144	11	14	44,319	21,644	6
East Kilbride: Moncrieff	561	55	46	128,366	74,660	190
East Kilbride: Mossneuk	249	12	-	24,801	17,001	108
East Kilbride: Old	645	61	31	-	74,890	20
East Kilbride: South	203	22	-	61,551	49,581	122
East Kilbride: Stewartfield	29	5	-	14,493	7,000	6
East Kilbride: West	272	23	-	51,371	37,923	30
East Kilbride: Westwood	320	30	-	-	51,164	40
Hamilton: Cadzow	385	56	35	109,207	82,509	88
Hamilton: Gilmour and Whitehill	117	26	-	37,545	28,824	7
Hamilton: West	185	31	-	65,266	39,752	69
Hamilton: Hillhouse	357	40	-	78,891	58,526	153
Hamilton: Old	452	68	16	-	90,798	45
Hamilton: St John's	488	51	59	-	76,105	232
Hamilton: South	156	19	20	53,259	38,895	10
Quarter	92	11	-	28,379	14,770	-
Hamilton: Trinity	257	17	-	55,372	33,077	-
Holytown	146	23	17	51,742	31,722	73
New Stevenston: Wrangholm Kirk	83	11	17	41,059	24,005	7
Larkhall: Chalmers	83	5	-	26,824	19,830	120
Larkhall: St Machan's	316	57	35	-	62,522	120
Larkhall: Trinity	151	16	26	46,575	30,626	120
Motherwell: Crosshill	263	41	47	77,681	59,380	55
Motherwell: St Margaret's	347	15	-	43,311	24,452	10

Congregation	Com	Eld	G	In18	M&M	–18
Motherwell: Dalziel St Andrew's	452	63	41	140,299	79,030	65
Motherwell: North	127	25	25	52,083	35,036	90
Wishaw: Craigneuk and Belhaven	119	25	-	-	27,832	10
Motherwell: St Mary's	659	92	58	-	88,862	452
Motherwell: South	384	63	53	90,012	63,828	170
Newarthill and Carfin	209	27	15	71,637	47,916	67
Newmains: Bonkle	107	17	-	-	20,429	13
Newmains: Coltness Memorial	176	20	12	-	36,559	6
Overtown	253	30	49	68,686	28,813	150
Shotts: Calderhead Erskine	389	28	29	87,885	56,166	6
Stonehouse: St Ninian's	381	54	41	-	9,205	170
Strathaven: Avendale Old and Drumclog	516	50	35	119,730	83,567	22
Strathaven: Trinity	908	124	78	200,536	129,971	-
Uddingston: Burnhead	263	23	8	50,377	33,746	45
Uddingston: Old	420	48	35	147,998	81,969	40
Uddingston: Viewpark	389	66	16	118,550	65,267	150
Wishaw: Cambusnethan North	404	31	-	74,409	47,780	55
Wishaw: Cambusnethan Old & Morningside	370	33	17	65,772	62,010	130
Wishaw: Old	184	21	-	37,306	20,792	35
Wishaw: South Wishaw	274	26	19	78,756	60,976	50

18. Dumbarton

Congregation	Com	Eld	G	In18	M&M	–18
Alexandria	227	22	22	-	41,245	27
Arrochar	58	-	6	-	11,139	-
Luss	95	16	10	51,053	34,260	-
Baldernock	172	13	-	33,698	23,128	-
Milngavie: St Paul's	809	94	92	208,833	116,484	141
Bearsden: Baljaffray	350	24	34	90,370	51,055	45
Bearsden: Cross	763	-	22	-	97,938	-
Bearsden: Killermont	570	52	49	-	88,236	75
Bearsden: New Kilpatrick	1,264	118	95	319,463	175,042	30
Bearsden: Westerton Fairlie Memorial	328	37	49	101,140	61,333	48
Bonhill	495	-	-	-	39,562	-
Renton: Trinity	244	-	-	30,184	14,418	-
Cardross	380	-	28	117,448	49,404	-
Clydebank: Faifley	177	-	34	41,786	21,587	-
Clydebank: Kilbowie St Andrew's	234	21	23	43,479	19,012	98
Clydebank: Radnor Park	110	15	12	44,748	28,985	-
Clydebank: Waterfront	151	23	-	50,844	34,820	31
Dalmuir: Barclay	164	18	-	44,392	18,983	21
Craigrownie	135	17	-	31,734	25,887	4
Garelochhead	146	-	-	-	39,347	-
Rosneath: St Modan's	100	13	26	27,432	15,410	4
Dumbarton: Riverside	453	60	36	101,707	68,815	11
Dumbarton: St Andrew's	101	18	-	29,855	18,357	-
Dumbarton: West Kirk	141	22	-	-	33,607	139
Duntocher: Trinity	190	25	44	38,158	24,108	-
Helensburgh	827	65	32	214,810	123,093	30
Rhu and Shandon	258	21	28	-	38,097	8
Jamestown	174	20	15	-	27,925	-

Congregation	Com	Eld	G	In18	M&M	–18
Kilmaronock Gartocharn	202	10	-	25,628	18,758	8
Milngavie: Cairns	339	34	-	-	87,649	17
Milngavie: St Luke's	356	15	-	80,272	51,205	15
Old Kilpatrick Bowling	225	16	-	-	39,847	66

19 Argyll

Congregation	Com	Eld	G	In18	M&M	–18
Appin	85	11	20	27,766	17,998	2
Lismore	39	-	-	14,992	8,454	-
Ardchattan	86	9	-	24,463	18,445	8
Ardrishaig	120	17	30	33,498	21,784	-
South Knapdale	31	4	-	-	6,805	-
Barra	31	3	-	6,304	9,328	-
South Uist	51	7	-	15,611	10,824	6
Bute, United Church of	463	37	29	68,056	51,362	16
Campbeltown: Highland	359	29	-	-	28,212	12
Campbeltown: Lorne and Lowland	707	41	25	108,404	53,630	76
Coll	18	3	-	6,698	2,456	-
Connel	113	-	9	39,170	27,230	-
Colonsay and Oronsay	12	2	-	-	5,323	-
Craignish	46	-	-	-	4,852	-
Kilbrandon and Kilchattan	92	19	-	32,345	23,067	6
Kilninver and Kilmelford	53	10	-	-	7,130	6
Cumlodden, Lochfyneside and Lochgair	71	12	14	-	12,062	-
Glenaray and Inveraray	97	16	-	28,367	21,273	1
Dunoon: St John's	115	24	32	44,909	28,346	-
Kirn and Sandbank	284	31	-	-	36,508	15
Dunoon: The High Kirk	285	33	25	-	42,378	-
Innellan	53	-	-	16,875	10,332	-
Toward	49	-	-	-	13,354	-
Gigha and Cara	32	6	-	8,870	7,640	3
Kilcalmonell	39	12	-	11,253	6,927	1
Killean and Kilchenzie	117	13	17	23,565	13,240	25
Glassary, Kilmartin and Ford	90	10	-	15,246	15,794	8
North Knapdale	47	6	-	26,895	20,580	23
Glenorchy and Innishael	41	6	-	-	7,640	-
Strathfillan	41	6	-	12,422	5,815	-
Iona	13	6	-	-	8,659	2
Kilfinichen & Kilvickeon & the Ross of Mull	27	4	-	8,674	7,429	-
Jura	24	5	-	7,652	3,220	-
Kilarrow	40	15	-	24,292	18,032	6
Kildalton and Oa	79	9	-	-	26,705	12
Kilchrenan and Dalavich	35	9	-	14,892	11,082	16
Muckairn	111	18	-	26,672	17,840	-
Kilfinan	29	-	-	6,676	4,725	-
Kilmodan and Colintraive	77	9	-	14,140	13,777	15
Kyles	86	20	-	27,173	19,331	3
Kilmore and Oban	430	41	23	74,954	58,689	35
Kilmun, Strone and Ardentinny: The Shore Kirk	169	15	13	-	34,762	-
Kilninian and Kilmore	22	5	-	11,992	6,356	-
Salen and Ulva	32	5	-	13,309	8,999	9

Congregation	Com	Eld	G	In18	M&M	–18
Tobermory	62	12	-	30,186	19,780	13
Torosay and Kinlochspelvie	25	3	-	-	4,361	1
Lochgilphead	121	16	23	36,441	23,498	35
Lochgoilhead and Kilmorich	57	-	-	24,274	22,576	-
Strachur and Strachlachlan	106	11	11	19,723	19,668	-
North and West Islay	112	25	8	35,905	28,679	13
Rothesay: Trinity	299	33	10	56,928	38,238	55
Saddell and Carradale	179	14	19	24,903	23,180	18
Southend	213	15	14	30,681	19,228	-
Skipness	18	2	-	12,484	4,022	1
Tarbert, Loch Fyne and Kilberry	97	11	18	37,481	23,156	5
Tiree	72	10	-	-	12,509	3

22. Falkirk

Congregation	Com	Eld	G	In18	M&M	–18
Airth	139	9	18	82,690	26,241	42
Blackbraes and Shieldhill	148	21	18	30,209	19,498	-
Muiravonside	172	22	-	-	27,731	2
Bo'ness: Old	315	24	10	66,220	35,955	50
Bo'ness: St Andrew's	356	18	-	50,368	52,450	5
Bonnybridge: St Helen's	289	14	-	-	33,261	12
Bothkennar and Carronshore	194	18	-	36,370	22,037	-
Brightons	571	32	53	137,901	80,672	190
Carriden	368	38	21	54,102	40,118	-
Cumbernauld: Abronhill	183	12	23	55,355	46,684	12
Cumbernauld: Condorrat	284	25	33	71,659	47,449	101
Cumbernauld: Kildrum	247	24	-	40,651	37,649	220
Cumbernauld: Old	302	42	-	65,740	48,657	67
Cumbernauld: St Mungo's	154	29	-	41,006	28,560	14
Denny: Old	298	38	20	59,625	39,300	15
Haggs	219	23	-	34,988	22,108	44
Denny: Westpark	403	32	24	93,689	64,038	102
Dunipace	320	25	-	56,536	37,686	54
Falkirk: Bainsford	116	14	-	-	23,500	90
Falkirk: Camelon	172	13	-	-	45,594	15
Falkirk: Grahamston United	501	40	22	-	42,389	44
Falkirk: Laurieston	195	17	20	65,505	23,219	2
Redding and Westquarter	124	12	-	-	15,246	-
Falkirk: St Andrew's West	389	28	-	77,734	53,785	20
Falkirk: St James' *within Grahamston fig.*	*	17	-	-	22,696	-
Falkirk: Trinity	506	-	16	-	99,759	-
Grangemouth: Abbotsgrange	321	50	-	62,866	48,086	101
Grangemouth: Kirk of the Holy Rood	299	25	-	57,267	35,149	15
Grangemouth: Zetland	513	72	50	112,847	67,358	198
Larbert: East	599	53	29	129,995	79,838	237
Larbert: Old	280	18	-	80,816	49,187	70
Larbert: West	334	30	32	70,281	48,581	89
Polmont: Old	342	26	38	-	58,669	50
Slamannan	97	6	-	-	18,728	24
Stenhouse and Carron	312	31	-	-	47,298	6

Congregation	Com	Eld	G	In18	M&M	–18
23. Stirling						
Aberfoyle	71	5	12	15,991	16,239	3
Port of Menteith	54	7	-	-	10,142	-
Alloa: Ludgate	283	20	23	77,566	46,618	12
Alloa: St Mungo's	319	43	32	-	46,267	20
Alva	430	54	30	79,259	49,169	57
Balfron	126	15	-	48,373	23,797	8
Fintry	99	11	16	19,481	19,622	2
Balquhidder	47	4	-	13,110	8,227	4
Killin and Ardeonaig	82	8	9	29,280	14,513	7
Bannockburn: Allan	260	33	-	62,260	27,926	-
Cowie and Plean	149	10	-	15,660	7,482	-
Bannockburn: Ladywell	354	18	-	-	18,488	21
Bridge of Allan	653	50	68	100,329	77,074	73
Buchanan	93	7	-	16,944	13,108	6
Drymen	244	21	-	81,074	44,737	40
Buchlyvie	153	14	15	25,424	20,762	20
Gartmore	59	12	-	-	16,956	2
Callander	494	25	27	109,601	65,991	80
Cambusbarron: The Bruce Memorial	275	19	-	-	40,454	32
Clackmannan	339	25	23	101,150	46,959	54
Dollar	225	25	54	89,982	57,809	3
Glendevon	28	3	-	-	3,406	-
Muckhart	80	8	-	20,132	19,629	12
Dunblane: Cathedral	766	72	35	227,898	125,422	199
Dunblane: St Blane's	294	28	32	-	60,378	26
Lecropt	139	16	-	37,843	22,943	8
Fallin	242	7	-	-	18,256	78
Gargunnock	119	9	-	19,549	22,438	15
Kilmadock	85	12	-	-	15,961	6
Kincardine-in-Menteith	73	5	-	18,131	11,316	6
Killearn	322	20	43	80,872	63,632	55
Kippen	179	14	19	28,167	23,553	8
Norrieston	90	9	10	22,082	17,313	2
Logie	486	52	28	91,811	62,735	96
Menstrie	319	20	23	56,848	43,423	11
Sauchie and Coalsnaughton	404	24	12	54,242	34,876	6
Stirling: Allan Park South	155	27	-	47,754	29,236	100
Stirling: Church of The Holy Rude	136	18	-	-	32,186	-
Stirling: Viewfield Erskine	219	20	23	40,020	21,213	7
Stirling: North	330	26	22	-	39,000	28
Stirling: St Columba's	427	52	-	109,612	59,686	100
Stirling: St Mark's	157	9	-	25,450	21,510	27
Stirling: St Ninian's Old	597	60	-	106,334	58,460	76
Strathblane	164	16	40	80,663	44,933	40
Tillicoultry	538	60	32	-	59,490	72
Tullibody: St Serf's	325	22	25	-	35,220	12
24. Dunfermline						
Aberdour: St Fillan's	342	17	-	-	51,000	10

Congregation	Com	Eld	G	In18	M&M	–18
Beath and Cowdenbeath: North	195	21	15	-	38,001	11
Cairneyhill	92	17	-	27,886	16,179	-
Limekilns	227	31	-	82,321	48,885	30
Carnock and Oakley	152	19	25	56,940	36,871	4
Cowdenbeath: Trinity	263	25	8	66,866	47,404	22
Culross and Torryburn	61	12	-	49,579	34,305	20
Dalgety	485	43	22	122,351	79,716	110
Dunfermline: Abbey	604	60	-	146,958	85,785	112
Dunfermline: East	79	6	-	68,252	12,554	60
Dunfermline: Gillespie Memorial	130	25	13	-	27,455	18
Dunfermline: North	138	16	-	30,116	21,121	1
Dunfermline: St Andrew's Erskine	166	20	14	50,290	31,203	3
Dunfermline: St Leonard's	301	25	26	73,988	49,628	45
Dunfermline: St Margaret's	225	-	9	79,462	47,066	-
Dunfermline: St Ninian's	142	16	23	47,955	31,217	8
Dunfermline: Townhill and Kingseat	210	22	23	68,275	43,482	30
Inverkeithing	212	-	-	61,423	43,805	-
North Queensferry	50	6	-	19,272	9,886	6
Kelty	236	19	27	60,981	50,428	10
Lochgelly and Benarty: St Serf's	368	-	-	62,345	42,825	-
Rosyth	205	19	-	37,956	23,319	8
Saline and Blairingone	144	16	15	-	31,139	15
Tulliallan and Kincardine	252	29	36	58,137	42,420	70

25. Kirkcaldy

Auchterderran Kinglassie	295	-	15	51,875	39,121	-
Auchtertool	62	-	-	-	5,949	-
Kirkcaldy: Linktown	226	-	32	66,308	39,094	-
Buckhaven and Wemyss	232	-	21	47,391	34,187	-
Burntisland	269	35	22	-	38,870	40
Dysart: St Clair	401	28	14	33,737	40,341	40
Glenrothes: Christ's Kirk	179	16	21	37,843	21,569	4
Glenrothes: St Columba's	384	46	-	61,024	39,964	86
Glenrothes: St Margaret's	255	24	28	61,969	35,983	50
Glenrothes: St Ninian's	206	28	16	78,707	44,491	12
Kennoway, Windygates & Balgonie St Kenneth's	586	46	47	99,310	61,052	15
Kinghorn	260	15	-	76,484	49,185	10
Kirkcaldy: Abbotshall	450	-	-	84,961	48,072	-
Kirkcaldy: Bennochy	397	38	15	-	53,686	15
Kirkcaldy: Pathhead	324	34	39	74,512	46,410	130
Kirkcaldy: St Bryce Kirk	326	30	21	81,989	67,791	31
Kirkcaldy: Templehall	129	13	15	35,409	18,355	-
Kirkcaldy: Torbain	196	31	-	47,013	30,206	60
Leslie: Trinity	143	14	-	-	17,739	-
Leven	471	-	34	102,947	64,982	-
Markinch and Thornton	562	-	-	92,305	57,667	-
Methil: Wellesley	271	25	17	65,522	29,938	118
Methilhill and Denbeath	172	19	33	29,882	22,519	6

Congregation	Com	Eld	G	In18	M&M	–18
26. St Andrews						
Anstruther and Cellardyke: St Ayle	374	34	34	91,144	51,178	15
Kilrenny	94	13	-	32,811	20,843	-
Balmerino	112	12	-	-	14,655	-
Wormit	171	-	30	50,159	23,322	-
Boarhills and Dunino	129	7	-	25,976	16,378	-
St Andrews: Holy Trinity	299	24	31	187,896	65,967	70
Cameron	88	11	12	22,917	13,731	6
St Andrews: St Leonard's	423	45	19	118,768	80,935	24
Carnbee	84	12	13	13,994	10,728	1
Pittenweem	210	12	16	23,795	15,510	2
Ceres, Kemback and Springfield	334	21	16	-	68,629	37
Crail	310	23	44	53,762	28,180	6
Kingsbarns	62	7	-	19,757	11,609	-
Creich, Flisk and Kilmany	72	8	-	19,581	20,140	-
Cupar: Old and St Michael of Tarvit	481	32	23	134,918	79,900	42
Monimail	82	10	-	20,901	14,760	4
Cupar: St John's and Dairsie United	632	50	32	-	71,573	6
East Neuk Trinity	300	27	50	84,523	52,451	10
St Monans	241	12	24	61,674	46,604	17
Edenshead	351	23	12	-	38,282	-
Falkland	117	12	-	-	25,720	-
Freuchie	130	20	20	28,591	14,950	1
Howe of Fife	285	20	-	58,627	41,489	13
Largo	299	33	20	89,310	52,703	1
Largoward	42	6	-	9,441	2,557	10
Leuchars: St Athernase	288	24	19	-	38,744	13
Lindores	335	27	-	-	31,383	4
Newport-on-Tay	334	34	-	75,165	45,460	35
St Andrews: Hope Park and Martyrs'	504	44	22	121,728	96,740	10
Strathkinness	86	10	-	22,033	10,442	-
Tayport	220	15	-	-	35,092	-
27. Dunkeld and Meigle						
Aberfeldy	158	12	-	-	27,892	154
Dull and Weem	144	12	12	-	20,821	3
Grantully, Logierait and Strathtay	126	10	6	33,524	27,363	2
Alyth	646	-	23	88,983	54,673	-
Ardler, Kettins and Meigle	376	26	34	-	32,646	9
Bendochy	72	12	-	27,696	16,489	-
Coupar Angus: Abbey	260	15	-	43,648	25,537	30
Blair Atholl and Struan	108	14	-	16,951	22,611	-
Braes of Rannoch	18	3	-	-	7,097	-
Foss and Rannoch	78	8	-	10,044	10,140	3
Blairgowrie	800	45	38	117,670	75,241	112
Caputh and Clunie	137	15	-	20,533	23,708	25
Kinclaven	123	11	15	23,844	13,455	5
Dunkeld	319	30	-	102,140	69,568	-
Fortingall and Glenlyon	49	8	-	16,447	12,762	4
Kenmore and Lawers	49	6	21	-	18,408	8

Congregation	Com	Eld	G	In18	M&M	–18
Kirkmichael, Straloch and Glenshee	75	5	-	17,908	12,330	4
Rattray	267	15	-	40,203	22,920	10
Pitlochry	314	32	23	78,551	56,967	27
Tenandry	37	9	-	21,787	18,884	-

28. Perth

Aberdalgie and Forteviot	171	12	-	-	11,459	11
Aberuthven and Dunning	189	17	-	50,100	33,519	50
Abernethy & Dron & Arngask	268	28	34	38,062	36,891	10
Almondbank Tibbermore	247	16	20	-	29,577	2
Methven and Logiealmond	153	14	-	-	16,108	5
Ardoch	170	17	28	44,546	22,316	22
Blackford	92	12	-	22,780	17,320	54
Auchterarder	543	37	43	166,155	91,779	35
Auchtergaven and Moneydie	473	24	19	-	35,520	-
Redgorton and Stanley	308	15	31	43,809	29,315	43
Cargill Burrelton	118	19	18	27,286	22,931	15
Collace	107	6	13	17,178	9,148	8
Cleish	179	10	13	40,361	28,674	10
Fossoway: St Serf's and Devonside	197	15	-	55,815	35,132	12
Comrie	395	-	19	102,849	70,687	-
Dundurn	49	7	-	19,178	10,312	-
Crieff	576	34	26	-	63,075	10
Dunbarney and Forgandenny	521	31	27	90,026	56,053	103
Errol	247	21	30	52,325	29,424	55
Kilspindie and Rait	63	6	-	12,000	8,070	-
Kinross	652	34	39	122,330	72,814	134
Mid Strathearn	349	-	14	53,389	51,309	-
Muthill	242	22	13	41,152	32,760	16
Trinity Gask and Kinkell	39	4	-	-	5,886	-
Orwell and Portmoak	370	34	28	68,138	54,675	40
Perth: Craigie and Moncrieffe	543	35	28	66,473	58,950	79
Perth: Kinnoull	365	34	25	-	51,460	53
Perth: Letham St Mark's	455	9	19	121,949	68,983	70
Perth: North	826	44	37	241,347	127,768	63
Perth: Riverside	64	-	-	-	24,528	-
Perth: St John's Kirk of Perth	443	-	-	106,934	66,255	-
Perth: St Leonard's-in-the-Fields	402	31	-	83,185	53,906	4
Perth: St Matthew's	726	29	19	117,988	58,334	126
St Madoes and Kinfauns	273	-	-	54,642	46,557	-
Scone and St Martins	816	49	48	111,939	70,660	47

29. Dundee

Abernyte	83	11	-	19,869	13,521	10
Inchture and Kinnaird	147	27	-	38,043	30,774	10
Longforgan	172	19	16	-	31,679	5
Auchterhouse	127	11	13	-	18,769	8
Monikie & Newbigging & Murroes & Tealing	442	22	10	-	35,988	5
Dundee: Balgay	307	33	-	61,336	39,450	10
Dundee: Barnhill St Margaret's	692	51	63	-	95,076	30

Congregation	Com	Eld	G	In18	M&M	–18
Dundee: Broughty Ferry New Kirk	601	44	36	105,798	63,983	91
Dundee: Broughty Ferry St James'	125	10	15	-	18,663	29
Dundee: Broughty Ferry St Luke's & Queen Street	355	37	18	33,353	45,260	15
Dundee: Broughty Ferry St Stephen's & West	271	23	-	50,586	30,349	-
Dundee: Dundee (St Mary's)	501	40	-	81,941	58,870	-
Dundee: Camperdown	120	10	-	30,178	20,789	10
Dundee: Chalmers Ardler	165	16	-	82,552	51,715	95
Dundee: Coldside	189	15	-	47,045	35,357	117
Dundee: Craigiebank	139	9	-	24,468	18,876	54
Dundee: Douglas and Mid Craigie	106	9	-	19,652	15,789	100
Dundee: Downfield Mains	248	22	21	81,249	54,317	121
Dundee: Fintry	84	7	-	52,988	30,936	60
Dundee: Lochee	455	22	27	72,276	50,083	251
Dundee: Logie and St John's Cross	191	13	23	72,408	45,327	20
Dundee: Meadowside St Paul's	273	26	16	67,994	32,160	20
Dundee: St Andrew's	401	42	23	118,188	67,796	16
Dundee: Menzieshill	238	14	-	-	26,701	14
Dundee: St David's High Kirk	198	40	20	-	32,360	30
Dundee: Steeple	200	29	-	123,416	79,010	43
Dundee: Stobswell	357	35	-	60,223	45,132	-
Dundee: Strathmartine	229	22	21	49,561	27,997	3
Dundee: Trinity	381	30	24	-	36,965	47
Dundee: West	259	27	23	68,803	53,183	-
Dundee: Whitfield	36	5	-	-	9,202	40
Fowlis and Liff	136	11	-	-	28,252	22
Lundie and Muirhead	263	25	-	45,035	30,497	40
Invergowrie	248	45	36	62,666	40,652	12
Monifieth	970	57	42	130,202	95,885	82

30. Angus

Congregation	Com	Eld	G	In18	M&M	–18
Aberlemno	192	10	-	27,618	16,533	14
Guthrie and Rescobie	210	10	10	24,478	15,579	13
Arbirlot	131	8	-	41,637	15,811	1
Carmyllie	92	12	-	-	15,522	-
Arbroath: Knox's	226	18	-	-	24,745	30
Arbroath: St Vigeans	458	40	14	-	45,252	95
Arbroath: Old and Abbey	404	28	-	80,358	64,650	80
Arbroath: St Andrew's	517	36	38	143,813	83,191	75
Arbroath: West Kirk	667	73	40	89,766	69,305	20
Barry	182	8	17	-	16,130	3
Carnoustie	291	20	17	-	48,777	11
Brechin: Cathedral	428	29	30	-	51,813	20
Brechin: Gardner Memorial	416	17	-	45,955	38,006	14
Farnell	109	-	-	9,300	9,722	-
Carnoustie: Panbride	610	31	-	-	48,966	20
Colliston	165	5	9	19,213	11,635	4
Friockheim Kinnell	132	-	19	20,715	3,832	-
Inverkeilor and Lunan	107	6	17	20,371	15,310	1
Dun and Hillside	373	45	33	-	36,454	4
Dunnichen, Letham and Kirkden	225	15	16	-	27,073	1

Congregation	Com	Eld	G	In18	M&M	–18
Eassie, Nevay and Newtyle	191	14	16	24,384	21,348	30
Edzell Lethnot Glenesk	326	25	22	36,792	32,063	10
Fern Careston Menmuir	96	9	-	12,403	13,864	12
Forfar: East and Old	491	45	43	-	73,506	27
Forfar: Lowson Memorial	580	46	30	-	68,539	220
Forfar: St Margaret's	452	24	13	84,327	46,972	95
Glamis, Inverarity and Kinettles	333	27	-	52,398	45,596	11
Kirriemuir: St Andrew's	241	18	25	52,714	31,237	35
Oathlaw Tannadice	116	7	-	19,691	17,878	3
Montrose: Old and St Andrew's	579	39	18	85,306	53,185	32
Montrose: South and Ferryden	381	-	-	46,190	37,727	-
The Glens and Kirriemuir Old	912	65	32	-	71,548	150
The Isla Parishes	133	-	12	28,328	30,511	-

31. Aberdeen

Congregation	Com	Eld	G	In18	M&M	–18
Aberdeen: Bridge of Don Oldmachar	178	12	-	48,032	33,260	86
Aberdeen: Craigiebuckler	715	66	24	-	68,511	80
Aberdeen: Ferryhill	307	43	-	82,199	54,152	100
Aberdeen: Garthdee	182	13	-	24,949	19,409	45
Aberdeen: High Hilton	289	28	14	55,649	32,950	50
Aberdeen: Holburn West	317	41	32	83,395	70,751	14
Aberdeen: Mannofield	912	100	41	-	92,583	15
Aberdeen: Mastrick	204	21	-	-	32,622	1
Aberdeen: Middlefield	94	5	-	6,967	3,474	-
Aberdeen: Midstocket	423	40	47	-	60,566	50
Aberdeen: Northfield	141	9	17	25,530	19,429	2
Aberdeen: Queen's Cross	403	40	17	126,100	85,720	11
Aberdeen: Rubislaw	398	59	23	147,753	83,393	20
Aberdeen: Ruthrieston West	301	31	15	84,788	46,509	7
Aberdeen: St Columba's Bridge of Don	213	13	-	-	54,465	100
Aberdeen: St George's Tillydrone	82	9	-	12,213	10,798	4
Aberdeen: St John's Church for Deaf People	87	5	-	-	-	-
Aberdeen: St Machar's Cathedral	467	39	-	187,154	86,672	12
Aberdeen: St Mark's	422	37	43	124,450	101,817	18
Aberdeen: St Mary's	291	37	-	71,933	47,909	75
Aberdeen: St Nicholas Kincorth, South of	317	23	-	-	45,028	115
Aberdeen: St Nicholas Uniting, Kirk of	305	24	12	92,731	13,708	6
Aberdeen: St Stephen's	147	20	12	-	41,342	39
Aberdeen: South Holburn	409	39	35	86,449	68,012	6
Aberdeen: Stockethill	87	6	-	-	8,812	50
Aberdeen: Summerhill	115	17	-	27,935	18,961	3
Aberdeen: Torry St Fittick's	306	-	18	-	43,442	-
Aberdeen: Woodside	235	28	20	45,283	34,003	93
Bucksburn: Stoneywood	384	13	-	33,748	23,057	-
Cults	694	65	33	181,962	102,815	63
Dyce	873	53	38	-	63,372	145
Kingswells	308	23	16	48,002	33,770	7
Newhills	355	33	33	-	74,420	25
Peterculter	523	43	-	112,609	65,292	74

Congregation	Com	Eld	G	In18	M&M	–18
32. Kincardine and Deeside						
Aberluthnott	103	8	12	13,784	11,450	3
Laurencekirk	354	9	-	23,113	21,403	-
Aboyne-Dinnet	275	9	18	-	30,918	45
Cromar	190	13	-	27,607	25,896	2
Arbuthnott, Bervie and Kinneff	453	-	26	-	51,963	-
Banchory-Ternan East	502	27	22	82,386	66,296	144
Banchory-Ternan West	578	-	25	-	70,104	-
Birse and Feughside	199	15	-	-	32,340	24
Braemar and Crathie	178	25	-	-	39,204	45
Drumoak-Durris	371	14	-	56,240	41,969	25
Glenmuick (Ballater)	241	20	-	40,347	28,367	11
Maryculter Trinity	135	13	9	40,766	31,294	50
Mearns Coastal	222	-	-	23,424	19,071	-
Mid Deeside	537	34	23	70,050	41,409	8
Newtonhill	223	11	10	31,558	20,010	90
Portlethen	271	17	-	55,757	47,396	56
Stonehaven: Dunnottar	528	23	19	61,723	42,567	10
Stonehaven: South	227	9	-	-	16,767	11
Stonehaven: Fetteresso	539	38	25	-	94,580	142
West Mearns	418	19	22	-	36,275	-
33. Gordon						
Barthol Chapel	68	8	8	-	5,254	19
Tarves	253	15	29	45,019	26,628	52
Belhelvie	322	32	16	93,018	60,213	69
Blairdaff and Chapel of Garioch	298	25	11	40,016	21,622	8
Cluny	175	11	-	30,871	18,993	6
Monymusk	96	5	-	22,778	14,336	39
Culsalmond and Rayne	155	6	-	12,387	11,404	6
Daviot	140	10	-	-	8,988	8
Cushnie and Tough	232	10	-	27,754	18,312	1
Echt and Midmar	258	13	-	32,140	28,327	17
Ellon	1,332	72	-	175,371	93,922	137
Fintray Kinellar Keithhall	150	11	7	26,417	25,088	-
Foveran	241	11	-	44,175	37,364	11
Howe Trinity	473	18	32	78,049	52,636	17
Hunt Cairnie Glass	579	8	8	-	38,140	-
Insch-Leslie-Premnay-Oyne	330	29	14	-	27,989	90
Inverurie: St Andrew's	759	33	-	124,049	70,451	10
Inverurie: West	578	45	24	90,738	51,097	5
Kemnay	432	31	-	80,561	52,614	145
Kintore	643	34	-	-	57,821	50
Meldrum and Bourtie	382	22	34	66,393	50,284	-
Methlick	322	28	20	66,749	41,659	51
New Machar	389	19	-	51,333	49,078	25
Noth	216	8	-	23,243	13,180	1
Skene	1,103	63	38	153,604	83,774	138
Strathbogie Drumblade	397	35	21	58,689	43,916	15
Udny and Pitmedden	240	25	11	68,535	47,306	84

Congregation	Com	Eld	G	In18	M&M	–18
Upper Donside	323	18	-	31,848	30,337	25

34. Buchan

Aberdour	104	8	10	13,557	7,365	-
Pitsligo	79	-	-	22,217	8,192	-
Auchaber United	115	-	10	13,381	12,888	-
Auchterless	176	17	-	19,332	15,521	5
Banff	530	35	-	-	51,207	205
King Edward	136	12	9	29,057	11,971	2
Crimond	152	-	-	24,674	15,974	-
Lonmay	100	11	13	14,422	11,953	-
Cruden	375	-	15	44,437	30,519	-
Deer	563	20	16	48,559	45,012	39
Fraserburgh: Old	501	-	43	-	75,057	-
Fraserburgh: South	246	16	-	-	28,693	-
Inverallochy and Rathen: East	80	-	-	-	11,139	-
Fraserburgh: West	459	-	-	59,166	47,891	-
Rathen: West	69	8	-	11,908	7,346	-
Fyvie	173	14	16	39,845	28,385	-
Rothienorman	109	8	-	-	8,440	16
Longside	390	25	-	66,531	43,464	15
Macduff	570	29	31	100,540	56,201	133
Marnoch	353	18	11	35,427	26,181	83
Maud and Savoch	177	13	-	26,284	19,532	11
New Deer: St Kane's	282	14	7	-	34,496	-
Monquhitter and New Byth	261	19	9	28,327	18,631	2
Turriff: St Andrew's	447	25	13	-	28,955	86
New Pitsligo	254	-	-	-	15,647	-
Strichen and Tyrie	431	-	20	47,956	33,623	-
Ordiquhill and Cornhill	138	11	10	10,395	7,618	19
Whitehills	269	-	18	38,924	25,464	-
Peterhead: New	513	28	26	56,038	75,751	18
Peterhead: St Andrew's	388	24	19	50,352	31,727	28
Portsoy	300	-	19	76,523	26,197	-
St Fergus	150	8	7	15,700	8,787	-
Sandhaven	66	-	-	-	3,118	-
Turriff: St Ninian's and Forglen	525	22	16	85,352	46,569	30

35. Moray

Aberlour	202	13	30	44,433	32,049	-
Alves and Burghead	137	13	32	43,848	26,938	9
Kinloss and Findhorn	74	19	9	-	24,411	-
Bellie and Speymouth	332	23	27	65,717	49,906	90
Birnie and Pluscarden	202	20	22	-	29,494	15
Elgin: High	398	38	-	-	38,592	30
Buckie: North	330	33	28	55,796	39,069	14
Rathven	66	15	14	-	11,193	5
Buckie: South and West	218	-	29	51,972	24,863	-
Enzie	69	-	-	6,162	8,215	-
Cullen and Deskford	264	-	17	49,055	36,384	-

Congregation	Com	Eld	G	In18	M&M	–18
Dallas	44	6	8	15,779	10,291	1
Forres: St Leonard's	159	8	27	51,380	28,933	6
Rafford	41	5	-	12,079	9,485	20
Duffus, Spynie and Hopeman	219	-	10	74,801	38,557	-
Dyke and Edinkillie	167	19	13	30,244	22,833	16
Elgin: St Giles' & St Columba's South	484	-	39	132,864	73,070	-
Findochty	37	8	11	22,413	11,869	18
Portknockie	55	9	16	23,098	12,358	40
Forres: St Laurence	327	16	21	71,965	53,358	-
Keith: North, Newmill, Boharm and Rothiemay	444	44	16	34,996	59,163	-
Keith: St Rufus, Botriphnie and Grange	834	58	33	-	57,153	20
Knockando, Elchies and Archiestown	222	-	6	41,098	28,579	-
Rothes	272	17	13	40,249	27,749	18
Lossiemouth: St Gerardine's High	176	10	26	47,240	35,197	-
Lossiemouth: St James'	189	14	29	52,926	35,682	10
Mortlach and Cabrach	277	-	12	39,455	19,444	-
St Andrew's-Lhanbryd and Urquhart	322	38	20	63,134	48,154	10

36. Abernethy

Abernethy	135	12	-	48,253	30,962	47
Boat of Garten, Carrbridge and Kincardine	125	16	28	42,473	25,571	17
Alvie and Insh	68	6	-	26,898	23,517	25
Rothiemurchus and Aviemore	66	7	-	13,246	11,854	8
Cromdale and Advie	57	2	-	18,729	15,485	-
Dulnain Bridge	30	7	-	9,799	9,061	-
Grantown-on-Spey	181	13	-	49,454	26,418	28
Kingussie	82	17	-	23,833	18,969	17
Laggan	39	8	-	24,441	12,093	3
Newtonmore	65	12	-	33,580	18,492	25
Tomintoul, Glenlivet and Inveraven	126	10	-	21,227	18,456	20

37. Inverness

Ardersier	49	8	-	18,738	9,982	18
Petty	45	-	11	15,474	9,872	-
Auldearn and Dalmore	43	-	-	12,317	7,527	-
Nairn: St Ninian's	163	11	21	55,691	35,006	8
Cawdor	149	12	-	29,220	18,337	-
Croy and Dalcross	55	9	16	21,345	10,810	3
Culloden: The Barn	225	-	-	-	59,629	-
Daviot and Dunlichity	50	5	7	12,672	11,815	-
Moy, Dalarossie and Tomatin	33	5	11	8,037	7,660	13
Dores and Boleskine	50	6	-	16,014	11,693	-
Inverness: Crown	494	50	26	-	76,421	88
Inverness: Dalneigh and Bona	143	10	14	51,478	34,419	79
Inverness: East	219	25	-	114,481	76,232	43
Inverness: Hilton	222	11	-	76,824	46,592	37
Inverness: Inshes	226	16	-	-	93,192	115
Inverness: Kinmylies	67	8	-	41,272	41,969	60
Inverness: Ness Bank	524	44	30	147,511	88,215	163
Inverness: Old High St Stephen's	383	31	-	-	76,999	2

Congregation	Com	Eld	G	In18	M&M	–18
Inverness: St Columba	58	4	-	-	13,440	33
Inverness: Trinity	191	-	12	60,402	44,228	-
Kilmorack and Erchless	89	11	16	49,199	33,674	15
Kiltarlity	55	6	-	28,178	14,122	23
Kirkhill	72	10	14	25,700	16,181	14
Nairn: Old	360	47	16	116,062	67,327	52
Urquhart and Glenmoriston	98	8	-	69,494	36,548	20

38. Lochaber

Acharacle	32	4	-	21,033	10,479	12
Ardnamurchan	14	5	-	11,380	7,686	-
Ardgour and Kingairloch	46	6	12	13,268	7,796	3
Morvern	34	5	8	9,375	6,710	14
Strontian	25	3	-	6,276	3,993	8
Duror	29	6	14	12,303	9,391	1
Glencoe: St Munda's	41	8	-	14,853	9,640	-
Fort Augustus	64	9	-	17,328	13,234	3
Glengarry	27	5	13	-	7,884	6
Fort William: Duncansburgh MacIntosh	322	31	16	83,210	51,837	20
Kilmonivaig	53	14	10	-	18,217	10
Kilmallie	93	12	20	28,412	24,551	12
Kinlochleven	44	6	14	24,300	11,469	-
Nether Lochaber	39	8	-	15,179	12,455	-
North West Lochaber	77	12	10	-	20,137	17

39. Ross

Alness	65	9	-	29,870	16,792	14
Avoch	17	4	-	15,111	9,231	4
Fortrose and Rosemarkie	59	7	-	27,241	23,768	10
Contin	36	12	-	13,886	14,433	-
Fodderty and Strathpeffer	90	17	-	-	18,645	-
Cromarty	38	6	-	17,579	5,781	-
Resolis and Urquhart	74	9	-	-	26,447	6
Dingwall: Castle Street	133	13	-	60,458	30,189	12
Dingwall: St Clement's	164	31	17	78,037	39,157	24
Fearn Abbey and Nigg	38	5	-	-	18,036	-
Tarbat	32	4	-	-	8,843	-
Ferintosh	134	19	14	57,222	30,447	12
Invergordon	110	8	-	47,448	40,350	11
Killearnan	110	-	-	26,127	31,313	-
Knockbain	30	8	-	11,532	14,064	-
Kilmuir and Logie Easter	58	8	13	31,187	24,011	1
Kiltearn	52	8	-	35,764	20,340	6
Lochbroom and Ullapool	38	-	-	32,226	20,257	-
Rosskeen	110	12	9	44,235	37,484	42
Tain	87	7	13	55,108	30,134	8
Urray and Kilchrist	81	14	-	-	32,490	90

40. Sutherland

Altnaharra and Farr	22	-	-	-	5,774	-

Congregation	Com	Eld	G	In18	M&M	–18
Melness and Tongue	28	6	-	16,827	15,720	6
Assynt and Stoer	13	2	-	12,903	7,304	5
Clyne	55	-	-	-	17,998	-
Kildonan and Loth Helmsdale	30	6	-	11,564	9,436	-
Creich	18	6	-	11,584	12,992	-
Kincardine Croick and Edderton	29	6	-	14,804	15,367	-
Rosehall	20	2	-	10,079	7,491	-
Dornoch: Cathedral	296	29	54	-	70,234	45
Durness and Kinlochbervie	22	3	-	18,531	12,212	30
Eddrachillis	6	2	-	18,505	7,985	1
Golspie	36	8	4	29,093	30,877	-
Lairg	22	3	12	24,021	15,519	-
Rogart	12	-	-	-	9,475	-

41. Caithness

Congregation	Com	Eld	G	In18	M&M	–18
Bower	28	-	-	3,159	7,549	-
Halkirk Westerdale	41	7	9	12,580	8,670	-
Watten	17	2	-	6,115	7,495	-
Latheron	57	12	7	23,035	16,447	35
North Coast	39	10	17	20,777	13,351	5
Pentland	97	11	14	31,702	25,290	19
Thurso: St Peter's and St Andrew's	115	13	-	-	36,967	18
Thurso: West	166	23	21	55,327	33,234	12
Wick: Pulteneytown and Thrumster	182	13	25	61,818	39,380	15
Wick: St Fergus	191	25	21	46,075	35,175	2

42. Lochcarron-Skye

Congregation	Com	Eld	G	In18	M&M	–18
Applecross, Lochcarron and Torridon	53	5	7	35,950	21,364	12
Bracadale and Duirinish	39	9	5	-	18,832	5
Gairloch and Dundonnell	79	5	-	78,392	41,398	12
Glenelg Kintail and Lochalsh	86	-	9	35,716	33,132	-
Kilmuir and Stenscholl	46	-	-	-	23,262	-
Portree	84	11	-	69,283	42,489	11
Snizort	29	-	-	-	21,349	-
Strath and Sleat	117	8	-	97,887	60,468	-

43. Uist

Congregation	Com	Eld	G	In18	M&M	–18
Benbecula	64	11	16	-	25,473	18
Carinish	73	11	13	56,161	27,890	11
Berneray and Lochmaddy	28	2	9	17,788	12,034	-
Kilmuir and Paible	25	4	-	31,265	19,581	7
Manish-Scarista	28	3	-	33,765	24,120	6
Tarbert	71	7	-	-	38,676	12

44. Lewis

Congregation	Com	Eld	G	In18	M&M	–18
Barvas	69	8	-	84,008	48,192	25
Carloway	44	4	-	27,346	15,071	14
Cross Ness	60	4	-	38,713	30,689	53
Kinloch	32	4	-	38,258	25,403	24
Knock	24	1	-	29,137	18,090	8

Congregation	Com	Eld	G	In18	M&M	–18
Lochs-Crossbost	9	3	-	16,899	12,742	9
Lochs-in-Bernera	27	3	-	18,215	12,166	8
Uig	20	3	-	21,279	14,366	10
Stornoway: High	83	3	-	67,842	37,906	25
Stornoway: Martin's Memorial	324	11	-	159,508	86,929	70
Stornoway: St Columba	140	9	41	-	57,052	148

45. Orkney

Birsay, Harray and Sandwick	300	-	36	42,588	25,516	-
East Mainland	224	-	13	31,279	17,028	-
Eday	8	-	-	-	1,723	-
Evie	23	-	-	4,857	8,779	-
Firth	70	3	-	19,303	16,280	18
Rendall	44	-	-	9,339	8,379	-
Rousay	13	3	-	1,156	3,783	-
Flotta	23	5	-	4,304	3,214	3
Hoy and Walls	46	8	-	6,813	4,669	2
Orphir and Stenness	145	-	-	21,200	19,483	-
Kirkwall: East	347	-	24	-	45,348	-
Shapinsay	39	-	-	11,576	4,396	-
Kirkwall: St Magnus Cathedral	481	30	29	84,848	48,142	-
North Ronaldsay	7	-	-	-	982	-
Papa Westray	7	4	-	9,263	4,985	3
Westray	80	16	24	27,433	19,913	40
Sanday	44	7	7	-	6,491	-
South Ronaldsay and Burray	135	-	14	19,835	11,849	-
Stromness	280	30	13	-	28,505	1
Stronsay: Moncur Memorial	50	7	-	-	9,155	15

46. Shetland

Burra Isle	32	6	10	13,759	6,492	14
Tingwall	46	10	22	25,252	23,610	-
Delting	63	7	11	12,449	12,963	4
Northmavine	56	4	-	8,490	8,261	-
Dunrossness and St Ninian's	35	9	-	12,485	9,982	-
Sandwick, Cunningsburgh & Quarff	52	6	9	21,968	17,136	11
Lerwick and Bressay	305	24	8	72,128	49,739	34
Nesting and Lunnasting	27	4	-	5,135	5,532	-
Whalsay and Skerries	158	14	15	18,851	11,594	18
Sandsting and Aithsting	22	7	-	9,738	5,593	18
Walls and Sandness	28	12	-	-	6,613	7
Unst and Fetlar	74	8	17	17,855	12,351	5
Yell	25	8	12	-	7,539	-

47. England

Corby: St Andrew's	218	16	-	43,552	29,172	6
Corby: St Ninian's	280	13	-	41,753	23,078	5
Guernsey: St Andrew's in the Grange	174	18	-	73,059	44,994	14
Jersey: St Columba's	114	12	-	56,996	35,160	7
London: Crown Court	210	30	3	-	60,810	17

Congregation	Com	Eld	G	In18	M&M	–18
London: St Columba's	825	55	-	-	220,818	12
Newcastle: St Andrew's	104	13	-	-	7,932	21

48. International Charges

Amsterdam	364	15	-	-	-	20
Bermuda	496	41	-	-	-	70
Brussels	304	22	-	-	-	35
Budapest	27	6	-	-	-	22
Colombo	88	12	-	-	-	5
Costa del Sol	10	3	-	-	-	-
Geneva	220	13	-	-	-	25
Gibraltar	25	4	-	-	-	7
Lausanne	116	13	-	-	-	8
Lisbon	50	5	-	-	-	5
Malta	67	20	-	-	-	5
Paris	80	8	-	-	-	5
Rome	81	7	-	-	-	7
Rotterdam	182	16	-	-	-	54
Trinidad	244	-	-	-	-	-

INDEX OF MINISTERS

Ministers who are members of a Presbytery are designated 'A' if holding a parochial appointment in that Presbytery, or 'B' if otherwise qualifying for membership. 'A-1, A-2' etc. indicate the numerical order of congregations in the Presbyteries of Edinburgh, Glasgow, and Hamilton.

Also included are ministers listed in Section 6:

(1) Ministers who have resigned their seat in Presbytery but registered as Retaining or Employed (List 6-D);

(2) Ministers who have resigned their seat in Presbytery but registered as Inactive (List 6-E);

(3) Ministers serving overseas (List 6-J) – see also Presbyteries 48 and 49;

(4) Ordained Local Ministers and Auxiliary Ministers, who are listed both in Presbyteries and in List 6-A and List 6-B respectively; and

(5) Ministers who have died since the compilation of the last *Year Book* (List 6-P)

For a list of the Diaconate, see List 6-C.

INDEX OF PARISHES AND PLACES

Numbers on the right of the column refer to the Presbytery in which the district lies. Names in brackets are given for ease of identification. They may refer to the name of the parish, which may be different from that of the district, or they distinguish places with the same name, or they indicate the first named place within a union.

INDEX OF SUBJECTS